India
in
Sri Lanka

Between Lion and the Tigers

Other books by Avtar Singh Bhasin

1. Nepal's Relations with India and China, 1947-1992: Documents: Two Volumes (1994)
2. India-Bangladesh Relations, 1971-94: Documents: Two Volumes (1996)
3. Some Called it Partition, Some Freedom; Last 75 days of the *Raj* (1998)
4. India-Sri Lanka Relations and Sri Lanka's Ethnic Conflict, 1947-2000: Documents: Five Volumes (2001)
5. India-Bangladesh Relations, 1971-2002 Documents: Five Volumes (2003)

India in Sri Lanka

Between Lion and the Tigers

Avtar Singh Bhasin

Manas Publications
New Delhi - 110 002 (India)

MANAS PUBLICATIONS
(Publishers, Distributors, Importers & Exporters)
4858, Prahlad Street,
24, Ansari Road, Darya Ganj,
New Delhi - 110 002 (INDIA)
Ph.: 23260783, 23265523 (O); 27131660
Fax: 011-23272766
E-mail: manaspublications@vsnl.com
Web site: www.manaspublications.com

2004

ISBN 81-7049-210-6
Rs 795

Typeset at
Manas Publications

Printed in India at
Nice Printing Press
and Published by Mrs Suman Lata for
Manas Publications, 4858, Prahlad Street,
24, Ansari Road, Darya Ganj,
New Delhi - 110 002 (INDIA)

Welcoming

Geetika's brother Arjan

A Note on Sources

The forerunner of the present study is my publication "India-Sri Lanka Relations and Sri Lanka's Ethnic Conflict—1947-2000—Documents: Five Volumes" published in 2001. The text of the documents in the present narration is available in the above-mentioned publication. Readers who are interested in full text or the original may like to refer to them in that publication. Other sources used are also indicated in the main body of the book itself.

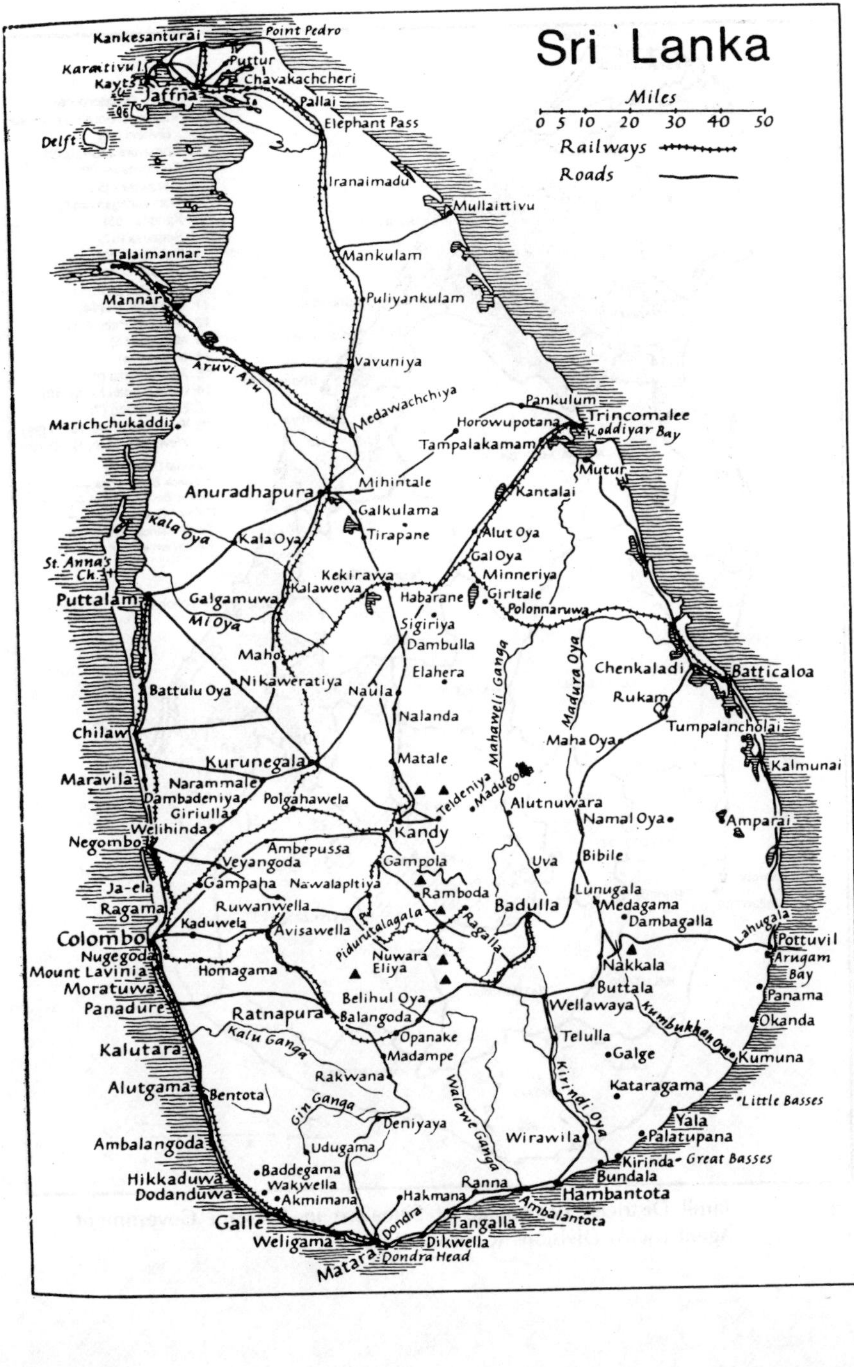
Sri Lanka
Miles
0 5 10 20 30 40 50
Railways
Roads
Kankesanturai
Point Pedro
Karaitivu I.
Puttur
Kayts
Chavakachcheri
Jaffna
Pallai
Elephant Pass
Delft
Iranaimadu
Mullaittivu
Talaimannar
Mankulam
Mannar
Puliyankulam
Aruvi Aru
Vavuniya
Medawachchiya
Pankulum
Trincomalee
Marichchukaddi
Horowupotana
Koddiyar Bay
Tampalakamam
Mutur
Anuradhapura
Mihintale
Kantalai
Galkulama
Kala Oya
Tirapane
Kala Oya
Alut Oya
Gal Oya
St. Anna's Ch.
Kekirawa
Minneriya
Kalawewa
Habarane
Giritale
Puttalam
Galgamuwa
Polonnaruwa
Mi Oya
Sigiriya
Dambulla
Mahaweli Ganga
Madura Oya
Maho
Elahera
Chenkaladi
Batticaloa
Nikaweratiya
Battulu Oya
Naula
Rukam
Nalanda
Tumpalancholai
Chilaw
Maha Oya
Kurunegala
Matale
Kalmunai
Maravila
Narammale
Madugoda
Dambadeniya
Polgahawela
Teldeniya
Alutnuwara
Giriulla
Namal Oya
Ampara
Welihinda
Kandy
Negombo
Ambepussa
Bibile
Veyangoda
Gampola
Uva
Ja-ela
Gampaha
Nawalapitiya
Ramboda
Lunugala
Ragama
Ruwanwella
Medagama
Badulla
Dambagalla
Colombo
Kaduwela
Avisawella
Pidurutalagala
Ragalla
Lahugala
Pottuvil
Nugegoda
Nuwara Eliya
Nakkala
Arugam Bay
Mount Lavinia
Homagama
Moratuwa
Buttala
Panama
Panadure
Belihul Oya
Wellawaya
Ratnapura
Balangoda
Okanda
Kumbukkan Oya
Opanake
Telulla
Kalu Ganga
Kalutara
Madampe
Galge
Kumuna
Rakwana
Kataragama
Alutgama
Bentota
Walawe Ganga
Kirindi Oya
Little Basses
Gin Ganga
Deniyaya
Yala
Wirawila
Palatupana
Ambalangoda
Udugama
Kirinda
Great Basses
Baddegama
Bundala
Hikkaduwa
Wakwella
Ranna
Hambantota
Dodanduwa
Akmimana
Hakmana
Dondra
Ambalantota
Galle
Tangalla
Weligama
Dikwella
Matara
Dondra Head

Tamil Districts: Percentage of Sinhalese in Assistant Government Agent (AGA) Divisions (Census 1981)

Preface

This study is the second part of my five-year research on India-Sri Lanka Relations. The first part "India-Sri Lanka Relations and Sri Lanka's Ethnic Conflict, 1947-2000"— a documentary study of the subject, was published in five volumes in 2001. The compendium contained official documents, which I collected both in New Delhi and Colombo. While most of the 1223 documents in that compilation are unclassified, there are several of them, which are confidential and Top Secret. The latter category of the documents was obtained in Colombo from highly reliable and well-placed sources. This work was well received both in academic and official circles, which encouraged me to persevere further with the study of the subject. The result is the present book.

During my research I made extensive use of the libraries of the Ministry of External Affairs, Government of India, Nehru Memorial Museum and Library, the India International Centre Library, Parliament Library, the National Archives, and the Central Secretariat Library all in New Delhi. In Colombo I made use of several research institutions and libraries, principally the National Archives of Sri Lanka, the National Library, Institute of Ethnic Studies, the Bandaranaike Centre for International Studies, the Lake House, and the Jayewardene Centre. I consider myself fortunate indeed that I succeeded in getting access to some private collections of important retired functionaries of the government.

In India and Sri Lanka, as part of my research, I interacted with several persons who were deeply involved in shaping the events or watching them from close quarters during the last few decades. For various reasons some of them did not wish to be identified, which is understandable. I respect their reservations and owe them a debt of gratitude. Some of the persons, I should particularly like to mention are Shri K. Raghunath, a former Indian Foreign Secretary, Shri Rajinder Puri, a journalist, Shri Mohan Guruswamy, journalist, and Lakhan Lal Mehrotra, formerly Indian High Commissioner in Colombo. In Sri Lanka Tilaka Attanayake, President of the World Buddhist Peace Foundation, Mr. P. Saravanamuttu, Executive Director, Centre for Policy Alternatives, Mr. Prematilaka Mapitigama, Secretary to the former President of Sri Lanka J. R. Jayewardene, Mr. KHJ Wijadasa, Secretary to the former Prime Minister and President Ranasinghe Premadasa, Mr. Sambandhan, and V. Anandasangaree of the Tamil United Liberation Front, and V.S. Sambandan, Resident Correspondent of the *Hindu* in Colombo were good enough to spare their valuable time to talk to me and educate me about the different perspectives on Sri Lanka's problems. I express my sincere thanks to them all. There are quite a few other persons who made their contribution in my understanding of the issues facing the Sri Lankan society. Without naming them I express my gratitude to them. However for the views and opinions expressed here I remain fully committed and responsible.

During my stay in Colombo I had the pleasure of meeting Mr. Neelam Tiruchelavan on several occasions. He not only allowed me the use of his library and personal papers but also articulated to me the Tamil perspective on the ethnic problem. He was a great steadying influence who believed that the destinies of the two communities, the Sinhalese and the Tamils were intertwined and they must find a modus vivendi to live together peacefully. He like many others of his notable contemporaries, both Tamils and Sinhalese, paid with his life for not flinching from that noble ideal, which was dear to his heart. I take this opportunity of paying my tributes to Tiruchelavan and to all those who became victims of the violence, which had been the bane of Sri Lankan politics for almost three decades.

Avtar Singh Bhasin

Content

‹1›

Sri Lanka and India

Sri Lanka (Ceylon), a 66,000 square-kilometre island in the Indian Ocean, south of the Peninsular India is separated from the Indian landmass by the narrow and shallow Palk Strait. The fact that merchant or naval vessels from the western coast of India to the eastern coast or vice-versa must circumnavigate the island underlines her strategic importance for India, and places the island in the Indian security perimeter.

Among the 19 million of the Sri Lankans, 69.3 per cent are Sinhalese who are all Buddhists and 15.5 per cent are Hindus who are all Tamils (ethnic Tamils as well as of Indian origin). The 7.6 per cent Muslims are both Tamils and Moors, the latter being of Arab descent. The 7.5 per cent Christians are Tamils, Sinhalese and Burgers. The two principal languages spoken in the Island are Sinhala and Tamil; English remains the language of the elite. The Sinhalese occupy south and central Sri Lanka; the Sri Lankan Tamils north and the east. The Tamils of Indian origin, who are also known as Plantation or Estate Tamils, came to Sri Lanka as indentured labour in the 19th century, and are settled in the Central highlands which are Sinhalese areas, where the British developed tea, coffee and other plantations. Now, of course, there are a large number of Tamils who live outside of these two regions, principally in Colombo and some other places in the South. Similarly, a substantial number of Sinhalese live in the Eastern Province where they were given state lands as part of the colonization programme.

For Sri Lanka, from colonialism to independence was a smooth transition. The weakness of the colonial rule, failure of the two principal communities to weld into a single politico-administrative entity visited it in the post-independence period. Historically, the two communities remained apart from each other and have lived in the island more as adversaries than an integrated community with Sri Lankan culture and ethos. The only common factor between the two communities is that both came to the Island from India before the advent of the Christian era. Over the centuries, the Sinhalese developed a new language for themselves and accepted Buddhism as their religion.

The Tamils on the other hand, continue to speak much the same language, follow the same religion in the same form and stick to much the same social customs as they came with, but with some local flavours to create a distinct Sri Lankan Tamil culture. In recent years, the Muslims among the Sri Lanka Tamils have distanced themselves from the larger Tamil constituency to forge a closer relationship with the Sinhalese on the anti-Tamil platform.

The Sinhala-Tamil problem in Sri Lanka is two-dimensional and each posed a different set of problems. When Sri Lanka attained independence on February 4, 1948, the Plantation Tamils enjoyed full voting rights as British subjects and were in a position to win elections to 7 to 8 Kandyan constituencies and influence another 14 results by strategic voting in the Kandyan central highlands. This was an anathema to the Kandyans, the Brahmins among the Sinhalese. To correct this insufferable position, the first thing that the Sinhalese did in the post-independence period was to restrict the citizenship rights and therefore voting rights to as few Tamils of Indian origin as possible. Despite ties of ethnicity, the Sri Lanka Tamils in the north and the east remained indifferent to the plight of their Tamil brethrens in the Kandyan areas. Similarly the Plantation Tamils by and large, remained sensitized from the ethnic problem that has led to so much of bloodshed. It is a different matter that often the Plantation Tamils too became victims of the anti-Tamil pogrom during the long history of ethnic conflict. Lack of cohesive approach between the two Tamils, prevented forging of a common constituency between them. In the present study we are mainly concerned with the problem of the Tamils who are settled in the north and the east provinces for more than two millennia and therefore claim, quite rightly, social, economic, cultural and language rights at par with the Sinhalese.

The two Tamil provinces constitute one-third of the island's surface area and contain the world's best and most strategic natural harbour, Trincomalee. About two million people occupy the two Tamil provinces. The rest of the population of the Island is cramped in 2/3rd of the remaining land area. The Tamil areas have a coastline of 3/5th of the entire coastline of the country. The 12.6 per cent Sri Lanka Tamils are 92 percent of the population in the Northern Province and 68 percent in the Eastern Province. It is the Tamils' concentration in the north and the east that is the bane of Sri Lanka's ethnic problem. Diffused minority communities present little problem than when they are concentrated in a particular region of the country. In the latter case, a minority even when it is a fraction of whole but has a very high educational and cultural consciousness, presents a unique problem requiring a unique response from the majority community and the Government. When that response fails to materialize, there is a problem on one's hands. It is further compounded when that society, with a distinct culture and language, had in the past enjoyed a long period of independent existence as a rival to the majority community.

Few nations today are socially and culturally wholly homogeneous. They are an amalgam of historical communities with a fairly clear sense of separate identity. They are acutely conscious of the various social, economic and political factors that brought about their present situation. When such a society faces a challenge of identity and ethnicity, it is not surprising. Break up of such states by application of the homogeneity principle could only spell disaster. It is essentially a problem of reconciling sub-nationalism with the broader concept of nationhood. It is this failure of the Sinhala State to provide a decent space to its Tamil minority to fulfill its distinctive linguistic and cultural aspirations that confronted the State with a problem that has bled it white during its more than five decades of existence as an independent State.

A parallel case was that of Pakistan, where failure to provide the required response to the ethnic Bengalis led to her final nemesis, and establishment of an independent state of Bangladesh. This development provided contradictory pulls in Sri Lanka where too the roots of the ethnic problem could be traced to the "Only Sinhala Policy" of S.W.R.D. Bandaranaike in

1956. The Tamils nursing a grievance against the majority Sinhala community's failure to appreciate its aspirations were greatly influenced by the events leading to the emergence of Bangladesh. The Sinhalese suspecting the Tamils of irredentist aspirations, determined to prevent the Pakistani fate, adopted policies, which only increased alienation of the Tamils. Unfortunately for the Tamils, India, which had acted as a midwife at the birth of Bangladesh, was unwilling to repeat her performance. It is interesting that by contrast India a more plural society in terms of language, religion and ethnicity, than Pakistan or Sri Lanka succeeded in preventing such a fate, due largely to her allowing all of them decent space within the larger Indian nation. But in both the neighbouring countries, however, India's role in the ethnic problem had been crucial.

Historical Threat Perception from India

At the time of independence, Sri Lanka was apprehensive of her future as an independent nation. She was worried that a small island with a small population, with much smaller resources was being left to deal with a new emerging nation, India, in the north with much greater resources in men and material. There was an additional creeping danger of international communism, which Sri Lanka's leaders detested. The perceived danger of India was so dominant on the Lankan mind that the British, saw it as a strategic advantage. One would do well to remember that about the same time, while demitting power in India, the British Defence establishment was very keen that the Andaman Islands in the Indian Ocean were retained under British sovereignty as naval and air bases for the defence of the Empire and the Commonwealth. Unfortunately, its efforts in this direction came a cropper because of opposition from the Viceroy of India Lord Louis Mountbatten. He feared any attempt in that direction would derail the very process of transfer of power in India, which was high on the agenda of His Majesty's Government and in which he had a personal stake. Rebuffed in India, the British General Staff dug its heels in Colombo and ensured that the independence of the Island was linked to the grant of defence bases on the Island. As it happened, the British Government before demitting power entered into defence arrangements with Sri Lanka, pledging its military assistance for the security of the Island nation "against external aggression and for the mutual protection of essential communications", in return for use of her naval and air bases.

Sri Lanka's fear of her security from the peninsular India, which was rooted in her history and psyche, dominated her thinking in the post-independence period. Colombo failed to take into account the new dimensions of the Indian policy in the post-1947 period. Independent India did not harbour any ambition or inclination to follow a policy that would endanger the independence or sovereignty of any country, least of all the small countries in her neighbourhood. Nevertheless, Sri Lanka continued to be obsessed with fear of Indian domination arising out of her historical experience. What added to her paranoia was that unlike in the past, she now faced a much bigger and united India with much larger resources, both human and material. The big country-small country syndrome came to haunt her as it did others in India's periphery.

There was indeed an element of dichotomy in Indian policy, which made its smaller neighbours uncomfortable. India while pursuing a policy of accommodation towards her smaller neighbours, could not give up the basic postulates of the policy dictated by geo-politics of the region. The fact that small states in her neighbourhood fell in her security perimeter and therefore must not follow policies that would impinge on the security of her bigger neighbour. They should not seek to invite outside power(s). If any one of them needed any assistance it should look towards India. India's attitude and relationship with her immediate neighbours depended on their appreciation of India's regional security concerns: they would serve as 'buffer states' in the event of an extra-regional threat and not proxies of the outside power(s). The challenge for independent Sri Lanka was how to get out of India's embrace without arousing Indian apprehensions or bile.

J.R. Jayewardene's early perception of India

In 1954, J.R. Jayewardene gave a peep into Sri Lankan thinking on this account. As a Minister in the Senanayake Cabinet, he had penned a memorandum for his Prime Minister who was preparing to host a Conference of the Prime Ministers of Southeast Asian countries in Colombo. In that Memorandum of March 19, 1954, Jayewardene predicted that India would dominate "the whole region south of the Himalayas stretching from Afghanistan to Indonesia". Giving vent to his grave apprehensions, he lamented the emergence of even a stronger India proceeding "from strength to greater strength, economically and militarily" without any "possibility of a splitting up". Reminding that in 1823, the United States had proclaimed her Monroe Doctrine he predicted grave "danger to our (Sri Lanka's) independence" if India did likewise and her rulers turned "imperialists". As an insurance against this danger he suggested:

> "It is therefore necessary to see that the states in this region are not cut off from the rest of the world from economic and military aid, such as Pakistan has recently secured from America. India should not be permitted to proclaim a 'Monroe Doctrine' in the Indian Ocean where she will play the role that the USA plays in the Atlantic".

In writing the above note, Jayewardene had come a long way from the views he held on the future of Sri Lanka in relation to India, in the forties when he saw the survival of his country only as an appendage to India. In a letter dated July 20, 1940, he expressed his feelings to Jawaharlal Nehru that while India, given her size could look after herself once she became independent, Ceylon might not, and expressed the possibility of his country being "bartered away by a peace treaty" following the War. Therefore, he believed the future of Sri Lanka "lies with India" and suggested a deputation to India to discuss his country's future with the Congress leaders.

Sharing Jayewardene's nervousness, Nehru advocated "a close federation of India, China, Burma and Ceylon". As the tide in the war turned in favour of Britain, India and Burma were promised independence, Ceylon too smelt independence for herself. Jayewardene talked no more of federation. In his letter of June 29, 1945, wishing to move away completely from his earlier position of association with India, Jayewardene told Nehru, "I do not think that either the State Council, or the country will accept anything less than has been promised to India and Burma, that is, the status of a free and equal partner in the Commonwealth of Nations".

The changed perception that Sri Lanka evolved of India in the post-independence period became an important determinant in Sri Lanka's foreign and security policies. The asymmetry between the two countries in terms of population, industrialization, technology, and armed forces contributed greatly to a sense of insecurity in Colombo. To face this asymmetry, Sri Lanka logically relied on extra-regional and regional counterpoises. The natural extra-regional props were Great Britain and the United States. India's adversaries—Pakistan and China—became regional props. With Britain she had a defence treaty signed in 1948, and to the Americans she offered facilities like the stationing of Voice of America broadcasting facilities, permission to use Trincomalee harbour and the like. On August 1, 1951, Sri Lankan Prime Minister told the House of Representatives that friendship with Great Britain was Sri Lanka's greatest security, and Sir John Kotelawala on May 26, 1955 said in a public speech that the "day Ceylon dispensed with Englishmen completely, the Island would go under India". Similarly, as time passed Colombo cultivated cosy relations also with Pakistan and China.

The regional props were seen more in use after the emergence of Sri Lanka Freedom Party on the scene in 1956 under SWRD Bandaranaike and his wife Sirimavo Bandaranaike. In addressing the inequiliberium, Colombo was eager to avoid giving any open or visible offence to India. This was also the time when Sri Lanka started taking keener and leading role in the non-aligned movement and other regional outfits. To win over the gratitude of Pakistan, she took an ambivalent position on Kashmir. During the Indo-Pakistan conflict of 1965, Colombo by sending identical messages to the two countries emphasized her equi-distance from Islamabad and New Delhi. In 1971, she was not convinced of Indian stand on Bangladesh and provided staging facilities to Pakistani aircraft ferrying between Dhaka and Karachi when India closed her air space to Pakistan. The 1962-Chinese attack on India and its aftermath gave an ample opportunity to Sirimavo Bandaranaike to display her diplomatic skills. She emerged out of this role with greater sheen without having to take sides. Her initiative enabled her to avoid giving offence to India without naming or having to condemn China as the aggressor in the Sino-Indian dispute. Playing statesmanlike role, Bandaranaikes held a worldview similar to Nehru's and adopted a common approach to important international issues like the Suez crisis and the Soviet intervention in Hungary in 1956. Colombo also made deft use of the policy of non-alignment, which it pursued vigorously under Sirimavo and kept not only India in good humour but also used it as a security umbrella. Actively pursuing the policy of non-alignment and choosing to be its chief spokesperson enabled Sri Lanka to secure for her influence in the non-aligned movement out of proportion to the Island's size and resources.

With the emergence of J.R. Jayewardene on the political scene in Sri Lanka in 1977, Colombo reverted back to a pro-West tilt while maintaining the pretence of and exploiting all the advantages of a non-aligned country. By now the ethnic problem was getting menacing. The Tamils had the previous year vowed to seek a separate state for them and no longer be petitioners in the court of the Sinhalese. The militancy, too, gained ascendancy among the Tamil youth. A number of militant movements sprung up with uncompromising agenda. They threatened to marginalise the leadership of the moderate Tamil United Liberation Front. After race riots of 1983, under the pressure of Indian Parliament and the state government of Tamil Nadu, India became quite active in Colombo bidding good-bye to the policy of "benign neglect" of ethnic Tamils. She became actively involved in helping to find a solution to the intractable ethnic problem.

Unable to stand the Indian pressure which at times looked quite daunting, Sri Lanka turned to the West in obvious disregard of India's security sensitivities and ignored the regional strategic fundamentals intrinsic in a situation of proximate and asymmetric power balance. Apprehensive that India would fill the vacuum in the Indian Ocean should the big powers were forced to withdraw from the waters around her, Jayewardene's enthusiasm for "Indian Ocean as a Zone of Peace" declined sharply. He was quite happy with the presence of the big powers in the waters around the Island, to keep India's ambitions under check.

Sri Lanka was, similarly no longer willing to extend support to the call on all nuclear states to refrain from stationing nuclear weapons on the territories of other states. There were enough straws in the wind to give an early signal that Lanka was using non-alignment to camouflage her pro-West policies. In 1981, Colombo lifted the nine-year; old embargo on foreign warships calling at Trincomalee. This was a green signal for the Americans to use the facilities of one of the best harbours in the world, in the Indian Ocean, for their ships to anchor and soldiers to rest and recreate. There was no dearth of reports that the United States was seriously considering making Trincomalee a naval base in South Asia. The contracting of the Trincomalee Oil Tank Farm to a consortium of companies acting as proxy to the western interests made India feel uncomfortable. It led to a lot of misunderstanding between the two countries. The new agreement with the USA in 1983, under which the Voice of America was given expanded facilities on the Island and which sought to exclude the jurisdiction of Sri Lanka over its administration, operation and maintenance was the straw that broke the camel's back. India was apprehensive that the United States with its satellites and new facilities on the Island had acquired capabilities to gather strategic information. India was unhappy that Colombo in the pursuit of antagonistic policies was not only disregarding India's security and strategic interests, but was also being disrespectful of the regional power and sought to spite it.

On the bilateral plane, the relations between the two countries immediately after their independence were impacted by the citizenship question of the Tamils of Indian origin or Plantation Tamils who were brought to the Island in the nineteenth century by the British planters. India's initial stand that since the Tamil labour had made a great contribution to the economy of the Island, and were settled there for almost a century, uprooting them would create a human problem of great magnitude, was not appreciated by Sri Lanka. She was adamant on evicting them lock stock and barrel back to India. India was accused of chauvinism and hegemonism in not accepting her people back and trying to foist them on a small country in order to dominate it. India, finally, felt compelled (Agreements in 1964 and 1971) to take a substantial number of them back. The agreements did help to restore Colombo's some confidence in New Delhi, but at the cost of Plantation Tamils. At the start of the decade of eighties, India declared the issue closed despite the fact that enough people had not applied within the stipulated time frame for the Indian citizenship to complete the Indian quota. It was at this time that Sri Lanka was facing a new problem of ethnic Tamils in the north and the east provinces. India's gradual involvement in the ethnic conflict on the side of the Tamils put the Sri Lankan Government on the defensive. With the ethnic conflict escalating, Colombo chose to tone down its stridency on the citizenship question and found it prudent not to take on the Government of India on this issue. Showing political acumen, Colombo adjusted to the changing realities by agreeing to grant citizenship to all remaining persons of Indian origin. Despite the political dust raised by the final settlement, the mood in Colombo was melancholy, with the ethnic problem still looming large on the horizon.

Another issue, which at times bestirred the relations between the two countries related to the Kachchativu Island in the Palk Strait. Anxious to resolve the issue without letting it snowball into a major crisis, India conceded Colombo's claim to the island. It, however created domestic problems for India with the Tamil Nadu Government. The Indian fishermen from Tamil Nadu who traditionally fished in and around the Kachchativu Island for a rich catch felt cheated. This often led to problems with Sri Lankan authorities, who enforced their writ on these waters and prevented Indian fishermen from poaching in the area. Despite the state government of Tamil Nadu protesting to the Government of India against harassment of the Tamil Nadu fishermen by Colombo, Indian Government repeatedly advised Chennai to prevail upon the Indian fishermen to remain within the Indian waters thereby helping in avoiding unpleasantness in relations with Sri Lanka. Chennai unable to discipline the fishermen have continued to blame the Government of India for having surrendered India's claim on Kachchativu and asked for its retrieval from Colombo.

Despite clear enunciation of Indian policy in regard to fishing in the Palk Strait, clashes between the Indian fishermen and Sri Lankan Navy continue to occur at regular intervals. The Government of India for obvious reasons of domestic politics, on a routine basis had been making the minimum necessary noises in Colombo to keep Fort St. George in good humour.

❮2❯

Sri Lankan National Consciousness

The British, after their conquest of the island, treated Sri Lanka as one single unit of administration under one central authority. Paradoxically, the administrative unity failed to create either a cohesive Sri Lankan society or a national consciousness. A large number of Tamils, due to their advancement in education and preferred treatment from the British, had taken up employment in the civil services to emerge as a special privileged social class. The Sinhalese on the contrary remained a backward feudal class, lacking in modern education, steeped in agriculture and other rural vocations. The two communities moving in two different economic streams failed to merge into an interactive society, capable of promoting a national consciousness.

Not too much to bind them, created emotional cleavage between the two communities. With different cultural backgrounds they drew their sustenance from two distinctly different sources of history. Their epics and heroes are different. The hero of one is the foe of the other. Their victories and defeats overlap. Their failure to find a common hero in history, who could equally inspire valour and pride in both was to be a major contributory factor in preventing them from being welded together as a nation. Yoked together by the British the two communities came closer to each other but one as a numerical majority and the other as a minority. It is no wonder that when the British were leaving the Island in 1948, the Tamil minority was apprehensive of its future.

Efforts of the Donoughmore Commission to create an interactive society by the introduction of provincial councils and delegating to them some important and crucial functions of the central government failed to achieve the desired objective. An important recommendation of the Donoughmore Commission, that the central legislature met besides in Colombo, also in Kandy and Jaffna periodically was not implemented. It is one of those missed opportunities of history that nations rue and lament in retrospect. It was not that the Tamils alone felt unhappy with the highly centralised set-up, the Kandyan Sinhalese, who considered themselves a league higher than the rest of the Sinhalese, too were upset since their suggestion made to the Donoughmore Commission for the creation of three autonomous regions representing the Tamil, Kandyan and other Sinhala interests was not accepted.

Tamils' efforts to salvage their position on the eve of the transfer of power came a cropper. They struggled in vain for constitutional safeguards against the Sinhala majority rule, which looked inevitable given the demographic composition of the population. When the proposal of the Soulbury Commission to suggest a suitable mechanism for the transfer of power were being given final touches in London, the Tamils made another valiant bid to convince the British of their apprehensions. On September 11, 1945, in a meeting with the Colonial Secretary G.H. Hall, G.G. Ponnambalam of the All Ceylon Tamil Congress (ACTC) insisted that in Sri Lanka no party alignment cutting across communities had emerged in history and "race, religion and caste" dominated the Island's politics. Ponnambalam while not advocating abolition of the adult franchise put forward the plea that it was precisely the adult franchise, which had worked against the minorities. He pointed out that under the restrictive franchise "that held the field between 1834 and 1931 the Sinhalese never on any single occasion held more than 50 percent of the seats in the State Council". However, he added, since the "introduction of adult suffrage in 1931 the Sinhalese had always, and under the present constitution would continue to have a preponderant majority in the Council". He therefore advocated "weighing the representation of the minorities at the centre on some such lines, as were proposed by Lord Wavell for meeting the Moslem claims in India". Ponnambalam was heard and assured that the British Government would not be unmindful of their interests. But luck ran out at the end. Their demand for 33 per cent weightage was rejected. Describing the findings of the Soulbury Commission that the Eastern societies being "plural" and "antagonistic" wherein the principal problem of government is protection of minorities, as unexceptional, the Tamils lamented that the Report disregarded its own facts and had "put forward a Constitution which will result in still further oppressing the Tamils and other minorities".

The Tamils were on the horns of a dilemma. If they did not endorse the constitutional proposals as a prelude to the British withdrawal from the Island, they feared censure at the hands of the Sinhalese for prolonging the colonial rule. In a no-win situation, they joined the Sinhalese members in endorsing the constitutional proposals in a vote in the State Council in November 1945. This did not stop them from condemning the Soulbury Report and the White Paper on Constitutional Reforms in its special session held on November 4, 1945 in Colombo's Town Hall.

On January 15, 1946, continuing their tirade against the constitutional reforms, the Joint Secretary of the All Ceylon Tamil Congress S. Sivasubramaniam in a letter to British Prime Minister Attlee whined that the new Constitution sought to set up "an irremovable communal oligarchy in perpetual power" and paved "the way for an immutable succession of Sinhalese Buddhist Prime Ministers".

The British Government was not impressed and regarded opposition to the reforms any thing more than "the still-born policy of rump of dissatisfied (Tamil) politicians". Nevertheless London remained anxious that there should be no miscarriage of justice and that the Tamils were not given an avoidable reason for nursing a grievance at a time when the British were leaving. It decided to have another look to the proposals. But the Colonial Secretary Creech Jones when he consulted the Governor in Colombo was advised, "against any reopening" of the issue.

Seen in this background, the new Constitution made a false start and had in it the seeds of Tamil antagonism. The Tamil juxtaposed their apprehensions with those of the Muslims in India who appeared too close to their goal of a separate homeland and hoped for some such success. They were too painfully aware that no community had succeeded in either wresting a democratic constitution from the domination of another nation or establishing representative institutions from within, without guarantees for the securities of the minorities wherever such a problem had arisen. Majorities are perceived to be oppressive and tyrannical and minorities always dread and fear that their interests and rights, unless clearly and definitely safeguarded by statutory provisions, would suffer and be prejudiced. This apprehension is, however, enhanced all the more when communal majority and minority are pitted against each other. It was this perceived fear of the Hindu majority that led to the partition of India in 1947 and it was this fear of the majority that the Tamils were seeking to insure against through statutory safeguards but to no avail.

The Soulbury Commission, which gave the island a new Constitution on the eve of the transfer of power and lasted until 1972, did make an effort, however limited, to allay Tamil apprehensions by providing certain safeguards. The Constitution stipulated that the Parliament would not enact discriminatory legislation against a particular ethnic or religious minority to which all other groups were not simultaneously subjected. The Prime Minister was expected to nominate members of the minorities to the nominated seats and also consider giving them representation in the Cabinet. However it failed to prevent the inevitable majority factor of the Sinhala community having full play in independent Sri Lanka that has haunted the two communities since then. The citizenship laws, which were practically the most important first measures undertaken by the new Sinhala Government, sought to deprive a vast majority of the Tamils of Indian origin of their citizenship and throw them out of the island. This shook the Plantation Tamils and was an oblique signal to the Sri Lankan Tamils too that they too needed to watch out.

The inevitable having happened, the Tamils did not try to meet the challenge head on. They tried to make the best of the bad bargain. Instead of taking up the cudgels for their brethren, the Plantation Tamils, they considered it prudent to fall in the mainstream of the country's politics and seek an alliance with the only Sinhalese party, the United National Party (UNP) in the hope of finding a *modus vivendi* for coexistence between the two communities. It was with this in mind that the All Ceylon Tamil Congress (ACTC) went in for an alliance with the UNP by joining the D.S. Senanayake Government despite the fact that this caused a split in the Tamil community. In December 1949, Samuel James Velupillai Chelvanayakam, parted company with the ACTC and founded his own party—the Ilankai Tamil Arasu Kadchi (ITAK)—popularly known as the Tamil Federal Party or the Federal Party, which became the standard bearer of the Tamil nationalism. ACTC gradually got wiped out.

The Federal Party's call for a federal setup issued at the first convention of the party, held at Trincomalee in 1951, was lost in the cacophony of Sinhalese majority politics. The Sinhalese response though equally robust was unfortunate and negative. They perceived the Tamil aspirations as irredentist, who on the eve of independence had knocked on the doors of the British, to safeguard their future rather than putting their faith in the sister community. The pugnacity of the unitary Sri Lanka State and Tamil urge for federalism, resulted in a clash between the state nationalism and Tamil sub-nationalism, the latter in course of time maturing into an attribute of nationhood, coinciding with the aspirations of the Tamils. The rising frustration of the Tamils, gradually found expression in the various liberation organisations, some peaceful, others not so peaceful and some even outright violent.

It was perhaps in this perspective that S.J.V. Chelvanayakam, father of the Tamil nationalism in Sri Lanka, moving an amendment to motion of thanks on the Governor General's address in the House of Representatives on November 26, 1947, asked "why the Tamils should not have the right to secede from the rest of the country if they desired to do so". But these were early days. The Tamils were repeatedly testing waters. They tried to assert themselves when a national flag for the new nation was to be decided upon. To the Sinhala proposal that the Lion flag be accepted as the official flag for the new Dominion, the Tamils strongly suggested inclusion of "Nandi" and "Crescent and Star" representing Hindu and Muslim sentiments in the proposed flag. But this too was ignored and instead a flag with a lion and two strips (instead of "Nandi" and "Crescent and star") to represent the minorities was thrust upon the reluctant

Tamils. They were dejected and warned that the flag adopted was a symbol of disunity of Ceylon.

The struggle for succession to the ailing Prime Minister D.S. Senanayake in 1951, in the ruling United National Party (UNP), acerbated the ethnic problem in the country. S.W.R.D. Bandaranaike, an Oxford educated and liberal aristocrat, considered himself the natural heir to D.S. Senanayake but was rebuffed and had no qualms in splitting the UNP. He formed the rival Sri Lanka Freedom Party (SLFP). The succession battle proved fatal for the ethnic peace of Sri Lanka and a disaster of the first order for the luckless inhabitants of the Island.

Though the new party failed to make a good showing in the 1952 elections, Bandaranaike decided to bide his time. In the 1956 elections indulging in populism, SWRD, in order to grab power, seized on the highly emotive issue of language and adopted a one-point programme for his party--"Sinhala Only" and proclaimed that within 24 hours of his coming to power he would make the language of the majority community the sole official language of the country. Ironically the same Bandaranaike before independence had realised and accepted the need for parity of treatment to both the languages as essential to bring about amity and understanding between the two principal communities. In changing his colours now, he was reaching out to a very important constituency of Buddhist clergy, who were the standard bearers of Sinhala chauvinism and culture. Even as the intrusion of religious obscurantism and fundamentalism in Sri Lankan politics gave dividends to S.W.R.D. Bandaranaike and his SLFP, it introduced a pernicious development in the body politic of the Island. From now on the Sinhalese nationalism adopted an increasingly strident religious overtone.

The influential and completely obscurantist sections of the clergy, in their self-proclaimed role of defenders of the faith against assorted and imaginary threats to the holy trinity—the country, the community and Buddhism—opposed any concessions to or compromise with the Tamils on any issue whatsoever. This policy naturally was to hit the Tamils the most. No wonder that the Tamils perceived this step as anti-Tamil since it sought to deny their language the equality of treatment and sought to hit, where it hurt the most—at their almost total monopoly on jobs in the government sector, the largest employer.

The UNP on the other hand initially tried to stick to the policy of parity of the languages, to keep the support of the traditional Tamil voters, but as the electioneering in the 1956 elections progressed and it found itself losing the Sinhalese vote bank to the SLFP, it too belatedly though unsuccessfully, tried to change horse midstream. The SLFP, of course, not only won the elections hands down on the slogan of "Sinhala Only" but also changed the rules of the Island's politics forever.

It is tragic that the Sinhalese political leaders in their shortsightedness gave up the prudent and well thought out policy of the early years of taking the Tamils on board, while walking the road to nation building. The Official Language Commission appointed on May 23, 1951, to determine the language policy of the State was mandated to suggest measures necessary for transition from English to Sinhalese and Tamil with the object of making the two languages official languages of the administration. It was a positive development, which was welcomed by the Tamils. In fact, the Muslims who had pleaded acceptance of English as their language instead of either Sinhala or the Tamil, were chided by the Commission, which observed: "It is well known that their home language is either Tamil or Sinhalese and it is highly unrealistic for them to act as if English has ever been or can ever be the home language of the large majority of them".

The "Sinhala Only" policy proved right the early forebodings of the Tamils that majority rule would reduce them to the status of a second-class citizen. This dreaded reality now stared them in the face. On January 20, 1956, the Tamil Members of Parliament decided to form themselves as a United Front to: (1) preserve their language and culture, (2) maintain the identity and freedom of the Tamil speaking people and (3) keep inviolate their traditional home. They called upon the Tamils to struggle for the creation of a Tamil State "which will offer to federate with the Sinhalese State on terms of complete equality if acceptable to both the nations or elect to remain independent". While being strident, the Tamils chose to remain unmindful of the fact that they, the 12 percent of the population, were demanding parity with 74 percent of the Sinhalese. On January 29, 1956, the Federal Party Working Committee realized that time had not yet ripened to call for independence "in the interest of the unity of Ceylon as well as in the interest of peace, concord and amity between Tamil and Sinhala speaking peoples". A day earlier on January 28, 1956, a conference of Jaffna lawyers had unanimously decided to form an assembly immediately to protect the Tamil language and the rights of the Tamil-speaking people of Ceylon. A former Minister S. Natesan, speaking at the conference said that it was testing time for the Tamil people who had for centuries lived and used their language in Ceylon without hindrance and on terms of complete equality with the Sinhalese. On February 20, 1956 the Tamil speaking Northern and Eastern Provinces observed *hartal* in protest against the decision to declare Sinhala as the only official language of the country. Taking note of the agitated mood of the Tamils, the Government on May 3, 1956 decided to defer the introduction of the legislation to make Sinhala the sole State language of Ceylon. A 13-member sub-committee was appointed to advise on the steps necessary for an early switchover from English to Sinhala for the transaction of all official business and other related issues. But it had no powers to alter the principal provision of the draft legislation, that Sinhala should be the only official language.

Mr. Bandaranaike, later told a press conference that the question that Sinhala should be the official language was a settled one and "we are not prepared to discuss that". The sub-committee would however, consider what steps should be taken to provide for the "reasonable use" of Tamil as well as other languages. To soften the Tamil opposition he offered to co-opt Tamil members on the Sub-committee. "But they seem to be precluded at the moment, because the basic assumption that Sinhalese should be the one official language is unacceptable to them", the Prime Minister said.

On May 3, 1956, the leader of the Ceylon Tamil Congress G. Ponnambalam moved an amendment to the speech from the Throne pleading for the retention of parity between Sinhala and Tamil languages in the national curriculum. He said: "Tamil has been the indigenous language of Ceylon for over 2000 years and if you now try to eradicate it by a stroke of legislation, it would be an utter negation of democracy". He described the move to "impose Sinhalese on an unwilling and dominant minority" as "retrograde and anachronistic". Ponnambalam was unsparing in his criticism of the move to declare "Only Sinhala" as the official language of the country and went on to say that this move would "deny the Tamil speaking people a rightful share in the independence of the country, constitute a gross violation of their fundamental rights, relegate them to a position of subservience and condemn their language and culture to gradual extinction in Ceylon". Prime Minister Bandaranaike in his reply speech on May 4, 1956, tried to take the edge off the ruffled feelings of the Tamils and blamed the present situation on the conflicting pronouncements and assurances of the previous Prime Minister John Kotelawala, which had irritated the two communities and caused excitement. The Sinhalese, he said, genuinely feared that in the present context, if the Sinhala were not adopted as the sole official language, it would result in its extinction.

On May 29, 1956, in the teeth of opposition from the Tamils, December 31, 1960 was fixed the dead line for the switchover to Sinhalese as the State language of Sri Lanka while deciding to make some changes in the original draft Language Bill to accommodate Tamil. The Tamils refused to be propitiated. The Federal Party decided on a peaceful *satyagraha* on June 5, 1956, the day the Language Bill was to be presented to the Parliament. On May 18, a largely attended public meeting of the Federal Party in Colombo decided to hold a Convention of the Tamils to decide on a programme of direct action to preserve their language.

On June 14, 1956, the House of Representatives passed the Official Language Bill by 65 to 28 votes, declaring Sinhala as the only State language. Asking for its implementation by the end of December 1960, S.W.R.D. Bandaranaike while introducing the Bill in Parliament on June 5, had declared that he was determined to see that justice was done to everybody, but ignored the threat of *Satyagraha* by the Tamils. Its volunteers who protested the Bill, were roughed up both by the Sinhalese and the police. Its warning that "the struggle to secure for Tamil a status of equality with Sinhala would be carried out beyond the Island and, if necessary, the issue would be taken to the "United Nations" went unheeded.

The Tamils were not impressed by the verbal assurances of the Prime Minister. The Federal Party's Convention held at Trincomalee on August 18-19, 1956, described the "Only Sinhala" Act as "the most iniquitous and worst piece of injustice perpetrated on the Tamils". The convention condemning the new language policy said there was no difference between the 'Apartheid' act of the South African Government and the policy pursued by the successive governments in Ceylon in relation to the Tamils. The convention unanimously adopted a resolution, which became a benchmark in the Tamil struggle to secure equality of treatment for Tamil language and their own rightful place in the Island's polity. Its four main elements were:

(1) Replacement of the pernicious present Constitution by a rational and democratic one, based on the federal principle and the establishment of one Tamil linguistic state, incorporating all geographically contiguous areas in which the Tamil speaking people were numerically in a majority.

(2) Restoration of the Tamil language to its rightful place, enjoying parity of status with the Sinhalese as the official language.

(3) Repeal of the existing citizenship laws and enactment of fresh laws on the basis of a single test of residence; and

(4) Immediate cessation of colonizing Tamil areas with the Sinhalese.

❮3❯

Widening Gulf

The demand for merger of the Northern and Eastern provinces to create a Tamil homeland forcefully articulated by the Tamils, has since remained an anathema to the Sinhalese. It revived the historical memories of Sinhala-Tamil rivalry and aroused fears among the majority community of Tamil separatism. The Sinhalese were not unaware of the fact that as a small minority, the Tamils by themselves were no danger to the country's sovereignty or territorial integrity. But, there were across the Palk Strait another 50-60 million Tamils and if at any stage the two together joined up to create a pan-Tamil movement, it would then be difficult to stem the tide of Tamil nationalism. It was this outlandish fear of Tamil nationalism swamping them that provided the rationale for the Sinhalese to be unyielding. The noises made by the Federal Party led by Chelvanayakam, to titillate the Tamil nationalism as a counterpoise to Sinhalese chauvinism, were perceived as ominous warnings. The Tamils' attempt to break through the Sinhalese majority at the time of the departure of the British was recalled to question the intentions of the Tamils. The stridency of the Tamils against what the Sinhalese saw as legitimate restoration of the pride of place to their language, failed to evoke an understanding response from the majority community. The lack of mutual trust among the two communities and the discriminatory policies that flowed from the "Sinhala Only" policy, were to put the two communities on a collision path. It created that wedge which eventually blew up into an unending civil war. The backing that the SLFP received from the Buddhist clergy in its pursuit of pro-Sinhala agenda, not only strengthened the role of the religion in state politics but also denied any space to the minority Tamil community. The chauvinistic populism that overtook Sri Lanka split into several directions with all its ramifications.

The Sinhala colonization in the newly developed lands in the Eastern Province to dilute the Tamil majority too came to haunt the Tamils. They saw in it the Sinhalese hidden agenda to change the ethnic balance in favour of the majority community and added to their litany of grievances. The State, on the other hand, rejected the theory of Tamil homeland and said that the whole of the Island was home to all the Sri Lankan citizens, and no area could be considered exclusive homeland of any particular community. The Tamils, on the other hand, were not willing to make any compromise on the need to merge the Northern and the Eastern provinces to create a Tamil homeland. Such a Tamil state should stand to the rest of the country in a federal relationship of equality with the Sinhalese area. The demand was articulated on the platform of highly developed Tamil culture and the need to secure it from the onslaught of outside forces.

The upsurge in Sinhala chauvinism, or the Tamil nationalism, depending on from which side of the spectrum one perceived the problem, saw the first anti-Tamil riots in 1956. In the Eastern Province over 150 Tamils were killed by the Sinhalese settled under the state sponsored scheme of Gal Oya, in the district of Amparai. In his very first test as a leader of the Sri Lankan people, Prime Minister S.W.R.D. Bandaranaike, who though an enlightened cosmopolitan, liberal, Oxford-educated gentleman, was found wanting. He failed to rise above the ethnocentric forces. The obscurantist forces unleashed by him now refused to retreat or regress. Walking a tight rope, he was nevertheless keen to show the Tamils some accommodation to redeem his liberal image.

On July 26, 1957, Bandaranaike entered into a pact with the Federal Party leader S.J.V. Chelvanayakam (Bandaranaike-Chelvanayakam Pact). It sought to promise the Tamils regional councils with devolution of substantial powers— power to raise finances, use of Tamil in the north and east, authority to the regional council for the selection of suitable persons for the alienation of land in a particular area; constitution of Northern

Province as a separate region, Eastern Province being divided into one or more regional areas. But alas, it was not to be! The little he conceded was too much for the chauvinistic Sinhalese, who cried foul and ran for Bandaranaike's blood, demanding the annulment of the pact.

Most Tamils were willing to accept the agreement as an advance and improvement on the existing state of affairs. They were willing to work it out and build on it for improvement in the future. A couple of days after the signing of the pact, on July 28, 1957, the Federal Party at its convention at Batticaloa described it as "an interim adjustment", and declared that it remained wedded to the Party's ultimate objective of achieving a Tamil linguistic state or states within a Federal Union and ensuring parity of status for the Tamil language throughout the island. This was indeed a qualified acceptance of the pact and did not strengthen the Prime Minister's hands either. To that extent the Tamils cannot escape some responsibility for Sinhalese response.

On July 28, when the Tamils were holding their conclave in Batticaloa, S.W.R.D. Bandaranaike, whose house the Buddhist clergy besieged for capitulating to the Tamils, discounted fears of Tamil separatism. The "Sinhala Only" Act would remain untouched and there would not be any federal form of constitution for Ceylon, he assured the breast-beating clergy. He clarified that the regional councils would be subject to close supervision and control of the Central Government. He further added that their powers would be strictly and carefully defined by special legislation; the Sinhalese speaking people in the north and east would have their rights safeguarded; steps would be taken to ensure that the regional use of Tamil did not infringe on the position of the Sinhalese as the only official language and that colonization would be directly administered by the Central Government, except for the small development schemes initiated by the local bodies.

Neither community seemed happy. The radical Tamils dubbed the Pact as capitulation before the Sinhalese majority. The Sinhalese on the other hand, saw in the Tamil response whetting of their appetite while eroding the gains of the 'Only Sinhala' Act. Bandaranaike now found himself hamstrung by the dynamics of both the Sinhala and the Tamil chauvinism. The same forces, which had propelled him into power, now forced him to beat a hasty retreat. Bowing before the combined forces of the clergy and his party rabble-rousers, the beleaguered Prime Minister beat a hasty retreat and on August 12, 1957 he not only effectively buried the Bandaranaike-Chelvanayakam Pact but with it also the first attempt, even if a limited one, at reconciliation between the two communities.

Unencumbered by the Tamil baggage, the Government now fired yet another salvo in the pursuit of its chauvinistic agenda. It introduced new number plates with marking "SRI" on government owned vehicles. To the Tamils this was an affront indicative of Sinhalese determination to humiliate the Tamil minority. In April 1958, the Federal Party launched its *satyagraha* to protest the Government's decision on number plates. On April 9, 1958, Bandaranaike announced that the *satyagraha* launched by the Federal Party had made it impossible for him to implement the terms of the Language Pact in the way he had contemplated.

On April 10, 1958, the Executive Committee of the Federal Party issued a statement calling upon the Tamils to join in a non-violent mass movement organised on the Gandhian pattern. It said that the Prime Minister had left the Tamils with no choice but to struggle or be content with the position of a "disgraceful subject race". Bandaranaike, reacting swiftly to this move said that the Federal Party's *Satyagraha* would be a "tragic blunder". Holding an olive branch to the Tamils and wishing to resurrect the Pact he said that he was misunderstood by the Federal Party when he said that "certain actions of the Federal Party had created a situation in the country which did not make it possible to proceed with the implementation of the pact as contemplated, and therefore the pact had become a dead letter." He went on to hold the hope that there was still time to save the country with "restraint and statesmanship on the part of all concerned".

On April 11, 1958, an uncompromising Chelvanayakam announced that the Tamils had reached the "parting of the ways" and that they were prepared to be destroyed with honour rather than accept the subjugation of the Sinhalese. In an indication of intensification of the *satyagraha*, he said apart from defacing the symbol of "SRI" on buses, the Federal Party planned to refrain from paying income tax and property tax and travel on the national railways without tickets in order to court arrest and "fill the already congested jails in the country". The *satyagraha* launched by the Federal Party though peaceful provoked the Sinhala backlash. It led to major anti-Tamil riots in May-June 1958 throughout the Island. Hundreds of Tamils were killed and thousands rendered homeless.

On July 4, 1958, the Prime Minister keen on mollifying the Tamils but refusing to make any compromise on the language question, told the Parliament that although the pact with the Federal Party had been rendered a dead letter by the Federal Party's agitation against the "Sri" symbol on government vehicles and subsequent agitation all over the country, those things that the government considered fair and reasonable would be done, pact or no pact.

The echoes of Sri Lankan Tamils' fate reverberated across the narrow Palk Strait in the Indian State of Tamil Nadu where sympathies were expressed for them. Protest demonstrations were organised, and the Government of India was called upon to intercede with Colombo on their behalf. The Dravida Munnetra Kazhagam (DMK) demanded that a Tamilian be appointed the Indian High Commissioner in all those countries where there was a considerable Tamil population.

The Government of India followed a two-dimensional policy towards the Tamils in Sri Lanka. With regard to the Plantation Tamils it initially maintained that the Tamils of Indian origin who migrated to the Island in the nineteenth century as indentured labour and had made Ceylon their home were not Indian nationals and they should be allowed to stay on where they had been living, unless they qualified for Indian citizenship under Article 8 of the Indian Constitution. (This approach was later modified to take back some of them.) The other plank with regard to the Sri Lankan Tamils was that India considered the language problem of the Island and that of the ethnic Tamils as an internal matter of Sri Lanka, which should be resolved between Sri Lanka and her citizens. India was loath to be interfering in the internal affairs of a small neighbour and make herself vulnerable to the charge of interference.

The Bill for "reasonable" use of Tamil language, introduced in Parliament on July 17,1958, but rejected by the Tamils, was passed on August 8. Prime Minister Bandaranaike putting up a brave stand declared that the Bill sought to give to the Tamils "fundamental human rights as laid down by the United Nations" and if the people were opposed to the measure, the machinery of democracy was available to them at the next general elections and added sarcastically: "I wish them good luck". Entitled "The Act To Make Provision for the Use of the Tamil Language and Provide for Matters Connected Therewith or Incidental Thereto", provided for the use of Tamil as the medium of instruction in schools, for admission to public services, correspondence with Government and for prescribed administrative purposes in the Tamil-speaking Northern and Eastern provinces.

It is noteworthy that when the Bill was passed in Parliament on August 8, 1958 without a division, the Federal Party members were under house arrest and had rejected the government's offer to bring them to the Parliament under police custody to enable them to vote on the Bill. Chelvanayakam had described the Prime Minister's offer as "an affront to the dignity of the House" and added, "We deeply regret that the suggestion should have come from the Prime Minister". The Government, however, explained that the offer was made because of the Federal Party's demand for the release of the detenus to enable them to participate in the debate.

The Federal Party smelt an opportunity after the 1960 general elections, neither of the two Sinhala parties succeeded in securing an absolute majority in Parliament and neither could therefore form a government on its own strength. (It may be relevant to remember that in the meantime a Buddhist monk had assassinated S.W.R.D. Bandaranaike and the leadership of the SLFP had passed into the hands of his wife Sirimavo Bandaranaike.) Both the parties sought the support and cooperation of the Federal Party in the government formation. On March 30, 1960, the Federal Party in a statement set out the four minimum demands for its support:

1. Granting of regional autonomy for the Northern and Eastern provinces and delegation of powers to regional bodies for development oriented subjects. Pending the

establishment of the regional bodies state-aided colonization will be suspended.

2. Tamil to be recognised statutorily and administratively as the national language of the Tamil-speaking people in Ceylon. Tamil to be made the language of administration and of the courts of law in the Northern and Eastern provinces.
3. Amending of the Ceylon Citizenship Act of 1948.
4. Till such time as the question of citizenship and the franchise for the Estate Tamil population was settled, representation in Parliament for these people to be provided by way of nomination to 4 out of 6 appointed seats in Parliament.

It is significant that the ethnic Tamils, who did not lift a little finger in defence of the rights of the Plantation Tamils when their citizenship rights came under attack soon after independence of the country, now belatedly sought to take up the cudgels on their behalf. They, perhaps, tried to forge a new united Tamil constituency to fight the chauvinism of the Sinhalese. It was seen that whenever there were anti-Tamil riots, the Sinhalese in the South and in Colombo particularly, made hardly any distinction between the two and made all Tamils equally the target of their wrath. Even the Tamils with Indian passports were not spared. The mobs never make such fine distinctions. As we shall see, while the Estate Tamils could not make any substantial contribution towards the struggle of the ethnic Tamils, yet the Ceylon Workers' Congress leader S. Thondoman never shirked to speak on their behalf or intercede between the ethnic Tamils and the Sinhalese leaders for political compromise as and when an opportunity presented itself.

In the negotiations that followed between the Federal Party and the two Sinhala parties after the hung verdict, a coalition was built between the Federal Party and the SLFP. It was generally agreed that SLFP would restore the core of the Bandaranaike-Chelvanayakam Pact. The Tamils conveniently forgot that it was the chauvinistic streak of the SLFP since 1956 that was responsible for most of Tamils' misfortunes. The Governor-General, however, was not convinced of the durability of the alliance of convenience and dissolved the Parliament to the chagrin of both the SLFP and the Federal Party.

Nonetheless, the alliance endured the dissolution. Both the parties went into the new elections on the basis of their above understanding. But to the mortification of the Tamils, the SLFP came out of the July 1960 elections with its own majority, the Federal Party's support lost its sheen. To no one's surprise the SLFP, true to its past, did not feel obliged to accommodate the Tamils' viewpoint. On the contrary, relieved of the Tamil crutches, the SLFP did not have to look over the Tamil shoulders. It now followed ruthlessly the radical pro-Sinhala agenda which increased the Tamils' vows and with that their alienation. The Federal Party once again found itself on the agitational course.

As from January 1, 1961, Sinhala language replaced English as the official language of the country. The same day, the Minister of Justice, P.C. Fernando, striking a conciliatory note appealed to "all our brothers of the Tamil community" to accept the language policy of the Government in a spirit of friendship and goodwill. Assuring the Tamils he said: "I, as the Minister of Justice wish to assure the Tamil speaking friends particularly those in the Northern and Eastern provinces that nothing will be done by me which is likely to cause any embarrassment or hardship to them". He declared that the language policy of the government was not actuated by any other motives than "to preserve for the Sinhalese people in this small country their language which is so rich and so ancient and which is spoken and written only within the confines of this island".

Earlier, on December 20,1960, the House of Representatives had adopted an official motion by 68 votes to 2 making Sinhala the language of Parliament with arrangements for members, who did not know Sinhalese. While naturally the Sinhalese welcomed the switchover as the "dawn of new era of national awareness", the two million Tamils protested that the position of parity of status their language had enjoyed with Sinhala had gone. An official spokesman of the government announced that it would bring into force a series of regulations to ensure "reasonable use" of Tamil, especially in the administration of the Tamil speaking Northern and Eastern provinces.

The Tamils found the above sop inadequate. On January 2, 1961 the Federal Party observed *hartal* in the Tamil speaking provinces as a protest against non-recognition of Tamil as an equal partner. *Satyagraha* commenced on February 20, 1961 and the administration in the two Tamil provinces found itself paralysed. But the government did not want to be seen negotiating "under duress" and decided to get tough to twist their arm. On March 1 the troops were airlifted to the North to assist the police to maintain law and order after the Governor-General had signed an order empowering their engagement in non-military duties. In "a massive show of strength" the troops did a flag-march on the streets of Jaffna and Batticaloa. The Jaffna Municipal Council adopted a resolution appealing the Government to withdraw troop-deployment. Forgetting the pre-election understanding with the Tamils, on March 4, 1961, the Prime Minister Sirimavo Bandaranaike appealed to the Federal Party leaders to stop what she called "their mischievous campaign", but promised that if they faced any inconvenience or hardship by reason of the implementation of the Official Language Act she would be ready to consider their difficulties. In a show of her firmness she declared "there can be no discussion while the *Satyagraha* movement is on". Refuting charge of Sinhalese chauvinism, she said that it was "extremely unfair" to accuse the Government of attempting to "inflict a Sinhala imperialism and thus destroy Tamil heritage". Trying to create wedge between the Tamil people and their leaders and to warn the Tamils of the serious consequences of confrontation she appealed to them, over the head of their leadership not to associate themselves with the activities of "unscrupulous politicians who think they can intimidate the Government into their way of thinking":

> "I want the Tamil people to realise that if they do identify themselves with the Federalists, they will soon create a hostile barrier between themselves and the Sinhalese people as a whole, the consequences of which it will be difficult to estimate."

The fulminations of the Prime Minister did not register on the Tamils.

There were talks between the Government and the Federal Party leaders but the gulf refused to narrow down. On April 7, 1961 the leader of the House of Representatives C.P. deSilva told the House that the government was unable to consider the demands of the Federal Party because they were in conflict with the provisions of the Official Language Act and the Tamil Language Special Provisions Act. So uncompromising were the Sinhalese parliamentarians, that they took the Minister of Justice to task for even holding talks with the Federal Party when the Prime Minister had announced no talks with them until the *Satyagraha* was withdrawn. They urged the government to quell what they termed "the rebellion in the northern and eastern provinces with a firm hand", since it posed a serious threat to the integrity and unity of the country. The Tamil leaders in Parliament, on the other hand, disabused the notion of the Sinhalese members that the demand for a federal constitution was a demand for separation and cited the examples of Switzerland, the USSR and India to say that a federal form of government would make-for greater unity of diverse linguistic and cultural groups. The Federal Party leader E.M.V. Naganathan reiterated that in democracy no government could rule over a people without their consent, and in so far as Tamils were concerned they had withdrawn their consent. Bullets could not conquer their spirit. The Tamil people were united to a man and they would not surrender, he said and warned that by denying the right of self-determination to the Tamil people, the Sinhalese people were undermining their own security as a nation.

Failing to get any succour, the Federal Party converted its *Satyagraha* into a civil disobedience movement from April 15, 1961. Chelvanayakam inaugurated a parallel postal service in Jaffna district and acted as the first postmaster to sell a large number of stamps and stamped envelopes. The Party announced its intention to set up an independent police service. The government was quick to point out that the new twist in the campaign showed that the Federal Party was separatist, which it denied.

The Government on April 17, 1961 proclaimed a State of Emergency, and in what looked like an all out war, arrested all the top leaders of the Party, which was also proscribed. On the same day, the Prime Minister warned the Tamil leaders that they would be held responsible for the consequences arising out of the measures that the government might be forced to take. On April 25, 1961, the Estate Tamils too decided to join the other Tamils and went on strike to press for a settlement of the language issue. The Government replied with a string of stringent measures to control the unrest. On April 26, general mobilization was ordered. The government called out on active service nine units of Volunteers and Reservists of the Army, Navy and Air Force and the Home Guards.

On April 26,1961, the Prime Minister made a belligerent broadcast blaming the Federal Party for the economic and political unrest in the country, and called upon the people (the Sinhalese population) to unite to meet the challenge. When the House of Representatives debated the Emergency on May 4, 1961, the Government took the position that a political solution was not possible as long as the Tamil leaders stuck to their present views. The Government left nobody in doubt that the State of Emergency would continue as long as the Federal Party's agitation did not end. A Tamil member not belonging to the Federal Party, M. Sivasithamperam fervently pleaded with the Government to create a friendly atmosphere to help a negotiated settlement of the language issue. He said that the Tamils wanted to live and work together with the Sinhalese as equal partners in the state and not as second-class citizens. They had started the *satyagraha* only after they had explored all avenues of peaceful settlement. A majority of the Tamils were opposed to a separate state. "The Government is welcome to give its own explanation, but if there is anyone who wants to divide the country, it is the Government by treating the Tamils as not being part of the nation", he asserted. Sounding a note of warning Sivasithamperam said that the feeling was growing among the Tamils that the only way for them to preserve their language, culture and self-respect was to find a separate course. Every citizen had the fundamental right of self-determination and whether the Tamils would exercise that right and live and work under one Government depended entirely on how the Government settled the language problem, he said. Government's half-hearted efforts at conciliatory approach were sabotaged by the radical position taken by the clergy, he lamented.

Yet, again the Sinhalese chauvinism was at worst. A feeble attempt for devolution of powers at the district level through the District Council Bill had to be abandoned since it was not acceptable to the diehard Sinhalese. In the meantime, the Government too went through its nationalisation agenda, which included education, petroleum business, the Lake House group of newspapers etc. The agreement on the question of citizenship for the persons of Indian origin signed with India in October 1964 (Sirimavo-Shastri Pact) with a provision for repatriation of 5,25,000 Plantation Tamils to India, though eased tension in Indo-Sri Lanka relations, was as much a rude shock to the Plantation Tamils as to the ethnic Tamils. The Plantation Tamils were appalled that the Pact would render them refugees and force them to leave their homes and hearths to an uncertain future in India.

In December, 1964, Sirimavo Government hit by defections was defeated in parliament. The Federal Party stung by its recent experience refused to rescue the Government by voting for it. In the ensuing elections held on March 22, 1965, the Federal Party once again demonstrated its hold on the Tamils and bagged 13 of the 16 Tamil seats it contested besides winning one of the Muslim seats in the Eastern Province— in all 14. The older All Ceylon Tamil Congress managed to win only 3 seats. The electorates' verdict was a hung parliament, SLFP winning 41 against UNP's 66. Sirimavo exuded confidence to cobble a majority if only the Federal Party threw its lot with her SLFP, since she had the support of some other smaller parties and groups and promised every thing to ameliorate the grievances of the Tamils. Unfortunately, the past record of the Party did not inspire confidence among the Tamils and they would not bite the carrot she had dangled before them and this time they decided to throw their lot with the United National Party (UNP).

Senanayake-Chelvanayakam Pact

In return for Tamils' support, the UNP Government promised some conciliatory measures which were embodied in the Senanayake-Chelvanayakam Pact (March 24, 1965). It was an improvement on the earlier effort viz., the Bandaranaike-Chelvanayakam Pact of 1957. It envisaged a moderate degree of devolution at the district councils' level and a compromise on the question of land alienation for the Sinhala in the North and the East by setting out priorities on the basis of which land would be allotted to landless persons. It was a compromise formula in which Tamils were assured priority entitlement for allotment whether they lived in the northeast or elsewhere.

To give satisfaction to the Tamils on the language question, the Parliament adopted the Tamil Language (Special Provisions) Regulations, 1966. These regulations were published on December 26, 1965, in an Order Paper of the House of Representatives. To gain SLFP's acceptance to them a government spokesman clarified that these regulations were identical with those framed by the late S.W.R.D. Bandaranaike when he was the Prime Minister. The Government's hope that the SLFP led by the late Bandaranaike's wife would feel compelled to pledge support failed to materialize. The SLFP roped in the Lanka Sama Samaja Party, and the Communist Party to muster support against the new pact. The leaders of the three parties accused the government of having entered into a secret agreement with the Federal Party and of having accepted its fundamental aim, which sought to divide Ceylon into two separate and distinct state units. The clergy, who had during the elections played a leading role in turning the elections in favour of the UNP under the banner of Maha Sangh Peramuna, turned hostile and organised a major protest against the Regulations. The Opposition also came from the Plantation Tamils since they argued that the Tamils living outside the Northern and Eastern provinces would not enjoy the rights as were now being bestowed upon the ethnic Tamils in the two provinces. They demanded that unless these regulations also brought them within their ambit, the Ceylon Workers' Congress would not support them in the Parliament.

The agitation evoked mixed response and there were some untoward incidents of violence in Colombo necessitating deployment of the army. The Government declared some of the basic utilities as Essential Services and banned their workers from joining any call for strike. Emergency was declared throughout the Island. It was in this tense atmosphere that the House of Representatives debated the Regulations on January 8, 1966. J.R. Jayewardene, Minister of State who moved the motion for consideration of the Regulations said that the government was proud of the Regulations, since they could bring about the long-lost amity in the country. After a 4-day debate, on January 11, 1966, the Regulations were approved by the House by 95 votes to 54. During the debate the Prime Minister Senanayake strongly defended the Regulations stating that by implementing these Regulations they were not touching a word of the 'Sinhala Only Act' enacted by the SLFP Government. On the same night, the 30-member Senate also approved them by 18 votes to seven.

On June 26, 1966, in another conciliatory gesture to the Tamils, Prime Minister Dudley Senanayake graced the Federal Party's Convention on racial amity at Kalmunai in the Eastern Province. It was for the first time since the inception of the Federal Party that any Prime Minister had attended its convention which was attended by thousands of Tamils from all over the country. In his address to the Convention, Senanayake paid tribute to Chelvanayakam and said that Sri Lanka's struggle for independence had not led to bloodshed, riots, or bitterness because there was a racial harmony in Ceylon. There could not be socialism without national unity. If the Ceylonese wanted to enjoy the fruits of freedom, this racial harmony must be permanent. He declared: "Fate has called upon me to be instrumental in bringing about national unity and I will be very happy when every person in this country is able to say, this is his native land."

To satisfy his Buddhist constituency, which had expressed misgivings on the government's language policy, Senanayake on November 16, 1966, defended his policy and said the "basis for real unity has been established" by the steps taken by him in regard to language. He further added, "The official language is Sinhala all over the country, but Tamil now, as it was in 1956 too, is recognized a regional language of a national minority".

Unfortunately, the bon-homie did not last too long. The whole process of reconciliation was thwarted by the same imperatives of competitive chauvinism and populism that spelled the doom of Bandaranaike-Chelvanayakam Pact earlier. The new pact too evoked anti-Tamil sentiments. The UNP, like the SLFP in the past, developed cold feet. The Party realised that the Tamil constituency could soon be a millstone round its neck particularly when the SLFP had reverted full blood into anti-Tamil mode. It was the same old process of an uncompromising two-party competition for the Sinhala votes and a strategic failure of the majority community. It failed to realise that under its chauvinistic agenda and dispensation the two Sinhala parties were asking their fellow Tamil citizens who did not even share with them historical memories of a joint struggle waged by the two together against a common enemy in history to live in a unitary, centralised state of Sri Lanka, that was conceived as the collateral of a nation defined explicitly in terms of Sinhala identity. In other words, post-independent Sri Lanka State advanced the idea of a monolithic, unitary sovereignty but without corresponding development of equal citizenship over the exclusive rights of the majority community. Those who went about the task of building a Sri Lankan nation state succeeded in creating not one but two nations in one state. As the later events were to show, the transition from expression of separatist sentiment to a full-fledged separatist movement, which took about two decades since independence, decided the agenda of the State for the future and cost it dearly.

The die was cast with the emergence of United Front Government in Colombo in the 1970, comprising Mrs. Bandaranaike's Sri Lanka Freedom Party, the Trotskyist Lanka Sama Samaja Party and the Communist Party (Moscow) with 125 seats in the House of Representatives (out of 151). It was a signal for the ushering in of an ultra-Sinhala agenda. One of the most important and significant items on the Front's programme was to draw up a new Constitution to replace the one given at the time of independence by the British. The Tamils' foreboding seemed to come true. They found that the Government intended to enshrine in the proposed new Constitution, Sinhalese language as the only official language reducing Tamil to the permanent status of a second-class language. It was proposed to make special provision for Buddhism and dispense away with the features of the existing Constitution, which gave some protection to minority rights. Their demand for parity for the Tamil language was brushed aside as also the demand for a federal type of constitution to make some room for their sensitivities. The Federal Party countered with the hypothesis that with the lapse of the British rule, the Tamils were not bound by the majority rule of the Sinhalese, that they had a right to self-determination. The Government was in no mood to pay heed to these oft-repeated arguments of the Tamils, and went ahead with the business of the formation and adoption of a new Constitution. Not unexpectedly the Tamils were left disgruntled and sulking.

‹4›

Creeping Separatism

Continued Tamil disgruntlement and frustration with the majority's disdain of their grievances led to Tamil consciousness transforming into Tamil sub-nationalism and then into a Tamil nationalism. It convinced the Tamils, that mere devolution of powers would neither resolve their problems nor meet their aspirations. The rising influence of the Buddhist clergy was another stumbling block, since, it espoused the myth that Buddha had ordained that the Sinhalas were the chosen people with no space for the historical Dravidian foe. The anti-Tamil riots of the fifties, the legislative, administrative, educational, linguistic and employment discrimination, abrogation of the Bandaranaike-Chelvanayakam and Senanayake-Chelvanayakam Pacts, which were perceived as early attempts even though quite modest at meeting the minimal Tamil aspirations, convinced the Tamils in no uncertain terms that accommodation was not in the Sinhala nature. Since the majority community was not ready for a federal polity, they must escalate their demands to jolt them from their apathy. It was no wonder that the Tamils moved swiftly from the demand for autonomy for the Tamil Northern and Eastern Provinces to the goal of a separate and Sovereign State of Eelam by joining the two provinces. The events in the erstwhile East Pakistan from the language riots in the fifties to the formation of Bangladesh in 1971 had a profound impact on the Tamil psyche. They felt that their plight was analogous to that of the people of East Pakistan except that it lacked enough stridency.

To test the waters for any possible support in India, the Federal Party leader S.J.V. Chelvanayakam visited Chennai in

February, 1972. The extent of Indian support and intervention that the Tamils expected or desired was not spelt out. He met all the Tamil leaders particularly M. Karunanidhi and M.G. Ramachandran. Though Mrs. Gandhi had played a leading role in the creation of Bangladesh only recently, she was seemingly unenthusiastic for a similar role in the Island. The Sri Lankan Tamils refused to comprehend that the elements for separation of the two wings of Pakistan were inherent in the geography of that country. Besides, India had found Pakistan a petulant neighbour, which since inception had harboured hostility towards her and needed to be cut to size. East Pakistan was an extraordinary situation and therefore, invited an extraordinary response. No one in India was convinced that a parallel situation existed in the Island to justify Indian intervention. Mrs. Gandhi had ostensibly enjoyed a good rapport with Mrs. Bandaranaike, despite privately nursing a grievance against the latter for providing staging facilities to Pakistani aircraft during the Bangladesh crisis. Indira Gandhi was quite conscious that Sri Lanka under Sirimavo had emerged as the leading light of the non-aligned movement enjoying prestige disproportionate to the country's size and resources, and therefore any Bangladesh-type adventure in Sri Lanka stood ruled out particularly so close to the dismemberment of Pakistan.

It was not lost on the Indian leadership, that there was in Tamil Nadu itself a secessionist movement not too long ago. It was feared that any support to an irredentist movement for the Tamils across the Palk Straits could revive old ambitions of the Indian Tamils for a pan-Tamil state. Therefore there was nothing in Chelvanayakam's trip to Tamil Nadu that could have enthused him. It only helped to convince him that Sri Lanka's Tamils had to fight their battle on their own strength and on their own ground.

Formation of the Tamil United Liberation Front

There was no let up in the policies of the Government in Colombo, which would give some succour to the Tamils, to assuage their feeling of being discriminated against. On the contrary, Colombo kept needling the Tamils, not only by inflicting Sinhalese Buddhist hegemonism but hitting them hard where it hurt the most. In the name of nationalization, the Government resorted to the Sinhalising of the plantations, which shut on the Indian Tamils future avenues of employment. Though Sri Lankan Tamils were not touched by this action, it was seen as another significant anti-Tamil step. This was followed by the infamous system of "standardization" of marks for students seeking admission to universities in science-based courses, a subterfuge by which Tamil students with better marks were excluded from admission to preferred courses to make way for Sinhalese students with lower marks. During the five years period (1965-70) before the standardization system was introduced, Tamils had secured higher number of seats than the Sinhalese in prestigious courses like medicine and engineering. In medicine alone the share of Tamils was 53 per cent against 41 per cent for the Sinhalese and in engineering courses it was 50 per cent against 48 for the Sinhalese. During the 1970-76 period when standardization system was in operation the Tamil share in medical admissions went down to 33 per cent and in the engineering to 25 per cent. These percentages when seen against the fact that indigenous Tamils are only 12.6 per cent of the population against the Sinhalese 74 per cent, sounded reasonable. But psychologically it had a disastrous impact on the young aspiring Tamils, who valued merit and competition but found left out in favour of the middling. The resultant frustration in the Tamil youth provided natural and ready material for any radicalization of agitation for the Tamil cause.

During the same period, adoption of the new Constitution, which gave Buddhism the foremost place created a fresh irritant and a major contentious issue in the ethnic discourse. It brought home to the Tamils, majority of whom professed Hinduism, that they and their religion henceforth would not get equality of status, in a semi-theocratic state. Altogether, the new measures succeeded in creating a strong sense of alienation among the Tamils generally, and the Tamil youth particularly. In 1975, the Tamil United Front, formed earlier in May 1972, by the amalgamation of moderate Tamil parties, to provide a common platform for articulation of Tamil opinion, emerged in its new avatar as the TAMIL UNITED Liberation FRONT (TULF). By adding "Liberation" to its tag, Tamils put the Government on notice that they were entering a new stern phase in their struggle against the Sinhala State. They realised rather painfully, that the earlier policy of sharing power in coalition with the Sinhalese, in their desire to remain part of the mainstream politics and in the hope that better sense would prevail, did not bring the desired dividend. On the contrary, their being a junior partner with the majority community, created the impression among the latter that political aspirations of the Tamils were being fully met, by giving them a share in state power and Tamils being part of the ruling elite could not have any legitimate grievance. From Tamil United Front to the Tamil United Liberation Front was a big leap. Earlier on September 9, 1973 the TUF at its Trincomalee Convention had expressed itself that Tamils were "fully qualified to be regarded as a separate Nation by virtue of their language, culture, history, territory and innate and intense desire to live as a separate nation..."

The next step towards separation and secession did not take too long to be vocalized. After the passing away of Chelvanayakam in March 1973, the leadership of the Tamils had passed into the hands of Sivasithamperam and A. Amirthalingam. The state policies pursued since 1956, had already galvanized the Tamils to adopt a radical agenda in the quest for justice and fairness. In the process, a people content to be bureaucrats and professionals and seeking their socio-economic salvation through constitutional means, were forced unwittingly to a militant path. A spark was needed to ignite the flame of radical militant nationalism and it did not take long to surface. The tragedy surrounding the Fourth Tamil International Conference at Jaffna in January 1974 was enough to break the camel's back. The repression, with which the people attending the Conference were treated and burning of the Jaffna Library housing the priceless collection of Tamil literature, were seen as a challenge to Tamil nationalism. There was no looking back. Assassinations and bomb blasts became routine events in the life of the Tamil youth in the north. The Government and the Sinhalese were soon to get formal notice that the period of petition and *satyagraha* had passed into history and a new chapter was being ushered in, the Tamil struggle for dignity and equality. This was precisely the time when several militant organisations of the Tamil youth sprang up with no qualms about using violence as a tool, to vent their wrath and anger at the "iniquitous regime".

Vaddukoddai Resolution

The high point of Tamil dissidence was the Resolution adopted on May 14, 1976 at the Convention of the Tamil United Liberation Front at Vaddukoddai, which marked the watershed in the history of separatism in Sri Lanka. It emphasised the differentiations between the two communities in the historical perspective and lamented that overlooking the facts of history "power was transferred to the Sinhalese nation over the entire country on the basis of numerical majority thereby reducing the Tamil nation to the position of subject people". In the preamble, the Resolution said:

> "...Throughout the centuries from the dawn of history the Sinhalese and the Tamil nations have divided between them the possessions of Ceylon, the Sinhalese inhabiting the interior of the country in its Southern and Western parts from the river Walawe to that of Chilaw and the Tamils possessing the Northern and Eastern districts."

The Resolution, listed various grievances of the Tamils in terms of language, employment, education, religion, culture etc., and the series of efforts made by them to correct them, which only led to failures, repression and frustration. It expressed the resolve of the Convention for "restoration and reconstitution of the Free, Sovereign, Secular, Socialist State of Tamil Eelam based on the right of self-determination inherent to every nation", which it said had become "inevitable in order to safeguard the very existence of the Tamil Nation in this country". Northern and Eastern provinces were declared to be the areas constituting the Eelam State where every citizen was guaranteed equality of treatment, where the "pernicious practice of untouchability or inequality of any type based on birth shall be totally eradicated and its observance in any form punished by law". The Convention called upon the TULF to formulate "a plan of action and launch, without undue delay, the struggle for winning the sovereignty and freedom of the Tamil nation". Finally, it called upon "the Tamil nation in general and the Tamil youth in particular to come forward to throw themselves fully in the sacred fight for freedom and to flinch not till the goal of a sovereign state of Tamil Eelam is reached".

The Resolution was Tamils' war cry and a notice to the Government that they had waited for too long at the threshold, and now they had been compelled to cross it. There was now no going back. The Government indeed was alarmed at this unexpected development. In order to mitigate the seriousness of the situation, it tried to isolate the different elements constituting the Tamil United Liberation Front. The Prime Minister chose to accuse only the Federal Party, which, in the past, had spearheaded the campaign for a federal set up, for the new development. The TULF speaking on behalf of all the Tamils rebutted the charge against the Federal Party alone. In a letter dated May 25, 1976 to Sirimavo Bandaranaike, it repudiated that the Federal Party alone could be held responsible, since the decision for a "separate Free, Secular, Socialist State of Tamil Eelam was adopted by the Convention of all the Tamil parties." It said that the Government was behaving like colonial masters, who invariably accuse freedom movements as "anti-social and subversive".

To strengthen the Tamil resolve as reflected in the Vadddukoddai Resolution, the TULF contested the 1977 parliamentary elections on the platform of a separate State and a Tamil homeland and won hands down in the Tamil constituencies. It was however more than clear to every one that when, even, the moderate demands of the Tamils in the past had been rebuffed by the Sinhala radicalism, a demand for a separate state stood no chance of acceptance through constitutional means. The TULF leadership, which accorded primacy to constitutional methods, to achieve the goal of Tamil homeland, continued to participate in the parliamentary process, to the disillusionment of the youth who wanted a radical agenda. It was no wonder, that gradually it found itself losing ground in the face of new emerging trend of militancy, among the youth. It were the latter who had to bear the brunt of the discriminatory educational and economic policies of the Government, that had not only slammed the doors of higher education shut on them but also deprived them of the reasonable job opportunities.

It was about this time that many of the youth feeling suffocated in the moribund atmosphere, left the Island to find succour abroad— to India, Europe, Australia and North America where, in course of time, they formed influential lobbies. Since they left with a hurt feeling, they nursed a grievance against the Sinhala State. They were keen to support any movement aimed at changing the rules of the game in favour of their brethren behind home. The Tamil diaspora became not only a natural source of financial support for the militant movements back home but provided the intellectual and cerebral input. Later, however, there was no dearth of reports, that most Tamils living abroad were coerced into contributing to the coffers of the LTTE, at pains of threat to their relations in Sri Lanka, if they failed to contribute. A report prepared by the Mackenzie Institute of Toronto, Canada catalogued many such activities of the LTTE. According to the same report (and there were other reports too) LTTE engaged in drug trafficking too, which was a great money-spinner. Another activity, which was colateral to their militancy, was gun running. The LTTE developed a great expertise in this trade. They chartered ships, and ferried huge quantities of arms in support of their movement in the North, besides selling to other terrorist and insurgent outfits around the globe.

In the parliamentary elections of 1977, the SLFP Government was voted out of office in favour of the United National Party under J.R. Jayewardene. During the election campaign, Jayewardene pledged to set up a "righteous society" where all citizens would be equal. He held out an olive branch to the TULF, promising to remedy the Tamil grievances over language, education, jobs and colonization, and the promise was reiterated in the Governor General's speech in Parliament. But, the situation was marred by countrywide ethnic riots in which the Tamils, as always, were at the receiving end. What started as a clash between the police and a group of civilians in Jaffna, turned into a major countrywide conflagration. Apparently, defeated Sinhalese politicians cashed in on the TULF demand for Tamil Eelam to fan the flames of communal violence. It left more than 250, mainly Tamils, dead several hundred injured and with a trail of looting and arson. While the anger of the Sinhalese was mainly directed towards the ethnic Tamils, ironically it were the Estate Tamils in the Sinhalese majority areas especially Colombo, Kegalle, Kandy, Anuradhapura, Mannar and Trincomalee who bore the brunt of the arsonists' anger. They became easy prey, since, they were caught in Sinhala-dominated areas. As a measure of safety, 3,000 Tamils were evacuated in three ships to Jaffna, while many others were evacuated by air and rail. Those who could not leave had to be moved to refugee camps in those cities. The anti-Tamil riots gave legitimacy to ever-increasing violence among the crop of Tamil militants who felt convinced that the Sinhalese too needed to be taught a lesson or two to make them realize that violence was a double-edged sword.

The gravity of the situation was not lost on the Government. On August 23, 1977 the Leader of the House, Ranasinghe Premadasa winding up the debate in Parliament on the Government's policy statement, tried to appease the ruffled sentiments of the Tamils by suggesting:

> "Let us forget the past dark period. Let us find a fair and just solution to the problem. Let us not go into the rights and wrongs of the past. We seek your cooperation now to solve the issue. I do not think the problem is beyond solution.. ...Whatever be the political pressure, we are not going to yield to it. We are determined to implement the mandate. We have now a new environment. Let us march into a new era".

But the Tamils were hardly assuaged or swayed by this rhetoric. The TULF leader and Leader of the Opposition Amirthalingam refusing the bait "to forgive and forget" said:

> "We have been used as pawn in the Sinhalese political game. We had been victims of violence several times. Law and order is one thing for the Sinhalese population, and another thing for the Tamils. For the last 30 years we have tried to live in peace and harmony with the Sinhalese people. We are the most peaceful people. But we do not want peace at any cost, not at the cost of our honour, self-respect or freedom."

<5>

Rise of Tamil Militancy

India had looked at Sri Lanka's ethnic problem as her internal affair and followed a policy of benign neglect. The extent and seriousness of the 1977 riots in which some Indian nationals in Colombo also suffered, was a rude shock to New Delhi. Protests were lodged both in New Delhi and in Colombo. Prime Minister Morarji Desai too sent a personal message to his Sri Lankan counterpart expressing hope, that Colombo would take steps to restore Tamil confidence. For diplomatic reasons New Delhi's concern was confined to the Indian nationals. The Tamil Nadu Government had no such qualms. The State Legislative Assembly on August 24, 1977, unanimously passed an official resolution expressing its "rude shock" at the happenings in Sri Lanka, and urged the Government of India to pressurise the Sri Lankan Government the need to stop immediately "violence and atrocities which the Tamils in Sri Lanka are subjected to". The resolution called upon the Government of India and the Prime Minister to depute a representative of the status of a Cabinet Minister to Sri Lanka to find out the true state of affairs and have direct talks with that Government "by way of assuaging the feelings of the Tamils" there. New Delhi did not consider the suggestion of Chennai for deputation of a Minister to Sri Lanka as necessary, and responded by asking its High Commissioner Gurbachan Singh to tour the affected areas to restore confidence among the Tamils.

The UNP Government, pretending reconciliation adopted a new Constitution, which ostensibly sought to give greater attention to some of the concerns of the Tamils. To doubly assure the Tamils against infringement or even imminent infringement of their rights by the executive, afforded them Supreme Court's protection. But much of the good intentions were not matched on the ground, with the result that very little was achieved in terms of reconciliation. The Tamils remained as estranged as ever. The gap between government's promise and performance continued to widen, thus increasing the alienation of the Tamils providing further fuel to the Tamil militancy. The past too haunted both the communities and each remained as distrustful of the other as before. As the Tamil disillusionment with the Sinhalese State increased, their confidence and reliance in the efficacy of constitutional means eroded correspondingly. This naturally brought the stock of the parliamentary leadership of the Tamils into question thereby providing greater sheen to the militants.

The Liberation Tigers of Tamil Eelam or the LTTE, was one of the many militant outfits that sprung up as a byproduct of the historical Sinhala chauvinism. The roots of the LTTE went back as early as 1970, when the Tamil Students Federation was founded. It rechristened itself as the Tamil New Tigers and finally, in 1975 gave itself the tag of Liberation Tigers of Tamil Eelam (LTTE). From the very beginning violence became its creed. Its leader, Velupillai Prabakaran, consecrated the Tamil struggle with blood of a Tamil by personally undertaking the assassination of Jaffna Mayor Alfred Duriappah on July 27 1975. This was not only his first attempt at assassination but also the first of the ethnic conflict and that too of a Tamil by a Tamil. To tide over the financial problems in the early days, the organization indulged in bank robberies. It was thus in March 1976, that Prabakaran with his friends looted the state-owned People's Bank at Puttur in Jaffna. The booty was worth seven lakh rupees—5 lakh in cash and 2 lakh in gold.

Since then, the LTTE has never looked back. Despite heavy odds, it became the cutting edge of the Tamil national movement. The military wing of the TULF—Tamil Youth Front—remained a paper organisation, since it did not believe in the cult of violence. However, it did not fight shy of using the militancy of the Tamil youth to extract concessions from the government. The Tigers worked in concert with the other Tamil militant organizations until 1976, when it decided to charter its independent course to achieve the goal of 'Eelam' as propounded in the Vaddukoddai Resolution. While the Resolution was more of a strategy for the TULF to win elections, for the LTTE it was an article of faith to be pursued to its logical conclusion. The TULF remained wedded to parliamentary route to achieve its goal but LTTE had no compunction in using violence to reach the objective of Eelam. The sight of the politicians remaining wedded to the parliamentary route and struggling to extract some concessions from the State to gain some semblance of autonomy despite pledging themselves to Eelam only created contempt among the Tigers for their duplicity and non-commitment. Henceforth Prabakaran was to shun the politicians for he was convinced that they possessed convenient conscience.

Though India had as yet not committed herself in any manner to the Tamil cause, in Tamil Nadu there was some sympathy for the Sri Lankan Tamils and their sufferings. It provided them safe haven. There they could melt into local population due to shared language and culture and enjoy immunity from the Sri Lankan police and law whenever faced with the heat in Jaffna.

Victimised by police brutality, economic hardships generated by mounting unemployment, failure to get admission in universities despite scoring high in examinations, cultural and linguistic discrimination—gave birth to revolutionary odour among the youth which found concrete expression in militancy and guerrilla activism of the LTTE, bordering on national liberation struggle and finally degenerating into international terrorism. The personality clash between two of the LTTE's early leaders—Prabakaran and Uma Maheswaran led to a split in the organisation and the formation of a rival outfit, the People's Liberation Organisation of the Tamil Eelam (PLOTE) under the latter's leadership. Among the other militant organisations that sprung up among the Tamil youth were, Eelam Revolutionary Organisation of Students (EROS); the Tamil Eelam Liberation Organisation (TELO); the Eelam People's Revolutionary Liberation Front (EPRLF); the Eelam National Democratic Front (ENDLF) and many more. Some of these organizations even established contacts with other militant organizations abroad, particularly the Al Fatah, and received arms and training in their use. The adoption of violence as an instrument for redressal of grievances and killing of innocent Sinhala civilians, and later Tamils shattered the moral superiority of the militants and the high moral ground which the Tamils had so far occupied.

In November, 1978, the Political Committee of the LTTE issued a document entitled "The Struggle for Tamil Eelam and the Liberation Tigers", which articulated the need for its birth, its relevance and role for the future. It minced no words in providing ideological raison d'être for the type of activities in which it engaged itself in. It said:

> "The Tamil Liberation Tigers are the historical product of the Sinhalese chauvinistic oppression. They were the product of a revolutionary situation generated by the contradictions of national conflict. Caught up at the peak of national oppression, constantly victimized by police brutality for political actions, the revolutionary ardour of the militant Tamil youth sought concrete political expression to register their protest. Disenchantment with the political strategy of non-violence, confronted with the demand for revolutionary political practice, the Tiger movement gave its historical birth in 1972 as the armed resistance movement of the people. Structured as an urban guerrilla force, disciplined with an iron will to fight for the cause of national freedom, the Tigers launched a series of attacks against the armed forces of the oppressive regime."

Mincing no words, the LTTE declared the "establishment of a sovereign, socialist democratic people's government" as its primary objective, using the only "viable and effective path of armed revolutionary struggle" to liberate the Tamil homeland. LTTE was also clear that such an armed struggle could only be waged through "guerrilla warfare" for the present to be "gradually and systematically transformed into a genuine people's war of liberation" later.

The LTTE in a letter to Jayewardene clarified its character and role as an extra-parliamentary liberation movement and not a group of terrorists as the Government had tried to dub them. On the contrary, the letter charged the Government of indulging in "terrorist acts" by clothing itself with "extraordinary powers". Claiming a high moral ground, the LTTE asserted that they "were fighting for a noble cause, a right cause, the cause of national freedom of the oppressed nation". It was unfortunate that while the President appeared to accept the reasonableness of the Tamils' demands, yet he remained apprehensive of their motives. The state of mutual suspicion failed to break the Sinhala-Tamil impasse.

Such acrimonious discourse could hardly have brought the two communities any closer. Gradually drifting apart, the trust between the two communities became the casualty. On August 6, 1979 President Jayewardene voiced the Sinhalese apprehensions of the Tamils and said:

> "... The main thing is for them (Tamil leaders) to trust me and for me to trust them. The fears that the (majority) Sinhalese have is that give them (Tamils) something, they will use it to get Eelam. They have to give up that (separatist) cry".

Anton Balasingham, the LTTE ideologue, while further articulating the LTTE thinking in 1983, in a thesis entitled "Liberation Tigers and Tamil Eelam Freedom Struggle", reiterated that the LTTE were fighting only for the complete independence of the Tamil homeland. He accused President Jayewardene of being misled by what he perceived the TULF thinking that the Tamils were not serious in their demand for Eelam. Therefore, the President, in believing that the Tamil militant youth were a misguided lot, was either being cynic or he suffered from misperceptions, claimed Balasingham. Putting forth eloquently the viewpoint of the Tamil youth, Balasingham justifying the "revolutionary armed struggle" said:

> "Plunged into the despair of unemployed existence, frustrated without the possibility of higher education, angered by the imposition of an alien language, the Tamil youth realised that the redemption of their plight lay in revolutionary politics, a politics that should pave the way for a radical and fundamental transformation of their miserable conditions of existence. The only alternative left to the youth under the conditions of mounting national oppression, the youth rightly perceived, was none other than a revolutionary armed struggle for the total independence of their nation".

The LTTE in its relentless struggle to project itself as the sole representative of the Tamils successfully discredited or destroyed almost all the other rival Tamil militant outfits to emerge as the single most important entity without which no solution of Sri Lanka's ethnic problem was possible. It succeeded in gaining defacto international recognition. It organised itself as a state within the state by controlling territory, organising civil and criminal administration in the areas controlled by it and collecting taxes. The people of Jaffna respected the LTTE as much as they dreaded it, and its unquestioned leader Velupillai Prabakaran. The LTTE marginalized all moderate, democratic Tamil opinion and no Tamil leader of any consequence dare accept a solution not acceptable to it. The Tigers had in their armoury a potent weapon which enabled it to mystify everybody else—the cyanide capsule—which set them apart from all other militants. It, too, symbolized LTTE's superiority over all other groups. It was a curious blend of rational obscurantism, absolute nihilism and revolutionary commitment.

Sinhalese reaction to Tamil militancy

The UNP Government like the SLFP earlier, failed to respond positively to the Tamil aspirations. Thondoman, the leader of the Plantation Tamils and President of the Ceylon Workers' Congress had in his own way made several attempts to bring the ethnic Tamils and the UNP closer. But his efforts bore no fruit since the Sinhalese invariably retracted from their promises made to them. Even before the 1977 elections when UNP required the support of the Tamils to dethrone the SLFP Government, Thondoman had worked a reconciliation between the Tamils and the UNP. Jayewardene had promised to take effective steps to redress their grievances. That understanding was reflected in the UNP manifesto too. But unfortunately, the gap between promises and fulfillment refused to narrow down. Thondoman gave vent to his frustration on this account in his speech made in the Sri Lankan Parliament on August 4, 1983, when the House discussed the anti-Tamil riots. He said:

> "There is one thing I must say. As far as the Tamil leaders are concerned, so many Members here were trying to show that they are very unreasonable, that they had been very obstinate. That is not the case. I am

sorry to say as far as my knowledge goes that is stretching too much. In fact Tamil leaders have been very reasonable. They have been cooperative with every government that was in power. They negotiated and came to an agreement with the SLFP and there was the Bandaranaike-Chelvanayakam Pact. It was the government of this country at that time, which was unable to honour it. Again, when Mr. Dudley Senanayake took charge of the Government, they came to an understanding with him. Although they asked for extreme demands, they never hesitated to come to terms by negotiations."

In the face of such plain speaking, the Sinhalese leaders chose silence as their best defence. The inevitable result was marginalization of moderate Tamil forces. Thus, the traditional Tamil leadership, which played an important role in democratically articulating the Tamil grievances over the years, was completely rendered irrelevant in the political equation. With the emergence of the militant youth groups, violence in support of the Tamils' well known demands became order of the day, inviting repressive measures from the government and dispatch of army units to the north to bolster the police force already deployed in strength. Since both the police and the army were for all practical purposes completely Sinhalese, they resorted to repressive measures on a scale not normally deployed against the civilian population thus inviting the charge of genocide. The decline of the moderate leadership was in direct proportion to the rise of the militancy. Soon the whole Tamil question appeared to head for an impasse. The killing of a close associate of Prabakaran, Shankar at the hands of Sinhala police on November 27, 1982 was the first fatal casualty of the LTTE guerrilla in action and became a landmark event in the violent history of the LTTE. Since then the day is commemorated as Heroes' Day, when Prabakaran issues a special message for his cadres, which also gives inkling into his mind.

Anti-Tamil Riots of 1983

The year 1983 was one of the most tragic years in the history of ethnic conflict in Sri Lanka. Prabakaran had returned to Jaffna from Tamil Nadu fully in command of the organization.

The LTTE had also spread its wings in other parts of the world apart from India. It had an office in London. It submitted a memorandum to the Non-aligned summit conference meeting in New Delhi in March, 1983. To announce his return and gain full control of the Tamil movement from the TULF, he issued an *obiter dictum* preventing the Tamils from participating in the voting for the local bodies elections in May, 1983. It was a frontal challenge to the full-blooded participation of the TULF in the elections. Violence had gripped the north. In January, a UNP worker was killed in Vavuniya, the next month a police inspector and the month after that an army vehicle was ambushed. In the wake of worsening law and order situation, Thondoman wrote to the President pointing out the inadequacy of the steps taken in the previous five years to resolve the ethnic strife in the country, and reminded him that "this issue has to be resolved, not only in the interest of the Tamil community, but in the larger interest of national unity and development". In April 1983, three UNP candidates for the local bodies elections were shot dead in Jaffna district. In view of the LTTE dictum of boycotting the elections, the Tamil voters in the north stayed indoor on the polling day. The police and polling stations were attacked killing many Sinhalese. The Sinhalese press reporting these incidents called upon the Government to deploy larger units of the security forces in the Tamil north and eliminate the Tamil terrorist menace. On July 9, 1983, President Jayewardene told the *Daily Telegraph* of London that there "are no areas of negotiations as long as the terrorists are active". He summed up the government position vis-à-vis the TULF and the militants thus:

> "We are not interested in the terrorists' views. We are going to eliminate them. It is no longer possible to argue, debate or talk with them. They must give up their violence. The TULF also, it appears, don't want to talk to them. We have been moving a lot with the TULF. We used to have dialogues and so on. They used to speak on behalf of the terrorists. But now all that is going to cease. Not on the political issues. We will still talk to them as M.Ps and so on. But on the terrorist issue, this we are going to deal with ourselves....because unless the terrorists are eliminated, the TULF is useless. They are in fear of their lives. They say one thing to me and

> something else to somebody else. I am sorry for them. They wanted the Development Councils. We gave it to them. Of course, we have not transferred all powers, the money and so on. We are doing it. We don't do it quickly. It can't be done overnight. Laws have to be passed. Something entirely new, it applied to the whole island. We are doing it. Now we are going to the fullest extent in giving autonomy to their Development Councils. The language question also. If they want a political solution, that is the political solution."

In the interview he sounded pugnacious and truculent. When his interlocutor pointed out the inadequacy of the steps taken to ameliorate the situation in Jaffna, the President shot back:

> "I have tried to be effective for some time, but cannot. I'm not worried about the opinion of the Jaffna people now. We were thinking we must act in a way so they will support us. Now we can't think of them. Not about their lives or of their opinion about us. Nothing will happen in our favour until the terrorists are wiped out. Just that. You can't cure an appendix patient until you remove the appendix. This is the firm determination that I have come to now."

The uncompromising and defiant mood of the Head of the State was indeed desperate. But desperation never resolves issues of political nature. The President blinded with state power was unwilling to see beyond his nose and take steps that would exterminate the root cause of violence. Not that he was unaware of the problem, but populism and competitive Sinhala politics, which dominated the polity and brought the two communities to a collision course and cramped him into submission before the forces of Sinhala chauvinism. One cannot forget that both, S.W.R.D. Bandaranaike and Dudley Senanayake before him, had unsuccessfully tried their luck at making peace with the Tamils. J.R. Jayewardene was indeed endowed with craft and guile, but not with courage to test the tested waters once again and put his political career at stake.

He nevertheless wanted to appear to be doing enough to respond to the Tamil aspirations. On July 20, 1983, the President met leaders of some of the political parties who responded to the invitation for the Round Table Conference to find a solution to the ethnic problem. The Conference was however, deferred to another date in response to the Ceylon Workers' Congress suggestion for enlargement of the agenda to make it more comprehensive by including all the concerns of the Tamils. But the events of July 23, 1983 intervened: the LTTE killing 13 Sinhalese soldiers in an ambush of a military convoy near the University of Jaffna. The consequent reprisals against the Tamils by the Sinhalese led to tragic consequences for all, sucking in even the Plantation Tamils and Indian nationals. It was an anti-Tamil pogrom that became a watershed in the history of ethnic conflict in Sri Lanka. No authentic figures of people killed were available. Approximately 2000 Tamils in Colombo area alone were reported killed. The goriest of the killings took place on July 25 and 27 when their fellow Sinhala prisoners massacred 53 Tamil inmates of the Welikade prison. The estimated value of the property lost or damaged during the disturbances was over 2,000 million Sri Lankan rupees, about 79,000 persons were rendered homeless, and over 1,50,000 persons lost their jobs and the plantation industry, principally tea, suffered huge losses with an estimated tea stocks worth SL.Rs.50 million going up in flames.

Despite destruction on a large scale, the Government reaction was halting and clumsy. Though the riots started on the 24th July 1983, the curfew was not imposed till the evening of the next day. Timely action could have prevented major losses to life and property. Neither the President nor any important functionary of the government visited any of the refugee camps to show sympathy to the victims of the riots, which could have soothed the hurt feelings of the Tamils.

The Secretary General of the TULF, A. Amirthalingam, described the LTTE ambush on the security men as a product of the atmosphere of interminable harassment of the Tamils on their hands and the government's failure to redress the grievances of the Tamils against the security forces. President Jayewardene, speaking to the nation three weeks later (22 August 83), conceded that "there has been growing tension between the Sinhalese and the Tamil people in the last thirty-five to forty years", but blamed the violence on the Tamils for advocating separatism.

Speaking of the Indian interest in the problem, the President said:

> "...for the first time, the Central Government of India has specifically stated that they do not support the separation of our country and will not help in such a movement and further that they stand for the unity and integrity and the independence of Sri Lanka."

Though sounding conciliatory, perhaps on account of the scale of the violence and its impact on the Tamils and national and international opinion, President Jayewardene remained adamant vowing that in future too, "we will not have any talks with any Party that wants to advocate the separation of Sri Lanka". He did not come forward with any concrete suggestion that would resolve the ethnic problem, the root cause of separatism of the Tamils. Far from taking any conciliatory measures to alleviate the hurt feelings of the Tamils, in August 1983, the moderate TULF was proscribed. It, thereafter, shifted its base to Chennai in Tamil Nadu, India. The government came up with an amendment to the Constitution, which disqualified the sitting Tamil members for their failure to take an oath, giving up separatism as a means to redress their grievances.

6

Indian Involvement in the Ethnic Conflict

The Government of India faced a great dilemma in Sri Lanka. It had pledged to maintain the territorial integrity of Sri Lanka and therefore, could not lend support to any demand for Tamil Eelam. At the same time, the way the Tamil problem in the country had snowballed, it led to an emotional upsurge in Tamil Nadu in favour of the Tamils of Sri Lanka. Thousands of people took to streets demanding stern measures to stop the genocide of the Tamils. Protest demonstrations were held in front of the office of the Sri Lanka's Deputy High Commission in Madras. The Indian Parliament, too, did not remain unaffected. There were emotionally charged debates in support of the Tamils. The Members, cutting across party and linguistic lines, believed that the Tamils had not only been deprived of their due share in the administration of the country but also their culture and language had been denied its rightful place. It was articulated by the Members of the Parliament that the Tamils had suffered repression and untold atrocities not only now but in the past too at regular intervals.

In the face of upsurge in Parliament and in Tamil Nadu, the Government of India was compelled to take serious note of the developments in Sri Lanka and reconsider its policy of benign neglect. The arrival of thousands of Sri Lankan refugees in Tamil Nadu in the wake of anti-Tamil riots only sharpened the edge in favour of the Tamils. The TULF under proscription and its members staying out of the Parliament were cooling their heels in Chennai and stoking the anti-Lankan sentiments among the Tamils in South India. Various militant groups too had moved their camps to the Indian state and found themselves welcomed. For the next couple of years, Tamil Nadu became their base. Funds were openly and freely raised for their activities and Tamil politicians of the state backed their own favoured groups. The Chief Minister of the state M.G. Ramachandran, emerged as the patron of the LTTE. There was no dearth of funds hereafter. According to B.G. Deshmukh, a former Cabinet Secretary and Principal Secretary to Prime Minister Rajiv Gandhi noted, "the state government gave them all help and full freedom not only of movement but also of collecting money for arms. In fact, M.G. Ramachandran, the Chief Minister (of Tamil Nadu) openly gave a huge donation for this purpose. The militants defiantly imported arms from outside, which resulted in their free availability throughout Tamil Nadu." (*A Cabinet Secretary Looks Back*: Harper Collins: 2003: p.334)

Soon, Tamil Nadu became not merely a sanctuary but a backyard of Sri Lankan militants. Arms and ammunitions were freely ferried across to northern Sri Lanka from Tamil Nadu. It became the base for ensuring that the militant movement in Sri Lanka was not short of supplies, of strategic and non-strategic material, necessary to keep the military machine of the militants well oiled and supplied. Indian fishermen unhesitatingly were available to provide the logistical support for their movement. In short, the Sri Lankan Tamil outfits had free run of Tamil Nadu and found themselves above the law. No wonder, soon they became a problem for the state's law and order machinery. Since most of the groups were rival groups, internecine warfare among them became a routine affair. Street brawls among the militants, and between Indians and militants were no longer uncommon, which was conducive neither to the long-term interests of the militants nor of the local people and state. One of their activities, which attracted adverse attention, was drug trafficking. Free flow of funds led to abnormal rise in real estate prices in the Tamil Nadu capital, which was also the subject of adverse comments. For some time their activities were tolerated in the hope that enjoying the Indian hospitality they would feel obliged and cooperate with the Government of India in finding a solution to the ethnic imbroglio. But soon it was discovered that the militants were oblivious of the New Delhi's concerns. The fiasco of the Indian effort at the highest level to find a solution to the ethnic problem during the SAARC summit in Bangalore in 1986, made New Delhi realize the futility of its policy of appeasement towards them. Soon it was aware of the extent of local clout that the militants particularly Prabakaran had built for himself and his movement. When on November 8, 1986, government cracked down on all militant leaders including Prabakaran, arrested them and seized their arms and ammunition, while Colombo for once felt elated that New Delhi had at last responded to its entreaties and acted tough, it too laid bare the limitations of Indian government's ability to deal with them sternly. In Tamil Nadu, the arrests raised a lot of commotion and the political circles felt disturbed that the government was wielding the big stick against the repressed Tamils. The government had to return the confiscated equipment to buy the peace locally.

Colombo's elation too was short-lived. It realized that New Delhi had mortgaged itself to the local politics to an extent that it had become difficult for it to shed the burden of Tamil politics. New Delhi was in a quandary, since it found that Colombo too had become unmindful of the India's strategic interests and was leaning heavily on the western countries while professing non-alignment. Dubious western private agencies were not only advising the government but also actively helping in canalizing arms from equally dubious sources. India had considered Sri Lanka as falling within her security perimeter in South Asia. That perimeter stood threatened and breached. New Delhi, while finding itself unable to act domestically, decided to act tough with Colombo.

New Delhi wished to convey a message to Colombo that India, as a regional power could not follow a hands off policy and be a hapless spectator in her own backyard. She had a right to intervene in the settlement of a potentially destabilizing conflict of a neighbouring state to prevent its cascading impact in the region, or to deny an opportunity to any outside power to fish in troubled waters.

Active involvement of India in Sri Lanka's ethnic strife could be traced to Indira Gandhi's return to power in New Delhi at the beginning of 1980. Her exit from power in 1977 coincided with the exit of another woman Prime Minister in Colombo, and emergence of Jayewardene on the scene. There had developed some sort of cosy relationship between the Nehru-Gandhi family and the Bandaranaike family since the fifties under S.W.R.D. Bandaranaike and Nehru. This relationship continued thereafter under Sirimavo Bandaranaike and Indira Gandhi, despite the fact that India was miffed at the former's role during the Sino-Indian conflict in the Himalayas in 1962 and the Bangladesh crisis in 1971. Sirimavo's dexterity and adroitness ensured that there was no damage to the relationship on the surface, and particularly at the personal level. Jayewardene, on the contrary, failed to strike a similar personal chord with Indira Gandhi. In the pre-independence days, he was very close to Nehru and the Congress Party and later used his old Congress connections and particularly, the fact of his having attended the Ramgarh session of the Indian National Congress in 1940 to his best advantage. He developed major reservations towards India after the withdrawal of the British power from South Asia. As pointed out at the outset, India in his eyes became a major bully in the region, with ambitions to dominate the smaller countries in her periphery. He therefore thought it was necessary for smaller countries to devise strategies to contain Indian hegemony.

Mrs. Gandhi took personal dislike of Jayewardene for attempting to slight her for no particular reason when she was out of power during 1977-79. In the 1977 election campaign, he indulged in avoidable witticism at the cost of Mrs. Gandhi though the target was Sirimavo Bandaranaike. He was reported to have told an election meeting at Galle that there was a cow and a calf in India and a cow and a calf in Sri Lanka. The remarks received wide publicity in India and hurt Mrs. Gandhi who was in political wilderness. She was possessed of a long memory. When she returned to power in January 1980, his remarks rankled in her mind. Besides, during the short-lived Janata Party regime in New Delhi, 1977-79, there was bonhomie between the Janata Party leaders and the UNP leaders in referring to the events in the two countries in the previous couple of years under the two women prime ministers. They drew critical parallels much to the dislike of Mrs. Gandhi. During his state visit to New Delhi, J.R. Jayewardene speaking at the state banquet on October 27, referred to the recent change of governments in India and Sri Lanka and said:

> "I will not go into recent history, but there are many parallels that can be drawn between the events that took place in your country during the last two years and the events that took place in our country during the same period. You may not know but my one and only son was put into jail and up to date he has not been charged for any offence.... I was not put into jail because our position was too powerful to put the leader of the opposition into jail, as they did in the case of Morarji Desai".

Mrs. Indira Gandhi was not the one who would forget such gibes and banter easily. She kept a critical watch on the events taking place around her. On August 27, 1979, replying to a letter of 22 August, 1979, from the Tamil Co-ordination Committee based in London, which drew her attention to the violence being perpetrated on the Tamils in Sri Lanka she lamented, "the Janata Party is going out of its way to be friendly with the present Government of Sri Lanka". Against this background, her return to power in New Delhi in January, 1980, marked a watershed in India's relations with Sri Lanka. India had thus far gone out of its way to accommodate the concerns of her small neighbour by seeking to remove any irritant in the bilateral relations. The agreements of 1964 and 1974 on the question of persons of Indian origin were an attempt to accommodate Colombo, even when it marked a reversal in the policy pursued until then that Sri Lanka was responsible for all the Tamil immigrants who had settled there since the 19th century. India also looked the other way benignly, despite pressure from the Tamils in India when Colombo adopted discriminatory policies against the ethnic Tamils. There were ethnic riots in the past too but India chose to regard them as their internal troubles. Henceforth, it was all to pass. India from now on was to take more active interest to make up for past neglect. On resuming power in New Delhi, Mrs. Gandhi too found that the security environment was getting fragile due to the pro-West policies of Jayewardene.

Mrs. Gandhi, perceptive as she was, had quietly studied and felt concerned at the noticeable militancy gradually creeping among the Sri Lankan Tamil youth. The younger elements were getting convinced that while petitioning Sri Lankan Government for their due share in the governance of the country, they must be willing and able to fight it out, if there was no other way. Despite the uneasiness about events in the Island, India did not consider it desirable to be seen to be interfering directly in the internal politics of the Island. Nevertheless Mrs. Gandhi was loath to discourage the Island Tamils in their struggle. Too many Sri Lankan militant youth were drifting aimlessly in Tamil Nadu who if organized and trained could pose a serious challenge to Jayewardene government. India not only looked the other way when they organised and trained themselves in the use of firearms and other tactics of guerrilla warfare to be able to wage an armed struggle back home, if necessary, but also decided to provide them the necessary training and wherewithal. As the number of refugees increased after the 1983 unfortunate riots, the training camps became more pronounced and conspicuous and New Delhi's contribution in running them too became translucent. Yet New Delhi chose to deny its own involvement and their very existence on the Indian soil. Over time, as militant activity increased on the Island, the strength and number of training camps in India too increased and they became more and more detectable. They were well documented by the Indian and international media, which provided incontrovertible evidence of their existence, official Indian connivance and active support. Obviously, such camps could not continue to exist and flourish unless the Government of India supported and funded them. It naturally raised the ethical question whether such camps were justified? Were these not the facilities for the Sri Lankan Tamils to train themselves for armed incursion in their country? Was it not promotion of cross-border terrorism, a charge made by India later against Pakistan? But this pro-active policy was justified because New Delhi felt that Colombo was indulging in discriminatory policies against the Tamils impacting adversely the Indian Tamils. But once India decided to move away from the policy of benign neglect to one of treading on the slippery path of pro-active policy on the side of the ethnic Tamils in Sri Lanka, India could not help slipping deeper and deeper into the quick sands of murky Sinhala politics.

M.R. Narayan Swamy, in the biography of Prabakaran (Konark: 2003) provides an interesting insight into such camps and training provided to them. He believed that the LTTE was a reluctant participant in such camps. According to him the

RAW, the Indian intelligence agency had initially concentrated on Tamil Eelam Liberation Organisation (TELO), Eelam Revolutionary Organisation of Students (EROS), People's Liberation Organisation of Tamil Eelam (PLOTE) and the Eelam People's Revolutionary Liberation Front (EPRLF) for training. In such a scenario, the LTTE did not want to be left out since it was the expectation that India at the end would not only provide funds and arms for their struggle but also the impetus as in the case of Bangladesh. In the words of Narayan Swamy:

> "Amid all this politicizing and away from media glare, Indira Gandhi's decision to arm and militarily train the Tamil militants began to be carried out. It was such a covert mission that even senior officials of her foreign ministry were not aware of. In a few months, however it became an open secret. The Research and Analysis Wing (RAW) made the connection with Sri Lankan guerrilla groups. Their leaders reached Tamil Nadu along with busloads of fleeing Tamils. Besides the TULF, the militant groups were also allowed to open political offices in Madras and Madurai. It marked the beginning of an Indian involvement that New Delhi would rue in the years to come." (p. 90)

Narayan Swamy talking of LTTE's reluctance said:

> "Prabakaran was in Jaffna when word came to the LTTE through a Sri Lankan Tamil intermediary that New Delhi was preparing to militarily train Tamil militant groups. The Indian decision troubled Prabakaran because he feared it would undermine the LTTE's supremacy. The LTTE considered itself a genuinely homegrown group built brick by brick by Prabakaran. He had apprehensions that India's involvement would elevate the other Tamil groups to the same level as the LTTE, both tactically as well as strategically. Being obsessed with centralized control, Prabakaran did not like the idea of being bracketed with groups he considered far less consequential than the LTTE." (p. 91)

According to Narayan Swamy, it was Anton Balasingham, his alter ego, who clinched the issue in favour of the Indian offer. "He was astute enough to understand that rejecting Indian training would not only be a loss in military terms but would amount to a political hara-kiri."

Again, Narayan Swamy believed that the Indian military training had a magic impact on the Tamil youth, who hitherto were reluctant to join the militancy in large numbers. He said:

> "India's covert involvement in the Sri Lankan Tamil cause dramatically altered the dynamics of the separatist movement. From being a ragtag band of loosely trained rebels the organizations began to acquire a cutting edge and focus. Prabakaran's initial hesitation to accept the Indian offer had an unexpected benefit for other less effective rebel groups, which now began to attract hundreds of young men waiting to go to India for training. One middle-ranking guerrilla said: 'Until 1983 I found it difficult to attract people into the Tamil movement. Once India entered the picture, there was such a rush for joining our struggle that I found it difficult to control the crowds'." (p. 94)

The Indian move was in line with what had happened in Bangladesh. There too India had trained the people from the then East Pakistan and then backed them to mount an attack on the eastern region to help in the creation of Bangladesh. This move of India raised similar hopes among the Tamil youth that India after all had decided to go in for the final kill.

Nevertheless Prabakaran remained concerned at Indian intervention in the Tamil problem which he thought it was for the Tamils themselves to fight out, analysed Narayan Swamy. Swamy said:

> "Amid growing speculation that New Delhi might militarily intervene in Sri Lanka, he (Prabakaran) made it clear that the need of the hour was for Tamils to fight their own war." 'Would you suggest military intervention (by India)?' he was asked. He replied: "We have the courage, confidence and determination to fight and win our freedom. We should fight and free ourselves. But we do need India's support and sympathy." India, he added should recognize the "fair and legitimate demand of our people and accept our right to self-determination." (p.103)

What made Prabakaran look to Indian help with such reservations? He was not fully sure of Indian commitment to the cause of Tamil Eelam. India while training the Tamils in guerrilla warfare, had repeatedly committed herself to Sri Lanka's territorial integrity and sovereignty. She too had agreed to facilitate a peaceful solution to the ethnic problem within the four walls of the Island's Constitution. The Indian Prime Minister had appointed G. Parathasarthy as her Special Envoy to conduct talks with Colombo to facilitate a solution to the intractable problem. She had placed her bet on the TULF leadership to lead the Tamils' struggle. It was Amirthalingam who was more in New Delhi than any other Tamil leader and giving leadership to the Tamils in the eyes of everybody. New Delhi appeared to be acting more on his advice and batting on behalf of the TULF, than any one of the militant leaders. In fact, their voice was hardly heard in New Delhi nor were they ever seen in the Indian capital. Prabakaran who was ever suspicious of the TULF since the aftermath of the 1977 elections, could hardly be faulted if he placed no reliance on the peaceful negotiations being promoted by New Delhi. He interpreted the RAW exercise as a tactical move, which would put enough pressure on Colombo to make concessions to the TULF. To that extent, Prabakaran could perceive that he and the LTTE and other militant organisations were being used for the benefit of the TULF. And he had nothing but contempt for the latter.

❮7❯

Anti-Tamil Riots of 1983

In May, 1983, there were anti-Tamil riots on a large scale. In conveying its concern to Sri Lanka, New Delhi expressed its distress, particularly on the regulation, which sought to dispense with the need for an inquest before disposal of dead bodies. Colombo was left in no doubt that India's feathers had been ruffled. The Indian High Commissioner in Colombo who was at that time in New Delhi was asked to return to Colombo immediately to convey the concern of the Government of India at the highest level.

When the news of official Indian concern in what Sri Lanka thought was an internal matter was leaked to the Colombo media, all hell broke loose. Colombo in a demarche to the Indian High Commission reacted angrily and expressed its disapproval of "Indian interference" in the domestic affairs of Sri Lanka. Colombo was also somewhat intrigued at the Indian disapproval of the emergency regulation regarding disposal of dead bodies, since a similar regulation was also in force in 1971 when India far from protesting had actively and militarily assisted Colombo in tackling the emergency situation in the south of the country. To remind India that she too had a similar problem, officials in Colombo maintained that they had desisted from making comments on similar events in India out of concern for good neighbourly relations. Stung by the Sri Lankan reaction, a spokesman of the Indian Ministry of External Affairs in New Delhi on July 21, 1983, tried to douse the fire of Sri Lanka's anger. He said, while India rejected any charge of interference, it valued the historical ties between the two countries. A couple of days later on July 23, Mrs. Gandhi in the course of her press conference in Chennai sought to assure Sri Lanka that India was "against any secessionist movement in any sovereign country" and did not "condone terrorism". Nevertheless, as she held out the assurances of non-interference, she repeated her distress at the latest developments. That the Government of India was under pressure from Tamil Nadu was evident from what she said at the press conference: "I am aware of the great concern of the people of Tamil Nadu at recent developments regarding the Tamil population in Sri Lanka".

In the statement made in the Lok Sabha on July 27, 1983 by the External Affairs Minister P.V. Narasimha Rao, Tamil Nadu factor was oozing out. Underlining Indian concern and compulsions, he said: "developments affecting the Tamil population in Sri Lanka give rise to feelings on the Indian side and can create situation of strain". He did not distinguish between the Sri Lankan Tamils, Tamils of Indian origin or Tamils who were Indian nationals since all were the victims of mass brutality and state's neglect in handling the riots. The members representing the cross-section of the political parties and states were harsh in their criticism and berated the government for its failure to safeguard Tamil interests. Rao's suggestion that he intended to discuss the situation with the Lankan Foreign Minister A.C.S. Hameed who was expected in New Delhi on July 30, for the meeting of the SAARC Foreign Ministers failed to pacify the members. Taking note of the strong sentiments in the Parliament, Prime Minister Indira Gandhi lost her patience and did not wish to wait for the arrival of the Sri Lankan Foreign Minister to take up the issue. The next day, July 28, when the Rajya Sabha was still debating Sri Lanka, she telephoned President Jayewardene and expressed her "grave concern" on behalf of the "Members of Parliament and the people generally all over India and especially the people of Tamil Nadu and the South", on the events in his country. To accentuate Indian anger and concern at the developments, an exasperated Prime Minister suggested an immediate visit by the Indian External Affairs Minister Narasimha Rao. Jayewardene could sense Mrs. Gandhi's mood. He felt it wiser to listen out India than to enter into confrontation. He was not unaware of the mood in Tamil Nadu. He had closely followed the proceedings in the Indian Parliament where members were in an embattled frame of mind and cried for Sri Lankan blood, while berating the government for being soft on Colombo.

Rao left for Colombo the same evening and returned to Delhi in the early hours of July 30. He reported the outcome of his visit to the Lok Sabha on August 2, 1983. He conceded that India's "diplomatic expression of concern was unfortunately made an occasion for a virulent press campaign against India as though we had interfered in Sri Lankan internal affairs". Rao, overcoming the personal snub administered to him by Prime Minister Premadasa (he made him wait for 20 minutes in his ante-room, before receiving him), remained as objective as possible in giving his assessment of the situation in Sri Lanka. For record he tried to segregate the problems of Tamils of Indian origin from those faced by the Sri Lankan Tamils, he made it clear that "India cannot be impervious to the sufferings of large number of people in our immediate neighbourhood, though separated by boundaries of nationality and citizenship". The underlying message was that the differentiation between the two Tamils was only a matter of semantics.

Sri Lanka though quite miffed at India's undue concern for the Tamils had still accepted Rao's visit to prevent further downslide in relations between the two countries. Yet, Jayewardene was upset with "double standards" in India's approach to the problem of militancy and terrorism. He carefully watched the measures India had adopted to deal with similar situations in India and concluded that his measures were no different from those of India and therefore, was anxious to tick off New Delhi for her undue concern. According to press reports leaked to the media (Daily *Sun*, August 1, 1983), while preparing to receive Rao, President Jayewardene addressed his Cabinet before his arrival and desired his Foreign Minister to: "ascertain from India how they solved their communal problem when the extremists asked for a separate state." To convey Colombo's hurt feeling he told his Cabinet: "We will ask India what help they can give us—we will ask the same from the Soviet Union and the United States—we will ask all our friends how they can help us settle these problems. If India, by some chance, even decide to invade us, we will fight—we may lose but with dignity. Then we will go into exile and come back to our country later".

Colombo at this time was agog with a report circulated by the New Delhi correspondent of the UPI from Colombo itself that Sri Lanka had asked for military assistance from the USA, the

U.K., Pakistan and Bangladesh. It, however, turned out to be a false alarm. The UPI correspondent was expelled from Colombo, but not before it created alarm in New Delhi. Panic ridden Mrs. Gandhi telephoned Jayewardene to reassure Colombo of India's bona fide and that it meant no harm to Sri Lanka. Jayewardene tried to convince her that Colombo had not approached any country for any assistance in combating the Tamil militancy. New Delhi did not wish to leave anything to chance. According to press reports quoting an authoritative source in New Delhi, India took the precaution to assure the four countries suspected of having been approached that while India was deeply concerned at the developments in the Island, she had absolutely no intention of intervening. At the same time, she too wished to leave them in no doubt that India would not tolerate intervention by any other country within or outside the region. The implications of Indian stand were not lost on any one that outside intervention might compel India to intervene militarily. In doing so the Government of India wished to localise the issue and avoid at all cost any outside involvement or intervention and reiterated the doctrine of regional security in which India had a dominant role and position.

This doctrine of regional security and India's central role in that was emphasized by Prime Minister Indira Gandhi when she spoke in the Lok Sabha on August 5, after the External Affairs Minister had replied to the debate on the situation in Sri Lanka. She said:

> "As you know, we have made it clear in every forum and in every possible way that India does not pose any threat to Sri Lanka, nor do we want to interfere in their internal affairs. I reassured the President (of Sri Lanka) on this. We want the unity and national integrity of Sri Lanka to be preserved. At the same time, I pointed out to the President that developments in Sri Lanka affect us also. In this matter India cannot be regarded as just any country. Sri Lanka and India are the two countries who are directly concerned. Any extraneous involvement will complicate matters for both our countries. We live in the region where many forces are at work, not all of who wish India or our neighbours well. Forces of destabilization are at work. Hence, we must make every

effort to minimize any opportunity for foreign elements to weaken us."

Sri Lanka while feeling assured, was left uneasy. Colombo was betting on outside help to scare New Delhi away to stop espousing Tamil cause. The message now from New Delhi was loud, clear and ominous. The President for once appeared convinced that the threat of possible outside intervention would not frighten New Delhi. On the contrary it would ensure what Colombo thought it was seeking to insure against. In the changed scenario, Jayewardene realized that New Delhi needed to be reassured of Colombo's bona fides. On August 6, 1983, he personally telephoned Mrs. Gandhi to say, "rumours that had been spread regarding Sri Lanka requesting military assistance from foreign countries were untrue". An official spokesman asserted a day earlier (August 5) in Colombo that such reports and rumours "appeared to be aimed at destroying the close ties of friendship that existed between Sri Lanka and India." He was categorical that Colombo had not asked for military assistance against India from any country. He expressed his government's "distress" at such report(s). In support of his contention, he referred to the denial of the State Department of the USA that Colombo had approached for any military assistance.

The discussions in the Indian Parliament on the 4th and 5th August, 1983, on the EAM's visit were marked by an emotional upsurge. Jayewardene was compared by some to Hitler whose "soul survives in some parts of the world". The members cutting across party lines highlighted the plight of Sri Lankan Tamils and called for stringent measures to tackle the problem of Tamils in Sri Lanka.

Violence continued to grip Sri Lanka. Gradually, India's assertion of concern for Sri Lankan Tamils became more pronounced and strident. Colombo was compelled to take note of the fact that India was no longer a disinterested party, and would not and could not, watch the events from the sidelines. Compulsions of domestic politics and pressure of parliament was leaving fewer options for New Delhi. Colombo for once felt it had become essential to reassure New Delhi that Colombo was doing its best to resolve the ethnic problem. Jayewardene decided on personal diplomacy. He sent his brother H.W. Jayewardene to New Delhi as his Special Envoy to explain Sri Lankan position.

While listening to HW Mrs. Gandhi too made use of the opportunity to affirm to Colombo yet again that India posed no threat to the sovereignty or territorial integrity of the Island. On August 12 (after the visit of H.W. Jayewardene) Mrs. Gandhi told the Lok Sabha that she had conveyed to Jayewardene that India stood for the "independence, unity and integrity of Sri Lanka", and did not wish to "interfere in the internal affairs of other countries". Lest such an assurance should make Colombo complacent towards the plight of the Tamils, she issued an oblique warning adding for the benefit of Colombo that "because of the historical, cultural and such other close ties between the people of the two countries, particularly between the Tamil community of Sri Lanka and us, India cannot remain unaffected by such events there". Sri Lanka was therefore put on notice that henceforth welfare of the Tamil minority who enjoyed ethnic and cultural affinities with the people of Tamil Nadu was a matter of direct concern to India. That Colombo felt compelled to concede India's locus standi was no longer a matter for speculation.

While in New Delhi, the President's brother gave a detailed resume of the efforts made by Colombo to resolve the ethnic conflict. Some of these were implementation of laws relating to the District Development Councils, the use of Tamil as a national language, amnesty for the Tamils, repeal of draconian laws, discontinuance of army's role in curbing ethnic violence in the north, etc. Finding Colombo on the back foot, Mrs. Gandhi felt bold to tell her interlocutor that they were not enough "to meet the aspirations of the Tamil community". To placate Mrs. Gandhi, H.W. Jayewardene expressed Colombo's willingness to "consider any other proposals, which would give the Tamil minority their due share in the affairs of their country, within the framework of a united Sri Lanka". She saw in this a window of opportunity to get a toehold for India as a peace broker in the ethnic conflict of a country, beleaguered and tormented by internal dissensions. To Mrs. Gandhi's pleasant surprise, Colombo was willing to trust India. H.W. Jayewardene, after consulting with his brother, conveyed Colombo's acceptance of India's good offices to resolve the country's ethnic conflict.

Impact of Indian Involvement

It is ironic that when Sri Lanka initially adopted policies of discrimination against the Tamil minority during the premierships of S.W.R.D. Bandaranaike and his wife Sirimavo Bandaranaike, the Indian leaders—Nehru and Mrs. Gandhi—had apparently best of relations with them, India did not even attempt to use their influence to get the Tamils a fair deal. While negotiating with Colombo on the future of the Tarnils of Indian origin during the three decades following the independence of the two countries, India was loath to take up the question of discrimination against the ethnic Tamils, which had become a major domestic issue in the Island's politics, particularly since 1956. This, despite the fact that India against her past stand and in the interest of the Tamils of Indian origin had made a major change in her policy in 1964 to accommodate Colombo and accepted a substantial number of them for grant of Indian citizenship and repatriation back to India. Those were the days, when perhaps the Tamils too wanted to keep India out. They had chosen to be part of the mainstream politics of the country. They remained aloof from the citizenship question of the other Tamils. They were content to be the junior partners in the Sinhalese dominated governments in the hope of getting a fair deal by working within the system and fight their own battle, despite several setbacks and occasional bouts of violence against them.

In 1971, India extended military assistance to Mrs. Bandaranaike to bail her out of the J.V.P. insurrection in the south. One has to remember that it was Sirimavo's discriminatory policies in the seventies towards the Tamils that reached their nadir and accentuated the ethnic problem. She was the darling of the Indian establishment on the non-aligned platform, the movement of which she was the leading light that berated South Africa and Israel at the drop of the hat for pursuing fascist and racist policies overlooking Sri Lanka's record at home. India failed to nudge Sirimavo into being more benevolent towards her ethnic minority, which had ties of language, race, religion and culture with the people of an important state of the Indian Union.

Paradoxically, it was the return to power of the UNP government under J.R. Jayewardene who had campaigned during the 1977 elections on the policy of reconciliation that led to the dismantling of some of the discriminatory regime put in place by Sirimavo Bandaranaike. Tamil language was given its due recognition and the standardization scheme for admission to universities in premier courses, which had worked against the

Tamils, was abandoned. But it was too little too late. Already in 1976, the Sri Lankan Tamils had adopted the Vaddukoddai Resolution asking for separation and a sovereign Eelam State. Militant movements of the Tamil youth had taken deep roots. They had abandoned the policy of petitioning Colombo and vowed to secure what they thought was their rightful due by frontal confrontation.

It was not until the anti-Tamil pogrom of 1983 and the uproar that it created in Tamil Nadu and in Parliament, that New Delhi felt compelled to sit up and take cognizance of it as a problem affecting her. At this time there were other external factors, which made India feel besieged. Soviet Union after the death of Brezhnev had come under great pressure in Afghanistan. Pakistan as a front line state, had once again become darling of the American establishment and was feeling buoyant with fresh dose of American military and economic aid. She had blatantly chosen to extend support to the various militant movements in India, particularly in Punjab and Kashmir. Beleaguered India discerned with deep anxiety that Sri Lanka had chosen to involve outside powers and agencies impacting the security of peninsular India.

The Indian decision to get involved in finding a solution to the ethnic problem greatly invigorated the Tamil community, which had practically given up any hope of peaceful resolution of its problem with the Sri Lankan Government. The Tamil members were already staying out of the Parliament for failing to take an oath of allegiance to the "unitary" Constitution under a new amendment. On August 14, 1983, Appapillai Amirthalingam, Secretary General of the TULF, on a visit to New Delhi said that his party would reconsider an earlier decision not to negotiate with Colombo in view of the qualitative change in the situation. Their sagging spirits were revived that India with her tail twisted by the compulsions of domestic politics would mount the required pressure on Colombo to make it see reason. They felt it was now the turn of Colombo to seek accommodation with them. They could afford to stand on the high moral ground and wait for things to happen. Appointment of G. Parthasarthy, a Tamil as interlocutor to interface with Sri Lanka further boosted their self-esteem. They felt they could count on his Tamilian background to forcefully argue their case in Colombo. The designation of "Special Envoy of the Prime Minister of India" apparently vested enough authority and prestige in his person to be taken seriously by Colombo.

Despite feeling euphoric, the Tamils did not fail to notice that while offering to intercede on their behalf, New Delhi had assured Colombo respect for their sovereignty and territorial integrity. This was in conflict with their dream of Eelam, which they expected India to fulfill somehow. But by so doing, India intended to convey to the Tamils a message too that while she was anxious that they got their due, they should not misconstrue Indian involvement to mean Eelam. India was careful not to promote at this stage any secessionist ambitions of the Tamils. She herself was faced with a number of militant and separatist movements within the country and any support to such an agenda of a community in a neighbouring country would have been a wrong signal.

Describing the acceptance of "good offices" as a breakthrough in the Lok Sabha on August 18, 1983, Rao however cautioned that "good offices by their very nature are not capable of being defined in cut and dried terms. They could take different forms in different times and on different occasions in regard to different questions...", and a final solution would come after negotiations and as a package worked out between Sri Lankan Government and the Sri Lankan Tamils. Prime Minister Mrs. Gandhi was more forthcoming and her remarks in Parliament were music to the ears of the Tamils. Speaking in the Lok Sabha the same day (August 18), while she quoted the Tamil leader Amirthalingam to welcome India's offer of good offices as introducing "a basic change in regard to negotiation between his party and the Government of Sri Lanka", she indicted Colombo thus:

> "For many years, he (Amirthalingam) and his party has sought fulfilment of the legitimate rights and aspirations of the Tamil people of the Island within a united Sri Lanka, but had failed to get any hopeful response. On the contrary, the Tamils have been increasingly harassed, and the latest outrages against them have left them totally without confidence in negotiations. Mr. Amirthalingam and his colleagues did not find it possible to come to the negotiating table on the basis of the past offers. However, he feels that as a result of India's efforts, the picture has changed and,

although differences between the two sides remain deep, there might now be some possibility of a solution".

Mrs. Gandhi did not mince words to convey to Colombo that New Delhi could not ignore compulsions of domestic politics: "I am particularly aware of the deep emotions of our brothers and sisters in Tamil Nadu over these tragic happenings...the agony of Tamils in India and elsewhere is that of our entire nation. The brutality and insensate violence to which the Tamils of Sri Lanka have been subjected were vividly described by Amirthalingam in his talks here. My Government and I personally have been conveying our own anguish and concern to the Government of Sri Lanka".

The people at large in Jaffna were ecstatic at Mrs. Gandhi's pronouncements. The Jaffna residents in a letter of August 23, 1983, to Mrs. Gandhi congratulated her on this development, which they described as an "expert handling of President Jayewardene". The majority community, however, did not look at this development with any equanimity. There was no political consensus on Indian involvement and the Sinhalese remained skeptical. The *Sun* said on August 25, 1983:

> "Lankans who have experienced five centuries of colonial domination would naturally be averse to any foreign power giving them advice on how to run their affairs—however much altruistic it may be".

On 3rd September the paper editorially said:

> "India cannot and must not think that it could play a role in solving Lanka's ethnic problem. It must not once think of playing politics with a friendly neighbour".

Anura Bandaranaike of the SLFP was apprehensive that this might set a precedent for the future. Because of his personal regard for Mrs. Gandhi, he felt "absolutely confident" that she would never permit any intervention in Sri Lanka's affairs. Nevertheless he felt concerned that a precedent had been set for outside intervention. In the background of Indian intervention in 1971 to quell the JVP insurrection, which was invited by Sirimavo herself, she sounded more conciliatory of Indian role as an intermediary who should not be applying any pressure but "just explore possibilities and see where they (differences) can be narrowed down". Vouching for Mrs. Gandhi and describing her line as correct, Sirimavo added: "I happen to know personally that she will never encourage separatists, like some other countries might".

The members of the Indian Parliament did not share the Government of India's optimism for a solution. They continued to harbour misgivings about the intentions of Sri Lankan Government since the past record of Colombo did not inspire much confidence and it was felt that the Tamils in the north particularly remained vulnerable to the highhandedness of the State's security forces.

Not confident of Colombo's intentions, there were some voices in India seeking deployment of multi-national peace force or an Indian peace keeping force to give the Tamils a better sense of security. But India was not convinced of either the need or the efficacy of such a force. On August 24, 1983, addressing the Consultative Committee of the Parliament, Narasimha Rao rubbished such a proposal and cautioned that deployment of a "multi-national peace keeping force drawn from various countries" could only "trigger off adverse reactions". Besides that, the record of such forces had not been noteworthy. At this stage, India was not too sanguine about the role for an Indian peace keeping force either. The Indian Defence Minister, R. Venkataraman speaking in Chennai on September 20, 1983, had described the demand as "ridiculous" and said that neither the leaders of the Jaffna Tamils nor those of the people of Indian origin had made such a demand as they knew of its consequences. Negotiations being the most prudent course, Venkataraman called it unfortunate that some people in Tamil Nadu should criticise the steps taken by the Indian Prime Minister to help the Sri Lankan Tamils. Dismissing the view that a mere threat of armed intervention by India could have prevented the killings of Tamils, he warned that on the contrary Sri Lanka would have been compelled to seek assistance from other countries and put paid to chances of peaceful solution. Dismissing any parallel between the situation in Sri Lanka and Bangladesh, he said in the latter case there was a specific request for intervention from the people of that country, besides provocation by Pakistani attack on India. It is tragic that a few years later India was to forget this well considered view of her defence minister, and rushed into a situation where angels feared to tread.

❮8❯

India's Mediatory Role

G. Parthasarthy, a Tamil himself, as pointed out above was designated as the Special Envoy of the Prime Minister invested with sufficient authority and prestige, initially played into the hands of the TULF leaders. He failed to recognise the ground realities and the limits that he could go to. On August 26, 1983, he handed over to President Jayewardene an 8-point proposal calling for merger of Northern and the Eastern provinces, after taking out the Muslim majority district of Amparai to be constituted a separate state. Given the past history of Sri Lankan hypersensitivity towards constituting a united Tamil state comprising the two provinces, his mission was a non-starter. Colombo completely ignored his proposals. A press release issued by the Presidential Secretariat did not even take note of them. Later, when TULF leader Amirthalingam met President Jayewardene on September 3, fresh proposals were discussed between the two, which were welcomed by the spokesman of the Ministry of External Affairs who confirmed that the TULF leader would visit India to acquaint the Indian Prime Minister with the nature of his discussions with President Jayewardene.

Between the first visit of Parthasarthy in August 1983, and the second in November, there was an all-party conference in Colombo, which ended in fiasco because of the boycott of the conference by the SLFP. In any case there was little meeting ground in the talks between the TULF and the government principally because of latter's insistence that TULF abjured its separatist agenda before entering the talks, and the TULF refusing to accept any pre-condition. The impasse led the government to initiate its own measures to resolve the Tamil problem and hence the All-Party Conference. Though there was no specific agenda for the Conference, President Jayewardene had identified five specific areas for discussion—the Tamil Language Special Provisions Act, the Development Councils Act, Education, Employment and Measures to eradicate terrorism. Six parties were invited to the Conference. These were: the ruling United National Party, the main opposition Sri Lanka Freedom Party and the Mahajana Eksath Peramuna, Lanka Sama Samaja Party, Communist Party of Sri Lanka, and the Ceylon Workers' Congress. As stated above, the Conference hardly transacted any business. Except the ruling UNP and the Mahajana Eksath Peramuna no other party responded. The SLFP further muddied the Conference atmosphere by insisting that the government clarify whether the meeting between the Plantation Tamil leader Thondoman and Uma Maheswaren, a militant leader living in exile in South India constituted a deviation from the Government's committed policy of not having talks with "terrorists" or other groups, which did not disavow separatism.

Meanwhile, Parthasarthy was anxious to make another attempt at reconciliation. The hawks in the UNP remained opposed to his mission altogether describing it as constituting foreign interference. The President saw it prudent to play safe. He postponed his second visit billed for October-end. This visit, finally, took place from 7th to 10th November 83. Meanwhile Thondoman, on return from his Indian and US visits told a press conference in Colombo on October 23, that TULF leader Amirthalingam whom he met in India, had requested him to represent the interests of the Sri Lankan Tamils also in Parliament, since they stood debarred from it. He warned that the Tamil issue in Sri Lanka had become the concern not only of Tamils in India but the world community and that what was happening in the North was not viewed as terrorism by the Indian people but as armed resistance against the policy of oppression of the Sinhala forces.

After the second visit of the Special Envoy, Parthasarthy, from 7th to 10th November, the Indian External Affairs Minister P.V. Narasimha Rao clarified in the Lok Sabha on November 17, that his mission was not one of mediation; he was only "acting as a channel of communication between the Sri Lankan Government and the leaders of the TULF in order to help find a common basis for a solution by narrowing down the differences between the two sides".

An important development went unnoticed amidst this flurry of political activity. The militants and elements wedded to Eelam were getting frustrated with the TULF, whom they described as a party, which had been entrapped by the Parthasarthy mission. The General Secretary of the Tamil Eelam Liberation Front, M.K. Eelaventhan told Anita Pratap (*Sunday*, December 11-17,1983) that the TULF leadership was very "mellow and exhausted" and had outlived its utility. He said:

> "For the last 35 years they have made excellent speeches in Parliament in Tamil and English, complete with facts and figures but it still has not made an iota of difference. It is not that Tamils lacked in oration or in factual presentation, we find it impossible to deal with Sinhala leaders who have preconceived notions, who are prisoners of their prejudices. I think it is a blessing in disguise that President Jayewardene has brought in the sixth amendment that has kept the TULF out of Parliament. Now events are compelling them to launch a violent or non-violent mass struggle outside Parliament".

Eelaventhan rejected any political solution short of Eelam and said, if TULF were to accept anything less than that their leadership would be wiped out. He wondered if the Government of India would pressurize the TULF into accepting any proposal not acceptable to the Tamils generally. He lamented the helpless situation of the TULF, who could not go beyond "what the Indian Government offers" to them. A few months later, on March 11, 1984, (*Sunday*) Prabakaran spoke in the same vein while speaking also to Anita Pratap. He lamented that the parliamentary system not only failed the Tamils but also "aggravated" their plight. Giving the LTTE's perspective, Prabakaran disabused any notion that their movement was separatist but one for independence based on the right to national self-determination. He contested the view that the militants were terrorists fighting "for a division or separation of a country". He prided in the fact that they were, "fighting to uphold the sacred right to live in freedom and dignity. In this sense we are freedom fighters and not terrorists". Giving a new vision of the state of Eelam, the LTTE supremo said:

> "Tamil Eelam will be a socialist state. By socialism I mean an egalitarian society where human freedom and

individual liberties will be guaranteed, where all forms of oppression and exploitation will be abolished. It will be a free society where our people will have maximum opportunity to develop their economy and promote their culture. Tamil Eelam will be a neutral state, committed to non-alignment and friendly to India, respecting her regional policies, particularly the policy of making the Indian Ocean a zone of peace."

Meanwhile, the militant Tamils had built up a major international network of support through the Tamil diaspora, which carried their grievances in the councils of the world and international media. Soon the diaspora became a major source of funding for the Eelam movement spearheaded by the LTTE, both out of commitment and through coercion. As time went, the Diaspora became more uncompromising on the Eelam question than the Tamils in Sri Lanka. Unmindful of the consequences, it became the powerhouse of the LTTE until 9/11 dealt a body blow to militancy wedded to violence.

The final proposals emerging out of the efforts of the Indian Special Envoy G.Parthasarthy were contained in a document called, 'Annexure C'. These proposals were finalised after a series of discussions at various levels and between various leaders including the Tamils to make them acceptable to all shades of opinion. 'Annexure C' had suggested devolution of powers at the regional and district levels as well as measures to neutralise the disadvantages imposed on the Tamils by the pursuit of 'Only Sinhala' policies of the past, discriminating against the Tamils and their language. Missing in this proposal was the earlier suggestion of merger of the two Tamil provinces to create a Tamil State. It came up for discussion at the All-Party Conference in January, 1984. The Conference achieved nothing beyond appointing two committees to consider various aspects of the grievances of all the communities and to find solutions to them and to examine the causes of ethnic violence, terrorism and measures for their eradication. The Conference was marred by withdrawals and boycott by various groups and parties on one pretext or the other. It may be recalled that the President had visited New Delhi in the later part of November, 1983, to attend the Commonwealth Heads of Government Conference and used the opportunity to hold discussions with the Indian leaders on the various aspects of the 'Annexure C' and obtained Indian assurance against secession and commitment to Sri Lanka's independence, integrity and sovereignty. G. Parthasarthy too had obtained assurances from the TULF leaders who happened to be present in New Delhi at the same time that they would give up their call for a separate state, if an acceptable solution to their problems was worked out.

One of the principal reasons for failure of the All-Party Conference was President Jayewardene deviating materially from the 'Annexure C' proposals and his adoption of dilatory tactics to ensure that the Conference did not come to grip with the substantive Tamil question. In presenting a Memorandum to the Conference, the President spoke of the impasse on account of "two contradictory and apparently inflexible positions taken up by the two sides—on the one hand, "the District Councils and no more" and on the other hand "Regional Councils and no less". He was critical of the Tamil position since he said, "TULF position is one that admits of no possible compromise". On September 30, 1984, A. Amirthalingam speaking at the plenary session of the resumed All-Party Conference while criticizing the very manner in which the Conference was being organised, described the Tamil proposal for Regional Councils as reasonable since it was already a compromise from their mandate "for an independent State" to a "Union of States within the framework of a united Sri Lanka". He emphasised that though it did not fully satisfy the aspirations of the Tamils, yet TULF was "willing to recommend it" to the Tamils "subject to the unit being the Tamil linguistic region consisting of the Northern and Eastern provinces, with devolved legislative and executive powers over specified listed subjects, including the maintenance of internal law and order in the Region, the administration of justice, social and economic development, cultural matters and land policy". He rejected the proposal for District Councils which permitted only inter-district coordination as also the proposal for a Second Chamber, which he felt was "calculated to defeat the objective of devolution". Surely Amirthalingam was going beyond the 'Annexure C' in asking for the merged Regional Council for the north and the east.

The proposals that the President placed before the Conference in the form of a draft Bill, were acceptable neither to the Tamils nor to the Sinhala parties. Within the government, there was also a lack of unanimity. The President had to dismiss his Minister of Industries and Scientific Affairs, Cyril Mathew, for publicly criticising his proposals. It was once again more than clear that no Sinhala leader of any hue was willing to concede any space to the Tamil aspirations. Both the TULF and the SLFP rejected the Bill for their own reasons — one accusing the government of conceding too much, other too little. The SLFP continued to suspect the Tamils for their separatist leanings, and any accommodation to them was nothing but the first step towards disintegration of Sri Lanka, particularly after the adoption of the Vaddukoddai Resolution in 1976. The government, on another plain too remained quite articulate in peddling the Tamil demands in the international fora as secessionist and separatist in nature. The TULF leader, Amirthalingam, speaking at the All-Party Conference on December 21, 1984 warned,

> "Time is running out. Tamil areas are under virtual siege. Normal life has come to a standstill. Death, arson, rape and looting stalk these areas. Starvation is staring the poor in the face. This is the grim reality of the situation in the Northern and Eastern provinces. We are constrained to state that the two Bills before this Conference do not embody any scheme of autonomy which could be accepted by the Tamil people or their accredited representatives, the Tamil United Liberation Front."

Though the Sri Lankan Government was feeling greatly embarrassed at the continuing violence which had attracted adverse international attention, it was easy for it to explain its position on the Tamils' secessionist plank. On September 24, 1984, speaking in the United Nations General Assembly, Foreign Minister A.C.S Hameed, after a narration of the background of the problem stood on the high moral ground and justified his country's position thus:

> "No government in independent Sri Lanka has tried harder to resolve this problem by accommodating the claims of the minority Tamil community. On the one hand, the government has been severely criticized by the majority Sinhalese community for the efforts and concessions it has made. On the other hand, the representatives of the Tamil minority proclaim to the outside world that their

civil and human rights have been violated and their answer, therefore, is a separate State. Perhaps this dissatisfaction of both the majority and the minority communities is in itself evidence that the Government has been both balanced and impartial in its handling of this difficult question...(and) for the Government and the people of Sri Lanka— and among these people I include the overwhelming number of the minorities in our population —the independence, territorial integrity, sovereignty and unity of Sri Lanka are not negotiable. In short, under no circumstances can we or will we accept the division of the country."

Efforts of G. Parthasarthy failed to produce any concrete results. Attempts to promote further talks between Colombo and the TULF were non-starter, since Sri Lanka insisted that before she entered into any meaningful discussions with the TULF, it should abjure demand for Eelam and come to the mainstream of the national political life. As pointed out earlier the TULF too remained debarred from Parliament, since it failed to take an oath pledging allegiance to the unitary Constitution. The impasse in Colombo led President Jayewardene to make use of his visit to New Delhi in November, 1983, for the Commonwealth Prime Ministers Conference for summit level discussions with the Indian Prime Minister. As stated above the TULF leaders, who were in Delhi, were also involved in the triangular discussions. But the package offered by the Sri Lankan government involving regional councils and some devolution of powers for local autonomy, remained as before unacceptable to the Tamils.

The Tamils remained adamant on larger Regional Council comprising the two Northern and Eastern provinces instead of a separate council for each of the two provinces as offered in the 'Annexure C'. They were also averse to the referendum to ascertain the wishes of the people for merger of district councils into regional council, since it would only inflame ethnic passions and increase tension. On the question of referendum, though the President was prepared to relent, the colonization scheme in the newly developed areas continued to bother the Tamils. They were apprehensive that it would tilt the ethnic balance in favour of the Sinhalese, in otherwise traditionally Tamil majority areas. In her talks with Jayewardene, Mrs. Gandhi assured her interlocutor that India wanted Sri Lanka to preserve her territorial integrity by arriving at a fair and equitable settlement of her ethnic problem. He was also assured that India had no desire to interfere in Sri Lanka's internal affairs and condone any violent acts. But at the same time, she expected Sri Lanka to meet the legitimate aspirations of the Tamil community to ensure peace and tranquillity for the good of all the communities.

Ethnic violence once again broke out in April, 1984. Seven persons were killed when troops opened fire in Jaffna after the Tamil militants threw a bomb at an army truck, injuring 15 soldiers. In another incident, seven militants lobbed a bomb at the Bank of Ceylon branch at Point Pedro and escaped with Rs. 9,65,000. An eighteen-hour curfew was in force in Jaffna, following incidents of bomb blast and arson by Tamils and retaliatory firing by the troops killing two and injuring several. In the midst of growing violence, Jayewardene was becoming impatient with the Indian role, which he felt only encouraged Tamils' intransigence. On April 9, 1984, he expressed his frustration at the Indian role at a UNP rally saying no outside force, "not even one hundred Indias will be able to subjugate Sri Lanka".

A worried Government of India was constrained to express its anguish in the Lok Sabha on April 3, 1984, for lack of progress on the political front. On the contrary, India was being accused by Colombo media of interference in Sri Lanka and providing arms and training to the militants. India contradicting such reports felt it necessary to assure Colombo of her commitment to the Island's unity and integrity, and opposition to secession and all forms of violence. While saying so, as in the past, it was made abundantly clear that India had an abiding interest in the restoration of peace and harmony in Sri Lanka, since developments in that country affected India closely. To allay India's fears on the eruption of violence, on April 15, 1984, President Jayewardene sent his Special Envoy, Lalith Athulathmudali, to New Delhi who apprised the Indian leaders of the progress achieved at the All-Party Conference and prospects for the future. He unsuccessfully tried to assure India that all was well.

On April 6 and May 7, 1984, the situation in Sri Lanka came up for discussion in the emotionally charged two Houses of the Indian Parliament for the umpteenth time. The members from Tamil Nadu were particularly agitated and did not fight shy of suggesting extreme military steps to deal with the situation. The External Affairs Minister in vain counselled cool and levelheaded approach to the problem. Giving a resume of the discussions held with the Sri Lankan Minister of National Security who had visited New Delhi from April 12 to 15, as the Special Envoy of the President, the External Affairs Minister Narasimha Rao maintained that the recent violence had caused New Delhi a lot of anguish. Rao articulated the "deep concern felt throughout the country over the offensive by the army at present underway in the Northern and Eastern provinces and over the political dialogue". He regretted that the deployment of a large number of troops in Jaffna was aggravating ethnic tension. In the unending cycle of attacks and counter-attacks, the lives of many innocent people had been lost. He was unhappy that the atmosphere for a political dialogue had been vitiated. Rao also informed the members of Colombo's compulsions as conveyed by Athulathmudali for taking action against the Tamils to avoid the backlash of ethnic violence in Sinhala majority areas in the south and in the plantations against the Plantation Tamils. Rao's efforts to cool passions of the Tamil members of Parliament did not appear to succeed. They described the government's inaction as a "betrayal" of the Tamil cause. Members from other states while sympathising with the Tamils were not convinced of any other option except the political one. They did not favour a military alternative or call to the United Nations as prudent. Despite taking a charitable view of Colombo's predicament, New Delhi felt embarrassed by the anti-Indian stance of Colombo. The External Affairs Minister felt compelled to regret it in his intervention in the Lok Sabha on April 6:

> "It is unfortunate that in this tense atmosphere senior leaders of the United National Party, particularly the Prime Minister, have chosen to contribute to an anti-India build up to which the local media have given prominent coverage. We on our part, have conveyed to the Sri Lankan Government that the allegations made against India are baseless, we have reiterated our commitment to Sri Lanka's unity and integrity and have stressed the urgency of continuing the political dialogue with seriousness so that a viable political settlement can be arrived at."

The Indian reiteration of her commitment to the unity and integrity of Sri Lanka went home. On April 19, 1984, Lalith Athulathmudali, making a statement on his visit to New Delhi assured his Parliament:

> "I am happy to inform this House that the leaders of India, the President, and Prime Minister, the Foreign Minister and the Defence Minister and even the men in the street again and again reiterated their commitment to respect our unity, integrity and sovereignty as Sri Lanka. They all wished to leave me in no doubt about this matter."

Bolstered by repeated Indian assurances to the Islands' unity and integrity, Sri Lanka felt emboldened to deal with the Tamils in her own way. But Tamil Nadu factor worried them. Jayewardene on a visit to China soon thereafter (April, 1984), reportedly told the Chinese President Li Xiannian, that there were no problems between Sri Lanka and the Central Government in India on the unity of the Island but indicated that the position taken in Tamil Nadu had created difficulties for Colombo. He was stated to have conveyed to Beijing that various political parties in Tamil Nadu were attempting to take advantage of Sri Lankan situation at the upcoming elections in the state "expressing views totally against international standards of conduct". In this context, he mentioned the "march to Sri Lanka" organised by some Tamil Nadu politicians, and Mrs. Gandhi's assurance that she could not stop them marching on the Indian territory, but if they tried to cross the water into Sri Lanka by boat, she would stop them. "She did that", President Jayewardene told the Chinese leaders as a proof of Central Government's sincerity. Continuing he strongly asserted: "we will not allow our country to be divided", but pointed out to the Chinese that Colombo needed the support of both the Government of India and of Tamil Nadu to tackle the problem of terrorism. In this context, he pointed out to the Chinese leaders the importance of Chinese sympathy and understanding. When President Jayewardene thanked President Li for China's understanding and support on the ethnic issue, President Li responded with remarks that it was China's duty to support its friends and there was no need to thank the PRC for that.

❮9❯

India's Concern at Escalating Violence

At the popular level, the plight of the Tamils in Sri Lanka agitated the minds of the Indian public, particularly in Tamil Nadu. They demanded some meaningful action by the Government of India to alleviate their sufferings. The Sinhala army had been ruthless in its handling of the situation in Jaffna. Indian External Affairs Minister Narasimha Rao on May 7, 1984, conceded in the Rajya Sabha that India had conveyed to Colombo her anguish at the "senseless killings" in Jaffna. He regretted the presence of a large number of troops in Jaffna, which had aggravated the ethnic tension. To take the edge off members' criticism, Rao said that India had stressed on Colombo "the need to take measures to defuse the tension such as reducing the presence of the army, which resulted in incidents affecting the civilian population". While saying so, Mr. Rao was not unmindful of Sri Lankan compulsion to take action in order to avoid Sinhala backlash in Sinhalese areas in the South and in the Plantations against the Tamils.

Rao's indulgent statement did not prevent tongue lashing in Sri Lankan Parliament. The very next day (May 8), the SLFP leader Anura Bandaranaike "unequivocally" condemned Rao for his statement. He described Rao's statement as an "unwarranted interference", and sought clarification if India had indeed asked for troops reduction in Jaffna. The Sri Lankan Minister for National Security, Athulathmudali, relying on semantics ducked the opposition attack. He insisted that what India had said was their opinion and not any request for withdrawal. He maintained that the Government had received no specific request for "withdrawal" of troops, nor the Indian Minister used the word "withdrawal" in his statement.

India's espousal of the Tamil cause, the misunderstanding on the lease of Trincomalee Oil Tank Farm, the Voice of America broadcasting facilities, the military assistance from Israel and other dubious agencies from the West and South Africa, Sri Lanka's India bashing for providing arms training facilities to the militants on the Indian soil erected between the two countries a mountain of suspicion, which could only be tunneled with trust and understanding. Regrettably, both the elements were missing. Sri Lanka repeatedly questioned India's right to ask for reduction in her troop-deployment in Jaffna, and advice on other issues like the Oil Tank Farm and VOA. Ranasinghe Premadasa had no qualms of conscience in using ill-tempered language against the Indian leaders when demanding return of the Tamil militants, alleged to be operating from the Indian territory. He often alluded to developments within India like the situation in the Punjab to justify action against the Tamil militants and army deployment. He even challenged India to "openly invade" Sri Lanka and not play "hide and seek". President Jayewardene, too, never lagged behind his Prime Minister in this respect, though he preferred to use a little more civilised language. His statement of April 9, 1984, at a UNP rally in Colombo, that no outside force, "not even one hundred Indias will be able to subjugate Sri Lanka" or calling upon his people to spread the message that "Sri Lankans are a race that cannot be subdued", were made to convey Colombo's determination to meet the Indian challenge on the ethnic question head on.

Sri Lanka remained miffed with India for what she thought Indian encouragement and support to Sri Lankan Tamils in terms of military training and refusal to repatriate those operating from Tamil Nadu against the interest of the Island. On May 24, 1984, speaking in Parliament in the debate on the extension of Emergency, Premadasa once again gave vent to his frustration and said:

> "India should not play hide and seek with us. India should invade us openly and we are prepared to lay down our lives to defend our country...there may be some henchmen here who are prepared to be governed by India, but the majority of Lankans would prefer to die."

Next day (May 25), speaking again in Parliament in the debate on the Trincomalee Oil Tank Farm, Premadasa was unrelenting. Taking a high moral ground he said Sri Lanka had not encouraged the Punjab militants or given them refuge in the country. He questioned India's reservations on the lease of the Oil Tank Farm to a Consortium of foreign companies. He reminded India that when she signed a friendship treaty with the Soviet Union and received arms and equipment from that country, Sri Lanka did not question India's right to do so and therefore, India had no right now to object to Sri Lanka contracting the Farm to any country or company of her choice. Speaking in concert with his Prime Minister, Cyril Mathew, Minister for Industries and Scientific Affairs said, if India signing the Treaty with the Soviet Union and receiving arms from that country did not amount to deviating from the policy of non-alignment, how could Colombo's status as a non-aligned country be eroded by a similar action. Again on May 31, President Jayewardene said in Hong Kong that Sri Lanka would accept help "from the devil to break the back of the terrorist problem" in his country. He lamented that Colombo had not been able to get "the United States, Britain and India to help" Sri Lanka and therefore "we have to get help from somewhere. We can't be political waifs". Nevertheless, in a rare conciliatory gesture towards India, perhaps because he was on the soil of a third country, he went out of his way to give India a clean chit by saying, "I personally have no fears as long as India is free, united, democratic and under the influence of the Congress leaders".

Sri Lankan fulminations made New Delhi sit up. An official spokesman of the Ministry of External Affairs on June 1, 1984, expressed pain and surprise "at these outbursts against a friendly country which has gone out of its way to offer friendship and goodwill to the Government and the people of Sri Lanka". He warned:

> "All this seems calculated to do harm to the long-standing friendly relations between our two countries. Far-sighted people in Sri Lanka will, we hope, see to it that irreparable damage is not done to these relations. Is the Indian bogey being raised to mislead and divert attention from the ethnic question in Sri Lanka? All this could undermine the peace process."

The Government of India asked its High Commissioner to make "a suitable demarche" with the President and convey Government of India's feelings of hurt.

The Indian warning apparently went home. On June 5, 1984 Premadasa in a conciliatory gesture to underline Sri Lanka's affection for India, recalled the statement of the former Prime Minister D.S. Senanayake of December 9, 1948 while introducing the Indian Residents (Citizenship) Bill in Parliament:

> "India should realise that we are greatly attached to her. That may be due to cultural relations between the two countries: it may be due to the fact that Buddhism was brought here from that country. Whatever the reason be, we have a great deal of affection for India, and for its people a great love. It is therefore, painful to us to find that affection and that attachment is all forgotten, and that right is not given consideration, but that might is sought to be imposed".

Lest Sri Lankan affection should be misconstrued, in the same breath, he wished to tell India that it was all pass and now India stood condemned for harbouring "Sri Lankan terrorists" in Tamil Nadu. The signal was quite clear. Premadasa sought to convey that mere sentiments could not wish away ground realities of the situation. He again drew parallel with the situation in Punjab where the Government of India was fighting terrorism and reminded India that Indian terrorists did not draw succour from Sri Lanka. On the political plane, an impasse appeared to have been reached in Indo-Sri Lanka relations. Colombo appeared determined not to concede any space to India on the Tamil question.

As the political ground in relations between the Tamils and the Sinhalese appeared to cave in, violence intensified. In August 1984 Sri Lankan army went on a rampage in Jaffna, resulting in heavy loss of civilian life and property. On August 8, 1984, Ram Niwas Mirdha, the Minister of State in the Ministry of External Affairs, reported to the Lok Sabha "sharp deterioration in the security situation in the northern part of Sri Lanka resulting in large scale loss of human life and property". Indian agony was reflected in Mrs. Gandhi's speech from the ramparts of the historic Red Fort in Delhi on the solemn occasion of the anniversary of the Indian independence (August 15). Referring to developments in Sri Lanka, she told the audience:

> "The situation in Sri Lanka is quite grave and my heart is full of grief for those innocent people who are being attacked without having done anything wrong. There are extremists and terrorists there as well and it is evident that a government is required to counter them. But the manner in which a particular community is being attacked for the last so many years has come in the way of restoration of peace and the situation had gradually deteriorated. We do not want to interfere. We do not want to put any obstacles in the unity of another country. That would not be in our interest. We want our neighbouring countries to be stable and friendly towards us. We extended our hand of friendship and offered help in having a dialogue and arriving at some conclusions acceptable to all."

The unusual step of the Indian Prime Minister, recalling regretfully the developments in a neighbouring country on a solemn occasion was not lost on her audience. Next day (August 16), the Indian Parliament was informed that the situation in Sri Lanka had taken a "grave turn", and the Island army had gone berserk. New Delhi was panicky lest it should lead to renewed influx of refugees in Tamil Nadu, where there were already 40,000 of them. The Government of India repeated for the umpteenth time that:

> "The ethnic problem in Sri Lanka cannot be solved by military action. It is a political problem involving the just rights of the Tamil minority and only the determined pursuit of the political process of consultations and mutual accommodation can lead to a constructive way out. This has been our view all along and we have repeatedly conveyed it to the President of Sri Lanka".

While saying so, New Delhi yet again assured Sri Lanka that it stood for her integrity and unity but wanted violence to end. To address Colombo's grumble, Indian Minister of State for External Affairs extended an assurance that India had "taken steps to curb activities which may be directed against Sri Lanka from our soil". Not letting Sri Lanka off the hook, the Minister bewailed at the involvement of outside agencies in the country and cautioned "this can only aggravate matters not only in Sri Lanka but also in the region". Having taken the involvement of outside agencies seriously, India thought it fit to express its "deep concern" to the leaders of some important involved countries.

‹10›

Rajiv Gandhi takes over

The tragic events in India in the later half of 1984, leading to the assassination of Prime Minister Indira Gandhi, overshadowed developments in India-Sri Lanka relations. Sri Lanka felt India had for once met her nemesis. The funeral of Mrs. Gandhi in New Delhi was attended by world leaders, among them was President Jayewardene. Taking advantage of the morose pervasive in New Delhi he wished to drive home the point that India's espousal of the Tamil cause was unwarranted. On November 3, 1984, after Mrs. Gandhi's funeral, Jayewardene issued a statement drawing a parallel between the aftermath of the assassination of Mrs. Gandhi by a few extremist Sikhs and the events that followed with the assassination of 13 Sinhala soldiers in July, 1983, resulting in anti-Tamil riots in their wake. Jayewardene said:

> "In India, some Sikhs are agitating for a separate state, Khalistan. In Sri Lanka some Tamils are doing the same, seeking to establish "Eelam". Both movements have spawned terrorists who now operate on their own momentum. In both countries, the central governments seek to settle any dispute that may exist constitutionally and peacefully. The Indian and Sri Lankan governments accuse foreign countries of seeking to interfere. In India, the terrorists who committed the assassination were Sikhs. In Sri Lanka, they were Tamils. In India, the victim was a Hindu. In Sri Lanka, 12 of the victims were Buddhist Sinhalese. In India, a few enraged Hindus massacred innocent Sikhs. In Sri Lanka a few enraged Sinhalese massacred innocent Tamils."

Having drawn the parallel, he reminded India that the situation there was no different from the one prevailing in Sri Lanka, and extended "full support to Prime Minister Rajiv Gandhi", in the hope that he would also understand the situation in Sri Lanka and extend India's "full support" to his country.

Rajiv Gandhi felt humiliated at the parallel drawn by Jayewardene and wished to disabuse him at how ludicrous and absurd his perceptions were about recent happenings in India. In his letter of November 20, 1984, Rajiv told Jayewardene that the two situations were "not comparable", and mincing no words told the President curtly that he was greatly "distressed" at the comparison. So miffed was Rajiv that he did not want to leave Jayewardene in any doubt of his intention to stay committed to the earlier policies pursued by his mother. He told Jayewardene bluntly and candidly:

> "Because of the long historic, cultural and personal ties between the peoples of Sri Lanka and India, developments in Sri Lanka unavoidably affect us, especially in our state Tamil Nadu, where 55 million Tamils live. The tragic events of last year and this year in which there was a large-scale loss of life and property, had sent waves of anguish and concern in Tamil Nadu and elsewhere in India. Some 40,000 Sri Lankan Tamil refugees are still with us. The great majority of them have taken shelter with their friends and relatives in Tamil Nadu. In Parliament, I had myself witnessed the depth of feelings in our country on the situation in Sri Lanka..."
>
> "Your recent statement since your return from New Delhi has been brought to my notice. More recently, your Foreign Minister in a conversation with our High Commissioner has repeated unfounded charges about India sheltering or giving succour to Sri Lankan militants. You yourself drew a parallel between your political problem and Indira Gandhi's assassination, which has distressed me greatly. The two situations are not comparable."
>
> "I am aware of the magnitude of the ethnic problem in your country and the efforts you yourself have embarked upon since the last year to find a satisfactory political

solution to it. The basic approach of my government in this regard remains unchanged. The ethnic problem in your country is for you to resolve; we have not interfered and we do not wish to interfere in any way. I should like to reaffirm my Government's unflinching support for Sri Lanka's unity and integrity. We do not encourage or favour separatism and are firmly opposed to all forms of violence and terrorism. I have been greatly distressed by the events of last few days, which have caused loss of so many lives and widespread suffering."

He stressed upon Colombo the need to successfully conclude the process of political negotiations since India believed "an early settlement would satisfy the Tamils and wean away the overwhelming majority of the militants" from violence.

Sri Lanka refused to be browbeaten by the sternness of the new Prime Minister's mood. She remained defiant. On the ground there was no let up in violence; rather it escalated. On December 11, 1984, Rajiv Gandhi once again felt the need to caution Colombo of India's uneasiness at the deeply deteriorating situation. This time India's concern was direct. Many Tamils of Indian origin were "among the victims" of the ethnic violence. Colombo was admonished that its "Surveillance Zone in the narrow Palk Strait has been used to attack, harass and apprehend innocent Indian fishermen who have enjoyed traditional fishing rights in these waters". Its significance was not lost on Sri Lanka. The warning had come almost on the eve of the All-Party Conference scheduled to meet in Colombo on December 14, 1984 to evolve a negotiated political solution to the ethnic problem. It was seen by many as applying pressure on Colombo not to let the opportunity go awry and clinch some settlement acceptable to the Tamils.

As in the past, the Indian warning went unheeded. On December 13, 1984, Foreign Minister A.C.S. Hameed in a defiant tone accused New Delhi of turning a blind eye to the violence perpetrated by the Tamils, which in fact had invited retribution from the security forces in the discharge of their duty. While denying that the Indian fishermen had been attacked or harassed by Sri Lankan security forces, Hameed said that the Indian High Commissioner had been invariably informed of the violations of the Sri Lankan waters by Indian fishermen and any similar violation in future would continue to invite action on the part of her security forces. Justifying the creation of a "Surveillance Zone" in the Palk Strait, Hameed said, "with the escalation of terrorist activity the Government of Sri Lanka was compelled, in the interest of its own security", to proclaim such a zone which was "entirely within the internal and territorial waters of Sri Lanka". He once again accused India of encouraging "terrorists" by allowing them the use of Indian territory to mount propaganda and attacks on Sri Lanka. Elaborating on this theme he said:

> "As the Government of Sri Lanka has repeatedly stated these terrorist activities have been nurtured and controlled by terrorist organisations, which have received facilities in Indian territory. Terrorist leaders live openly in Tamil Nadu, make statements to the Indian press and are received by leading Indian political personalities. Terrorist leaders address public meetings and advocate the setting up of a separate state and are supported by some of the politicians, even in Indian Parliament, making a standing mockery of New Delhi's repeated declarations of respect for Sri Lanka's sovereignty, unity, integrity and stability."

In a show of defiance, Hameed sought to tick off Rajiv Gandhi by reminding him of India's internal situation and use of "emergency powers" in response thereof. He said:

> "It is a matter of record that terrorist activities in Punjab and other parts of India are condemned by the Government of India and its leaders. The Government of India has been compelled to apply emergency powers and special legislation on a selective basis to combat these activities and restore its authority. India has often charged neighbouring countries of harbouring, providing facilities and encouraging these terrorists. However, the Government of India has chosen to turn a blind eye to the activities of Sri Lankan terrorists on Indian territory and a deaf ear to the repeated representations of the Government of Sri Lanka regarding terrorists who are not only engaged in hostile activities against Sri Lanka, but also publicly proclaim responsibility for their campaign of terrorist violence."

Hameed was at pains to remind Rajiv Gandhi that his "tone and substance can only encourage the terrorists and their supporters both in India and in Sri Lanka to pursue further their nefarious activities".

It was an error of judgment on the part of India to have raised the issue of Indian fishermen in the context of unresolved ethnic question, even if it was intended to create space for deeper Indian involvement in Sri Lanka's problem. The problem of Indian fishermen had a history of its own. The agreements signed with Sri Lanka on June 28, 1974, March 23, 1976, July 31,1976 and November 22, 1976 not only fixed the maritime boundary between the two countries, but settled all other attendant matters including that of fishing and exploitation of marine resources between the two countries. India had conceded the claim of Sri Lanka on the disputed Island of Kachchativu in the 1974 Agreement. It was the fond hope of everybody that with the maritime boundary between the two countries determined, the fishing jurisdictions too stood settled. Unfortunately, as far as the fishing was concerned there remained a lot of confusion, which created too many avoidable misunderstandings. New Delhi cannot escape the blame for that. In his statement to Parliament on July 23, 1974, clarifying the contents of the June 28, 1974 Agreement, the Indian Minister of External Affairs had said, "I wish to remind the Hon'ble Members that in concluding this Agreement the rights of fishing, pilgrimage, and navigation which both sides have enjoyed in the past, have been fully safeguarded for the future". Since the Indian fishermen had always fished in these waters in the past, the Minister's statement gave a false assurance to the Indian fishermen. However, Article V (2) of the agreement signed on March 23, 1976 provided "Each party shall have sovereign rights and exclusive jurisdiction over the continental shelf and the exclusive economic zone as well as over their resources, whether living or non-living falling on its side of the aforesaid boundary." The clarification provided by New Delhi to Tamil Nadu later was that, while the Indian fishermen were free to visit Kachchativu to dry their nets and for pilgrimage, no fishing was allowed in the Sri Lankan waters as defined in the Agreements of 1974 and 1976, underscored the confusion created by the earlier Indian statement in 1974.

As the ethnic problem underwent a sea change in the eighties, from a peaceful to a militant movement embracing violence as its creed, the Palk Strait became a live artery for the Sri Lankan Tamils wanting to use Tamil Nadu as a sanctuary and a support base for their activities in Jaffna. Tamil militants, particularly of the LTTE variety, used the Indian fishing boats under the guise of Indian fishermen for their various illegal activities whether to ferry men in and out of Jaffna, or for smuggling of strategic commodities like fuel, arms and ammunition and other similar type of equipment. Later, after the Indo-Sri Lanka Peace Agreement of 1987 when the Government of India put stringent curbs on the activities of the LTTE in India, the role of Indian fishing boats and fishermen became all-important for the LTTE. Some fishermen whether out of commitment, or for greed or under threat from the LTTE indulged in activities other than fishing and ran into trouble with the Lankan Navy, keen to cut LTTE supplies and starve them of the necessary wherewithals. As relations between India and the LTTE came under strain, often LTTE craft posing as Lankan patrol targeted the Indian fishermen to obfuscate them. The Indian fishermen blamed the Sri Lankan Navy for harassing them thus creating misunderstanding in bilateral relations. To prevent Indian fishermen from fishing around the Kachchativu Island, the officials both of the Central Government and Tamil Nadu Government several times advised them that while they were free to visit Kachchativu to dry their nets and for pilgrimage, they were not to fish there since those waters belonged to Sri Lanka but without much success.

The problem of Indian fishermen in the Palk Strait was further complicated by the speech of the Minister of Internal Security P. Chidambaram, when he told the Lok Sabha during the debate on the budget of the Ministry of External Affairs that the Indian fishermen had "every right to fish in every part of the waters of the Gulf of Mannar, the Bay of Bengal and the Palk Strait". Whatever the legal position, the fact remained that a large number of Indian fishermen continued to intrude into the prohibited waters because the area was rich in prawns and it was the question of their livelihood. Some others went in for reasons other than fishing. In either case, it created a problem in relations between the two countries. It was only on March

23, 1992, that the Government of India in replying to a question in the Rajya Sabha explicitly and unequivocally said that traditional right of access and pilgrimage to the Island of Kachchativu did not include the right to fish in those waters. But that did not put an end to the problem and it continued to bedevil relations between the two countries. Therefore, to have warned Sri Lanka now for harassing the Indian fishermen was misplaced.

Rajiv Gandhi's deeper involvement in Sri Lanka's ethnic conflict

At the beginning of 1985, the situation in Sri Lanka seemed as despondent and gloomy as ever. The failure of the All-Party Conference was a great disappointment. Not that there were great expectations from the Conference; nevertheless, its mere existence gave some hope that a negotiated settlement, acceptable to all would be found. Indian Minister of State for External Affairs in his statement in the Lok Sabha on January 22, 1985, blamed the President, the Sinhala parties and the Buddhist clergy for this and said it was "a matter of grave disappointment and frustration" since it was feared that continuation of the present situation "may not permit the return (back home), in safety and honour, of many Sri Lankan Tamils who have taken refuge in India". The escalation in the level of violence was equally a matter of concern to India, which continued to raise its voice, particularly when it was having an adverse impact on the Indian fishermen operating in the Palk Strait. India continued to flog the issue of Indian fishermen and accused the Sri Lanka's Navy of mounting harassment of the Indian fishermen, and even violating the Indian territorial waters.

Sri Lankan response to the repeated Indian accusations of harassment of the Indian fishermen put India on the back-foot. On February 17,1985, the Indian High Commissioner in Colombo met the Foreign Minister Hameed to express Indian concern over reports of the Sri Lankan Navy killing two more Indian fishermen. Hameed proposed joint patrolling by the navies of India and Sri Lanka in the Palk Bay to prevent such incidents. He denied involvement of their navy in these clashes. The Sri Lankan Foreign Minister told the Indian High Commissioner S.J.S. Chhatwal, that Lankan Navy was not involved in the clashes, but he did not rule out the possibility of Tamil militants masquerading as Sri Lanka's Navy personnel engineering the clashes to create ill-will towards Sri Lanka in India. He proposed that if the navies of the two countries cooperated and communicated with each other and jointly patrolled the Palk Bay such misunderstandings could be avoided. The Indian response to such suggestions remained muted for obvious reasons. Sri Lanka declared that joint patrolling would, besides curbing the movement of "terrorists", also help check the flow of refugees. To repeated Indian pleas of curbing violence against the Tamils and finding a political solution, Sri Lanka continued to hold India responsible for her failure to cooperate. On the contrary, Sri Lanka accused India of encouraging violence by providing facilities to the Sri Lankan Tamils to operate from the Indian soil to carry on their activities against them. In his letter of March 1, 1985 to Rajiv Gandhi, Jayewardene made a frontal attack on India and said:

> "I ask you very little. Let us forget the issue of training camps; the existence of Sri Lankan terrorists in South India, their plotting and planning. I ask you to help me to prevent them from coming here with arms; at the same time could we not also prevent Sri Lankans from seeking refuge in your country? If we can agree on a common scheme to do this, by some form of mutual or combined surveillance, it will enable me to withdraw the Armed Services from combat; to suspend the operation of the Terrorist Act; and to help the north and east of Sri Lanka to return to normalcy. Surely, you can take this step forward which will help stop this taking of life and damage to property and the resumption of civilized life in your most friendly neighbour."

Jayewardene tried to strike a personal chord with Rajiv Gandhi by invoking his friendship with the Nehru family and said: "I need hardly mention that it is not only as the President of Sri Lanka that I am writing to the Prime Minister of India, I am writing as a friend of the Nehru family, you being the third generation that I have known since I became acquainted with your grandfather when I entertained him at my home in Sri Lanka in 1939, and I was his guest for a few days at his home in Allahabad when I attended the Ramgarh Session of the Congress in 1941..." Jayewardene in a chastened mood held out an olive branch by offering to hold a summit meeting with the Indian Prime Minister to resolve the issue. His request was cold-shouldered.

The growing violence in Sri Lanka was the subject of animated but heated debates on a number of occasions in both houses of Indian Parliament. The government, too, made several suo moto statements to apprise the Parliament of the latest developments in Sri Lanka from time to time. The members were greatly agitated at the lack of spirited response from the Government of India to the sufferings of the Tamils. They were unhappy with the Prime Minister's mere expression of his and his Government's outrage at the events in the Island. The continued influx of refugees that had accompanied the deterioration in the situation caused great concern to Parliament and the Government of India. The Tamil Nadu government, also reeling under the financial impact of refugees' burden, made several representations to New Delhi for effective steps to curb their inflow. On March 14, 1985, the Lok Sabha was informed that since the beginning of February 1985 a total of 2,722 families comprising 11,225 members had arrived in Rameshwaram as refugees from Sri Lanka. The refugees were also a source of numerous social evils and created law and order problem for the Tamil Nadu government.

Towards the end of March, Indian Foreign Secretary Romesh Bhandari, visited Colombo. On March 29, 1985, the Rajya Sabha was informed of the discussions held by Bhandari in Colombo. It was clear that the question of refugees figured prominently in those discussions. Bhandari conveyed the concern of the Prime Minister that the "conditions must be created for refugees to go back to Sri Lanka in safety and with honour". A few days later, on April 10, 1985, replying to the debate on the budget of the Ministry of External Affairs in the Lok Sabha, it was stated by the Minister of State in the Ministry of External Affairs Khursheed Alam Khan that due to ever growing influx of the refugees, their number now stood at more than 90,000. On April 25, Sri Lanka again figured in the Lok Sabha when the Prime Minister said that the Tamil Nadu Chief Minister M.G. Ramachandran had personally expressed his concern to him on the continuing influx of the refugees. Four days later, on April 29, Minister Khursheed Alam Khan made yet another statement in the Lok Sabha on the situation in the Island and after expressing his concern at the ever deteriorating situation said the "violence which had somewhat slackened is again endemic" and there were reports of "large scale violence in the Eastern Province involving Muslims and Tamils". The number of refugees, he said, had gone to almost a lakh, imposing on India a heavy social and economic strain. He again highlighted the plight of the Indian fishermen who he said had been deprived of their livelihood. He said India had felt concerned about the situation in Sri Lanka on other counts also. Listing other areas of concern the Minister said:

> "We are aware about the intrusion of foreign agencies in Sri Lanka. This is a very serious thing because we do not want any foreign agency so near our country and particularly the SAS, which is providing training to the commandos or the Mossad, which is a notorious agency like the CIA. Therefore, we never want that these agencies should be allowed to come into Sri Lanka. We have made this very clear to the Sri Lankan Government. Similarly, we do not appreciate that they have allowed a broadcasting station to the Voice of America to be installed there; it will not be in the interest of this region and we want that this region should be free from all such agencies. Just as we want that the Indian Ocean should be a zone of peace, similarly we don't want any kind of intrusion into our region."

On May 3, 1985, the Prime Minister reconfirming to the Rajya Sabha that the number of refugees who were spilling over into India had reached a figure of almost 100,000, expressing his anxiety said:

> "Our concern is for the Tamils in Sri Lanka. The concern is not only of people in the south but it is the concern of everyone in India. We have to see that the refugees go back, go back in honour, go back in safety, go back with the security of expecting and getting full freedom to express themselves, to work, to live within the integrity of Sri Lanka".

On the same day (May 3), Khursheed Alam Khan again spoke about the Sri Lanka developments in Parliament and repeated litany of Tamil woes but clarified to the House explicitly what India expected Sri Lanka to do to remedy the situation and demanded:

> "Now, very often question is asked as to what we have told the Sri Lankan Government as to how to deal with this issue. We feel unless there is first a cooling off period, it will be very difficult to find a political solution to this problem. If there is a cooling off period, the atmosphere will be conducive for discussions and dialogue aimed at finding a political solution. We feel that it is necessary that Sri Lankan troops should be sent back to barracks. They should be replaced by a civil administration. The policy of settling of Sinhalese in the predominantly Tamil areas should be given up — 30,000 Sinhalese families are to be settled in these areas. This will create further complications in future. It is also necessary that the Sixth Amendment should be withdrawn because that amendment is causing a lot of problems. As I said earlier, there should also be removal of restrictions on "prohibited" and "restricted" zones so that fishermen can go out and do their fishing. I have already mentioned about the intrusion of the foreign intelligence agencies. It is a matter of great concern to us and therefore, it is necessary that they should take note of it."

India kept up her pressure and gave no respite to Colombo. On May 7 1985, in a letter to President Jayewardene, Rajiv Gandhi squarely blamed Colombo for the plight of the Tamils and sermonized "if successive governments in Sri Lanka since independence had shown the necessary vision and spirit of accommodation, I am confident that your country would have been spared the agonies it is facing today."

Refusing to accept the charge of encouraging terrorism in Sri Lanka by providing refuge to the Tamil militants and by allowing the use of Indian soil, Rajiv Gandhi said:

> "You ask whether we could not prevent Sri Lankans from seeking refuge in my country. I am afraid the answer is entirely up to you. Nothing would give us more satisfaction than the creation of conditions in Sri Lanka, which would not force your Tamil citizens to

> seek refuge in our country. We would like them all to go back to their homes, but they will only return when they feel secure in Sri Lanka".

Rajiv Gandhi remained skeptical of the suggested summit meeting unless it was well prepared. Jayewardene, despite his defiant attitude was a worried man since the voice of Indian concern grew shriller by the day. India's highlighting of the refugee angle had particularly, an ominous ring. Nevertheless, Rajiv despite his reluctance for a summit meeting found himself hosting Jayewardene on June 1, 1985, and to his utter surprise he found the President quite mellowed and amenable. The talks in New Delhi once again underlined the continued importance of India's good offices and need for a negotiated settlement within the framework of Sri Lanka's unity and sovereignty. The President promised that he would declare amnesty for the Tamil militants and withdraw troops from the Northern Province if they surrendered arms and peace was restored. He indicated the line on which he envisioned a political solution. First, there should be elections for the constitution of district councils followed by more rights and powers to these councils. Later, he said, "we might consider setting up a coordinating council". The New Delhi summit exuded some optimism in Colombo and on June 21, 1985 Sri Lankan Parliament was informed that the government was "able to see some light at the end of the tunnel". The statement made on behalf of Sri Lankan Government by Vincent Perera, Minister of Parliamentary Affairs, sounded optimistic:

> "...India's President His Excellency Zail Singh and Prime Minister Rajiv Gandhi had both agreed that they will not support terrorist acts conducted against Sri Lanka from Indian territory. His Excellency the President has appealed to the Members of the Government, Parliamentary Group and all those who live in this country as well as others, to be patient while the government takes such measures as are necessary based on the talks in India to achieve peace in this country in our life-time and stop the killings of innocent men and women. In fact, Sri Lanka's stand right along was that terrorism in Sri Lanka could not be eliminated so long as the terrorists were allowed to direct operations from Indian soil."

❮11❯

Thimpu Talks

Following the New Delhi Summit on June 1, 1985, a 4-phase framework for a cease-fire between Sri Lankan Government and the Tamil organizations through the good offices of the Government of India was announced in Colombo. The National Security Minister, Athulathmudali, told a press conference in the capital that Government troops would adhere to the cease-fire but warned counter-action if any "splinter rebel group" did not fall in line. He acknowledged India's role in facilitating the cease-fire arrangement and indicated that depending on Tamils desisting from any hostile activity, Colombo would take some other steps as well to restore normalcy particularly in Jaffna peninsula. The Army Commander, Brig. Wannasinghe, was more forthcoming and told newsmen in Jaffna that security check-points in the peninsula would be removed, fishing allowed in the prohibited zones within five km of the shore, and plying of vehicles on certain roads in the security zones would also be allowed. Athulathmudali, adding a jarring note, said that the present situation was only a "cessation of hostile incidents" and not "cease-fire". "In law you can have cease-fire only between two parties which control territories", he added. Taking credit for initiating the peace process, he maintained that the cessation of hostilities was a "direct outcome of the process that began on February 9" (when he had called on Rajiv Gandhi in New Delhi).

On their part the Tamils, represented by the Eelam National Liberation Front (ENLF), an amalgam of all the Tamil parties including the LTTE, said in Madras: "we will not provoke, but if there is provocation we will retaliate". The spokesman of the

ENLF remained skeptic about the outcome of the negotiations but announced suspension of any violent activity so as not to create any embarrassment for the Indian Government. Following Jayewardene's visit to New Delhi, a Sri Lankan delegation consisting of legal experts and led by his brother H.W. Jayewardene had visited New Delhi on June 15-16, 1985, to sort out the legalities of the issues involved. The Government of India gave an indication of the nature of the talks held with this delegation to the Lok Sabha on July 24. It was stated that while President Jayewardene and Prime Minister Gandhi discussed the ethnic issue and its impact on bilateral relations, the delegation led by his brother held talks with the Indian Attorney General on matters relating to devolution of powers under Sri Lanka's Constitution.

Thimpu, the Bhutanese capital was chosen as a venue for the talks not only because it was a neutral territory, but also it was expected that its isolation provided a perfect setting. At the Thimpu talks in July-August, 1985, the Tamils were represented by all shades of opinion — the TULF and the militant organisations comprising Liberation Tigers of Tamil Eelam (LTTE), Tamil Eelam Liberation Organisation (TELO), Eelam People's Revolutionary Liberation Front (EPRLF), and Eelam Revolutionary Organisation of Students (EROS) under the banner of ENLF, which was formed some time ago under Indian prodding so that all the Tamil groups could present a united front in their struggle. The LTTE was a reluctant member of the front and joined only when its rival TELO under the leadership of Uma Meheswaren walked out. The PLOTE, however, joined the talks as an independent body. Prabakaran remained skeptical about success of the talks. He did not wish to be seen enthusiastic since in his opinion there was no chance of success. He had lost all faith in the fairness of Colombo and in any case unlike TULF, he stood for nothing short of Eelam, which would not be offered to him on a platter in any negotiated settlement. In any case, the talks were being held with the precondition that any solution emerging would have to be within the framework of the Sri Lankan Constitution. Hence, in Prabakaran's view the futility of the talks.

In the first round in July, 1985, the Tamils rejected the government's proposals, which they said were nothing but rehash of the ones placed before the All-Party Conference the previous year. Specifically, they neither recognised the notion of a homeland for the Tamils nor the right of self-determination. The leader of the government delegation Hector Jeyewardene asked Tamils to come up with their own alternative. The Tamils were, however not ready for this eventuality, and only enunciated four principles on which any solution of the ethnic problem must be based. These were:

1. Recognition of the separate national identity of the Tamils;
2. Respect for the integrity of the traditional Tamil homeland;
3. Recognition of the right of self-determination for the Tamils;
4. Citizenship rights for all (Indian) Tamils who had chosen to make Sri Lanka their home.

The first round of talks was adjourned on July 14, to meet again in August. Hector promised to come back with fresh proposals after consultations in Colombo on the points raised by the Tamils.

In his report on the first round in Thimpu made to the Cabinet, Hector reportedly said, "If the demand that the political settlement should recognise the right of Tamils to self-determination extends to the point of an absolute right, it can only mean the totally unacceptable claim to a separate State by whatever name it is called". On the other hand, Jayewardene was of the opinion that if this meant a "reasonable degree of autonomy" under the existing Constitution, the government would be willing to grant such an "autonomy."

To forestall any possible opposition of New Delhi to their demand for a separate Tamil state comprising the Northern and Eastern provinces, the Tamils dashed off a letter to Rajiv Gandhi on July 26,1985, articulating their apprehensions and drawing a parallel from the contemporary events in India. The letter said:

> "The composition of the Indian polity is such that no single group, linguistic or otherwise can impose its will on the other and seek to destroy the other. The situation in Sri Lanka is different. Seventy-four percent of the population are Sinhalese and can, in the absence of

adequate constitutional safeguards, set at naught any scheme of Government that may be granted to minority nationalities."

"A linguistic state is the basis of the Indian Union. Even your Punjab Accord provides for the redrawing of state boundaries enabling Hindi speaking villages which are contiguous to be included in the state of Haryana, while Chandigarh and some adjoining areas are to be included in Punjab. If the Government of Sri Lanka is genuine in its desire for a solution of the Tamil problem, they should agree to the same principles being adopted and all contiguous traditionally Tamil speaking areas in the Northern and Eastern Provinces being included in one unit."

The TULF requested the Indian Prime Minister to understand the Tamils' compulsions and consider these matters "affecting (their) very existence" with an open mind.

When the Thimpu talks resumed in August, as expected, the government delegation rejected the demands articulated by the Tamils the previous month. It showed its readiness to consider them within the framework of a united Sri Lanka, and her Constitution, which guaranteed to all communities however small their number, their rights in respect of culture, language and religion. Making light of the Tamil demand for self-determination, H.W. Jayewardene said:

"All governments in Sri Lanka since independence have recognised the right of all citizens, irrespective of their race or religion to participate in the democratic process of electing the government of their choice and of participating through their elected representatives in decisions regarding the framework of government and in the management of their own affairs. This is the only sense in which the Government of Sri Lanka recognises the principle of self-determination in the business of government. The right of self-determination is exercisable within the existing constitutional framework by all the citizens in Sri Lanka in respect of their political, economic, social and cultural affairs. One group of people living in an independent, sovereign state does not have the right to determine their future political status independently of the rest of the people living in that country and do not have the right to secede from the existing state to form and establish an independent state".

The Government delegation too was not prepared to accept the Tamils as a distinct nationality. It was articulated that nationality is derivative of the state and not related to language or religion. The nationality of an individual signifies the quality of his being the subject of a certain country, of owing allegiance to that country and of being entitled to its protection. The demand for a Tamil Homeland was, too, rejected which apart from other reasons was untenable for it had not been made on behalf of all the Tamils, a substantial number of which were Indian Tamils and Muslims. Besides it was pointed out statistically that even the Sri Lankan Tamils were distributed in substantial numbers all over the Island. In Colombo, alone they were 9.77 percent and in the Sinhala heartland Nuwara Eliya 12.48%. The government delegation too did not concede the right of the Sri Lankan Tamils to represent the Indian Tamils whose problem and aspirations, it was maintained, were different from those of the Sri Lankan Tamils. Besides, it was pointed out that the Indian Tamils had their own representatives to articulate their demands. They therefore, did not need any intervention on the part of the Sri Lankan Tamils to look after their interests.

Having responded to the four principles of the Tamils, H.W. Jayewardene went on to demand a complete renunciation of all forms of militant activity. He wanted all training camps whether in Sri Lanka or abroad (meaning India) to be closed down and return to the constitutional and peaceful methods for articulation of political demands.

Notwithstanding the rejection of their four principles by the Government, the Tamil delegation remained adamant. On August 15, in a joint statement to the conference, the Tamils went on to repeat the same four principles as fundamental to any solution of the Tamil problem. While saying so, it left a window of hope open, saying:

"The enumeration of the basic principles, which are inalienable rights of our people, does not entail that we are opposed to any rational dialogue with the Government of Sri Lanka. We wish to make it absolutely clear that any meaningful discussion for a lasting solution to the Tamil national question cannot be worked out unless the Sri Lankan state recognises these inalienable rights".

With each side taking a hard line, failure of the Conference stared everybody in the face. This brought Romesh Bhandari, the Indian Foreign Secretary, scurrying to Thimpu to salvage the talks. Shuttling between the two camps to narrow down the differences, he failed to make much headway with the Tamils. Tamils failed to understand that for domestic compulsions India could not endorse some of their demands like right of self-determination, nationality and homeland since there were many separatist movements in India harping on similar aspirations and agenda. They even accused Bhandari for failure to appreciate the Tamil aspirations and working for his own personal aggrandizement by trying to force them to accept anything less than the Tamil state of their concept.

Trying in vain with the Tamils to dilute the four "cardinal principles" spelt out by them for any meaningful talks, Bhandari had better luck with H.W. Jayewardene and persuaded him to offer a set of proposals, which at least partially fulfilled the demands of the Tamils. As a result, on August 16, Sri Lankan delegation presented at Thimpu new proposals titled: "An Outline of the Structure of the Sub-national units of a Participatory System of Government". The preamble broadly indicated the rationale of the proposals saying:

"The object of the present proposals for devolution is to ensure a greater sharing of power by all the people and their maximum participation in identifying their needs and problems and in deciding upon matters vitally affecting their interests. While enabling people at the local level to plan and to implement their solutions for problems, the proposed devolution seeks to maintain the political and economic unity of the nation, in the interest of the prosperity and good government of all parts of Sri Lanka."

The Tamils remained as obstinate as ever. India realized but refused to acknowledge the limits of her persuasive power over the Tamils. The next day in a joint response the Tamil delegation unanimously rejected the proposals stating:

> "The 'new proposals' do not recognise that the Tamils of Sri Lanka constitute a nation. The 'new proposals' do not recognise that the Tamil-speaking people have the right to an identifiable homeland. The 'new proposals' do not recognise the inalienable right of self-determination of the Tamil people. And finally the 'new proposals' do not secure the fundamental rights of the Tamil people and any solution to the Tamil national question is inseparable from the resolution of the problems of the plantation Tamils in the Island. And accordingly the 'new proposals' fail to satisfy the legitimate political aspirations of the Tamil people."

> "The four basic principles that we have set out at the Thimpu talks are the necessary framework for any rational dialogue with the Sri Lankan Government and are not some mere theoretical constructs. They represent the hard existential reality of the struggle of the Tamil people for their fundamental and basic rights. It is a struggle which initially manifested itself in the demand for a federal constitution in the 1950s and later in the face of continuing and increasing oppression and discrimination found logical expression in the demand for the independent Tamil State of Eelam or Tamil Eelam."

Whatever little chance, if at all, the Conference had of success, was ruined by an unfortunate development outside of the Conference. On August 17, 1985, the Tamils walked out of the Conference in protest against the massacre of Tamils in Vavuniya and Trincomalee. In an orgy of violence at Sambantivu and Arankatti, two villages in Trincomalee, the security forces killed about 200 Tamils. A spokesman for the Eelam National Liberation Front described the attacks as premeditated and with a view to intimidate the Tamils into submission at the Thimpu talks and force them to accept the proposals put forward by the government which were rejected by the Tamils. Abrupt end of the Thimpu talks disappointed New Delhi which had staked its reputation on finding a meaningful solution to the ethnic problem. It was for the first time that the two parties had come face to face across the table at the behest of India. It was also the first time a united delegation of all shades of Tamil opinion was represented in talks with Colombo. India had expected that with some luck, there would be an end to violence in the Island. It was unfortunate that the talks broke up because of eruption of violence. This was the last thing that India had bargained for.

New Delhi proposals

In yet another effort to salvage the situation, Government of India requested both the Sri Lankan and the Tamil delegations to come to Delhi on their way back to Colombo from Thimpu, to make a fresh bid to break the stalemate.` H.W. Jayewardene agreed to come to New Delhi while he asked other members to proceed to Mumbai and wait for instructions before leaving for Colombo. The Tamils refused to oblige on the pretext, as Prabakaran later clarified to Anita Pratap of the Calcutta based *Sunday* (September 29-October 5, 1985), that Tamils could not be seen to be negotiating peace when other Tamils were being massacred in Vavuniya.

After initial discussions in New Delhi with the Indian Prime Minister Rajiv Gandhi, H.W. Jayewardene summoned the rest of the delegation to New Delhi, which was still awaiting instructions in Mumbai. This was a signal for a fresh round of discussions with the Indian officials. On August 30, 1985, the Indian and Sri Lankan officials signed an agreement. The next day a press release of the Government of India said:

> "Dr. (H.W). Jayewardene had detailed and constructive discussions with the Foreign Secretary Shri Romesh Bhandari. A comprehensive paper has been drawn up covering all issues of importance and relevance. The detailed draft paper could serve as the basis for negotiations towards a mutually agreed accord by the parties concerned".

The next most difficult task was to obtain acceptance of the new proposals by the Tamils who were in no mood to cooperate. The latter now suspected India of buying the Sri Lanka line. The Tamils drummed up the boggy of military build up in the north and the east to terrorize the Tamils as a good enough reason to withhold cooperation. Colombo deprecated the Tamil cry of military build up as a propaganda stunt. On December 13, 1985, General Ranatunga, General-

Officer-Commanding the Joint Operations Command denied any build up of the army. President Jayewardene, when asked by New Delhi based fortnightly *India Today* (December 15), how he proposed to solve the ethnic problem, said: "the answer to this question lies in Rajiv Gandhi's own words that the ball is in the Tamils' court. We have already given them a working paper and we are awaiting their response. The ball is in their court. If they return it we will play. But so far nothing has been put to us".

Despite accepting Indian mediatory role, Jayewardene remained skeptical of Indian bona fide as a neutral intermediary. He questioned in the same interview India's compulsions to allow the Tamils to operate from India. In exposing the hypocrisy of the Indian position he asked: "Then why does India allow Tamil militants to operate from its territory? Your government wants the Sikhs to be sent out of the United Kingdom, Canada and other countries. How would India appreciate it if I keep the Sikh killers of Mrs. Gandhi in Sri Lanka?" He believed that the Tamil problem was a military problem and "to be tackled militarily". He justified his country's arms build up since he expected danger both internal and external. He said: "We are doing all this (military build up) because we are facing threats from outside and within our country. We fear that somebody might invade us, so we must have arms build up. We are preparing against any invasion". That he remained convinced of a military solution and it was the fear of India which was holding him back, was clear when he said:

> "I am not fully prepared to tackle Jaffna. I want to finish first other provinces. It is not difficult to handle Jaffna. We can cut off food and supplies to the peninsula and flush out the terrorists in a month's time. But will India support our action?"

On 20th February, 1986, Sri Lankan President recounted to the opening session of Parliament the administrative action taken by the government to remove the Tamils' grievances, which had created alienation among them and said:

> "Since 1977, the government had made Tamil a National language in the Constitution; amended rules governing entrance to the Universities and removed any racial bias

governing those rules; removed the regulations prescribing racial considerations governing entry to the Public Services and promotion in the Services. District Councils have been created and District Ministers appointed. The TULF accepted them and worked them for two years and contested elections. Last year they withdrew from them as sufficient powers and finance had not been allotted to them."

The President then went on to list various efforts at negotiations to find a solution to the ethnic problem and in this category mentioned his talks in Delhi with Rajiv Gandhi, the Thimpu talks, the New Delhi Talks, the All-Party Conference etc.

Talking about the agreement arrived at during discussions between Colombo and New Delhi in August last year, Jayewardene said that India was in agreement with the position that "the full implementation of any Agreement will be conditional upon compliance inter alia with the acceptance by the Tamils of the Constitution of Sri Lanka" and "in particular the provisions dealing with the Official Language, the National Languages, the National Flag and the National Anthem" and that the Tamil militants would "desist from such action, abjure violence in the future and disband their cadres and groups engaged in acts of violence", that the Tamils would "close down training camps in Sri Lanka and abroad". It was further agreed with New Delhi that the militants would surrender their arms "within a period of one month to the authorities specified by the Sri Lankan Government". These were comprehensive arrangements. Very stringent conditions were imposed by the Sri Lankan Government and accepted by the Government of India on behalf of the Tamils. That the Government of India did not succeed in enforcing any of the arrangements or conditionalities arrived at with Colombo should have been an abject lesson for New Delhi. But New Delhi refused to learn anything and was condemned to repeat the same mistakes later.

New Delhi's announcement of an Understanding with Colombo pressed a panic button in the Tamil camp. They were apprehensive that should the Government of India take a position, which did not meet their minimum demands, the Tamils would be in a very difficult position to retain the goodwill of the Government of India. They considered the Indian goodwill vital in their interaction with the Sri Lankan Government, since on their own, they had drawn a blank in Colombo during the previous four decades. Yet the Tamils were not prepared to go by Indian advice. Their strategy, henceforth, was to draw New Delhi away from Colombo by playing the Tamil card a little more dexterously and deftly.

‹12›

Towards Confrontation

That Sri Lanka had strong reservations about Indian mediatory role was articulated by Colombo on more than one occasion. If Colombo continued to involve New Delhi in the Island's ethnic problem it was not its expectation that New Delhi would be an uninterested mediator. It had little doubt that under pressure of Tamil Nadu politics, India's mediatory role was weighted in favour of the Sri Lankan Tamils, yet she could not wish India away. India was a powerful neighbour and her fifty million Tamils lent all support—moral and material—to the Tamils of Sri Lanka, besides a safe sanctuary. There were by now around 125,000 Sri Lankan refugees in Tamil Nadu. Sri Lanka was not unaware of the potential of the refugee factor. It was the catalyst for creation of Bangladesh only a decade and a half ago. Colombo was apprehensive of the Indian role. Sri Lanka calculated if India could not be kept out, it was necessary to neutralize her by involving her in the Island's problem. India despite initiating strong measures including deployment of security forces to tackle her own militants' problem, did not take kindly to Colombo employing equally strong measures to tackle Tamil militancy and was breathing down Sri Lanka's neck to solve the problem politically and through negotiations and discussions. On April 18, 1986, President Jayewardene told Radio Australia that India's role in solving the ethnic problem in his country was "vital because it is helping the terrorists". Asked whether he believed that militants were getting help from the Indian Government, he had told the Radio:

"I don't know, but I mean their materials, the guns etc., were coming with the knowledge of Tamil Nadu. They accuse Pakistan of helping their Sikh terrorists. We've accused India and they have not denied it. We know it is there, we can prove it's there".

Asked by the Radio who was Sri Lanka's better friend between "India, which is trying to bring about a peaceful settlement, or Pakistan which is supplying military assistance", the President had no hesitation in pointing to the latter as a "better friend", while accusing India of "double standards". Attributing once again his failure to tackle the Tamil militancy to the Indian factor, Jayewardene said: "With the huge continent of India backing them; that's our problem". Addressing a May Day rally in Colombo on May 1, 1986, he called upon India to help wipe out terrorism by closing terrorist bases in that country. The President received an enthusiastic applause from the crowd when he declared, "military solution was the answer to a military question. One cannot preach non-violence to those who come with the gun". The President's outburst came at a time when an Indian delegation led by Indian Minister of State, P. Chidambaram, was in Colombo holding talks to resolve the ethnic problem. Mr. Chidambaram ignoring the Presidential fulmination conceded that the latest proposals from Colombo handed over in New Delhi in April laid down the parameters within which a solution could be worked out. "We thought it better to talk man to man and know the Sri Lanka position. We will seek to find out, during the talks, the distance Colombo can go", Chidambaram said. On May 4, 1986, Colombo presented another set of proposals, which were declared to be final. On the crucial question of merger of the Eastern and Northern provinces, the government came forward with a modified formula of institutional framework to provide for the provincial councils in the north and east to consult each other and act in coordination on matters of mutual interest and concern.

Throughout this period when consultations were in progress between the two governments, there was deterioration in the law and order situation with militants' action inviting military reprisals and *vice-versa*. It was a vicious cycle with no end. On January 19, 1986, two policemen were killed in an ambush and in a reprisal action, security forces gunned down 23 Tamil youth. The month of February 1986, had witnessed another bout of violence in the two provinces. In March 1986, Colombo banned fishing in the northern coast to prevent any movement in the area, which Colombo felt would not allow the militants to move men and material from Tamil Nadu to Sri Lanka. In May, Tamil militants carried out a series of bomb explosions in Colombo one of which took place in the Central Telegraph Office killing 11 people and wounding another 100. This invited sustained military campaign by security forces against the militants, who intensified their retaliatory attacks in the Eastern Province against the Sinhalese. In June, the security forces launched a combined attack on the Jaffna peninsula with helicopters and aircraft thus laying siege to the entire peninsula. So intense was the military campaign that the Amnesty International in September 1986, accused Colombo of serious atrocities against the Tamils and indulging in systematic violation of human rights. But this siege was short lived. The government was forced to lift it under sustained international pressure. The counter-attack launched by the militants was no less furious, which contributed in no small measure in Colombo's decision to lift the siege.

India's stepped up efforts

As a result of the Indian efforts represented in the visit of Indian Minister of State, P. Chidambaram and Romesh Bhandari, from 29 April to May 4, 1986, (Romesh Bhandari had by now retired as Foreign Secretary but was engaged as the Special Representative for Sri Lanka), Sri Lanka offered some fresh proposals for resolution of the ethnic problem. India now had a new External Affairs Minister, P. Shivshankar. Immediately after taking over the new assignment, he said on May 12 that Sri Lanka's latest proposals contained "crucial gaps" on core issues like law and order and Tamil demand for the merger of the Northern and the Eastern provinces. Shivshankar warned yet again "unless Sri Lanka takes decisive steps to accommodate Tamil aspirations, the political process which has been restarted after a gap of time, may suffer a setback". New Delhi once again came under sustained pressure in Parliament and demand for some military action was the underlying creed. On May 13, External Affairs Minister P. Shivshankar, candidly told Parliament "some of the solutions as have been suggested by the Honourable members would prove disastrous" but appreciated the domestic concern and said:

> "...I am not unmindful, and the Government of India cannot be unmindful of the fact that this ethnic minority has a blood relationship with a large segment of our society. We owe certain obligations because of a neighbouring country and also owe obligations because it has an effect over a large segment of our society..."

The Minister added that while there was "some agreement on issues like the overall structure for devolution of powers and land settlement policy, there are still a number of crucial gaps in the formulations on core issues like law and order and on the nature of the relationship between the present Northern and Eastern Provinces, which are issues to which Tamils attach great importance". It was clear that the Government of India was not convinced that the new formulations would satisfy the Tamils and hence it was reluctant to put them to the Tamils for their considerations. The Indian High Commissioner, J.N. Dixit, had a day earlier (May 12) told President Jayewardene that while India felt that Colombo's formulations were progressive, India would wish Colombo to improve on them. He also conveyed Indian concern at the escalating violence and urged Sri Lankan Government to work out a quick solution, which would end the violence. (Dixit met other ministers too who were involved in the resolution of the Tamil problem including Athulathmudali). In reply, Jayewardene drew Dixit's attention to the increasing incidents of violence and emphasised to him that no solution could be worked out unless the violence ceased. It was a vicious circle, one would not cease without the other, but what would come first, remained elusive.

Within a few days, there was resumption of operations against the Tamils in the north, which according to the statement of the Indian Ministry of External Affairs included "indiscriminate aerial bombing and strafing of the Jaffna peninsula". New Delhi too failed to receive clarifications sought from Colombo to the latter's proposals. The response of the Tamils was hardly encouraging to New Delhi. The Government of India was batting with the TULF's brief. It was clear to it that the Tamil militant groups had a different agenda and that they were not even willing to sink their inter-group differences to strengthen the TULF in presenting a united Tamil stand. New Delhi was peeved that despite acting as a mediator, it had little or no influence on militant groups. There was no one in Tamil Nadu either, who could perform that task. India was also getting bad name internationally for appearing to be siding with Tamil militants, thus compromising its role of an honest broker or facilitator. The *Washington Post* on May 12, 1986, said that the terrorist movement in Sri Lanka would die if India cracked down on illegal Tamil activities and stopped the flow of weapons across the Palk Strait. The weekly, *Intelligence Report,* compiled by the Mid-Atlantic Research Associates quoted Indian sources as claiming that "domestic political factors" constrain Prime Minister Rajiv Gandhi from actions, which could "increase his unpopularity" in Tamil Nadu.

In responding to the criticism for large-scale deployment of her armed forces, Sri Lanka maintained that there would be no need to deploy the security forces in the Tamil areas once violence by the militants ceased and normal conditions returned to the Northern and Eastern provinces. On May 14, 1986, Sri Lanka's Minister of National Security told Independent Television Network in Colombo:

> "...the moment terrorists give up the path of violence then there is no role for the military to play. I have said repeatedly that there is no military solution to this problem. Unfortunately, the pro-terrorist newspapers in South India liked to be conveniently deaf to such statements of mine".

Castigating the Government of India, Athulathmudali said that those "who preach to us about (the futility of) a military solution are really preaching to the converted. They should really be preaching to the LTTE, or taking action against the LTTE because the LTTE has demonstrated that they are not interested in political discussions or a political solution." Drawing on Indian experience (the fate of the moderate Punjab leader Sant Harchand Singh Longowal, who negotiated with the Government of India for a political solution of the Punjab problem and was later shot dead), Athulathmudali said it were the terrorist groups who were an obstacle to peace. On May 19, the Indian Ministry of External Affairs yet again issued a statement expressing its distress at the reports of violence in Jaffna peninsula including indiscriminate aerial bombardment and strafing of the Jaffna city, which had "resulted in the destruction of a hospital and a large number of civilians killed and many hundred wounded". On May 20, Athulathmudali in a statement in the Parliament expressed contempt on reports of large scale destruction by the security forces in the Jaffna peninsula, and giving photographic evidence said how the statement of a "foreign government (read India) from which one would expect a commitment to facts" was distorted and at variance with the ground realities.

On May 21, the Indian High Commissioner J.N. Dixit called on President Jayewardene to convey to him India's concern at the deteriorating situation. He candidly told Jayewardene that if the military operations did not stop, then India's offer of good offices stood jeopardized. The President mincing no words too snapped back that as long as the militants continued with their acts of violence it was not possible to stop military operations against them. During the hour-long talks, the President refusing to buckle insisted that Colombo's halt to military campaign depended on the Tamil militants calling off their acts of violence. He clarified for the benefit of the High Commissioner that Colombo would provide further formulations on the fresh proposals for provincial autonomy if there were an absolute guarantee that no further clarifications would be sought. The implication of the Sri Lankan stand was clear that India lacked both the will and the ability to prevail on the Tamils either to accept what was a reasonable solution or to call a halt to their acts of violence and was simply engaged in browbeating Colombo. Sri Lanka was chagrined at Indian pressure without corresponding pressure on Tamil militants to cease violence. For Colombo it was "partiality and one-sided" approach that cast doubts on the genuineness of the preferred "good offices". It was Sri Lanka's perception, which was repeatedly articulated that India's control on the Tamil militants was tenuous. This was the underlying message that Athulathmudali wished to convey when he told Sri Lankan Parliament on May 20, that "their (LTTE's) published statements, their private commentaries, their pamphlets, everything show that they are against the ongoing Indian efforts. But strange enough, they are not being condemned by India".

Notwithstanding these accusations and motives attributed to the Government of India, Colombo conceded that India had thwarted a move by the LTTE to unilaterally declare independence. On June 14, 1986, Sri Lanka media carried a story that Tigers who had scored a success against their main contender, the Tamil Eelam Liberation Organisation (TELO) had thought the present juncture to be their best opportunity to declare the UDI since it would scuttle peace initiatives and focus all attention on them. Colombo appeared for once convinced that India's assurances of respecting the Island's sovereignty and territorial integrity were indeed genuine since New Delhi on learning the LTTE's intention for UDI, had talked the LTTE hierarchy out of any such misconceived move.

More worrying for New Delhi was the factional fights among the Tamil guerrilla groups, which broke out in the north and seemed to cut the ground from underneath TULF's feet thereby undermining the moderating role of India. The series of factional fights ended in favour of the LTTE— the best organised, armed as well as most violent and intransigent of all the militant organisations. At least 175 Tamils died at the hands of fellow Tamils. Among the dead was the leader of the TELO, the only group previously capable of challenging the LTTE for military control or influence in future negotiations with the government. Every one felt that the ascendancy of Tigers made prospects of future talks for a negotiated settlement more difficult if not impossible, which, the future events proved prophetic. Worst, it undermined the mediating role of India. Since most of the Tamil separatist groups had their political headquarters in the South Indian state of Tamil Nadu, New Delhi now had the additional potential problem of having a guerrilla army beholden to no one in a position of strength on its territory. The hold of the Tigers on the Tamil Nadu public opinion was demonstrated the previous year when India had to reverse her own decision to deport two of the Tigers' leaders. Internecine clashes among the Tamil militants mirroring Jaffna attacks rocked Chennai. The Central Telegraph Office in the city and an Air Lanka airliner parked at the Chennai airport became the targets of bomb attacks. American weeklies, *Time* and *Newsweek* reported that Tamil eelamists were intent on wrecking Indian sponsored peace efforts. In the face of these adverse developments, reports were rife that Sri Lanka's President had made approaches to friendly countries for more arms aid to face the insurgent threat. Already Pakistan had trained 1600 Sri Lankan armed personnel. Israeli advisors had provided training in intelligence gathering techniques and western commandos were training the security forces in advance counter-insurgency measures.

Faced with an impossible situation, the Government of India advised Sri Lankan government and the Tamils "to act with restraint", and to help the on-going peace process. The Indian High Commissioner conveyed this advice to Colombo. The Tamil groups were administered similar advice in Chennai, at a meeting with the External Affairs Minister P. Shivshankar. The Tamil Nadu Chief Minister M.G. Ramachandran, Union Home Minister Buta Singh and Minister of State P. Chidambaram also attended the meeting. The Indian ministers flew into Chennai for the meeting instead of meeting the Tamil groups in New Delhi, where they were encamped for two days trying to meet them in vain. An Indian government statement said that the Indian ministers had told the armed groups not to oppose or interfere in the current negotiations. They were told that the Government of India considered it imperative that the current negotiations proceeded unhindered till a solution was found. According to an *AFP* report, LTTE leader Prabakaran assured India that the militants would not stand in the way of the TULF reaching an agreement with Colombo. The daily *Hindu* reported from Chennai, Indian Foreign Secretary, A.P. Venkateswaran, had separately advised the Tamils that they should not expect the Government of India to support their demand for Eelam. India would work for an equitable political settlement for them. New Delhi was irked with the militants for calling the TULF General Secretary Amirthalingam a "traitor" and attacking TULF whom India kept in the vanguard for any negotiations with Colombo. India was also convinced that if there was any chance of successfully negotiating with Colombo, it was conceivable only with the TULF at the helm of the affairs.

During the talks between the TULF and the Sri Lankan Government in July-August 1986, the latter agreed to further concessions, which were incorporated in the proposals sent to the Government of India in September. President Jayewardene reporting on the talks to Sri Lankan Parliament on February 19,

1987, said: "These proposals included the draft constitutional amendments, the draft Provincial Councils Bill, Schedules setting out the Reserved, Concurrent and Provincial Lists, as well as detailed memoranda dealing with Law and Order, Land and Land Settlement and Education. The subjects of Finance and Administration were discussed but not finalised".

As the talks between the TULF and Sri Lanka Government continued in Colombo, there appeared a ray of hope that a settlement acceptable to all the parties would emerge. On October 15, 1986, Rajiv Gandhi speaking to journalists at the National Press Club in Canberra (Australia) described Colombo's proposals as "fairly good" and expected any sticking point to be sorted out during the SAARC Summit in Bangalore. He exuded confidence that the Tamils would accept them when presented to them. In order to make sure that Sri Lankan Tamils accepted the new proposals, New Delhi wanted the All India Anna DMK government in Tamil Nadu to give its nod in principle. On October 8, 1986, a team of Indian officials headed by P. Chidambaram met the senior leaders of the AIADMK in Chennai who promised full cooperation. Earlier M.G. Ramachandran, Chief Minister of Tamil Nadu had told the American media in the United States where he had gone for medical treatment that he welcomed Sri Lanka's initiative to resolve the issue. "India and Tamil Nadu are anxious that a peaceful solution should be worked out", All India Radio had quoted Ramachandran as saying. He assured that the state government and the Tamil Nadu opposition would support any solution acceptable to Sri Lankan Tamils. On November 11, 1986, Minister of State in the Ministry of External Affairs K. Natwar Singh told the Lok Sabha that the proposals refined by the TULF in consultation with the legal experts and officials of the Government of India were now under discussion among the various Tamil groups, which would finally be conveyed to Colombo. He once again reiterated the conviction of New Delhi that "only a negotiated political settlement can resolve the ethnic crisis in Sri Lanka in a manner, which would ensure that the Sri Lankan Tamils obtain their legitimate rights within the framework of the unity and integrity of this neighbouring country". Meanwhile on November 15, 1986, Jayewardene speaking at the SAARC Summit at Bangalore called upon the member countries (reference was primarily to India though not named) to realise that Sri Lankan Government and the people of Sri Lanka "are committed to uphold throughout the Island the Rule of Law" and to "protect democratic institutions". However, on the sidelines of the Bangalore Conference, Rajiv Gandhi and Jayewardene reached an understanding to reconstitute the Eastern Province by removing the Sinhalese majority Amparai district. The truncated province would have separate Provincial Council, like the Northern Province. It was indicated that at some future date modalities of linkage between the two provinces could be worked out. The Tamils, as always, appeared to have their reservations on these proposals. After further discussions between the Indian officials and the Tamils, it was agreed to seek further improvements in the proposals under consideration.

To promote some understanding between Colombo and the LTTE, New Delhi felt it would help if Prabakaran talked in person with President Jayewardene during the SAARC Summit in Bangalore in November 1986. It was through the intervention of Tamil Nadu Chief Minister, M.G. Ramachandran, that Prabakaran had condescended to the meeting. But contrary to all expectations and to New Delhi's embarrassment and disappointment, the meeting was a complete disaster. Far from responding positively to Jayewardene's proposals for a settlement, Prabakaran told the President that he stood firm on his demand for Eelam to which no compromise was possible. That the Indian officials including the Indian Minister of State for External Affairs, Natwar Singh, were upset bothered him the least. He had the audacity to accuse the Indian officials of going back on Mrs. Indira Gandhi's promise to stand by them. He wondered if India was "genuinely" interested in the welfare of the Tamils any more. India was peeved at Prabakaran's affront but could do little since he had become too powerful for the Indian government. India unsuccessfully tried to clip his wings by confiscating LTTE's communication equipment, which had to be returned under pressure of sympathy that he evoked in the people of Tamil Nadu in the wake of his hunger strike. But message went home and he decided to shift his base back to Jaffna to keep his independence of action for the pursuit of his goal.

Nevertheless, India persisted with her efforts to find a solution to the intractable problem. On December 16, Indian High Commissioner Dixit briefed President Jayewardene on the discussions between New Delhi and various Tamil groups and also with the Government of Tamil Nadu on the proposals earlier given by Colombo. While informing him that two Ministers of the Government of India, P. Chidambaram and Natwar Singh, would visit Colombo from December 17, he reassured the President that:

> "...the present emphasis and approach of the Government of India regarding Sri Lanka's ethnic problem is to evolve a package of proposals, which will be fully responsive to basic Tamil aspirations and which would remove the genuine historical apprehensions of Sri Lankan Tamils. At the same time the Government of India would like to ensure that such a package of proposals does not erode Sri Lanka's unity and integrity".

During the visit of the two Indian Ministers to Colombo from December 17-19, 1986, a six-point proposal was finalized, which they carried back home. The December 19-proposal, as it came to be known, raised a lot of hope for a breakthrough. The proposal came quite close to meeting Tamil demand for some sort of merger of the Northern and the Eastern provinces. No sooner had the Indian team left Colombo, than it was apparent that Colombo was having second thoughts. Colombo media, quoting official sources put out suggestions that attributed the December 19 proposal as emanating from India to give the impression that India was imposing a certain solution. On January 1, 1987, Indian High Commission felt compelled to issue a statement decrying the motivated propaganda and refusing to "get involved in a tendentious discussion about developments which have occurred following the departure of the Indian Ministers". The statement asserted that India had "at no stage in the discussions since 1983 put forward any proposal on its own unilaterally" and that "whatever proposals the Indian Ministers carried back for transmission to the Tamil side were result of a general consensus based on discussions with the Government of Sri Lanka". Before the December 19 proposal could achieve any concrete results, the atmosphere had become vitiated through both a tendentious press campaign in Colombo and large-scale violence and military action by the security forces.

❮13❯

Confrontation in Jaffna

In January 1987, the question of LTTE's control of the Jaffna peninsula and the possibility of it declaring Eelam figured prominently in Sri Lankan Parliament. On January 4, Colombo based *The Weekend* carried a lead story saying:

> "The Liberation Tigers of Tamil Eelam are on the road to setting up a de facto administration in the Jaffna peninsula from this month. They will among other things set up their own banks, licence vehicles, issue driving licences, deploy a traffic police force, establish a postal service, operate a public transport service, licence video cinemas and introduce other forms of taxation. Already, its Food Inspectors are issuing licences for meat stalls, fish markets, bakeries, and hotels for a fee. A television station "Nidarshan" (Freedom) goes over the air weekly for six hours. People's courts have been set up in the peninsula's 116 *gramasevaka* divisions. They have taken over the functions of the police and also settling disputes..."

On January 6, 1987, this and similar stories appearing in the media were brought to the notice of the Parliament by Anura Bandaranaike, son of Sirimavo Bandaranaike and Leader of the Opposition in Parliament. A day earlier, the Minister of National Security Lalith Athulathmudali told the *Sun* that all factual reports show that the LTTE "while avoiding the word UDI, is in fact in the process of unilaterally declaring independence." He warned that the people must make no mistake about it. Anura Bandaranaike said that the fact that the LTTE had been able "to gather the resources, ammunition, and cash and the personnel necessary to run a parallel administration to that of the Government of Sri Lanka" was an important fact, the importance of which "cannot be maximised or minimised." Anura warned "if you do not act now it will be too late for your Government or any other Government in the future to eradicate not only the threat of Eelam but also the threat of terrorism".

The Minister of National Security conceding that the situation was serious said a number of steps were contemplated to meet the challenge. One among them was said to be temporary suspension of fuel supplies to Jaffna, since the activities of the militants were dependent on this all important item. Colombo remained mistrustful of New Delhi's reaction, despite the fact the measure was of a non-military nature. Colombo's uneasiness was not off-beam since India insisted it was an exercise of a military option. Taking a dig at India and to chastise her, Athulathmudali said:

> "I am on the point that those who are urging a peaceful settlement seem to forget that the path of pressure now must be on the terrorists, not on the people of Sri Lanka, not on the Government of Sri Lanka, which would love to have a peaceful negotiated settlement. But who is obstructing a peaceful settlement? It is not the Government of Sri Lanka. It is not the members of Parliament here. The people who are obstructing the negotiating of a settlement are the very people who are trying to set up UDI in Jaffna today. So the world and all these countries must realize this. Now gradually this is being realized. We are not going to ignore the UDI step. Whether they call it UDI or not, no government in Sri Lanka can ignore that. We have taken a measured, limited response, where not one item of food has been touched, is today being represented by radio stations across the waters as an economic blockade. Now we have got nowhere near that. One item has been selected and a step has been taken and opinion across the waters is roused up as if we are going to do some kind of a terrible thing. We are not doing that kind of thing, but we cannot allow these steps, which are going on without pressure to stop them, without making some kind of response. We are going to make and we have to make appropriate response."

On January 8, 1987, Sri Lankan Parliament was again seized of the Jaffna situation. The Opposition chose to make a frontal attack on the Government. Anura Bandaranaike, blaming the situation squarely on the Sri Lankan Government, said that it had gone out of its way to antagonise India and draw its ire and wrath. The ruling party blamed it on the LTTE's intransigence and failure of India to prevail on the militants to give up violence. The embargo on fuel supplies was justified only as a means to derail the LTTE plan to set up a civil administration in Jaffna peninsula. The government's apology for its failure, as always was the support LTTE drew from across the Palk Strait and perhaps New Delhi's own failure to exercise any sort of moderating influence on the LTTE. It said:

> "How can you blame the Government of Sri Lanka without ignoring the nature and the quality of the threat from the terrorists? You can speak about a military solution, this, that and everything. When they have foreign bases, when they have foreign sources of supply, when they have a large number of people who feel sympathetic to them, it is not an easy task."

That Colombo was stating the obvious was more than true. If the ethnic violence refused to abate or go away both the Tamils for their uncompromising attitude and India for failing to persuade them to a compromise, must share responsibility. The Tamils, assured of Indian backing, adopted an intransigent attitude that until Eelam or something bordering Eelam was not achieved they would not give up violence. The moderate Tamils represented by TULF failed to restrain the militants' rhetoric. All efforts made so far, whether between the governments of India and Sri Lanka or between the Tamils and Colombo, failed to bring the two parties closer to each other. As pointed out above, even the Bangalore discussions, the previous year, on the sidelines of the SAARC Summit had failed to bridge the gap between the Tamil expectations and what Colombo was prepared to concede. There was no light at the end of the tunnel; in fact the tunnel appeared to be getting lengthier all the time. The Government of India for reasons of domestic politics found itself unable to persuade the Tamils to accept Colombo's proposals, which it had considered "fair and reasonable" as a starting point. New Delhi appeared unconcerned if her own credibility was getting eroded internationally in search of an elusive peace while pandering all the time to the obduracy of the Tamil militants. The non-military option pursued by Sri Lankan Government, including the fuel embargo in the north to derail the LTTE's efforts to introduce its civil administration, had upset India who demanded it be rescinded.

Following the failure of Thimpu Talks, the Government of Sri Lanka had come to believe that India had lost control on the Tamil militants and unable to perform her role of a mediator or even facilitator and that unless the LTTE were militarily defeated or at least weakened there was no hope of a negotiated settlement. As the Sri Lankan military offensive launched at the beginning of January 1987 gathered momentum it met with equally fierce LTTE response. The civilians, both the Sinhalese and Tamils suffered the most. Sri Lankan soldiers on a killing spree put to death 100 innocent Tamils. LTTE was hardly any way behind in this regard. The balance for once appeared to be in favour of Colombo.

Meanwhile, the Government of India unable to forsake the Tamils midstream, tried to build up pressure on Colombo once again. On February 9, 1987, Colombo was put on notice that if the current military operations continued unabated and if the fuel embargo were not lifted, "India would not be able to resume discussions with the Tamil militants". Nevertheless, India in order to stay in the game, clarified that "while this is for the present, India remains willing to resume the peace process if and when these actions are withdrawn..." India, however reiterated "the proposals which emerged on December 19, after the visit of Mr. Natwar Singh and Mr. Chidambaram to Colombo, must clearly be affirmed by the Government of Sri Lanka as a basis and only a starting point for further negotiations". The underlying message conveyed was loud and clear that India's solidarity with the victims of the ethnic conflict remained intact and that no attempt would be made to pressure or persuade the Tamils to accept any kind of political package found unacceptable by them.

As the army action escalated, the strife-torn Northern Province was placed under 36-hour curfew. With the train services suspended, and the fuel supplies cut, the electricity situation too looked grim. On February 12, 1987, Sri Lanka gave a 7-point response to the Indian message of February 9 calling for cessation of hostilities, but made it clear that it was predicated on the "clear understanding that all further discussions to be held, or solutions to be evolved, shall be within the framework of the independence, territorial integrity and unity of Sri Lanka". Essentially, Sri Lanka demanded the militants to give up violence, lay down arms, and accept a peaceful political solution. The Indian High Commissioner responded that unless the military action was not suspended, India was unable to resume her good offices. On February 12, Prime Minister Rajiv Gandhi in a TOP SECRET message conveyed to President Jayewardene his "distress" at the military operations and termed it a "dangerous political signal." Since Jayewardene always pretended to be following the path of Mahatma Gandhi, Rajiv Gandhi derisively remarked: "Your ambiguity on the 19th December-proposal and the military solution that you seem to be seeking lead us to believe that you have rejected the non-violent path of Mahatma Gandhi". On March 3, and March 4, 1987, Rajiv Gandhi intervening in the debate on the President's Address in the two Houses of the Indian Parliament lamented Sri Lankan vacillation.

On March 14, to persuade Colombo to relax the economic blockade of the Jaffna peninsula Rajiv Gandhi sent Dinesh Singh, a senior Member of Parliament to Colombo as his Special Emissary. This had the desired impact and the blockade was lifted on March 17. When the Lok Sabha again discussed Sri Lanka on March 18, 1987, the members were in an agitated frame of mind. Some of them did not hesitate to use unparliamentary language for President Jayewardene, which had to be expunged from the record of the proceedings on the Speaker's orders. There was even demand for internationalization of the issue to gather wider support. Once bitten, twice shy. Minister Natwar Singh counselling patience, however, warned against any such action and said:

> "It is Government's view that it would be inappropriate to internationalise the issue because we know from the past experience that in international organisations, if matters of this kind go, extraneous elements enter into it; big powers take position with regard to their regional

or global interests and if I may respectfully say, in the international fora generally simple things are made difficult and difficult things are made impossible."

On April 23, 1987, the Parliamentary Group of the ruling United National Party adopted a resolution calling upon the government "to annihilate terrorism and terrorists of Sri Lanka from now on...in order to create a suitable peaceful environment which is necessary to consider any political solution". The resolution requested the "Prime Minister of India to arrest the murderous Sri Lankan terrorists living on Indian soil and hand them over to Sri Lanka". Premadasa alluding to the present situation in the north said it "was much more than a war. What they could now do was to give the President as the Commander-in-Chief of the armed forces the fullest support and strength in tackling the problem in the light of the new developments". Persisting with his accusations that there were terrorist bases in India, he asked India "to hand over the terrorists who are enjoying protection on Indian soil". TULF chief Amirthalingam, finding himself helpless and marginalized, appealed for the "use of India's good offices to bring about a genuine cease-fire" to end the conflict between the Tamils and the Government. As the situation worsened, Colombo felt more and more desperate and blamed its inability to check the violence on India. On May 31, 1987, Prime Minister Premadasa appealing to Rajiv Gandhi said:

> "Please do not attempt to interfere in the internal affairs of this country. Do not put your finger into our affairs. If you cannot help us in this time of trial to control the terrorist murderers then all we ask you is please, do not obstruct our action against terrorism".

His bitterness and frustration was betrayed when he recalled his telling Mrs. Indira Gandhi that it would be better if India openly invaded Sri Lanka than give covert support to the terrorists to murder the country's innocents.

LTTE escalates violence

On February 20,1987, the Sri Lankan Parliament accepted a motion for the extension of emergency by another month by 116 votes to one. The Island had been continuously under a state of emergency since May 1983. An exasperated Premadasa repeated the charge that "terrorists were able to wage this war against us because of the shelter they got in India, in Tamil Nadu and elsewhere".

With the peace process facing heavy odds, the LTTE took matters in its hands. On April 17, Tamil militants killed 100 Sinhalese in the Eastern Province. The next day the official spokesman of the Government of India expressing his "profound sorrow and shock" unequivocally condemned the killings, blaming the deteriorating situation on Colombo. India found herself unable to prevail on the Tamil militants to desist from violence. Paying no heed to Indian embarrassment, the LTTE on April 20 raided a village in district Trincomalee and killed 18 Sinhalese and on April 21 there was a serious bomb blast in Colombo's main bus terminal in which 100 were killed, and 300 injured. India condemned the bomb blast and the killings. But this was no consolation to Colombo. Sri Lankan Prime Minister Premadasa hoped "that it had opened the eyes of the world, particularly India's". He told the Sri Lankan Parliament on April 24 "the government will not talk of a political solution hereafter until peace was restored to the country". Its response was large scale military operations accompanied by aerial attacks on the militants, which naturally resulted in large civilian casualties. Sri Lankan army appeared to be making all-round gains for what appeared to be a final strike to decimate the LTTE. In the face of repeated advice for restraint from India, Jayewardene in his Top Secret message to the Indian Prime Minister discounted figures of civilian casualties and hoped that "the badly battered LTTE may be a little more receptive to talks". He stressed the need to impress upon the LTTE that "they are no longer invincible". He however, assured Gandhi that Colombo had not closed its doors to a political settlement and that Sri Lanka was "anxious to go ahead with the provincial councils proposal and elections". While pursuing a military option Jayewardene personally assured the Indian Prime Minister that his friendship towards India and affection towards him "remain undiminished".

Under intense pressure from the Tamil members of Parliament and from Tamil Nadu generally, the Government of India remained blind to the violence of militants and was content to describe them as only "misguided". It refused to see the rationale of Colombo's action imposing "harsh economic and communication blockade and large scale military action" (Rajya Sabha—May 8, 1987). New Delhi warned Colombo "any victories through violence will be short-lived and illusory". In the Parliament, Gopalsamy from Tamil Nadu described the Government of India's approach as "spineless", and "cowardice". He described the Sri Lankan action as a "slap" on India's face. Members threw caution to the winds and often used derogatory language for the Sri Lankan President. Minister of State for External Affairs, Natwar Singh, found himself against heavy odds in defending the patient approach of New Delhi. He regretted India had "not been encouraged at all by the attitude of the authorities and the Government there in recent weeks in a situation which, by their actions they are aggravating and they are making the lives of the citizens of Sri Lanka who are Tamils, a painful existence, which this House condemns, this country condemns and the Human Rights agencies are condemning and we are trying our best".

Wilting under intense pressure from the aggressive tone of the members, the Minister hinted that India might have to consider the exercise of military option the result of which could be disastrous. He said:

> "We do not think a military solution that the Sri Lanka Government is contemplating is going to help. Consequences in Sri Lanka would be extremely grave. And if that military activity was to be expanded further by our doing something, then this whole region gets involved into a geopolitical situation which we would like to avoid."

‹14›

The Crisis Peaks

During the month of May, 1987, the Indian Parliament was constantly seized of the Sri Lanka question. New Delhi spent countless hours reviewing the situation. New Delhi articulated its concern at the deteriorating situation on two counts, which it had expressed repeatedly in the past, viz., denial of basic rights to the Tamils and India's ties of ethnicity with the Tamils of Sri Lanka. Natwar Singh in one of his speeches in Parliament said:

> "The two things make the Sri Lankan situation very grave and almost of daily concern to the Government of India. That is why Government is constantly reviewing the Sri Lankan situation and we are in constant touch with the government and the Chief Minister of Tamil Nadu. Of the two things, one is that nearly 2 million Tamils live in Sri Lanka. They have made their contribution to the development and advancement of Sri Lanka in all walks of life. They are part of Sri Lanka and that they should be denied their basic rights in their own country is to us an outrageous state of affairs. We cannot ignore the feelings of 2 million Tamils because as Shri Kumaramangalam said people of Tamil Nadu and other parts of India have relationship with the people living there and they are subjected to violence that is being perpetrated upon them by the authorities and the Government of Sri Lanka.
>
> "Now, the second point is the international environment. Sri Lanka is a small country, our neighbour and there what we see? Around Trincomalee, naval activities take place from time to time, which cause us concern. Within

> Sri Lanka as the hon. members have said, there is the involvement of Israel, there is the involvement of Pakistan. Arms have come; we have read reports from South Africa. Other countries were involved. The KM services of the United Kingdom are training the Sri Lankan army."
>
> (Lok Sabha, May 11, 1987)

Despite deep concerns, the Government of India remained committed to a peaceful negotiated political solution. The Prime Minister addressing the Congress Parliamentary Party ruled out the use of military option in Sri Lanka. But there was a sense of exasperation in dealing with Colombo. Natwar Singh, feeling irritated and peeved, complained that it was difficult to do serious business with the Government, which changed its mind so often. "How do you conduct business with people who go back on what they have said?" asked the Minister.

About this time, as things seemed to go out of control, Colombo launched a very quiet and subtle propaganda drive in India to win friends and influence people among the intellectuals and people in high places who could influence New Delhi in favour of Sri Lanka. Cyril Ponnamperuma, the Science Advisor to Jayewardene, visited New Delhi and met among others Sharda Prasad, Information Advisor to the Prime Minister; Dr. B.P. Pal, agricultural scientist; Raja Ramanna, Chairman of the Atomic Energy Commission and some other dignitaries in his "personal" capacity. In reporting to the President the success of his visit Ponnamperuma in a Memorandum of May 17, 1987, said that these meetings were important because all these scientists and policy makers had access to the Prime Minister of India and were committed to "use their influence to help Sri Lanka in this crisis". Giving his assessment of these gentlemen, he told his boss that between Karunanidhi and MG Ramachandran, the latter was a lesser evil. He found a "tremendous fund of goodwill on the part of the Indian people towards Sri Lanka" and there was a growing feeling of disgust among Indians for the Tamil terrorists. He recommended that Colombo should work for a strong lobby in New Delhi and Chennai to work in favour of Sri Lanka. Finally, he told the President that the persons he had spoken to were ready to "influence the situation in a private, non-political capacity".

The situation on the ethnic front continued to deteriorate. Violence on a large scale claimed many lives. Colombo was confident that for once it had an upper hand and a little push could deal a deathblow to the LTTE. On May 26, 1987, the combined strength of the Island's armed forces was unleashed in the North. The area was placed under a 24-hour curfew, and about 5000 young Tamils were shipped out of the North to facilitate the military operations. Indian intelligence sources reported that the President's order was to raze Jaffna to the ground in a "fight to the finish". Confirmation came on May 27, when Jayewardene, inaugurating the building of the Bank of Ceylon headquarters in the capital mincing no words declared that he had ordered the security forces to fight until Jaffna was liberated.

India had yet another change in the Ministry of External Affairs. Narayan Dutt Tiwari became the new incumbent. On May 26, an appalled External Affairs Minister said that as a result of the action of the security forces in the north, four thousand Tamils had been killed and there was the apprehension of an increased flow of refugees flowing into India, adding to the already unbearable burden on Tamil Nadu. A nervous Minister apprehended mounting "influence of external elements inimical to security, stability and peace in the region". High Commissioner Dixit kept the telephone lines between the two capitals busy. The developing scenario was too disconcerting for New Delhi to sit back. There were intense consultations in New Delhi. It was decided to call off the Sri Lankan bluff by issuing an oblique warning that if Colombo failed to review its misguided policy of military approach, India would also be compelled to review her policy on the issue. On May 28, in a statement, Prime Minister Gandhi said:

> "The horrific loss of innocent life of this magnitude is totally disproportionate to the avowed aim of exterminating the Tamil militant groups. The calculated and cold-blooded slaughter of thousands of Sri Lankan citizens by their own government cannot promote a solution. It is a gross violation of every tenet of human rights. The international community must impress upon the Sri Lankan authorities the imperative need for restraint."

> "While India was patiently and painstakingly working towards a political solution, it is apparent now that the Sri Lankan Government was buying time for pursuing the military option. The present offensive is part of this plan. India has done everything to find solutions compatible with the unity of Sri Lanka. But by mercilessly bombing a defenceless people and spreading misery, on the basis of only ethnic difference, Sri Lanka is itself putting its unity and integrity in jeopardy. From the rubble and ashes there can only arise the total alienation of an entire people, a more determined militancy, and more extreme options. The time to desist from a military occupation of Jaffna is now. Later may be too late."

When India's apprehensions and warnings were brought to the notice of the Sri Lankan President, he was enraged and according to J.N. Dixit said, "India can go to hell". (*Assignment Colombo*, p. 98). As the Tamils were being squeezed under the military offensive, the Government of India came under intense domestic pressure. Tamil Nadu was seething with anger. Parliament was getting aggressive. The Government found it impossible to keep it restrained. The crisis in Lanka was peaking. If Colombo succeeded in annihilating the LTTE, the bargaining chip, which the Tamils had forged together with all its drawbacks would be eliminated. They would be reduced to a non-entity and forced to accept whatever solution the Sinhalese Government offered. That too would spell the doom of the Government of India's Sri Lanka policy. Tamil Nadu, in general, would stand alienated. To salvage the remnants of that failed policy, it had become imperative for New Delhi to establish its credibility not only with the Indian Tamils and Tamil Nadu, but also internationally and with its neighbours. Small neighbours surrounded India. They needed to be told that India, an elephant could not be provoked beyond a point. Flexing muscles, New Delhi asked its High Commissioner to make it clear to Colombo that New Delhi would not let down the Tamils at this hour of their crisis. Should Sri Lanka persist with her military machine to eliminate the LTTE altogether, New Delhi would have no alternative but to provide the necessary logistical support to it, an euphemism for military intervention. The underlying message that India sought to convey to Sri Lanka was too bold and loud to go unnoticed in Colombo. India would not permit the military subjugation of Jaffna nor allow the Tamils to be brought on their knees.

What Colombo feared all along appeared to come to pass. Relations between the two countries reached almost breaking point with risk of military confrontation. India was worried at the deterioration of the situation in Jaffna, which she perceived, in the words of Dixit, as affecting "the peace and security in the region". (*Assignment Colombo,* p.106) To test the Sri Lankan determination and to put Colombo on notice that India meant business, India decided to break the economic blockade of the north by deciding to send supplies across the Palk Strait by unarmed fishing boats and sought Colombo's cooperation. This was denied. It was enough of an affront to the "regional super power," as Dixit explained to Deputy Foreign Minister Tyron Fernando at a dinner on June 5, the day the supplies were airdropped. In the words of Dixit:

> "I told him humiliating India by sending the fishing boats back had affected India's credibility with its own citizens in Tamil Nadu and the country's standing as a mediator who could safeguard the interests of Sri Lanka Tamils. I added that sustaining this credibility in the eyes of Sri Lankan Tamils was necessary as otherwise the ramifications would be a break-up of Sri Lanka. I stressed that, the jubilation (at India's failure to deliver the supplies by sea) and aggressive contempt for India in the Sri Lankan media had to be countered by Rajiv Gandhi to sustain his image as a person capable of handling negative acts against India, specially when he had been working very hard to bring about reconciliation between the Sinhalese and the Tamils." (*Assignment Colombo*, pp. 108-09)

High Commissioner Dixit ended his diatribe on a highly acrimonious and caustic note suggesting, if India had instead of airdropping relief supplies exercised the option of breaking the economic blockade by military action that would "have had much more serious implications for Sri Lanka and Indo-Sri Lanka relations".

Dixit in the coming days had to do a lot of explaining on the Indian action, which Colombo described as "naked aggression" on Sri Lanka's independence, and an "unwarranted assault" on her "sovereignty and territorial integrity". Expressing the travails of a small nation Sri Lankan Foreign Minister, A.C.S. Hameed bemoaned, "Sri Lanka had no military or other means of preventing this "outrage". On June 9, Dixit told protesting Sri Lankans that the action was an "inevitable necessity", because of the "tragic situation in the peninsula". He however, assured them that India had no "negative intentions towards Sri Lanka". Premadasa called it an act of "cowardice". The Sri Lankan media called the airdropping of supplies as a "raw and naked violation of Sri Lanka's independence and sovereignty". The UN Secretary General Perez de Cuellar said that he met the delegates of the two countries at the UN and hoped that the situation could be resolved by negotiations.

On June 7, Nepal expressed grave concern over airdropping of relief supplies by India and condemned it as a violation of Sri Lanka's territorial integrity. A Foreign Ministry spokesman said in Kathmandu that Nepal deplored the Indian intervention and would always condemn such violations of sovereignty. The Nepalese concern was quite understandable. Nepal, a small country was perpetually having one problem or the other with her big neighbour and did not wish to let the Indian action pass unchallenged. The Nepalese spokesman went on to suggest the appointment of an acceptable regional figure to find a solution acceptable to the two countries.

On June 9, an estimated eight thousand people of which one thousand and three hundred were Buddhist monks, staged a one-hour demonstration in front of the residence of the Indian High Commissioner protesting against the violation of Sri Lanka's air space and sovereignty. Among the demonstrators there were several prominent personalities, which included some of the ministers of the government. A memorandum handed over to the High Commissioner by the Ven. Gnanissara Thera stated:

> "We honour India which gave us Buddhism and which was the birth place of great religious teachers, learned men and philosophers. Although, we respect the Indian flag, we, as free Sri Lankans are not prepared to be subjugated. May the present short-sighted rulers of India realise human rights and freedom and give special consideration to this peaceful protest of ours. May the short-sighted rulers of India be far-sighted."

❮15❯

Towards a Peace Agreement

Sri Lanka realised for once the limits of defiance of a regional power much bigger in size and resources and the need to make peace with this reality. On June 15, as a first step towards reconciliation, Colombo entered into a formal agreement with New Delhi for receiving additional humanitarian supplies for distribution in the north thereby removing the immediate irritant that had led to the airdropping of the supplies earlier.

India had, since independence of Sri Lanka, watched silently the struggle of the Tamils to find a honourable space there. In the first instance, it were the Tamils of Indian origin who bore the brunt of Sinhala chauvinism when under the citizenship laws, it was decided to deprive them of Sri Lankan citizenship and throw them out. The alienation and estrangement that gradually seeped in among the ethnic Tamils towards the Sinhalese and the Sinhala state, invited retribution from the both which led not infrequently to anti-Tamil riots. Though initially their fate suffered benign neglect in New Delhi, gradually the reverberations were felt in India, particularly in Tamil Nadu. Indian Parliament was often rocked at their ill treatment. The ferociousness of the riots in 1983 against all the Tamils including the Indian citizens, made India give up the pretence of treating the ethnic problem as internal to the Island. Yet India was not ready to get involved completely. While pledging herself to the sovereignty and territorial integrity of the country, India was only willing to facilitate a solution acceptable to both the sides by promoting a dialogue between the two that had broken down because of perceived Sinhalese chauvinism. The initial Tamil enthusiasm about Indian involvement gradually got eroded, particularly among the militant sections, since they felt India had her own limitations and agenda, which limited her options. It could not be a party to the dismantling of the state, without which the dream of Eelam could not be realized. India too, felt frustrated since her interest was misunderstood and only led to Tamil rigidity. The Tamil constituency in India too remained despondent and Parliament disgruntled. While India found Colombo often grudging and stingy in accommodating the Tamils, the latter were no less obdurate and unyielding. The Government of India failed to goad the Tamils to accept a solution offered by Colombo and considered fair by New Delhi. It often found itself compromised and internationally found Indian image dented.

Colombo's latest military campaign and its roll-back under New Delhi's pressure gave food for thought to both New Delhi and Colombo to reconsider their inter-relationship. The state relations between the two countries had become hostage to the Tamil problem, which was impacting regional security. While Colombo was now convinced that the Indian factor had made a military solution of the ethnic problem out of question, it too was converted to the view that no political solution of the problem was realistically possible without India despite New Delhi's lack of adequate leverage with the Tamils, particularly the LTTE, the strongest guerrilla group. Given the plethora of Tamil organizations, Colombo found it impossible to deal with all of them or make all of them agree to any one solution. It concluded that it was not enough for New Delhi to just promote a dialogue. New Delhi must be made a party to any solution and it should be left to it to sell the same to the Tamils. Since New Delhi had repeatedly pledged itself to preserving and respecting Sri Lanka's sovereignty and territorial integrity, Colombo felt assured India would not prescribe a solution, which would be incompatible with the Island's Constitution. That India herself was facing similar separatist problems within the country was an added insurance. In the past, New Delhi operating on the periphery as facilitator got away when the Tamils chose to renege from any solution arrived at with Colombo. New Delhi was not unmindful of the fact that the Tamils had in the past too often been pigheaded not to accept solution considered fair by it or at least a starting point for negotiations, leaving it embarrassed. There was, consequently, a desire on the part of both the parties to work out their modus operandi afresh and find a solution, which would satisfy Tamil aspirations and fit into the four corners of the Sri Lankan Constitution.

The latest developments had chastened the Tamils, particularly the militants. They were not blind to the realization that without Indian intervention, they were almost decimated. Indian estrangement from Tamil cause would leave them once again at the mercy of the Sinhalese. Past history was not gratifying.

On June 21, A.C.S. Hameed, the Foreign Minister told Colombo's *Sunday Times* that "the problem cannot be solved without Indian participation in the negotiations because it is an internal problem with external dimension". It made it easier for things to fall in their place. Reconciled to the Indian factor, on June 15, 1987 Colombo formally entered into an agreement with India for receiving humanitarian relief supplies for distribution in Jaffna. To give no offence to India, Sri Lanka cautioned her naval personnel patrolling the Surveillance Zone in the north against entering Indian territorial waters when giving a chase to boats carrying LTTE cadres or supplies for them. The possibility of cadres attempting to "lure" the navy into Indian waters had not been ruled out.

There was yet another bout of acrimony between the two countries before they sat down to defuse the situation. Rajiv Gandhi belatedly, in a press interview to the weekly *India Today* justifying the violation of Sri Lanka's air space had said:

> "The situation deteriorated because Sri Lanka thought they could work on the military option. Sometime we wonder whether this whole exercise of getting the parties together across the table was not used by Sri Lanka to buy time for the military solution. This has caused the problem. They agree to something and then go back on that. They again agree partially but again change their mind. It is the Sri Lankan flippant attitude, which has caused all these tensions. There is a lot of vacillation on their part..."

These remarks coming from the Prime Minister of India when Sri Lanka was still smarting under the trauma of violation of her air space with impunity by a regional super power, endowed with much greater resources, both in men and material, stung

Colombo to the core and they did not wish to let it go unchallenged. On June 21, 1987, the Indian High Commissioner was summoned to the Foreign Ministry where the Acting Foreign Minister Tyron Fernando registered his protest. On the same day, the Ministry of Foreign Affairs in a statement described the Prime Minister's accusations as "incorrect and without foundation", and challenged "anybody to provide evidence of an occasion that Colombo had gone back on its word or given occasion for the remarks attributed to Mr. Gandhi."

Despite irritants, there were some straws in the wind to indicate that below the turbulent Indo-Sri Lankan waters, there were softer currents, capable of promoting a dialogue for a negotiated and peaceful settlement. Rajiv Gandhi gave first indication of this on June 29 when speaking at the luncheon meeting of the Indian Association of Foreign Affairs Correspondents in New Delhi. He said: "India was awaiting indications from Sri Lanka for a new initiative on the resumption of a dialogue on finding a negotiated settlement of the ethnic conflict". He added significantly that "the ball is now in Sri Lanka's court" and that the government was in touch with both Colombo and the militants. The implications were more than clear to both the parties. India gave enough indication that any settlement worked out between New Delhi and Colombo would be acceptable to the Tamils not excluding the LTTE. India would use all her resources to ensure that the Tamils did not spoil the party, at least this time.

While pursuing Indian peace initiative Colombo announced its intention to go ahead with its plans to hold elections to various local bodies and 16 vacant seats in the Parliament, which were lying vacant since the TULF boycott. India felt compelled to intervene once again to stop this affront. On July 1, Prime Minister Gandhi sent a personal message to President Jayewardene through High Commissioner Dixit to desist from going ahead with the planned elections until the ethnic issue was resolved. He warned that going ahead with the elections implied the very negation of the process evolved since 1983. He warned that in this context President "may carefully consider the implications of holding these elections unilaterally and then take a final decision". Expressing Indian intention for a peaceful political solution, he said this was possible only "if Sri Lanka

Government evolves a genuine solution which would meet the basic concerns of the Tamils", and added: "If Sri Lanka Government has any further ideas in this regard, India would be willing to cooperate on the basis of such ideas to evolve a compromise with the Tamils. The Prime Minister would like to have His Excellency President Jayewardene's reaction to this suggestion, if any".

The above message was clear and simple. Devoid of any tautology it went home. Colombo deciding to go along with New Delhi, accepted to formally implement the core of the various agreements that had been reached between Colombo and the Tamil groups and Colombo and New Delhi in the post-1983 period. For the Tamil militants, the Indian initiative was a God-sent opportunity. Since the last week of June, the LTTE had found itself pushed into a corner of the Jaffna peninsula in the Vadamarachi region and decided to return to the negotiating table to save itself from complete decimation. New Delhi apparently, had done its homework before embarking on the new peace initiative. First Secretary of the Indian High Commission, Hardeep Singh Puri, was sent to Jaffna to consult with the LTTE and gauge its mood. Hardeep though did not meet Prabakaran, but returned with the distinct impression that a somewhat chastened LTTE was after all not completely averse to a negotiated solution. Separately, N. Ram of the *Hindu* who was acting as an intermediary too received enough signals from the LTTE that it was open for an honourable settlement.

The heart of the understanding was that Colombo would in principle agree to the merger of the two Tamil provinces in the north and the east, to create the substance of the Tamil homeland. To enable Jayewardene to sell the settlement to the Sinhalese, it would be sugarcoated with a proviso that the future of the merged province would be decided through a referendum after one year in the Eastern Province alone. Since the Tamils did not enjoy a majority there, it left the possibility of a return to the status quo ante open. This was nothing short of a double deal. It may be pointed out that in the last couple of decades the Tamils in the Eastern Province had been reduced to a minority due to their exodus to foreign countries including India and the resettlement of a large Sinhala population there despite Tamil protests. Merger was a ploy to involve the Tamils in the search for a new political settlement. The referendum on merger after one year in the Eastern Province alone, was thrown in to assure the Sinhalese that once the peace returned to the Island, *status quo ante* would be restored. The Tamils were sure to protest and as expected they did, and accused India of bad faith.

Colombo media was agog with reports about the fresh Indian initiative. However on July 6, the Indian High Commission discounted such reports. It was feared that premature disclosure could lead to sabotage by the Sinhalese vested interest. The daily *Sun*, which had initially carried the report declared that it stood by its story. Meantime, the *Financial Times* of London got hold of the 14-point broad framework of the agreement and spilled the beans. The paper said a secret deal to "create a semi-autonomous Tamil homeland in Sri Lanka was close to agreement" and the Indian High Commissioner J.N. Dixit had returned to Colombo with the response of his Prime Minister. This was enough of an endorsement of the *Sun* story. *The Financial Times* went on to claim that an Indian diplomat had also held a secret meeting with the LTTE in the Jaffna peninsula. It was claimed that the proposals now worked out went further than any previous solution towards meeting the Tamil demands, which were largely supported by India. There was however a rider. The proposals did not enjoy the support of Prime Minister Premadasa, who was opposed to any accommodation with India. He was away to Japan and the agreement was hammered at his back. Some salient points of the 14-point formula were said to be the following:

* All parties agree to preserve the territorial integrity of Sri Lanka and its unitary constitution.
* The government recognises the multi-ethnic character of Sri Lanka. The distinctive cultural identity of the Tamil people and their rights in "their historic areas of habitation"—the closest any government has come to meeting Tamil demands for a "traditional homeland" in the Northern and Eastern provinces.
* Elections before the end of this year for nine provincial councils, each having its own governor, chief minister and board of ministers. Most significantly, the north and east will be combined to count one province.

* A referendum in the east within 12 months to allow the population—one-third Tamil, one-third Sinhalese and one-third Muslim—to decide whether it wants to remain merged with the north.
* The army will be confined to barracks and the Tamil rebel groups will lay down their arms.
* India will patrol the narrow Palk Straits between Sri Lanka and India to stop any further influx of arms or armed rebels from Tamil Nadu in southern India, home to 50 million Tamils.
* India will deport any Sri Lankan engaged in terrorist activity.
* The 125,000 Sri Lankan refugees in India will return to the Island, and Sri Lanka will confer citizenship on 100,000 Indian tea planters, now classified as stateless.

As the later events proved, the report was almost close to reality based indeed on well-informed sources.

The Tamil response, particularly that of the TULF, as speculated was positive, especially in view of the proposal for merger of the Northern and the Eastern provinces. A TULF spokesman said the offer to merge the east and the north was "a concession of fundamental importance and therefore a major breakthrough". Evidently, TULF was under the impression that the merger was on a permanent basis and not subject to review. Since the actual proposals were still under wrap, the media speculation was at its peak. The High Commissioner met President Jayewardene on July 17, 1987, when a number of Cabinet Ministers were also present. This was enough of a hint for the media to go to town in the background of reports that something was cooking. It was mentioned that Dixit had given some clarification to the Sri Lankan leaders to canvass support in favour of the Indian proposals.

The High Commission worried that premature disclosure could be injurious to the efforts underway was at pains to deny that any thing was at all cooking. It categorically stated that India had no fresh ideas to resolve the ethnic imbroglio, and therefore media reports were "incorrect". Giving reasons for the meeting the High Commission stated, "The meetings were only to provide clarifications about India's attitude on the ethnic question which was sought by the Sri Lankan side. The Government of India has not put forward any proposals so far". The High Commission while denying reports yet confirmed what was being speculated.

The toughened attitude of India as represented in the air-dropping of the relief supplies and their continuance, a reluctant Colombo falling in line, LTTE's chastened mood and its willingness to negotiate on certain conditions, India's categorical stand that she would not countenance any future economic blockade of the Tamil areas or for that matter allow any military action against Tamils to succeed, her displeasure at the induction of foreign military factors etc., all put together went a long way to convince every one that there was no alternative to a negotiated settlement.

Lalith Athulathmudali, Minister for National Security when asked to explain the rationale of the proposed agreement to the Executive Committee of the United National Party said on July 27 that the problem which was initially domestic, grew into an international problem "particularly with the involvement of India". He asked members to accept the reality of Indian involvement whether or not they liked it. He defined the four-fold obligations of India arising out of the proposed agreement thus:

1. "They (India) will patrol their own areas of the territorial waters in the Palk Straits as we have been doing in our own. They will do this to stop illegal transportation of goods, arms and people. This will not only affect the terrorists but also the traditional smugglers. I think this will severely affect the economy of Valvettithurai if the patrolling is successfully operated.
2. India will not allow anybody, be they terrorists or any other organisation, whose aim is a separate state in Sri Lanka to operate their activities from India.
3. India promises to dismantle all training camps and propaganda units of the separatist movement.
4. About 100,000 persons of Indian origin who had obtained their Indian citizenship and who could not be repatriated to India due to the suspension of the Rameshwaram-Talaimannar ferry service since 1984 would be repatriated to India."

Premadasa, who was abroad when the agreement was negotiated, was livid when on return home he learnt of the impending agreement with India on the ethnic question. At the Cabinet meeting on July 27, he had strong reservations on the signing of the agreement and called for a referendum if it had to be signed and wanted the formal signing ceremony postponed. There were rumours galore that the Prime Minister had resigned since he went to the Cabinet meeting in his private car. There were others in the Cabinet who equally opposed the proposed agreement. Dixit, on return to Colombo after a fresh round of consultations in New Delhi, had already confirmed to the President Rajiv Gandhi's travel plans for signing the agreement. The President had made up his mind. He was not receptive to any alternative suggestion. The agreement too provoked a great amount of opposition at the people's level, and the opposition even boycotted the signing ceremony.

In India, there was enthusiasm among the bureaucracy since it was seen as the Prime Minister's personal triumph. The proposed agreement was not to address merely Tamil issues. Sri Lanka was browbeaten into accepting what India perceived her security concerns — like the use of the Trincomalee port, future of the Voice of America broadcasting station, presence of foreign military advisors in Sri Lanka, etc. These were the one-sided obligations thrust upon Colombo. There was no reciprocity even for form sake to give an impression of a balanced document negotiated between two sovereign nations. It conveyed the imprint of a document imposed by a victorious power on a country vanquished in war. The main agreement, which sought to address the Tamil concerns, was an extraordinary document. It enjoined on Colombo various obligations on the dictation of New Delhi in favour of the Tamils. Strangely enough, the minority community remained as dissatisfied as the majority community chaffing at being goaded by a "regional bully" into accepting conditions perceived at undermining the country's sovereignty. India by signing the agreement and later committing her troops to underwrite its implementation, even in good faith, failed to take advantage of the experience of the interventionist policies of other countries.

On July 28, Prime Minister Rajiv Gandhi briefed leaders of various political parties about the impending agreement and said though LTTE had earlier accepted the proposals, was now apparently having a second thought. He said attempts to assuage the feelings of the LTTE were continuing but confirmed there was no change in his plan to travel to Colombo the next day. Evidently, he had decided to go ahead whether or not LTTE were satisfied. The TULF leaders have since maintained that they were shown the draft for the first time in New Delhi on the morning of the July 28, in the Committee Room of South Block by Kuldip Sahdev, Joint Secretary dealing with Sri Lanka in the Ministry of External Affairs. According to TULF leadership, they were not given a copy of the draft to carry away with them. All the copies were taken away after they had looked through and given their comments. The TULF had strong reservations on some of the provisions, particularly on the referendum after one year and only in the Eastern Province to decide the future of the merged province. That morning it was obvious to the TULF that New Delhi was determined to go ahead despite their reservations. To be fair to themselves, they decided to reduce their reservations into writing for posterity.

The reaction of the LTTE was important and crucial. New Delhi was therefore anxious to obtain its endorsement. But it was important that the projected peace plan was explained in proper perspective to the man who mattered the most, Prabakaran. Hardeep Puri, the First Secretary of the High Commission, who had earlier visited Jaffna and reportedly beholden himself to the LTTE was considered most suitable to perform this task. He arrived in Jaffna on July 19. By now only the broad contours of the agreement being negotiated with Colombo were available. There were many loose ends that needed to be tightened. Hardeep, therefore, could only give Prabakaran the broad perimeters of the settlement that was under negotiation between the two governments and succeeded in persuading him to come to New Delhi. New Delhi was reasonably confident that since the LTTE had initially signalled, through N. Ram, its readiness to accept Indian peace initiative, Prabakaran's acceptance was now a formality and he could not go back on his commitment and put India in the false.

Prabakaran, who had led a guerrilla life and had as yet not tasted any political power, failed to realize that important matters of state could not be subject to the whims and fancies of the changing moods and perceptions of individuals and taken lightly. Commitments once made unless held sacrosanct, business among countries would not be possible. It was this failure of the LTTE chief that was the bane of continuing conflict and was to prove disastrous for the peace of Sri Lanka. As we shall see during his career he made several commitments to gain temporary advantage or time, which he did not wish to honour. His promises and commitments were often strategic means to win the Eelam war. He did not suffer from qualms of conscience if he failed to keep his word. New Delhi's appeals and cajoling had little impact on the unyielding Prabakaran, who was fully conscious that he held the key to any settlement and that India would not go ahead without he being mollified. In deciding to come to New Delhi, Prabakaran, a shrewd tactician, was not unaware of the importance of the invitation. It was for the first time that he had received an invitation from the Government of India for talks on a crucial matter. It was not lost on him that it implied New Delhi's recognition of his organisation and his person as important elements in the settlement of the ethnic problem. In the past, this honour was reserved only for his bete noire, the TULF.

In New Delhi, the task of dotting every 'i' and crossing every 't' of the draft agreement was by now complete. Every one was keeping the fingers crossed while its contents were explained to Prabakaran. Soon it was discovered that the draft failed Prabakaran's test. He was also irked that New Delhi, despite being solicitous of his personal nod and bestowing on him the honour of a separate meeting (other Tamil leaders were met together), was not treating him as the sole representative of the Tamils. The conditional merger of the two provinces was equally distressing to him. He was appalled that the LTTE was required to surrender its arms. This would leave him and his cadres at the mercy of the Sinhala army, which had all along targeted the Tamils.

Prime Minister Gandhi had invested his personal prestige in the agreement and any setback would put him in a difficult situation politically, both at home and abroad. After his assumption of office of the Prime Minister, this was the first major problem in the realm of foreign affairs that he was called upon to handle. Success would catapult him in the big league and credit him of solving a problem that was festering since almost the independence of Sri Lanka. He was looking for a place in history and his officials were bending backward to ensure that he was not denied that honour. But Prabakaran was made of sterner stuff and once he had made up his mind, nothing could change it. The Indians were disappointed but warned him that he would be left out in the cold if he did not fall in line. Prabakaran, equally conscious of his place in history, refused to give in to New Delhi's fulminations despite every effort made to meet some of his last minute objections on security and upkeep of his cadres. He was even assured of a dominating role for the LTTE in the interim administration that was envisaged for the merged province.

On July 27, Velupillai Prabakaran rejected the proposals publicly and in toto. He described the agreement an act of betrayal and reiterated his resolve to continue with his armed struggle. Prabakaran based his concerns and disappointment on the provisions requiring the LTTE to surrender its arms. He was opposed to the disarming of his people until the government military camps in the north were dismantled. In a strongly worded statement, he blamed Rajiv Gandhi for having betrayed the Tamil trust. They had come to Delhi, he said, without any idea of the proposals, but had "walked into a trap". The LTTE, which so far had to reckon with the Sri Lankan army, might have to face the Indian army as well, he said prophetically. New Delhi disputed his contention that he was unaware of the details of the agreement. The fact that Puri could not have given him full and finer details of the agreement in Jaffna, was ignored. These were to be provided to him in Delhi where the draft was being finalized. And it was here after arrival in the Indian capital that he felt cheated when details and finer points of the agreement were shared with him.

That it was actually so, was also borne out by what the former Cabinet Secretary, B.G. Deshmukh, had to say in his book *A Cabinet Secretary Looks Back*. He said:

> "We wanted to keep the top leadership of the LTTE fully informed and Prabakaran was brought to Delhi for

> this purpose. M.G. Ramachandran and other politicians and N Ram of the *HINDU* said that the agreement would be acceptable to the LTTE, but many of us had serious doubts about its intentions and reliability. M.K. Narayanan, director IB (Intelligence Bureau) was one of them. But the director of RAW (Research and Analysis Wing) was quite confident: 'They knew LTTE better than anybody and they were sure to make the LTTE agree'. Rajiv Gandhi consulted General Sundarji (Chief of Staff of the Indian Army) who in his usual flamboyant style said, 'if the LTTE does not agree and wants to take on the Indian Army we will finish them within a week or ten days.' (p. 331)

There was gloom in the official circles. The officials in New Delhi, who were so far euphoric on the splendid task they had accomplished, were shell-shocked at the LTTE's reaction. An official spokesman of the Indian Ministry of External Affairs expressed Government of India's deep disappointment with the LTTE's response. He noted that all other Tamil groups had agreed to extend support and expressed the hope and confidence that the LTTE too would be prevailed upon to lend the necessary support. The spokesman assured the Tamils that the Government of India would make every effort to meet the legitimate aspirations of the Tamils in Sri Lanka. He, however, failed to take note of the TULF reservations, which though muted were serious. That the TULF did not wish to go public to avoid an open defiance of the Government of India was another matter.

Prabakaran had no such qualms and remained defiant. He was not bothered if the Government of India and the Prime Minister personally were embarrassed by his utterances. He told the Press Trust of India that the accord would remain "only on paper" since it had ignored the Tamil aspirations. Describing Rajiv Gandhi's decision to sign the accord as "disappointing and shocking", he said it amounted to "a stab in the back of the Tamils". He least expected the Government of India to "let down the Tamils" who had suffered immensely and were now totally exposed to the Sri Lankan army offensive. The LTTE leader reiterated that he would adhere to the truce, which was the core of the peace plan of the proposed accord, but would not lay down arms until the Sri Lankan army had dismantled their military camps in the north and moved to the barracks. Prabakaran repeated that he was "tricked" into coming to Delhi for talks. The Tamils were told that the Prime Minister wanted to hold talks with them to clear certain misunderstandings, but it was only on arrival that they were informed that an "unsatisfactory accord" was to be signed by the two governments. He wondered why the Government of India had toed the Sri Lankan line and tried to thrust a preconceived plan on the Tamils. He felt piqued that the entire Indian exercise in Delhi was aimed at getting Tamils' consent after the agreement had been negotiated and finalised and not for consultations to improve it to their satisfaction.

While other groups had chosen to give their acceptance of the proposals in writing, the LTTE felt there was no point in doing so as they were told their suggestions would not be included. "We were asked to accept the plan in toto without any change", the LTTE chief said and added that the LTTE could not be forced into accepting the proposals which gave them much less than in the past, particularly considering huge loss of lives and properties of Tamils during their struggle.

Apparently arm-twisted by the Government of India, a United News of India report later quoted a LTTE spokesman to say that Prabakaran denied having said that Mr. Gandhi had "betrayed the Tamils". In a statement issued late on the night of July 27, the spokesman who claimed that he was speaking on behalf of Prabakaran said that their leader had made no reference to Mr. Gandhi in his earlier statements rejecting the peace accord. The spokesman also denied that Prabakaran had said that the LTTE would have to face the Indian army in view of the rejection.

The Government of India was stunned by the reaction of the LTTE who now mattered more than the TULF. To propitiate Prabakaran, Rajiv Gandhi met him on July 28, and listened to his objections to see if any one of them could be accommodated. A statement issued in the name of Prabakaran after his meeting with the Prime Minister appeared conciliatory as compared to his earlier statements. But it gave clear indication that he had not accepted the agreement in the form it was going to be signed the next day. The statement said that the Prime Minister "listened to our concerns with keen interest and utmost sincerity". That the discussions were inconclusive was clearly admitted in the statement since it talked of discussions being resumed on return of the Prime Minister from Colombo after signing the agreement. What such discussions would achieve did not need much cyber power. As later events were to prove, LTTE was made to appear conciliatory and Prabakaran had no choice but to be obliging since he was under the five-star "hospitality" of the Government of India.

The assertion of J.N. Dixit in his book *Assignment Colombo* that the Tamil "approval was very much there, from the TULF at the one end of the spectrum to the LTTE at the other" is not borne out by fact on record. TULF's reservations were contained in its letter of July 28, sent to the Prime Minister on the eve of his departure for Colombo, and LTTE's reservations, nay rejection of the entire agreement, was well known publicly.

The Indo-Sri Lanka Agreement to Establish Peace and Normalcy in Sri Lanka was signed on July 29, 1987. While the main agreement addressed the issues of Tamil concern, the letters attached to it sought to take care of the Indian security concerns in the region. India, on her part agreed to deny training, military supplies and other facilities to the militants on her soil and deport those who were engaged in militant activities. The most crucial elements of the settlement were the merger albeit temporarily of the Northern and the Eastern provinces followed by a referendum in the Eastern Province alone after one year on future of the merger, the disarming of the militants and India undertaking the responsibility to ensure that they were disarmed if there was any problem in doing so. Just when the President of Sri Lanka and the Prime Minister of India were signing the all-important agreement, the Foreign Secretaries of the two countries were busy giving final touches to the blueprint for induction of the Indian armed forces in Sri Lanka, which arrived within hours of the signing of the agreement.

❮16❯

India and the Peace Agreement

The Agreement to Establish Peace and Normalcy in Sri Lanka was signed by the Prime Minister of India Rajiv Gandhi and the President of Sri Lanka Julius Jayewardene on July 29, 1987. It accepted that Sri Lanka was a "multi-ethnic and a multi-lingual plural society consisting *inter alia* of Sinhalese, Tamils, Muslims (Moors) and Burghers." The two Tamil provinces, Northern and the Eastern, were recognized as "areas of historical habitation of Sri Lankan Tamil speaking people together in this territory with other ethnic groups." Implication of this was not lost on the Tamils. Their claim to the two provinces as their exclusive homeland stood diluted. Besides the merger of the two provinces was conditional upon holding a referendum in the Eastern Province alone after one year. As explained earlier the Tamils did not have a majority in the Eastern Province, it was clear to them, that the merger would only be a temporary affair, a ploy to lull them into complacency for the present. The implementation of the agreement on the part of Sri Lanka was made conditional upon India undertaking to ensure that Indian territory was not used for "activities prejudicial to the unity, integrity and security of Sri Lanka". India agreed to undertake the disarming of the Tamil militants should they fail to do so themselves. An Annexure appended to the agreement had provisions to ensure free and fair elections to the merged Provincial Council, for the "surrender" of arms by the Tamil militants and provision for Indian peace keeping contingent to "guarantee and enforce the cessation of hostilities", etc.

Part two of the agreement contained letters exchanged between the Prime Minister of India and the President of Sri Lanka. In those letters Sri Lanka agreed to meet the Indian security concerns regarding deployment of foreign military and intelligence personnel in Sri Lanka, use of Trincomalee port for military purposes, lease of the Trincomalee Oil Tank Farm, operation of the foreign broadcasting facilities etc., in return for (i) India deporting Sri Lankan citizens engaged in terrorist activities from the Indian soil and (ii) India agreeing to provide military supplies and training for Sri Lankan security forces.

Speaking on the Sri Lankan TV on the day the agreement was signed, Rajiv Gandhi described it as an agreement "without parallel". Jayewardene speaking simultaneously was euphoric and saw the visit of Prime Minister in the series of visits starting with the landing of Prince Vijaya, son of Emperor Ashoka who brought Buddhism to their country centuries ago. He said:

> "This visit has been the most controversial visit by an Indian leader to Sri Lanka since Prince Vijaya landed on our shores 2,500 years ago. Prince Vijaya gave birth to the Sinhala race. The agreement that Prime Minister, Shri Rajiv Gandhi and I have signed, I hope will give a rebirth to the Sinhala race because we have been torn by conflict, violence, death and all the other depredations of human wickedness, specially in the North and the East."

When the *Hindu* asked President Jayewardene for a message for the Sri Lankan Tamils, he remarked: "The message is to forgive. I have forgiven them." The veteran leader sounded self-critical and admitting "mistakes" of his party, the UNP, along with various others in the Sinhala political spectrum said the "Only Sinhala policy" indeed was flawed. He recalled how true Sir Colvin R. de Silva was in the fifties when he said: "One language, two nations. Two languages, one nation".

The agreement lacked in sincerity on the part of both the signatories. What was intended was different than what had been put down on the paper. In para 6 of the annexure to the agreement, it was stated, "an Indian Peace Keeping Force (IPKF) may be invited by the President of Sri Lanka *to guarantee and enforce the cessation of hostilities, if so required*". (emphasis added) Quite evidently, the invitation to the IPKF was to be contingent on the need for it. The need could only have been felt if the implementation had got stuck or there were hurdles that needed to be removed. In fact as per paragraph 2.9 of the main agreement, the cessation of hostilities was expected to "come into effect all over the island within 48 hours of the signing of this Agreement". The "process of surrendering of arms" by the militants was to be "completed within 72 hours of the cessation of hostilities coming into effect." Vide para 4 of the annexure to the agreement the militants were to "surrender their arms to authorities agreed upon to be designated by the President of Sri Lanka".

Quite to the contrary, as the two leaders were signing the agreement, the Foreign Secretaries of the two countries were simultaneously dotting the "i's" and crossing the "t's" of the agreement in the form of Letters of Exchange inviting the IPKF "to bring about the cessation of hostilities". The letters were exchanged the same day the main Peace Agreement was signed, i.e. on July 29, 1987. It is interesting that on that very day both the leaders made statements on the Sri Lankan TV and jointly addressed a press conference, but did not give an inkling of the Sri Lankan request-letter inviting the Indian troops to help in the implementation of the agreement that had already been signed. The letters were kept confidential. Replying to a question if India had drawn up a plan "for sending any peace keeping force", Gandhi simply ducked it by saying "it depends on what they ask for". The fact remains that the Sri Lankan Foreign Secretary had already asked "appropriate military assistance to ensure the surrender of arms" and in addition, dispatch "with immediate effect" of "some naval vessels" to Colombo "to stabilize the situation and to preserve the unity, stability and integrity of Sri Lanka". It was not until the next day, July 30, while making a statement in the Indian Parliament on the agreement that the Prime Minister disclosed the landing of Indian armed forces in Jaffna that day.

That the President of Sri Lanka lacked sincere commitment to what he was signing, was more than apparent within hours. The most crucial provision of the peace accord was the merger of the Northern and the Eastern provinces to create a Tamil speaking Province. This was the demand of the Tamils right since the Island attained its independence in 1948. India was made to believe, and so it went on to assure the Tamils, that the provision of a referendum after one year was only a strategic move by the President to lull and placate the ultra-Sinhalese nationalists into accepting the agreement. As it turned out, it was intended to lull India and the Tamils, to be reneged later. On the same day, the agreement was signed the two signatories addressed a joint press conference. In the presence of Gandhi, Jayewardene made no bones about his real intentions. Answering journalists' questions he left no one in doubt, and certainly not the Indian Prime Minister that his commitment on the merger was tactical, since he told them that he would personally campaign and canvass against the merger at the time of referendum. So much for his commitment!

The agreement, like the proverbial elephant in the fable "Blind men and the Elephant", meant different things to different people. Tamils felt betrayed. Prabakaran was livid. Rajiv Gandhi was ecstatic since he believed he had achieved for the Tamils much more than they ever had been able to extract from Colombo. On August 2, 1987, speaking at a public rally in Chennai, he said: "This agreement secures everything that the Sri Lankan Tamils had demanded, short of breaking Sri Lanka's unity. In fact, it goes well beyond the initial demands of the Sri Lankan Tamils. Under the agreement, approximately one-third of Sri Lankan territory will be made into a single province where the Tamils will have a clear majority".

The officialdom around the Prime Minister patted itself on the back believing that it had succeeded in killing two birds with one stone—justice for the Tamils and a better security environment in the region. As later events proved, it neither secured justice for the beleaguered community nor succeeded in keeping external elements out of the region. Jayewardene was jubilant that he had cut the Indian support from under the feet of the Tamils and could now breathe easy. Sri Lanka's military establishment felt relieved that they no longer were required to face the Tigers and could retreat to their barracks and cut their losses. To the Buddhist clergy, it was a blow to the Sinhala pride. And to the common Sinhalese, it was a nightmarish throwback into history with a large-scale presence of the army of their historic foe, India. To the JVP, it was a *cause celebre*, which gave a new lease of life to their anti-India agenda. For the ruling UNP, it was a dubious achievement. For the SLFP, it was a petard to hang the UNP.

The manner in which the agreement was signed, was flawed. Ethnic problem was an issue between the Sinhala state and the Tamils, whether militants or otherwise. India had been sucked into the conflict because of the ties of kinship between the Sri Lankan and the Indian Tamils. Since 1983, when India first got involved in the ethnic problem, India insisted that she was only providing her good offices to facilitate a solution. There was no provocation, suddenly for India to become a direct party to the dispute by signing the agreement on behalf of the Tamils who, being kept out of the negotiating process, did not feel committed to it. India failed to realizse or did not wish to admit that ever since she became involved in Sri Lanka's ethnic problem, Tamil intransigence had increased considerably. They hoped that India's weight would browbeat Colombo into offering a package that would create a Tamil state, if not sovereign, at least bordering on sovereignty. The events leading to the birth of Bangladesh were fresh in their minds.

The agreement was signed after the ethnic conflict had already extracted a very heavy price. The democratic spirit of the Island's constitution was its first casualty. The country now had virtually turned into an authoritarian, anomalous of a civil society. It enjoyed draconian powers courtesy the Prevention of Terrorism Act. The civil liberties stood either abridged or subverted. The country was dotted with army and police check-posts. The capital city Colombo had such checkpoints at practically every street corner. Some 600 civilians were killed on the Sinhalese side, besides 500 to 600 deaths of the uniformed personnel. Many times more Tamils were killed and wounded. Over a lakh and fifty thousand Tamils were rendered homeless and were living in Tamil Nadu as refugees. The number of Sinhalese displaced was equally large. A permanent cleavage had permeated into the society, which stood divided in two distinct communities with no hope of getting united or even closer to each other. The defence was accounting for seventeen percent of the budget on the eve of the accord, as against 4 percent in 1976. The largest spinner of foreign exchange, the tourist traffic, was practically crippled. The commodity prices in world markets stood depressed thus affecting the economy severely. In this depressing social, political and economic quagmire, the agreement failed to bring the much-desired relief for the poor masses who were bearing the brunt of the conflict. The greatest gain of the peace accord for Sri Lanka was that the country that stood on the side of the Tamils, India, had been neutralised and won over on the Sinhalese side for the future, and Colombo could breathe easy.

But how did the agreement stand purely from the Indian point of view? It may be relevant to recall the reservations expressed by P.V. Narasimha Rao at the end of June 1987. In this connection following extract from J.N. Dixit's book *Assignment Colombo* (p.119) is quoted:

> "Though the Minister for External Affairs did not actively participate in these Core Group Meetings, he was present during the meetings chaired by the Prime Minister. I was asked to show the outline draft to him before I left for Sri Lanka, which I did. Narasimha Rao made three points about the whole process of negotiations about to start. First, we should not rush into this agreement. Second, we should carefully consider the wisdom of being direct signatories to this agreement. He was of the view that Sri Lankan Tamils should sign this agreement with Sri Lankan Government and we should just be guarantors. Thirdly, he felt that we must carefully assess whether the willingness of the LTTE and Sri Lankan Government to come to an agreement at that point of time was based on a genuine desire for peace and a durable settlement or was it just an interim tactical move. He asked me to keep these points at the back of my mind while negotiating the agreement."

(Dixit is factually not correct. Rao was heading the Ministry of Human Resource Development between September 1985 and June 1988. He did not return to the MEA until June 1988. Prime Minister perhaps wanted Rao being a former External Affairs Minister, and an elder statesman to be kept informed.

Nevertheless, this did not detract from the sound advice he gave to Dixit.)

It was the sagacious advice of an old war-horse. Dixit did not indicate whether he reported the advice of Rao back to the Prime Minister. Perhaps he did not think it necessary. Rajiv Gandhi had told him to brief Rao, which he dutifully did and that was it. All the three points he made, needed careful consideration at the highest decision-making level in the Government of India but tragically they were apparently not brought to the Prime Minister's notice, and ignored. Narasimha Rao, though an important member of the Cabinet, not being directly concerned with a matter of foreign policy was not involved in the decision-making process as evidenced by Dixit. That the agreement was rushed into, needed hardly any examination. It was concluded at a breakneck speed, in great seçrecy, and on the back of the very people whose interests it sought to protect. A hurriedly put together document was forced down the throat of the beleaguered Sri Lankan President. The latter sold the draft to his own Cabinet not only on the back of his Prime Minister but also blackmailing most other Ministers into submission at the pain of resignation.

The Tamils too were not involved in any detailed negotiation and neither their point of view was given any careful consideration. New Delhi was peeved at the Tamils' inability to work out a concensus among them to bargain with Colombo. Experience had shown that when in the past India had worked out some broad arrangement with Sri Lankan leaders and Tamils were asked to build on it, they failed to clinch the issue. New Delhi was left holding the crying baby and sing lullabies to them. Every time the Tamils had failed to agree among them or failed to negotiate with Colombo, they had looked to India to bail them out. It was felt that it was better that New Delhi took the matter in its own hands and work out an arrangement based on what had broadly been agreed upon in the past, piecemeal, between the Tamils and Colombo and between New Delhi and Colombo, in their various negotiating efforts. In New Delhi's calculations, the situation had come to a serious pass. Even the LTTE was at the brink of suffering a humiliating defeat. Any further attempt to leave the matter in the Tamils' hands was fraught with dangerous consequences, particularly when the situation had the potential to drag India into an active and open conflict. India was anxious to avoid an open military conflict with a small neighbour, having repeatedly sworn to respect its territorial integrity and sovereignty. New Delhi had reason to feel jittery at the developing scenario. It did not want to risk leaving the things to the Tamils for fear of another abortive round of negotiations. Nevertheless, it would have been most desirable to take the Tamils into confidence as the negotiations progressed with Colombo for an agreement that was to decide their fate. Not to have done that proved too costly, since for the failure none except New Delhi had to bear the brunt and stigma. India successfully silenced the Tamils into submission by cajoling and coaxing, but failed to win their unqualified approval to the agreement it had negotiated with Colombo. They remained uncommitted to the agreement in which India had invested her prestige. It was perhaps feared by New Delhi that if the Tamils were kept in the picture and consulted, the type of agreement that had been put together, had no chance of passing muster with them and hence the danger of its being vetoed by them. It was thought best to clinch the issue on their behalf and confront them with a *fait accompli.* Since the Tamils had put all their eggs in New Delhi's basket, they would have no alternative but to accept what was put on the plate for them, calculated India.

Nevertheless, New Delhi continued to maintain that the Tamils particularly the LTTE were consulted and they had agreed to its broad contours. As pointed out in the previous chapter, the Tamils in general and the LTTE in particular had serious reservations to the agreement that had been put together. Even in Colombo there were serious differences on signing the agreement. The Sri Lankan Prime Minister and most members of the cabinet were not in favour of signing it and had even suggested postponement of the signing schedule to another date so as to use the interval to work out a consensus. Even the President was not averse to a postponement, but it was pressure of the Indian High Commissioner who threatened him with 'now or never' scenario that made Jayewardene fall in line. Jayewardene persuaded himself into signing the agreement because he was aware that over the years New Delhi had got neckdeep into the problem and it could not pull out of it, unless a solution satisfactory to the Tamils was hammered out. Thanks to the Indian backing, the Tamil voice had become strident. Hence the need to suck India directly into the problem, negotiate a settlement with her and leave it to her to enforce it on the recalcitrant Tamils.

Taking cue from the past, India too felt that the Tamils were not capable of standing the pressure of the Sinhalese state, should India forsake them. New Delhi lived in a world of illusion that having contributed in the training, arming and financing of the Tamils, it had enough of clout with them generally and the LTTE particularly to arm-twist them. This was thought to be enough of a leverage to discipline the Tamils. India failed to remember that in the recent past, how despite Indian prodding, Tamils had contributed to the failure of the Thimpu Conference, and later when India had worked out with Sri Lanka an agreement they refused to have anything to do with that. Similar other Indian efforts to nudge or even goad the Tamils to come to some workable and negotiated settlement had been fruitless, and on a number of occasions Indian efforts to promote a dialogue had been sabotaged by them indulging in unprovoked violence. Of the militant organizations, the LTTE had an implicit faith in its violent methods to force a solution in favour of Eelam and it felt confident to pull on itself. Some of the blame for Tamil intransigence must lie at the doors of India. Having trained, supplied and financed the guerrilla movements of the Tamils, India aroused heightened expectations among them making them believe that if they pushed a little more, New Delhi could be made to get still closer to actual involvement and once its prestige was at stake, Eelam would not be far away. By signing the agreement now, India did put her prestige at stake, but on the wrong side and that was what was to prove the undoing of Indian efforts. Caught in this contradictory policy options, Government of India's efforts were doomed to failure. In the pre-agreement period it indulged in a policy, which was seen as promoting and abetting terrorism in a neighbouring country, a charge it frequently made against Pakistan. In the post-agreement period, it did not hesitate to use its force to push down the throats of the Tamils an Agreement, which they felt was fundamentally flawed and against their interests.

That the Sinhalese sentiments were outraged by the agreement was clear like daylight when the Prime Minister of India faced the wrath of a Lankan naval rating. He had a providential escape by timely ducking while inspecting a ceremonial guard of honour at the time of his departure home from Colombo. That the Indian community and the High Commission had to face angry demonstrations later, is another story. On return home, Rajiv Gandhi told the Indian Parliament that he had returned from a "momentous" visit. So enthused and excited was the Prime Minister on his success in signing the agreement that when a few days later on August 2, 1987, he received the PLO Leader Yassar Arafat at the Delhi airport, in his welcome speech he referred to the signing of the Sri Lanka agreement and described it as "an Agreement of the century"!

‹17›

LTTE and the Indian Peace Keeping Force

After the Indian army had been inducted into the Island as a follow-up of the agreement, it became obvious to everybody that the deadlines set in the agreement for various tasks were unrealistic. Prabakaran confined in Delhi until the agreement was signed, was allowed to return to Jaffna in the fond hope that he would volunteer to commit hara-kiri by disarming his cadres. His reasons for refusing to disarm were twofold. The first was the personal safety of the cadres. Without the peace returning and consolidating if the LTTE were to surrender its arms, it would be at the mercy of Sri Lankan army with no protection available. Secondly, should the objective of the agreement fail to realize, the Tamils would find it impossible to rebuild their armed strength again. Therefore, LTTE was anxious that a politico-structure of the Tamil state was established and the Tamil aspirations realized, before the LTTE were disarmed. The perceptions differed on the question whether peace should come first or the surrender of arms.

With every passing day the impossibility and enormity of the task stared everyone in the face. That the agreement was up against heavy odds was more than evident from the speech made by Prabakaran immediately after return to Jaffna on August 4. While making some conciliatory noises, from which India could draw a little solace, he declared to the Tamils:

> "The time is not very far off when the monster of Sinhala racism will devour this agreement. I have unrelenting faith in the proposition that only a separate state of

> Tamil Eelam can offer a permanent solution of the problem of the people of Tamil Eelam. Let me make it clear to you here, beyond the shadow of doubt, that I will continue to fight for the objective of attaining Tamil Eelam".

To propitiate New Delhi, Prabakaran made a token surrender of some obsolete arms to enable President Jayewardene make a much taller claim than was justified. In an address to the nation on August 6, the President said: "Yesterday those who have been carrying on a bloody battle against the democratically elected government of Sri Lanka for almost 12 years have handed over their arms in a symbolic gesture". Raising hopes for the future he said:

> "The terrorists have agreed to lay down arms, they agreed, in the future to act democratically and that they will come under the laws of Sri Lanka and under the Central Government of Sri Lanka. Therefore this Accord has, I think, for the first time after so many years established peace in our country or at least the beginnings of peace".

Despite many hurdles, both the countries at official level remained buoyed with the accord. World leaders did not wish to disappoint them by holding back their endorsement of the agreement, flawed as it was. This enabled the Minister of State in the Ministry of External Affairs, Natwar Singh, to claim international community's adulation for the Indian Prime Minister. The initial cease-fire and cessation of hostilities were enough of a reason for Natwar Singh to claim in the Lok Sabha on August 6, that the "implementation of the agreement has been remarkable by any standards than most people would have expected". When the accord came up for discussion in the Lok Sabha on the 11th and 18th of August, 1987 there appeared to be no national consensus on welcoming it. The opposition remained skeptical, particularly on the Government's failure to consult the Tamils. The ruling party and the AIADMK members were euphoric in welcoming it. Minister Natwar Singh disputed members' allegation that Prabakaran was not consulted beforehand. Making light of the delay in the surrender of arms by the LTTE, the Minister ascribed it to "acceptable flexibility".

He said that efforts were being made to minimise the differences among the Tamils. Justifying the agreement, the Minister concluded by saying:

> "If this problem had to be resolved, if an end had to be put to the ethnic conflict in Sri Lanka, if the security environment had to be prevented from getting worse, if the refugees had to go back, if the prisoners had to be released, and if the events that had darkened the life and menaced the future had to be terminated, then something like this agreement had to be produced. I want here to pay tribute to the two principal authors of this agreement, the President of Sri Lanka and the Prime Minister of India for having come out with a document which meets all the fundamental, basic demands of the Sri Lankan Tamils and the fact that the agreement has held for the last three weeks is a great tribute to all those who are involved in having it implemented. Here is an agreement in which there are no vanquished, only victors".

On August 19, speaking in the Parliament, the Minister once again expressed happiness that the agreement had not been violated since its signing, and touted that as an index of its success. To humour the LTTE, Natwar Singh conceded that the present agreement had been made possible "to some extent by the sacrifices made by the LTTE", and that the government was in constant touch with Prabakaran and had endeavoured to allay his fears regarding his own and his cadres' security.

The LTTE remained apprehensive. It clandestinely tucked away most of its heavy arms while making pretence of surrendering them. Prabakaran remained more than convinced that he could not dismantle the security apparatus which he had built over the years and which had been instrumental in putting the Tamil problem in such bold relief that every one was forced to sit up and take notice of it. In the gloomy scenario that emerged because of the stubborn stand of Prabakaran the implementation of the most important provision of the agreement, the surrender of arms by the LTTE, was never accomplished. If ever Prabakaran had any intention of surrendering arms, the terror unleashed by another equally determined but rival guerrilla organisation, the People's Liberation

Organisation of Tamil Eelam (PLOTE), against the LTTE in the fight for supremacy convinced him that he could not depend on anyone else but himself and for that he must not only stay fully armed but further strengthen himself.

In a momentous turn of events, the Indian Peace Keeping Force (IPKF) sent to enforce the agreement ended up in fighting the Tamil Tigers. It was an unfortunate showdown between a powerful regional military power on the one hand and the perceived forces of indigenous mass-nationalism, howsoever misguided, on the other. In retrospect, it soon became apparent rather painfully, that the Indo-Sri Lanka agreement and its consequential military intervention miserably failed to achieve its twin objectives of asserting India's hegemonic position in South Asia and of defusing the violence within Sri Lanka. India's intervention that lasted for almost two-and-a-half years left 1,155 Indian defence personnel dead. What was appalling was that the LTTE became the *bete noire* of the Indian Peace Keeping Force and the ethnic conflict between the Tamils and the Sri Lanka Sinhalese turned out to be an Indo-LTTE war if not the Indo-Tamil war. As the IPKF, operations expanded, most of the Tamil population, combatant or non-combatant decried it. The LTTE not only turned their guns on the IPKF but also targeted any Tamil who dared to cooperate with the Indian army. It followed a scorched earth policy in its fight against the IPKF and at the end ensured its exit from Sri Lanka in ignominy and opprobrium.

As early as September 20, 1987, the spokesman of the Indian Ministry of External Affairs accused the LTTE of engineering large scale violence in which 100 Tamils were killed in the Northern and Eastern provinces. On September 24, yet again the spokesman told journalists in New Delhi that LTTE had instigated Tamils in the northern town of Manaar to picket a camp occupied by the Indian troops and "the Indian Peace Keeping Force will be compelled to respond with even stronger measures if such violence is deliberately provoked by the LTTE". Notwithstanding the LTTE obduracy, India continued with its efforts to persuade it to enter the mainstream of the Island's political life by falling in line and staying within the parameters of the Indo-Sri Lanka Agreement. On September 23, 1987, in an effort to persuade Prabakaran, the High Commissioner Dixit had a six-hour meeting with him in Palaly to discuss his demands.

Prabakaran had all sorts of demands. They related to end of the Sinhalese colonization of Tamil areas in the Eastern Province, rehabilitation of the Tamils, closing of the police stations in the north, disarming of the Home Guards, closure of the army camps in the north and the east, release of the Tamil detainees, interim administration and monopoly of power for the LTTE etc. Prabakaran also wanted LTTE to be recognised as the sole representative of the Tamils. He later told a press conference jointly addressed by him and J.N. Dixit that he was given certain assurances by New Delhi, which had not been implemented and that he wished the High Commissioner to concede those demands. But the High Commissioner was not impressed and he merely agreed to forward his demands to New Delhi.

Despite differences of perception, an agreement was hammered out between the High Commissioner Dixit and Prabakaran on the composition of the proposed Interim Administrative Council for the merged province of the North and the East as envisaged in the Indo-Sri Lanka Agreement. It was agreed that out of the 12 members of the Council, the LTTE would have five seats against 2 each for TULF, Muslims and the Sinhalese. The Twelfth man would be the Chief Administrator-in-Council who would be appointed by Colombo out of a panel of three names submitted by the LTTE. The powers of the Administrative Council were broadly discussed and accepted by the LTTE and in return it agreed "to fully cooperate in the implementation of the Indo-Sri Lanka agreement" subject to the assurances given to him by the Prime Minister of India in July 1987. Finally, the arrangement for the Interim Administration collapsed on the question of nomination of the Chief Administrator. Prabakaran refused to accept the appointment C.V.K. Sivagnanam (Municipal Commissioner of Jaffna), one of the three names on the panel submitted by Prabakaran himself. He instead insisted on N. Padhmananathan former Assistant Government Agent in Batticaloa but Jayewardene refused to yield. The next crisis over the arrest of 16 LTTE cadres led by Pulendran for trying to smuggle in arms in violation of the Indo-Sri Lanka Agreement and their subsequent suicide spelt disaster for whatever was left of the agreement. It was enough of a reason for Prabakaran to decry the agreement altogether, and renege from the arrangement worked out for the establishment of Interim Administrative Council. On the question of surrender of arms, the LTTE predictably refused to be accommodative. Surrender of arms was imperative to give some semblance of respectability to the accord. On September 28, 1987, two months after the signing of the Accord, Lanka's Minister of National Security Lalith Athulathmudali said in a press interview that the Island's ethnic Peace Accord was like a steeplechase that was faltering at the second fence and "unless the tigers are made to accept the accord and its implications for the restoration of democracy in the North and East, then the accord is in danger".

These developments led LTTE to indulge in large-scale violence not only against the fellow Tamils, but also against the IPKF. The killing of half-a-dozen of Indian soldiers by the LTTE on October 6, 1987, led to the IPKF initiating "Operation Pawan" against it in which the IPKF suffered many casualties. These developments were a setback for the agreement and put the LTTE and the IPKF on a collision course. The clash of arms and collapse of the Interim Administrative Council even before it was put together was a great setback for the entire political process including the merger of the Northern and Eastern provinces. It effectively demonstrated Indian failure to exercise its clout with the Tamils and inability to implement an agreement, which it had forced both on the reluctant Sri Lanka state and the Tamils. Anxious to salvage the remnants of the agreement, New Delhi while failing on the LTTE front, continued to exert pressure on Colombo that it unilaterally implement some pieces of the agreement to give the impression that it was alive and kicking.

The LTTE did feel the heat of the "Operation Pawan" launched by the IPKF. An exasperated Government of India had already warned the LTTE of Indian determination to preserve the peace. The demonstration of the Indian will came as a shock to the LTTE who unable to withstand the pressure, in a desperate bid approached the Tamil Nadu leaders over the head of the Government of India for a halt to the military operations indicating its willingness to talk. On October 14, the spokesman of the Ministry of External Affairs in New Delhi described such moves only as "purely propaganda" in order "to try and generate support." The same day a spokesman of the Indian High Commission in Colombo announced that the IPKF had overrun Chunnakam, the LTTE stronghold in close proximity to Jaffna town. To prove that Prabakaran had reneged from the agreement with the High Commissioner following talks in September, the spokesman showed the journalists the minutes of the meeting between Prabakaran and Dixit. He insisted that India had used persuasion to get Prabakaran to surrender arms and bring him into the political mainstream. It was pointed out that "even after he broke the agreement" India, "tried to be patient. It is he who fired at the IPKF first at Jaffna and then at Tellipalai. It is after that, that India decided on a military operation to make him surrender the balance arms."

The PLOTE on October 4, accused the LTTE that its misguided tactics had diverted the direction of the Tamils' struggle from its goal. "Their ongoing barbaric actions against Sinhala civilian targets is only helping to raise communalism and divide the two sets of oppressed people", said the PLOTE statement signed by M.T. Maran, the group's Public Relations Officer in Sri Lanka. "On numerous occasions in the past, we have warned the LTTE that their incorrect strategies and failure to correctly identify the enemy will only lead to the destruction of our cause", Maran said. When Sri Lankan Minister of Lands and Land Development, Gamini Dissanayake, met the Indian Prime Minister in the Canadian city of Vancouver during the meeting of the Commonwealth Heads of Government, the latter described the failure of the LTTE to surrender arms as "unfortunate" but wanted Sri Lanka to be reassured of the "ability of the IPKF to deliver what is expected of them".

Failing to make the LTTE surrender its arms, the IPKF increased its pressure on it. This once again invited the odium of the Tamil Nadu politicians. The DMK leader in the Rajya Sabha on November 6, 1987, accused the IPKF of "butchering of all the Tamils in Sri Lanka" and called upon the Government of India to cease-fire. Some members while sparing the IPKF for tactical reasons because it had been given a difficult task blamed the Government of India "for their foolishness and the way

India has been bogged down into this affair in Sri Lanka". Emotions ran so high in the House that the Speaker had to intervene repeatedly to either "expunge" or order "not recording" at all some of the remarks made by members. On November 9, 1987, Prime Minister Rajiv Gandhi bemoaned in the Lok Sabha, LTTE's reneging from the agreement, which it had promised to support. Listing the dangers inherent in this attitude he said:

> "The LTTE's repudiation of the agreement, their attacks on Sinhalese and Muslims in the East and their murder of Sri Lankan soldiers threatened to produce a Sinhala backlash that would have destroyed the agreement and produced a cycle of violence worse than any the island had so far seen. The victims would have been mainly Tamils, especially in the South and the Central Highlands."

Unabated violence convinced Colombo that there existed a nexus between the LTTE and the JVP and the two together were "causing mass destruction of the Sinhala people in order to obstruct the implementation of the Indo-Sri Lanka Peace accord". On October 9, 1987, Chief Whip of the ruling UNP issued a statement quoting the President that "the LTTE-JVP combination have commenced a new operation against the Sri Lanka government and the Sinhala people". Exasperated at the failure of the IPKF to control the violence let loose by the LTTE, the statement blamed the Government of India for its failure to get the accord implemented, which "should have been accomplished by the middle of August". The UNP recapitulated for the benefit of the Government of India the following three tasks, which had remained unaccomplished:

> "A complete disarming of the LTTE and other terrorist groups in the North and the East;
>
> Return to election in the North and the East;
>
> Maintenance of law and order and the cessation of hostilities in the North and the East."

To put India on the mat, Sri Lankan Minister of Agricultural Development and Research and Minister of Food, Gamini Jayasuriya, speaking in the Parliament on the same day (October 9) on the situation in the North and the East reminded India that Sri Lanka had done its part of the bargain as called upon under the accord:

> "The Government of Sri Lanka has gone well beyond her own obligations under the Indo-Sri Lanka agreement. We began releasing terrorist suspects. We appointed an interim Advisory Council. We discussed 'Residual Matters'. We have now printed the Provincial Councils Bill. We have withdrawn our forces to barracks and watched as over 200 Sinhalese and 150 Tamils and even Muslims ended as cannon fodder to the adventurist terrorists—and all this under the protection of the 10,000 Indian Peace Keeping Force!"

India appeared to be tormented from all sides. It was now turn of the TULF to up the ante. In a letter of October 28, 1987, to the Indian Prime Minister it conveyed its dissatisfaction with the Constitution 13th Amendment Bill and the Provincial Councils Bill, since it claimed, the Bill did not meet the aspirations of the Tamils. The TULF pointed out that it was their expectation that before gazetting the Bills Colombo would consult with New Delhi as required under paragraph 2.15 of the Indo-Sri Lanka Peace agreement. They insisted this did not happen. They questioned the need for referendum after one year of the merger of the Northern and the Eastern provinces. Similarly, it was their expectation that the creation of the Provincial Councils and devolution of power to them would be effected through a constitutional amendment. They pointed out several lacunae in the Bills, which would work against the interests of the Tamils.

Unfortunately, non-implementation of the accord due to the obduracy and mulishness of the LTTE had left little space for the Government of India. It came under attack from within too. When the Rajya Sabha discussed Sri Lanka on November 6, 1987 for umpteenth time, the Tamil members as in the past were sore and unsparing in their scathing attack of the Government's policy in Sri Lanka. Murasoli Maran of the DMK opening the debate was bitterly acidic and described what was going on in the Island as "the butchering of all the Tamils" by the "so-called Indian Peace Keeping Force". He said:

"It is shocking to the whole mankind, shocking not only to the Tamils in Tamil Nadu but also to the Tamils living all over India and Indians living all over the world and it is something unheard of, something not ever thought of, something un-Indian, something brutal, something uncivilised which is going on there in Sri Lanka and it is being perpetrated by our own, our very respected armed forces."

V. Gopalasamy also of the DMK was so critical that most of his remarks were found unparliamentary by the Chair and not allowed to go on record. Aladi Aruna *alias* V. Arunachalam of the AIADMK was no less devastating. He said the AIADMK stood for the accord, but not "at gun-point". The Communist Party of India (Marxist) was equally critical. P. Upendra of the Telugu Desam Party said, "there is no parallel to what India is doing in Sri Lanka". M.S. Gurupadaswamy of the Janata Party said, "accord is in shambles" and the Indian army was fighting "our own kith and kin in a foreign soil".

The Government of India remained convinced that the agreement signed with Colombo was the only panacea to resolve the ethnic conflict. During the visit of Sri Lanka President to New Delhi in early November, fresh provisions for the Provincial Councils legislation were agreed (November 7, 1987). On November 9, Rajiv Gandhi re-emphasising to the Lok Sabha the merits of the Peace accord said:

"The agreement has been acclaimed internationally. There is a widespread consensus that the full implementation of the agreement will be of universal benefit. Tamil aspirations would be met, the unity and integrity of Sri Lanka preserved, and peace and stability restored to the region. Some of our important security concerns would also be met. Therefore, the Government of India are committed to the full implementation of this agreement. We believe that this resolve is shared by the Government of Sri Lanka."

Rajiv Gandhi, however, regretted that the LTTE had deliberately wrecked the agreement and indulged in large-scale violence despite the fact they were given a prime role and that the IPKF had to use its armed strength in response to their violence. Putting the blame on the LTTE, Gandhi said:

> "The unfortunate developments in Jaffna were not of our making. We reacted with a heavy heart when there was no alternative. We got the LTTE everything they wanted, disregarding the cost to our credibility with other militant groups and all communities including the Tamils. We overlooked the LTTE's vicious propaganda even before the outbreak of hostilities, not just against the agreement but also against India and the IPKF. In the Interim Administrative Council they were given a clear majority of seven out of 12, including a Chairman of their choice. Other Tamil militant groups were excluded at their insistence. While the Government of India has accommodated every concern of the LTTE, the LTTE have not honoured any of their commitments."

The Prime Minister's above statement came up for discussion in the Lok Sabha on August 10 and 11. The opposition members were critical of the manner the situation had developed. Even if some parties like the Communist Party of India supported the Peace accord, they were not happy that the Indian army had to be deployed against the very people who were sought to be protected. Members challenged the Prime Minister's contention that the accord was being fully implemented. Some members were derisive that like the other accords signed by the Prime Minister (the Punjab and Assam accords), this accord was fairing no better and was dead as dodo. Some called into question the wisdom of the government in signing the agreement itself instead of allowing it to be signed by the Tamils and finally not taking the Tamils into full confidence and obtaining their acceptance before hand. It was intriguing that the Prime Minister, whose statement of November 9, was under discussions, chose to observe silence at the end of the debate and left it to his junior Minister, Natwar Singh to defend him and the government on the floor of the House. Natwar Singh quoted the Communiqué issued at the end of the Commonwealth Summit in Vancouver, which described it as "an act of highest statesmanship" to defend New Delhi. The welcome given to the accord during the UN General Assembly session and by President Reagan when he received Prime Minister Rajiv Gandhi in the White House recently were flaunted as positive signals in support of the government policy in Sri Lanka. He disabused members of the impression that the agreement was arrived at in haste. He said: "A number of weeks of very hard work at different levels in Government, in different branches, was carried out. All these doubts, which assail the Hon. Members also assailed us, and provisions were made for every eventuality. But since agreements are made by human beings, they can be as perfect or imperfect as human beings are. If, as I said earlier, there is any way in which we can improve upon it, I am sure Government of India and the Government of Sri Lanka would like to look at it." He gave a resume of the government's efforts to propitiate Prabakaran but without success.

Failure of the accord to deliver had disillusioned Colombo as well. It was indeed a crazy situation. Premadasa who was from the start critical of the accord found his position vindicated and strengthened. On November 12, speaking in the Sri Lankan Parliament on the Provincial Councils Bill, he said that the mere passing of the Bill would not lead to its implementation. There are certain pre-conditions, which are to be fulfilled before the merged Northern and Eastern Provincial Council could be constituted. Praying that this did not come about, he said:

> "I examined this very closely because I am totally against the amalgamation and I am praying that this will never happen. Yes, of course, I will do every thing possible to prevent that because it is not fair, especially by the Muslim population who are living in these areas for generations. I know their plight."

The LTTE mounted further pressure to undermine the accord and the role of the IPKF. Posters appeared in Jaffna threatening all those who cooperated with the IPKF. Tired of being repeatedly accused by the Government of India for violations of the agreement to keep the cauldron of ethnic violence boiling, the LTTE decided to hit back. On November 18, 1987, Velupillai Prabakaran issued a lengthy signed statement. He accused the IPKF of engaging in a full-scale war against the LTTE. He lamented that the war had "brought disastrous consequences with a heavy toll of civilian casualties, immense sufferings to our people, severe disruption of socio-economic existence". He expressed remorse that "having engaged themselves in a war with violence, brutality and terror, the IPKF has lost its status as an instrument of peace but has assumed the role of a repressive invasion army, typically eliminating both the Tamil freedom fighters and innocent civilians". Prabakaran indicted India for mounting "a massive propaganda war to rationalize and legitimize her action". He termed the propaganda campaign as "vicious, malicious and distortion of the truth aimed to discredit" the LTTE in the "eyes of the Indian and world public opinion".

Prabakaran's wailing compelled the Government of India to offer him yet another opportunity to come clean on the surrender of arms. It declared a cease-fire for 48 hours starting from November 21. The LTTE response remained negative claiming it had surrendered most of its arms, a claim which the Indian spokesman on November 22 found "unacceptable" and "not only astonishing but a blatant falsehood". The spokesman insisted on the LTTE to surrender arms because "continued possession of arms by the LTTE not only prevented the implementation of the Indo-Sri Lanka agreement but endangered communal amity, safety and security of the Tamils elsewhere in Sri Lanka". The LTTE failing to respond to the 48-hour unilateral cease-fire, the IPKF resumed its operations.

India now not only "ruled out any talks" with Prabakaran, but announced that "there is no question of Prabakaran visiting Madras or New Delhi for talks with Indian leaders as has been speculated in a section of the press". At this juncture, India made an unsuccessful bid to wean away the LTTE cadres by offering them carrots in abundance in return for their surrender. On November 26, the Ministry of External Affairs said:

> "While the leadership of the LTTE continue with their hard line, self-centered attitude, there are indications that many cadres of the LTTE are keen to return to a normal and peaceful life. Government of India is deeply concerned about the welfare of these young cadres who have been mis-led by the leadership. IPKF therefore will offer the following facilities to all militant cadres who surrender to them:
>
> (a) Full security against threat to their lives to those wishing to stay under IPKF's protection till normalcy returns.
>
> (b) Free food and shelter.

(c) A monthly stipend

(d) General or vocational training to prepare the cadres for eventual employment/self-employment.

(e) Books and educational facilities for those wishing to resume their education.

(f) Facilities for placement for those not interested in self-employment.

The LTTE cadres did not find the Indian carrots palatable enough.

By now the strength of the IPKF had increased to 20,000. At the end of 1987 it was made known that Colombo would shortly take steps for the merger of the Northern and the Eastern provinces, elections to the Provincial Councils, election procedures, etc. Despite some progress in the implementation of the agreement on the Sri Lanka side, India remained disillusioned with the behaviour of the LTTE, who were holding the successful implementation of the Peace accord to ransom. The Indian frustration was palpable. It oozed out of the speech of Prime Minister Gandhi at Pudukkottai in Tamil Nadu on December 27,1987:

> "The agreement in Sri Lanka provides the basic framework for the settlement of all legitimate grievances of the Tamil people of Sri Lanka. It achieved much more than has ever been asked for, very much more than has been achieved before. The agreement has been accepted by all Tamils in Sri Lanka, all the militant groups, all the other except for one of the militant groups. The LTTE represents no one but itself. It has not been ready to come into democratic framework and it has been responsible for the killing of most of the militant Tamils and many hundred, thousands of innocent Tamils."

Sri Lanka had compromised her sovereignty in entering into the agreement with India in the hope that it would put an end to violence and usher in peace. There was however no end to her agony. The people were getting impatient. They had from the very beginning doubts about the wisdom of entering into such an accord. Colombo naturally directed its ire for its frustration on the IPKF. On December 3, 1987 Sri Lankan

Foreign Minister, A.C.S. Hameed lamented in the parliament that the IPKF who came in the country neither for "active combat" nor "to be engaged in in-fighting" could not perform the basic task envisaged in the agreement of July 1987 viz., "to supervise the peace-keeping operations" and "recover the arms and ammunitions from the terrorists".

Since the signing of the Peace agreement in July 1987, the leaders of the two countries had come a long way from the pre-accord days when they only traded charges between them. Now, despite problems at the ground level, there had developed a great deal of bonhomie among them. They could talk to each other in a relaxed atmosphere with and in confidence. India felt happy to invite and Jayewardene was even happier to accept the invitation of the Government of India to be the Chief Guest on the occasion of the Indian Republic Day celebrations in New Delhi in January 1988. To create the necessary friendly climate for the visit, the President was quite generous in giving his approval to several of the measures that the Indian Prime Minister had proposed to him through High Commissioner Dixit on January 13, 1988. He agreed to announce the merger of the Northern and the Eastern provinces, a plan to hold the elections to the Provincial Councils, decision to appoint one governor for the proposed merged province, association of the Indian Election Commission with the preparation and scrutiny of the voters' lists, non-exclusion of militant leaders in the election process, amnesty for Tamil militants etc., before his departure for New Delhi on January 25, 1988.

At the State Banquet in New Delhi for the visiting President, the Indian President served the Peace accord in good measure as an antidote for all the problems of Sri Lanka. He acknowledged Sri Lanka "as a multi-ethnic and multi-linguistic plural society in which the cultural and linguistic identity of each group has to be carefully nurtured". President Jayewardene in his reply went nostalgic and going down the memory lane recalled his connections with the Indian National Congress during the pre-independence days and his visit to Ramgarh in 1940 to attend the party's annual session. He extolled the virtues of non-violence but carefully skirted any reference to the Peace agreement. However, he added for good measure his determination "never to bend my knees to the insolence of violence; never to look to the right or to the left but to march straight on; always to follow 'Right for Right is Right' without fear of consequences and never to disown the poor".

It was not for nothing that the President avoided reference to the agreement, which he had himself signed only a few months ago. He was looking over his shoulders. He was conscious that back home, it had polarized further the already polarized society. The violence, if anything, had mounted manifold thus causing all round disillusionment. At the political level it had failed to create a national consensus. To add to his embarrassment, the Leader of the Opposition and President of the SLFP, the veteran Sirimavo Bandaranaike seeking to drag the visit into the realm of domestic politics of the Island cautioned India against being too euphoric about the agreement and said:

> "The Indian Government, the Indian Parliament and the people of India must reflect soberly and dispassionately on the circumstances of that visit (of Prime Minister Gandhi to Colombo to sign the agreement) and the consequences of that 'Accord'. ...
>
> At this critical juncture in our relations, the Indian Government and Parliament must face up to certain obvious questions. Has the Peace Accord brought peace? Has it not, on the contrary, hardened feelings among the majority community to the point where violence has now spread in most dangerous form to the South?"

The visit was made use of by Prime Minister Gandhi and President Jayewardene to discuss matters of mutual concern regarding the implementation of the agreement. High on the agenda was the need to start the political process in the context of continued strife in the Eastern Province and difference of opinion among Sri Lankan politicians regarding holding of fresh elections to the Provincial Councils at this juncture. It was agreed that the elections to the North-East Council would be de-linked from the elections to other provincial councils. Jayewardene agreed that in de-linking and postponing the election in the north-east, President would ensure that no blame was allowed to fall on the IPKF to avoid negative political impact. Unrelenting refusal of the LTTE to lay down arms and accept the amnesty too came up for discussion. Though the spokesman of the

Ministry of External Affairs refused to comment, the question of the duration of the stay of the IPKF in Sri Lanka was discussed. However, Rajiv Gandhi said that the IPKF would stay on in Sri Lanka as long as necessary. Earlier, Gandhi had maintained that the IPKF had gone to Sri Lanka at the invitation of Sri Lankan President and it would stay on there as long as the President desired. This change in the stance created a lot of trouble later.

18

Proposal for a Treaty of Peace and Friendship

Failure to disarm the LTTE, the key element in the Indo-Sri Lanka agreement was a source of great embarrassment to the Government of India. There were elements in Sri Lanka who felt that Colombo had not only been at the receiving end in the agreement, but had given away much more in the letters exchanged with the main agreement. Their grouse was that India had shoved unequal obligations towards Colombo. Sri Lanka was precluded from allowing the use of any of its ports to any third party, not to engage any outside military advisers, review the VOA agreement, joint lease of the Trincomalee Oil Tank Farm etc. India had not assumed any of the corresponding obligations, even cosmetically, which was customarily done in an agreement/treaty between two sovereign powers. Hence to deflect this charge of one-sided agreement, India indicated that she would not be averse to consider a treaty with Sri Lanka on the lines of the Indo-Soviet Treaty of Peace and Friendship assuming reciprocal obligations that would replace the letters exchanged with the agreement.

It was in the air that the question of treaty was discussed when Gandhi and Jayewardene met in New Delhi in November 1987. But on December 2, it was stoutly denied by New Delhi in the Lok Sabha. However, veteran Communist leader Indrajit Gupta persistingly asked "whether our Government considers it desirable that we should work to bring about some sort of a long-term treaty with Sri Lanka, a bilateral treaty, which would cover these areas of defence and foreign affairs. If so what steps are being taken? If not why not?" Once again the government adroitly said: "No proposal was brought by the distinguished President of Sri Lanka with regard to the treaty you mentioned". Still pressing his point, he asked if the Government at all considered its desirability, the Minister left no one wiser by saying that at the Government level, there was no such proposal though there was some speculation in the media.

During Jayewardene's visit to New Delhi in January 1988, the question of treaty was again on the horizon. Several days before the visit there were speculations in the Lankan media about the treaty being discussed during the President's visit. However, the press reports were not clear whether the President would carry the draft with him. The draft that was described to be clicking into shape was based on the principle of reciprocity. On January 25, the day the President arrived in the Indian capital, AFP carried a New Delhi datelined report quoting the Indian Prime Minister that India was willing to discuss Sri Lanka's proposal for a long-term friendship and cooperation treaty. The Indian news agency, Press Trust of India reported that New Delhi had an open mind on the proposal and would not shut the door to a discussion. It may be recalled that India had acted rather coolly when Colombo had first made the proposal in October 1987, saying it wanted first to ensure the full implementation of the July accord. India softened her outlook when Colombo clarified that the proposed treaty would be on the lines of the Indo-Soviet Treaty of 1971, which provided for mutual security and would serve as the framework for a future relationship. India was assured it would faithfully reflect the spirit and contents of the earlier Sri Lanka-India accord and of the letters exchanged therewith. In January 1988, at the end of the talks in New Delhi, Rajiv Gandhi himself confirmed that a draft of the treaty had indeed been received by New Delhi but added significantly "in something like this, we really need to go very deep into it". He did not appear to have any reservation in signing such a treaty.

Sri Lankan Minister of Land Development, Gamini Dissanayake who had accompanied his President and led the Sri Lankan delegation at the ministerial level discussions, confirmed to the media that there was some difference of opinion between the two. He described the differences in the nature of semantics. Meanwhile, Sirimavo Bandaranaike expressed her alarm at these reports. In a statement issued on January 26, when Jayewardene was still in New Delhi, she questioned the very need for a treaty. She said that the policy of non-alignment leaves no scope for a document of this nature.

Colombo was in a fix. It appeared to it that the treaty could get mired in another controversy. The agreement, the basic document had made no progress towards implementation and remained bogged in polemics thanks to the LTTE obduracy. The first priority was to see how to make it take off. Colombo felt that given the hostility of the general mass of people to the agreement, it was perhaps not desirable to go in for any kind of fresh document lest it should lead to another acrimonious debate. The question of treaty thus was allowed to remain dormant till the political climate improved.

It resurrected itself suddenly on September 13, 1988. Prime Minister Ranasinghe Premadasa was answering questions in Hong Kong to a group of Sri Lankans who wanted to know if the Indo-Sri Lanka Peace agreement had undermined the country's independence. He said: "I think an accord of this nature between two sovereign states should be reciprocal". He promised to work to bring about that reciprocity by signing a friendship treaty on the lines of the Indo-Soviet friendship treaty. He hoped that once that happened a lot of misunderstandings would be cleared "both nationally and internationally". Responding to this, the Indian High Commissioner in Colombo told the *Hindu* that India was quite willing to discuss such a proposal. India was well aware of Premadasa's preference for a treaty over the accord already signed and Colombo smarting under the notion of having been made to concede one-sided concessions to India, which had seemingly compromised her sovereignty. The above response of the Indian High Commissioner had become necessary at least for public consumption.

Premadasa assumed the Presidency of Sri Lanka at the end of 1988, to succeed Jayewardene. The change of guard in Colombo was quite disconcerting to New Delhi since the hostility of Premadasa to India generally and to the events of the last couple of years was well known. India was aware that she was no longer in control of the situation. For New Delhi it was necessary to work on a fresh response taking into account the new emerging political scenario in Colombo. Soon after Premadasa's assumption of the Presidency, Dixit had gone to New Delhi to prepare for such an eventuality to forestall the Presidential initiative in this direction. In the very first meeting that J.N. Dixit had with the new President (January 17, 1989 on return to Colombo after consultations with New Delhi), he conveyed to him the willingness of the Government of India "to consider the suggestion from Sri Lanka for a bilateral Indo-Sri Lanka Treaty of Peace and Friendship and Cooperation on the principles of mutual benefit and reciprocity." Premadasa expressed his happiness at the Indian initiative. He said "a draft of the Treaty would be conveyed to the Government of India in the near future." As noted above Colombo had in January 1988 conveyed a draft to New Delhi. Obviously, Premadasa was not happy with that document since it had Jayewardene's stamp.

On March 7, 1989, Sri Lankan High Commissioner in New Delhi Bernard Tilakaratna (who had in the meantime been designated his country's Foreign Secretary) on the eve of his departure from New Delhi, submitted to the Indian Foreign Secretary Shailendra Kumar Singh a draft treaty entitled: "Agreement to Consolidate and Expand Friendly Relations and Cooperation between Sri Lanka and India". The draft contained ten articles that sought to replace the letters that were signed by leaders of the two countries on July 29, 1987.

Reciprocity was the key element in the new draft. It was intended to give a practical shape to the promise President Premadasa had made to the people during the Presidential campaign the previous December. It was also part of the ruling United National Party's election manifesto. While most of the contents of the draft were innocuous, article IV (ii) that "each country will not permit its territory to be used by any person to commit terrorist activities or to advocate separatism in the other and will deport such person if such person is a national of the other country to that country", unpalatable to India. It sought to cast an obligation on India, which India's legal system could not sustain. India was prepared to commit herself not to let her territory be used for "terrorist activity directed against the other party." She was however not prepared for automatic extradition of any person, but to "consider request for extradition of any person involved in terrorist activity in accordance with existing arrangements". Sri Lanka's draft avoided commitment to the Indo-Sri Lanka agreement of July 1987, and only referred to it in the context of draft treaty being in replacement of the earlier letters exchanged. On the other hand, the Indian draft in the very first article reaffirmed the Parties' "determination to implement in its totality the Indo-Sri Lanka agreement and the Annexure thereto concluded on 29 July, 1987". These differences in perception on the scope of the new treaty and obligation for extradition perhaps stalled any meaningful negotiations between the two countries. It is a different matter that while India was quite comfortable with the agreement of July 1987 and the letters, Colombo felt suffocated but did not know how to respond to the complexities and conundrum that had been knit around the agreement. As long as Jayewardene graced the Presidency, India had a smooth sailing despite occasional needling from his wayward colleagues, which she soon learnt to take in her stride. But the change of guards at the Presidency was a completely new situation, which India had not bargained for, and was ill-prepared to face. Premadasa when asking the IPKF to pack up was virtually abrogating the 1987 agreement despite India swearing by it. Nevertheless, as a sop to India, Premadasa in his letter of June 2, 1989, asking for the withdrawal of the IPKF, was prepared to settle for a treaty for which he said, "we have submitted several proposals."

While trying to distance himself from the agreement, the President continued to insist that the Indo-Sri Lanka relations must be restructured on the pattern of the Indo-Soviet Treaty of Friendship and Cooperation, which he viewed as "a marvelous document", expressing the principles of "real understanding, cooperation and friendship." In talking to N. Ram of the *Hindu* (June 5, 1989) the President emphasised that a treaty and the Indo-Sri Lanka agreement must be understood as "completely different things". The accord was "for a specific purpose", while the proposed treaty was "for all times". The idea of a friendship or cooperation treaty was to put one country "on par with the other country" and he was keen on the idea.

On January 13, 1990, Indian High Commissioner in Colombo told journalists that India had "responded to a proposal by Sri Lanka to sign a friendship treaty by submitting a counter draft" on January 13, which was a "very forward looking" document. He said that it stressed "the sovereignty and equality of both nations and their willingness to cooperate with each other in a few fields of development". On January 18, 1990, Sri Lanka's State Minister of Defence, Wijeratne confirming that he had received an Indian draft said that a "friendship treaty with India can be signed next month if there are no controversial matters in the draft submitted by Indian Foreign Minister". Cautioning against any hasty action, he recalled to the journalists the experience of the July 1987 agreement, which he said, was signed in haste and then destruction followed. On the same day, January 18, the Indian High Commissioner separately briefed the Indian journalists based in Colombo and told them that the proposed draft was a "comprehensive document" which would take "the totality of our relationship into account." But the High Commissioner refused to be drawn into discussions on how the Indian and Sri Lankan drafts differed from each other. On March 15, 1990 the Indian Minister of External Affairs, Inder Kumar Gujral, confirmed to the Lok Sabha that while the response of Colombo to the Indian draft was awaited, the proposed treaty would "replace only the Letters Exchanged on July 29, 1987 at the time of the signing of the Indo-Sri Lanka agreement." On April 22, 1990 the newly appointed Sri Lankan Minister of Foreign Affairs, Harold Herat said that "we are going to initiate discussions" on the treaty with India.

As the IPKF was withdrawn, the Indo-Sri Lanka agreement of 1987 practically stood abrogated though India continued to swear by it for some more time. But to pin down Colombo to a formal relationship, the need for some arrangement was felt to be an unstated necessity. Despite the fact the two governments had the drafts of each other under their consideration, no progress to clinch the treaty could be registered. The sticking point, which was proving difficult to reconcile related to extradition of persons involved in violent activities. This was hinted at by the Minister of Foreign Affairs Harold Heart in Colombo on April 22, 1990 when he said, "there are some differences of perception," and referred to the article dealing with extradition of persons engaged in violent activities. Then he went on to recount other articles of the treaty, which he thought would present no problem of any kind.

As stated above, Colombo had clarified to the satisfaction of New Delhi that the treaty would only seek to replace the letters exchanged with the Indo-Sri Lanka agreement of July 1987, and not the entire agreement. If the proposed treaty could never take off the ground it was because there remained basic and serious differences on the question of use of the territory of one country by the nationals of the other for hostile purposes and their extradition. India wanted a provision whereby each country would consider the request for extradition on merits of each case and after going through the legal processes. Sri Lanka thought differently. She wanted that such persons should just be deported once the request was made. India's legal system would not allow such deportations as it would violate the ends of natural justice and circumvent the legal process and the courts. Since each side would not budge from its stated position on this ticklish question, the idea of treaty gradually went into limbo and got dropped altogether.

19

LTTE's Intransigence

It was unmistakably clear that the Government of India wielded enough clout with Jayewardene as long as he held office. It got many a thing done in favour of the Tamils by interceding with him. This too helped to give the impression that the agreement was being successfully implemented. Unfortunately, nothing seemed to go right for the agreement on the Indian side. The TULF who were the only hope of the Government of India, remained entrenched in Chennai and continued to make one demand after another on New Delhi instead of setting its own house in order. They had lost their initiative to the militant groups, particularly the LTTE. New Delhi was getting diffident and exasperated but could not get to rebuke the TULF publicly as that would have harmed its reputation which already was low enough in the eyes of both the militants and Colombo. The LTTE had refused to see reason and would do nothing that would lend an iota of respectability to the agreement. The LTTE too assessed that India having invested its total prestige in the agreement would do nothing to dilute it in any manner.

That India was feeling exasperated with both the TULF and the LTTE was not in doubt. On February 18, 1988 the TULF sent a telex to New Delhi asking it to ensure that Colombo took certain actions in relation to the constitution of the North-East Provincial Council and elections. An irked New Delhi felt that

> "...time had come to tell the TULF that instead of subjecting us to homilies on legal points most of which have been deliberately distorted by them, they should return to their constituencies and do grass-root level

political work amongst the Tamil people in the north and the east in order to look after and promote the interests of their community. It is strange that whilst the EROS, PLOTE, EPRLF and TELO are doing work amongst the people, the TULF instead of helping the cause of the Tamils, is issuing peculiar statements from Madras which is further complicating the situation along with the intransigence of the LTTE whom they basically fear because of which they can't return to Sri Lanka."

If Colombo was feeling impatient, it had every reason to do so. Domestic pressure was increasing since the IPKF operations gave no hope of their being able to tame the LTTE. The people at large and the government were coming to believe that the IPKF was not serious enough to go whole hog in dealing with the LTTE. India had her own difficulties arising out of domestic compulsions of Tamil politics. Already there were loud voices of discontent in the Indian Parliament about the IPKF operations, which had led to killings of the Tamils at the hands of the Indian army. The criticism was to intense and harsh that Minister of State Natwar Singh in his reply of March 18, 1988 in the Rajya Sabha regretfully said: "...but I do want to say that the IPKF is doing a great job under very difficult and complex circumstances and to attribute any motives to the Indian army which has a most marvelous record, is reprehensible and regrettable and should not have been done".

On the other hand, there was no dearth of people within and outside of Sri Lanka government who believed that India did not wish to eliminate the LTTE factor both for domestic and/or tactical reasons. This is confirmed now by a former Cabinet Secretary B.G. Deshmukh in his book *A Cabinet Secretary Looks Back* (2003). He wrote: "The fact, however, was that the army was fighting the LTTE with one hand tied behind its back. Its brief was to subdue the LTTE but not emasculate it to the extent that it would not be able to face the Sri Lankan army alone it if became necessary in the future in case the political situation so developed."

This was clear even then to any one who wished to see. There was the widely held perception that Prabakaran was allowed to slip out of the IPKF net thrice. India had her own difficulties. New Delhi was aware that Prabakaran's arrest would create fresh complications. The problem was how to handle him after his arrest? Since the IPKF was operating on behalf of Colombo, he would have to be handed over to Sri Lanka. Colombo was sure to try him for treason, and the consequences of this could be grave both for Colombo and New Delhi. Tamil constituency would be inflamed. The Indian Tamils and Tamil Nadu Government would find it impossible to reconcile to India acting as an agent of Colombo in facilitating his arrest. Above all, his arrest and incarceration would lead to the collapse of Tamil resistance and the bargaining chip to extract concessions from Colombo would collapse. Arresting him and bringing him to India was legally untenable. He could not be tried in India since his actions and violations were against Sri Lanka and her laws. The IPKF was operating for and on behalf of Sri Lanka. Keeping him under IPKF detention in Sri Lanka was an option, which was simply not available. It too would not have been countenanced by Colombo and created misunderstandings. New Delhi was neither unaware nor unconscious of the fact that if Colombo had invited New Delhi to intervene in the ethnic conflict, it was because it had no other choice. New Delhi feared the complete collapse of the LTTE would strangulate the Tamil struggle altogether. It would have given wrong signals to Sri Lanka. Given the odds against his arrest, it was best that even if Prabakaran came within the striking distance of the IPKF, he was allowed to escape the dragnet.

Under the circumstances, disillusionment with the prevailing uncertainty in the echelons of Sri Lankan government surprised no one. On February 25, 1988 the President in a report card presented to the parliament of the action taken by him to restore peace since the signing of the agreement did not show a very bright picture of the prevailing scenario and regretted that,

> "as a duty cast upon me as the Commander-in-Chief, I have to direct the members of the Security Services both from Sri Lanka and India to take arms against fellow human beings, our own citizens who have sadly taken to the path of violence in a democratic free society."

Rumours started floating in Còlombo that Sri Lanka and the LTTE had established contacts to reach a settlement outside of the Indo-Sri Lanka agreement. The move behind the back of the Government of India that "went against the grain of the Indo-Lanka agreement" hurt New Delhi. It made no secret of its strong opposition to any such move. High Commissioner Dixit remonstrating to the President told him that according to his information the Tiger emissaries had met a senior Minister in the Cabinet and discussed a peace formula. Later when speaking to journalists, the High Commissioner said that while India was keenly interested in promoting peace it could not remain inactive in the face of unilateral or bilateral moves aimed at bringing about a situation, which undermined the Indo-Sri Lanka accord or Tamil expectations. The unwritten message that the High Commissioner sought to deliver was that the future lay in finding a tripartite solution to the ethnic problem. When journalists asked High Commissioner Dixit what was wrong in both sides arriving at a mutually satisfactory settlement, he retorted the LTTE was not the Tamil people in their entirety, in the same manner that the JVP was not truly representative of the Sinhala people. Also, India had lost over 400 soldiers in a bid to stabilize Sri Lanka situation and working for peace in the Island. Nevertheless, Dixit confirmed that the President had reaffirmed his commitment to the India's "good offices".

The formula reportedly under negotiations comprised: "the postponing of elections for 5 years in the North and East; the setting up of an interim administration dominated by the LTTE in the north; the abdication of the Tamil claims on the Eastern Province; the re-demarcation of the Tamil areas; the establishment of three electoral units on an ethnic basis in the Eastern Province and the right of the Sri Lankan forces to retain hegemony over the east while the Tigers would control the north". While India could not possibly have any objection to this formula, it was stung to the core, since it sought to undermine her position, besides, eliminating all other Tamil factions particularly the TULF in which the Government of India had invested heavily. Fortunately, for India nothing much came out of these confabulations.

The LTTE and Colombo once again looked up to New Delhi. India rejected the LTTE's offer to negotiate but without preconditions. A LTTE report from Colombo of February 28, 1988 that the IPKF had called for a 24-hour cease-fire to disarm the LTTE, had to be scotched by New Delhi. Responding to the so-called offer of talks without preconditions, an official statement of the Ministry of External Affairs issued on February 29, 1988 quoting Prime Minister's statement of February 10, in the Consultative Committee of the Indian Parliament clarified that "we would welcome the LTTE joining the democratic political process provided it lays down arms and agrees to abide by the Indo-Sri Lanka agreement of 29th July, 1987." On March 2, the Prime Minister speaking in the Lok Sabha made no mention of any such possibility of talks with the LTTE and instead asked the latter to prove its claim to be the sole representative of the Tamils through the ballot by participating in the Provincial Council elections.

LTTE's activities were creating fresh complications for the Government of India. As LTTE's violence increased, particularly in the east targeting Sinhalese and the Muslims, Colombo was miffed with IPKF's inability to put down violence. President Jayewardene in a Top Secret message of March 5, 1988 drew Rajiv Gandhi's attention to the failure of the IPKF to pre-empt specific acts of violence involving large-scale massacre of Sinhalese and the Muslims, intelligence of which had been provided to the IPKF in time. To prevent another such incident, the President suggested deployment of Sri Lankan army, which had been withdrawn from the Northern and the Eastern provinces under the accord. On March 9, Prabakaran in a personal letter to Prime Minister Rajiv Gandhi once again made an offer of unconditional talks and said that he had nothing against the accord per se, but there was "legitimate fear of the chauvinistic attitude of the Sri Lankan regime, which had already thwarted the accord by failing to fulfill its commitment."

The Government of India in its efforts to put a brave face on the dismal and depressing scenario on March 17, 1988 claimed in the Lok Sabha:

> "Despite some of the more specific Tamil demands not having been met, the devolution package provided for

in the new constitutional arrangement, is far better than any thing offered to the Sri Lanka Tamils by the Government of Sri Lanka in previous arrangements and arrangements which were made but not implemented over the last 40 years."

On March 18, the Minister of State Natwar Singh assured the Rajya Sabha that despite LTTE's intransigence, the communication between New Delhi and the LTTE had not broken down and "there are various channels, there are various avenues, there are various organizations through which we are in touch with them." He was unequivocal that the LTTE had to surrender arms and accept the accord. He was quite open in recognizing the role that the LTTE had "played for the last four years", but the Minister was frank in telling the agitated members from Tamil Nadu that there would be no compromise on fundamentals.

No one was impressed by New Delhi's claim. On the contrary, LTTE came out with a most damaging indictment of the Government of India. In a statement issued on April 5, 1988 it charged India of splitting the Tamil movement and intervening militarily in Sri Lanka in order to gain diplomatic advantage for herself. It confirmed what Colombo always maintained, that in the pre-1987 period India had trained and armed the Tamil groups in India and allowed them the use of Indian territory for mounting insurgency in the Island. The statement was critical of the Indian intelligence agency, Research and Analysis Wing (RAW), for trying to eliminate the LTTE in collusion with the Sri Lankan army. Charging India of double-dealing, the LTTE statement said that in order to torment Sri Lanka, India threatened that she would supply modern sophisticated weapons including anti-aircraft guns to it (LTTE) to defeat the security forces of the Island. It was only then, the LTTE statement said that Jayewardene panicked and entered into the July 1987 accord, which "did not meet Tamil aspirations but only advanced India's commercial, political and other interests". The LTTE accusations were not empty rhetoric, but hard facts. Being part of the expeditionary force that received training and arms from India, the LTTE knew what was happening and their statement was an incontrovertible statement of facts, which greatly embarrassed India. The Government of India stood condemned for once before the bar of public opinion and looked for cover.

The next day, April 6, Natwar Singh making a statement in the Lok Sabha confirming payments made to the LTTE by the Government of India, chose to remain silent on the LTTE's charges, grave as they were. In the face of ever deteriorating law and order situation in the Eastern Province and the perception of Colombo that the IPKF were soft on the Tamil militants in view of the mounting pressure on the Government of India in the parliament from Tamil Nadu members, Sri Lankan Government introduced some elements of its security forces in the Eastern Province. New Delhi did not look at this deployment with equanimity. It was nevertheless forced to acquiesce and compromise in their deployment while denying in the parliament that anything was happening outside the Indo-Sri Lanka agreement. Meanwhile, the strength of the IPKF had touched 49,000. The deployment of Lankan security elements even in a limited way invited the wrath of the LTTE who on April 13, charged Colombo of violating the Indo-Sri Lanka agreement by their deployment and accused India remaining only a "bystander". LTTE conveniently forgot that it was their intransigence and cussedness that had brought the situation to this pass.

The roles appeared to reverse. In April 1988, Colombo media carried reports that India was negotiating with the LTTE behind the back of Sri Lanka. On April 17, 1988 the daily *Island* carried a report that Colombo had protested to the Government of India for striking a deal with the LTTE following reports that the Indian's had flown two Tiger leaders "Raheem" and "Johnny" from Madras to Vavuniya with a message for Prabakaran without taking Colombo into confidence. When India denied these reports, the *Island* on April 20, insisted that it stood by its story and quoted a highly placed Government official in Colombo as its source for its story. The story soon stood confirmed by the RAW. On April 27, 1988 one of the top RAW agents who was in touch with the LTTE in Chennai visited Colombo and met M.M. Gunaratne, Director General of Sri Lankan Intelligence. Based on his talks with the RAW Agent code named SUNIL, Gunaratne in a TOP SECRET memorandum informed President Jayewardene that RAW was holding negotiations with the LTTE for the past three months. RAW also informed Colombo that because of the disclosure of secret payments made to the LTTE by India, and because of his "arrogant and overbearing" conduct, High Commissioner J.N. Dixit was not presently "held in favour by the Indian Prime Minister, and therefore does not play any significant role in the process of negotiations". RAW agent SUNIL also gave a resume of his discussions with the LTTE in Chennai and the line of thinking being pursued to bring it into negotiating fold. LTTE had apparently stipulated that it would be prepared to surrender 700 of the estimated 1000 big weapons in its possession, retaining the balance 300 for the security of its cadres. Once this was accomplished, LTTE agreed to support the political process, surrendering the balance weapons gradually. The LTTE too demanded lifting of proscription and protection of the Government of India for its cadres. But Sri Lankan Government remained a little cynical about the figures of arms with the LTTE. On June 19, 1988, Sri Lanka gave New Delhi its own estimates of arms with the LTTE indicating that the arms with it were double than what it was prepared to admit.

The LTTE had other conditions to fulfill before it could agree to extend any cooperation in the implementation of the accord. One of the principal conditions imposed by it was for a grant of Rs. 100 crores (1000 million) from the Government of India for rehabilitation of the people in the North and the East and another Rs. 50 crores (500 million) for rehabilitation of the LTTE cadres. In return LTTE agreed to make a public announcement of the acceptance of the accord and join in the electoral process and contest the provincial council elections.

The slow pace of RAW-LTTE negotiations convinced Colombo that the latter did not mean business. As violence showed no sign of abating, Colombo questioned the usefulness of the presence of IPKF in the Island. Exasperated, Sri Lanka's Home Minister, K.W. Devanayagam on May 28, 1988 wrote to the Defence Minister of India, Krishna Chandra Pant, reminding him of India's obligations under the July 1987 agreement to get the LTTE to surrender arms. While Sri Lanka had fulfilled her obligations, India had failed to obtain the surrender of arms by the LTTE without which elections to the North-East Council could not take place, said the Home Minister. The failure of the IPKF to achieve this objective, the Home Minister said, was agitating the minds of the people who were questioning the need for its presence on Lankan soil. Sri Lankan concern at payments made to the LTTE by the Government of India was also underlined in the letter. The IPKF was accused of being partisan towards the Tamils who were intimidating the Sinhalese people.

It was obvious that the RAW and the High Commissioner in Colombo were both acting independent of each other and indulging in the game of one-upmanship. On June 14, 1988 Dixit met the President and requested him to make a public announcement that the elections in the Northern and Eastern provinces would be to only one Provincial Council. Not to be left behind, on the same day, the RAW agent SUNIL independently approached the President through the Sri Lanka's Director General of Intelligence, Gunaratne, and demanded virtually what Dixit had already conveyed. This was an important piece of political and diplomatic task, which should alone have been left to be handled by the High Commissioner. RAW's intervention showed lack of confidence in the High Commissioner. It corroborated what the RAW had earlier conveyed to Colombo that Dixit had lost confidence of the Prime Minister.

Be that as it may, Sri Lanka was willing to oblige provided the IPKF succeeded in obtaining the surrender of all arms and communication equipment from the LTTE. Since the LTTE was not sincere in the surrender of all its weapons, this effort like the many before came to a naught. Another issue, which proved a stumbling block, was the merger of the Northern and the Eastern provinces on a permanent basis. Finally, on June 30, 1988 the Presidential Secretariat issued a communiqué that the President of Sri Lanka had been informed by the Prime Minister of India that LTTE "has given indication of its willingness to lay down arms and cooperate in the implementation of the Indo-Sri Lanka agreement". The communiqué said if this were to happen, Colombo would be prepared to grant general amnesty "enabling their (militants) return to the democratic mainstream in terms of the accord and the latest constitutional amendment."

To convey the message that he was not bowing to any pressure, Jayewardene on June 30 in a separate statement said that the final merger would be decided after a referendum conducted in the Eastern Province alone according to the provision of the agreement. He told his Cabinet colleagues that the Government of India had agreed to the implementation of the accord "as it is". There was a mixed reaction to the Presidential communiqué and the LTTE's offer of surrender of arms to return to the mainstream of the political life of the country. The leader of the opposition in parliament, Anura Bandaranaike, had his doubts that India may have given some contrary understanding to the LTTE to buy peace, and described the move for merger without referendum as "immoral". He said, "We do not know the exact details of the so-called agreement (between the LTTE and Indian officials)." The left wing United Socialist Alliance (USA) welcomed the move if it helped in achieving peace. (The USA comprised of the left wing groups including Communist Party of Sri Lanka, Lanka Sama Samaja Party and the Sri Lanka Mahajana Party). The TULF Secretary General Amirthalingam, said that his party was still studying the implications of the communiqué and reminded that the TULF had been pressing for the merger of the two provinces and holding elections on the basis of the 1982 Electoral Register. A little skeptically he said since the Presidential declaration was conditional, everything would depend on the success of the talks between the Indian officials and the LTTE. Sri Lankan President and every one else had reason to be a little incredulous since the intelligence reports were not very encouraging. On July 4, 1988 the Director General of Sri Lankan Intelligence and Security, M.M. Gunaratne in a Top Secret note, quoting a mole reported to the President that the LTTE planned to hold back most of the arms, explosives and communication equipment; pretended to go along with the Provincial Council exercise till the bulk of the IPKF pulled out and then recommence their struggle with full force.

Since all this exercise was marred by suspicion and distrust on both the sides, nothing came out of it. The LTTE were disenchanted with the role of the Government of India, which could not get the President to agree to the permanent merger of the two Tamil provinces. LTTE once again resorted to India bashing since it now considered India the biggest hindrance to achieve its goal of Eelam. On July 9, 1988, the LTTE in a press statement accused the IPKF of waging an unjust war in which a large number of civilians have been killed, "women have been brutally raped, millions worth property destroyed and the wild life and jungles were devastated." The statement indicted India for believing that the temporary merger of the two Tamil provinces would solve the Tamil problem. It charged India of perpetrating greater atrocities on the Tamils than the Sri Lankan army and crushing the Tamil liberation struggle. This statement was a signal to the Government of India to end its efforts at reconciliation, which India regretted in her statement of July 12.

The LTTE in a separate memorandum submitted to the Indian government in New Delhi, stressed upon the need for a satisfactory resolution of the three basic issues: the permanent merger of the Northern and the Eastern provinces; the enhancement of the devolution package and a definite understanding regarding colonization. The paper indicated a pronounced shift from the earlier Tigers' negotiating position. This document was based on the premise that the Sri Lankan Tamils could aspire to only provisions that are incorporated in the Indian political system. This was on the basis of Indian Prime Minister Rajiv Gandhi's statement to the same effect. Secondly, the document relied on the fundamental acceptance of the Indo-Sri Lanka accord and to interpret those provisions in a favourable manner to Tamil aspirations. The LTTE said that the accord recognized that "the Northern and the Eastern Provinces had been areas of historical habitation of Sri Lankan Tamil speaking people, who have at all times hitherto lived together in this territory with other ethnic groups". As such the Tigers argued a permanent merger was necessary and the accord provision regarding the referendum in the east was unnecessary. It also said that if a referendum was held, it should be for both provinces together and not for one province alone.

The memorandum also made a detailed analysis of the 13th Amendment to the Constitution and the Provincial Council Act. It made specific suggestions as to how changes enhancing devolution could be made. In terms of colonization, LTTE pressed for permanent guidelines governing land alienation as available in the Indian state of Jammu and Kashmir, which had been given a special status in the Indian Constitution. Striving to draw a parallel, the Tigers demanded legal provisions that prohibited "outsiders" from acquiring land in Kashmir, thereby altering demographic pattern in the area. But all these arguments went beyond the provisions of the 1987 accord and were difficult to achieve. The Indian High Commissioner on July 12 regretted the LTTE's stance, and expressed India's determination to continue with its various efforts to persuade the LTTE to give up violence. It reiterated that New Delhi remained fully committed to implement the accord since it was a fair and practical basis to bring about durable peace and normalcy to Sri Lanka.

On July 23, 1988, Prime Minister Gandhi expressed his disappointment to the *Hindustan Times* editor H.K.Dua, that despite the fact that India provided the LTTE every opportunity to surrender arms and come to the mainstream, "unfortunately their response has not been positive". "If the LTTE aspires to safeguard and promote the interests of Tamils, it should give up violence and display the courage required to participate in the political process", said Gandhi. However, no change in the stance of the LTTE was perceptible. A week later on July 29, the LTTE in yet another statement said, "The Indo-Sri Lanka accord as a whole aids and abets Sinhala-Buddhist chauvinism. In such a situation, it is unreasonable and unjust for the Indian forces to engage in a war with our Organisation to disarm us".

❮20❯

One year after the Peace Agreement

Unfortunately, even after one year of the signing of the agreement, it had failed to take off the ground, inasmuch as its crucial provision, the disarming of the militants had not taken place and neither had peace returned to the Island, which was its fond hope. On the contrary, the LTTE had revolted against the agreement and was engaged in a bloody war with the IPKF that had been invited to ensure its implementation. Since the peace in the Island hinged on the implementation of this single provision, there was an allround sense of disenchantment. The elections to the North-East Provincial Council (NEPC) which were to be held within three months of the signing of the agreement and in any case not later than December 31st,1987 were nowhere in sight.

Failures in the north impacted adversely the developments in the south. The Sinhala radical forces led by the Janatha Vimukthi Peramuna (JVP) raised their head once again and spearheaded the Sinhalese backlash in the south. It was quick to take advantage of the Sinhalese mass consciousness on account of opposition to the presence of the IPKF and Tamil separatism. The Tamil Nadu factor that the agreement was expected to take care of, resurrected itself in a big way. The Indian army, which is a respected institution in the Indian psyche, came under severe attack repeatedly at the hands of the Tamil members of parliament and Tamil politicians in South India. It was accused of carrying out the killings of Tamils. The NEPC, even when belatedly constituted, to provide the locomotive force to propel the process of socio-economic reconciliation came in conflict with Colombo. The NEPC set up under duress from New Delhi was essentially a manifestation of the crisis management and failed to deliver reconciliation which was expected of it. The Council in its bid to project itself as the natural expression of Tamil nationalism, adopted policies, which were as stridently anti-Sinhalese as those of the LTTE. The Eelam People's Revolutionary Liberation Front (EPRLF), the party which emerged as the ruling group, failed to take independent stance on issues confronting the Tamil society and the country and failed to prove itself capable of standing on its own feet after the initial push. Instead it became more and more dependent on the IPKF. Even as IPKF was preparing to leave the Island a year later, neither the EPRLF nor the NEPC had found its feet on the ground and canvassed against its withdrawal. In a final act of desperation, NEPC adopted a highly objectionable secessionist resolution, which brought it not only in direct conflict with Colombo but also embarrassed the Government of India.

The expectation that the EPRLF would outmaneuver the LTTE by adopting a constructive and moderate agenda and project itself, as a democratic progressive alternative to the LTTE, failed to materialize. It chose the suicidal course of fighting the LTTE on its secessionist platform, something which it had unsuccessfully tried in the past. Therefore, for JVP to feel uncomfortable at these developments was not unnatural. On the other hand, these developments provided the cannon fodder for the JVP to target Colombo. It blamed Colombo for signing the Peace agreement with India "that betrayed our fatherland to Indian imperialism", and "allowed the aggressive Indian troops to take over a third of this country's territory." The JVP's propaganda could have been blunted by Colombo if it had some achievements to show for the IPKF in controlling the LTTE. On the contrary, the Sinhalese perceived the IPKF as being soft on the LTTE. Blaming everyone for the present situation, a JVP statement issued to mark the first anniversary of the agreement said:

> "The Indian imperialists and their local minions, specially those who have sought refuge under Indian imperialism such as the Jayewardene-Dissanayake clique of the UNP, the so-called United Socialist Alliance encompassing the Communists, Mahajana Sama Samaja and Nava Samaja

Parties, that are agents of the Indian imperialism, the EPRLF Tamil Eelam terrorists who are also agents of Indian imperialism, and their sycophants the so-called Independent Students' Union, the Thondoman clique, the Amirthalingams and all other traitors who draw their sustenance from Indian imperialism, scared and terrified and shivering over the great success of the people's struggle have launched a terrible conspiratorial plan of action to dull the edge of the peoples' fighting capacity."

Blaming the Indian High Commissioner for dividing the Sri Lankan opposition to strengthen the "Jayewardene-Thondoman clique", it pledged its support in the next Presidential election only to

> "a candidate put forward by a national liberation front having a national program based on total democracy and committed to abrogating the Jayewardene-Rajiv accord, driving away the Indian aggressive troops from the northern and eastern parts of Sri Lanka already occupied by them and abolishing the Provincial Councils that have heightened the ethnic inequalities, and aims to liberate the fatherland from the Indian imperialist grip".

To mark the first anniversary of the agreement, the High Commissioner agreed to join in an avoidable polemical press interview with the political stalwarts like Gamini Dissanayake, Minister of Lands and Land Development and Mahaweli Development and Anil Moonesinghe, a Member of Parliament from the Sri Lanka's Freedom Party. Minister Dissanayake blamed Tamil Nadu for stoking the fires of separatism in the Northern and Eastern provinces. Anil Moonesinghe had no difficulty in holding India responsible for all that went wrong and described the Indian intervention as simply "brutal and naked". Finally the High Commissioner was left holding the baby called Indo-Sri Lanka agreement in full public view.

On the August 29, 1988 the Rajya Sabha once again debated the Sri Lanka question. The Government came under attack as before. The Bharatiya Janata Party stalwart Jaswant Singh, who with his army background, considered himself a defence expert, said, "no country has ever benefited from a long war which is what we are ending up doing in Sri Lanka." Singh too doubted if India had an action plan "for creating such conditions that the IPKF can come back home." For him India had got stuck in the quicksands of Sri Lanka's ethnic conflict. P.V. Narasimha Rao, who had now returned to the Ministry of External Affairs laboured hard to defend the Government but apparently failed to convince the members that the government had at all a plan for the withdrawal of the IPKF from Sri Lanka. His suggestion that the withdrawal was linked to a political solution of the ethnic problem, which was nowhere on the horizon, convinced everyone that the IPKF appeared stranded on the Island indefinitely.

On the other hand, India kept up pressure on Jayewardene to take certain actions on his side so that some progress could be perceived. One of the items, suggested was election to the North-East Provincial Council. Hoping against hope that the LTTE could after all be brought to the negotiating table if more concessions were offered, Rajiv Gandhi asked Jayewardene to unilaterally issue a "Communiqué" promising amnesty to the LTTE if it abided by the agreement, improve the devolution package for the provincial governments, make Tamil operational as the official language and so on. On his side, Gandhi said that India had "taken into custody all hard-core LTTE cadres in Tamil Nadu under the National Security Act of India". But he could not claim any success for India towards implementing the agreement on the Island. Indian pressure on Jayewardene did work and he announced elections to the North-East Provincial Council and ordered the release of 115 Tamil political detainees. In the fond hope of a LTTE response, the IPKF announced a cease-fire for five days from September 15, 1988, which was extended by another five days. LTTE sensing Indian desperation, asked for a permanent cease-fire.

Bewildered by allround criticism, the LTTE decided to hit back and in order to deflect the accusations being hurled at it both by India and Sri Lanka, its Political Committee issued a lengthy statement on October 26, 1988 describing the Indo-Sri Lanka accord "a dead letter" since it failed in its "primary objective" of establishing peace and normalcy on the Island. Accusing the Government of India of desperate efforts to implement the accord by "unleashing all-out war" against the "liberation movement", the statement said:

> "For more than one year, our freedom fighters were able to put up a fierce and heroic resistance against one of the most formidable military machines in the world and successfully impressed upon the Government of India that military aggression, domination and terrorization cannot subjugate the will of a determined people who are fighting for a just and legitimate cause. The determined guerrilla resistance in the Tamil homeland and the violent rebellion in the Southern Sri Lanka clearly indicates that the vast majority of the population, both the Tamils and the Sinhalese, are vehemently opposed to the agreement."

Analyzing the causes of its failure, Anton Balasingham, Head of the Political Committee repeated the charge that it was an imposed agreement arrived at disregarding "the wishes, aspirations, fears and hopes of the people of the Island, particularly the Tamil speaking people".

As the Indian pressure to bring the LTTE into the peace process mounted, its determination to resist the IPKF, correspondingly strengthened. In the past, it was Colombo that was critical of the IPKF failure to deliver. As the conflict deepened, the latter also came under acerbic and harsh criticism of the Tamils in Jaffna. They accused the IPKF of many human rights violations and making capital out of Tamil misery and misfortunes. In October 1988, fifty faculty members of the Jaffna University issued a statement accusing India of arming the militants right from 1983 and thereby marginalizing the people. The actions of the militants went calculatedly unchecked and though India was the common patron of all the militants, divisions and antagonisms between the various groups grew at a rapid pace, culminating in annihilations of the Tamils, the University teachers said. In a fit of resignation the academics and intellectuals wailed that even if the elections were held to the Provincial Council of the North-East, the Tamils had little hope that anyone could function as a representative of the people. They lamented that the future elections would be decided by the manner in which India and the different groups perceived their own interests. They were convinced that the "outcome of elections cannot resolve problems arising from habits that have been exacerbated by the prevalence of murder and assassination."

❮21❯

Presidency of Ranasinghe Premadasa

The elections to the office of the President were due towards the end of 1988. President Jayewardene decided to retire from active politics leaving the field free for an impulsive Prime Minister Ranasinghe Premadasa to emerge as the President of Sri Lanka in December 1988. As part of his election manifesto, he had committed himself to ask the IPKF to pack up and go back home. As Jayewardene prepared to lay down his office, the future of the Indo-Sri Lanka agreement was a cause for concern in New Delhi. India was not unaware of the fragile nature of the commitment of the new President to the accord. Jayewardene had signed the accord with India in July 1987 in the teeth of his opposition. Talking to the BBC on December 13, 1988, an irritated Jayewardene threw up his hands and said "there was nothing to either renegotiate in the Indo-Sri Lanka Peace accord or abrogate it, since the accord was now a *fait accompli*". On the future of the IPKF, the President said: "Sri Lanka had done her part of the accord and a new President could ask the Indian forces to withdraw immediately or on a phased basis provided that he was satisfied that the Sri Lankan forces could meet the present situation". As the reign of the Indian *bete noire*, Premadasa loomed large on the horizon it was painfully clear to New Delhi that the days of honeymoon in Sri Lanka were over.

The writing on the wall was clear and bold, and India did not fail to read it. The Indian High Commissioner, J.N. Dixit rushed to New Delhi and gave the Prime Minister his assessment of the emerging political situation on the Island. In order to pre-empt the President on the question of IPKF's withdrawal, Dixit on return to Colombo informed the President that in addition to the two battalions of the IPKF already withdrawn, another two battalions would leave the Island soon. He also conveyed that India would be prepared to consider an Indo-Sri Lanka Treaty of Peace, Friendship and Cooperation on the principles of mutual benefit and reciprocity. Notwithstanding the friendly and conciliatory noises made by New Delhi, the noises emanating from Colombo were not devoid of shrillness, making New Delhi uncomfortable and exasperated. Earlier it had to contend with the LTTE. Colombo at least sounded friendly. Now the situation, changed on both the fronts. If India felt besieged, she had no one except herself to blame.

The IPKF's failure to disarm the LTTE in terms of the July 1987 agreement and bring them into the political mainstream was being articulated at the highest level in Sri Lanka more frequently now than ever before. The manner, in which the newly appointed Tamil Chief Minister of the North-East Council Perumal, seen as the protégé of New Delhi functioned, left much to be desired. He behaved as if he was answerable to New Delhi and not Colombo. After being appointed the Chief Minister he went over the heads of the Sri Lankan leaders to New Delhi and met Indian leaders including the Prime Minister and Tamil Nadu Chief Minister to discuss with them the emerging political scenario in the Island. New Delhi did nothing to disabuse him of his indiscretion. No Chief Minister of an Indian state would be allowed such latitude by New Delhi. Yet here was a Chief Minister of a province of another country doing just that with the indulgence of Indian leaders. The rebuke from New Delhi was not only missing, he was feeling emboldened after being received in New Delhi at the highest level. Earlier too, before the 1987 accord with Colombo, Sri Lankan Tamil leaders headquartered in Chennai negotiated with Colombo through the Government of India from that city freely taking positions on the ethnic issue on the advice of New Delhi. It is unfortunate that New Delhi instead of discouraging such a trend was seen to be approving it by its participation in the talks with the Tamil leaders.

Taking advantage of the developing estrangement between Colombo and New Delhi, the LTTE too sensed opportunity to snipe at New Delhi. It decided to project India as an interested party interfering in Sri Lankan affairs to promote her own strategic interests, while Tamils suffered. It approached the UN Human Rights Commission in Geneva challenging India's bona fide, holding her responsible for "continuous occupation and repression" in the north "under the cover of peace keeping operations". Its letter of February 7, 1989 sought to convey to the world that the

> "Tamil people are deeply disillusioned and disappointed with India's policy and have lost all trust and hope in the Government of India. They are convinced that the Indian administration has aggressive and hegemonistic designs in the region with the purpose of consolidating its strategic and geopolitical ambitions rather than to secure the interests of the Tamils. India has lost the status of impartial mediator and a peace maker."

Mounting further pressure, on March 21,1989 LTTE accused the IPKF of the massacre of 300 civilians in their renewed offensive by the deployment of heavy arms and tanks. On April 3, it sought to throw cold water on the North-East Council elections. Its press release said: "the puppets of the Indian Government who participated in this fraudulent elections are in New Delhi, complaining to the Indian Government that adequate powers have not been devolved to the provincial councils". The LTTE claimed that while in the IPKF operations hundreds of Tamils had been killed, it too had in the month of March 1989 alone killed 57 Indian soldiers and wounded 60, capturing 32 of their weapons, besides killing 11 Sri Lankan service personnel. When a week-long cease-fire was announced as from April 12, the LTTE ridiculing it said if it were the intention that LTTE would surrender its arms, then it was an exercise in futility. A press release issued by the Political Committee of the LTTE on April 11, branded the IPKF as an "occupation army" engaged in the killings of the Tamils and reminded the President that he had "unwittingly" failed to realize that the IPKF was "the enemy of the country".

The LTTE fusillade fitted into the new administration's strategy to get rid of the IPKF. If the LTTE could come to the negotiating table, the rationale for the IPKF's presence would be knocked out. On April 13, the new Foreign Minster, Ranjan Wijeratne sought to reach out to the LTTE and said: "We are pleased to invite the leadership of the LTTE to have talks with the government". Having a dig at India he added, "when a nation is wrecked by internal conflict, only outsiders will reap the benefits". To the Government's utter surprise the LTTE did not take long to respond. On April 15, it responded to the Government's call for talks. Colombo instantaneously responded the next day and asked the LTTE to "nominate an accredited representative to discuss necessary arrangements to facilitate a dialogue anywhere in Sri Lanka". The public reaction was a bit cautious. Two Colombo papers, the *Island* and the *Sun*, provided a rough indication of the public mood when they advised circumspection in falling into the LTTE trap. The political circles also remained cautious. The question that was hotly debated was what the two sides, with so much dividing them, could negotiate about and whether any agreement was possible at all. Successive Sri Lankan governments had been constrained by the forces of Sinhalese nationalism and chauvinism from making any concession to the Tamils. Sinhalese nationalism had become more militant over the years, especially after the formation of the JVP and Premadasa had very little leeway to show accommodation to them.

Though the LTTE desire for talks came as a surprise to everyone, especially in the context of LTTE's response of April 11, terming the government offer of cease-fire as an "exercise in futility", both sides had been exchanging feelers for the past few months and the Eelam Revolutionary Organisation of the Students (EROS) was one of the channels of communication. At the first meeting between EROS delegation and the Sri Lankan President in March, both sides had apparently agreed that the LTTE's participation was essential to any peace package. During his visit to Colombo earlier in April the EROS', leader Balakumar met President Premadasa twice and also contacted Anton Balasingham who was then in Australia, to sound the LTTE out. It was significant that the LTTE's offer of talks came in the context of references by the Sri Lankan Government to the withdrawal of the IPKF. The departure of the IPKF and a reduction in India's role seemed to be the most important point of convergence between Colombo and the LTTE.

Taking advantage of the President's anxiety to get the IPKF out of the Island, the LTTE had maneuvered and outwitted India. Failure of New Delhi to tailor its response to the developing situation and continuous pressure on the LTTE to surrender its arms to enable India to claim some implementation of the 1987 agreement, which had virtually remained stalled since its signatures, had already turned the LTTE hostile towards India. In a new twist to the events, the LTTE in an out-flanking move informed Premadasa that it was willing to fall in line if the IPKF were to withdraw from the Island. It was a double-edged sword that the LTTE sought to wield—it would help it to avenge its humiliation at the hands of the IPKF and once bereft of the IPKF support, the north-east administration would collapse thus enabling it to fill the vacuum. For Premadasa also it was God-sent opportunity—it would ensure return of peace to the Island and the President would redeem the most important pledge of his and his party's election manifesto to throw the IPKF out of the Island.

It was no less significant that the LTTE made the offer for talks after observing that the IPKF had on its own begun the process of pull out and the demand for its speedy de-induction had been gaining momentum even otherwise. In the LTTE's calculation, its initiative could bring it some credit for something, which in any case appeared to be happening. It would allow the LTTE to have a last laugh and in the end its adversary India, which did everything to humiliate it would stand humbled and discredited!

The unexpected twist in the tale stung India to the core. Its efforts for peace in the Island epitomized in the Indo-Sri Lanka agreement of July 1987, seemed aborted after the sacrifice of hundreds of soldiers. The principal party, which had invited India in Sri Lanka, had turned its back on her. At home, the Tamil constituency too had turned hostile. The Parliament was not placated either. There was more humiliation in store for India. The LTTE made it publicly known that it would not observe cease-fire till the IPKF left Sri Lanka. Tragically the initiative passed into the LTTE's hands. Reacting sheepishly to the unexpected developments, the official spokesman of the Indian Ministry of External Affairs said in New Delhi on April 17, 1989 that "talks are always good and India will support any move, which will lead to peace". Barely hiding his embarrassment, the spokesman in reacting to a question said, "If talks are held, it will come within the framework of the Indo-Sri Lanka agreement". The questioner appeared determined to embarrass the Government of India further and asked whether India was consulted before Sri Lanka Government made the offer for a dialogue to the LTTE. The spokesman, clearly discomfited, said the Indian mission in Colombo was in daily contact with both the parties at various levels. "We are involved in the process. We will study the offer and its acceptance and ascertain the veracity", he added betraying his lack of confidence.

It was clear to everyone that the LTTE having taken the driver's seat was pressing the escalator too hard and India was desperately trying to keep her toe on the brakes. On April 19, 1989 Sri Lankan Foreign Minister, Wijeratne announced that the talks between the Government and the LTTE represented by Anton Balasingham were scheduled to begin in the middle of the following week. The latter while confirming the timetable for the talks, drove another nail in the Indian coffin reiterating that the LTTE would not observe cease-fire until the IPKF left the Island. The LTTE said it asked for talks because it desired to see an end to the killings of the Tamil civilians. The implications were not lost on India.

On April 21,1989 the EPRLF Secretary-General, R. Padmanabha said that the LTTE had agreed for talks on the basis of three demands—the withdrawal of the IPKF; dissolution of the North-Eastern Provincial Council headed by the EPRLF and amending the Constitution along the Canadian model. However, the Foreign Minister, reacting to the EPRLF statement denied that LTTE had made any of the three demands articulated by Padmanabha but significantly added, "our talks will embrace all issues which will be mutually agreed upon". He also clarified that the discussions with Balasingham would only be preliminary-talks to prepare for substantive talks.

To allay any Indian apprehensions, President Premadasa had an unusually long conversation lasting 55 minutes with the new Indian High Commissioner Lakhan Lal Mehrotra, (successor to J.N. Dixit), after the latter had presented his Letter of

Credence. The President spoke of the need to remove any misunderstanding between the two countries and said that misinformation appeared to be a greater problem than misunderstanding. To add to India's tribulations the *Sunday Observer* of April 16,1989 carried a story that sought to blame IPKF and the EPRLF for the massacres of Muslims in Kinniyai and other places in the Eastern region of the North-East Province. The story said that the Muslims and the Sinhalese favoured deployment of Sri Lankan security forces instead of the IPKF, thereby eroding its credibility as a peace-keeping force. The unfortunate part was that the story was based on the briefing given by the Minister of Foreign Affairs and the Minister of State for Defence, Ranjan Wijeratne at the end of his tour of the eastern region. He had told the *Sunday Observer* that in Trincomalee, the Sinhalese residents blamed the EPRLF for the tension while in Kinniyai, the Muslims blamed it on both the FPRLF and the IPKF. Wijeratne had made similar statement on the state TV as well.

Nothing seemed to be going right for India. India was under attack from all sides, with no one to take cudgels on her behalf. In the midst of these not too happy developments, the Indian Foreign Secretary S.K. Singh made a dash to Colombo as Special Envoy of Prime Minister Rajiv Gandhi. He wanted to make a personal assessment of the new situation and the present status of the 1987 agreement, which Colombo wished to practically forget. He delivered a personal message of the Indian Prime Minister to the Sri Lankan President that covered "various aspects of the bilateral relations". A press release issued by the Indian High Commission in Colombo at the end of the Foreign Secretary's visit (May 1-3, 1989) said that "his visit represented the continuing dialogue between the governments of the two friendly neighbouring countries on matters of mutual interest". This included a review of the implementation of the Indo-Sri Lanka accord. However, the press release was conspicuous by the absence of any reference to the withdrawal of the IPKF from Sri Lanka even though the Indian Prime Minister Rajiv Gandhi had on April 25, 1989 told a high level meeting of Army Commanders in New Delhi that his government was contemplating withdrawing the bulk of Indian troops from the Island. He told the top brass of the Indian army, "India has to think seriously of getting back the bulk of the Indian peace-keeping force as soon as practicable". He added for good measure that though the IPKF had "done the nation proud...we should consider handing over control to the elected government in the North-East Province, so that they could protect themselves against any destabilization that might arise." The reference to the elected government of North-East Council for handing over control was mischievous since the IPKF were operating on agreement with the central government of the Island and not on behalf of the Provincial administration.

It was clear to India that she had lost the initiative in Colombo and was now at the receiving end. Nevertheless, New Delhi did not wish to give in so easily. It sought to remind Colombo that if the LTTE were coming forward to talk, it was the relentless pressure of the IPKF that convinced it that it had to negotiate. The question that the LTTE had to decide was whether to negotiate with New Delhi or Colombo and perhaps it had chosen in favour of the latter. It was in this context that the spokesman of the Indian Ministry of External Affairs on April 17, 1989 reminded Colombo that "the IPKF had never hindered any prospects of the LTTE and the Sri Lankan Government reaching a negotiated settlement".

The first round of talks between the LTTE and the Sri Lankan Government representatives commenced on May 4, 1989. Foreign Minister, Ranjan Wijeratne happily announced that the LTTE had assured the Government that it would not conduct any military operations while the negotiations were on. On his part Wijeratne also assured the LTTE that "as talks are going on, they will not be on the offensive" either. Taking Indian acceptance of the new development for granted, Wijeratne appreciated IPKF's cooperation in facilitating the airlift of the LTTE representatives to the talks from the jungles of the north to Colombo. He said, "We mentioned to them (the Indians) that the LTTE are responding to our peace overtures, and we would like them not to be inconvenienced". The use of the word "inconvenience" was unfortunate to say the least. IPKF was carrying on the dirty-armed campaign against the LTTE to ensure the territorial integrity of the Island nation. It was being made to lose face after sacrificing the precious lives of hundreds of her soldiers, and Colombo had no regrets. He further poured salt on the Indian wounds when he explained that contrary to what India might have to say, an eventual settlement need not be within the framework of the Indo-Sri Lanka agreement of 1987. Indicating the parameters of the talks, the Foreign Minister said the agreement arrived at with the LTTE would be within the framework of the "laws of the country, the Constitution and the approval of the people". Wijeratne conveniently forgot that the 1987 agreement was signed to uphold the inviolability of the same Constitution, which he was talking about. "We are talking to our countrymen, no one need tell us which way we should talk to our countrymen", he added. Referring to the visit of the Indian Foreign Secretary to Colombo he said that the Prime Minister of India in his message to the President had requested that they would "appreciate if they were kept informed about the developments". Condescendingly he sought to assure India "nothing will be held back. There are no secrets".

Addressing another press conference the next day May 5, 1989 Wijeratne clarifying the scope of the talks said, "our officials are meeting them to identify the issues and work out the modalities", and that "talks at the political level will commence shortly". In a series of communiqués issued by the Presidential Secretariat on the talks with the LTTE, India found herself being denigrated and ridiculed. Sri Lanka allowed the official communiqués to be used as vehicles for LTTE's indictment of the IPKF. In one of such communiqués issued from the Presidential Secretariat it was said on behalf of the LTTE that the IPKF had ceased to be a peace-keeping force and its role "today is that of an occupying army". In another Presidential communiqué of May 16, LTTE was quoted as accusing the IPKF of bringing about "untold hardship and suffering to the people of the North and the East" and virtually holding the IPKF responsible for massacring 5000 Tamil civilians. Not that the LTTE had not paid such 'compliments' to the IPKF in the past, but to have done so through the courtesy of the Presidential Secretariat was nothing short of scornful and disgusting for India.

Pitted against heavy odds, the Indian High Commission valiantly tried to rebut the unwarranted charges. On May 17, a High Commission statement noted, "that these communiqués make no reference to the circumstances in which the IPKF came to this country, the mandate the Governments of India and Sri have given to it jointly, the immense difficulties of their task and the enormous sacrifices it has been making in an attempt to preserve the unity and integrity of Sri Lanka". Regretting the contents and tenor of the Presidential communiqués the Indian High Commission said it was "our impression that the purpose of the current talks was not to provide a propaganda forum for the LTTE" but to bring "all concerned into the democratic process by giving up violence and accepting a commitment to the unity and integrity of Sri Lanka". The High Commission's regrets did not go unnoticed and the LTTE was quick to deny that it intended to use the communiqués to indict India. On May 18, the Presidential Communiqué on the talks quoting the LTTE denied that it wanted "to use this forum for purposes of propaganda or to create rift between Sri Lanka and India". It intended only to seek a negotiated political settlement at these talks. Colombo could not explain why the communiqués from the highest authority of the country instead of reflecting the tenor and trend of the talks had to carry the LTTE's point of view and what it thought of the performance of the IPKF or the role of India in the ethnic conflict. Refusing to relent in its propaganda campaign against the IPKF, the LTTE on May 20 in its own press release accused IPKF once again of intensifying its campaign of "military repression and terror" against the Tamils "in the occupied north-eastern region of the island". It blamed the IPKF's fresh campaign to the LTTE exposing "the atrocities of the occupation army" during the current peace talks.

The talks that opened on May 5, had continued till the end of the month. On May 30, the two delegations agreed that the "talks had opened the doors to greater understanding and appreciation of the issues involved and had laid a firm basis for future negotiations". It expressed the hope that the "Government would take early steps to bring peace and normalcy to the North and the East". Throughout the talks the LTTE delegation was led by its ideologue Anton Balasingham. A.C.S. Hameed, a senior Minister of Higher Education, Science and Technology and a former Foreign Minister led the Government side.

After the meeting on May 30, 1989, the two delegations met twice again on June 19 and July 2, 1989. On June 19, the LTTE spoke of the dangers to the peace process being posed by the massive conscription being carried out by the rival militant organisations like the EPRLF, ENDLF and TELO. On July 2, the LTTE sought to disabuse India of her efforts to belittle the achievements made by the two delegations during their month-long talks in May. The LTTE once again took the opportunity to commit itself to the "negotiated political settlement in the resolution of the problems facing the North and the East".

In the midst of this India-bashing by the LTTE, courtesy the Presidential Secretariat, the Indian Prime Minister sent his Principal Secretary B.G. Deshmukh to Colombo in the first week of July 1989. During his meetings with Sri Lankan leaders, questions like the IPKF's withdrawal, operations against the LTTE, the implementation of the devolution package and the assassination of the TULF leader A. Amirthalingam came up for discussion. The High Commission on July 15 described the discussions as "exploratory in nature". But from B.G. Deshmukh's own account of the meetings in his book *A Cabinet Secretary Looks Back* it was clear that the visit was a disappointing one. Deshmukh left the President in no doubt that India felt assured that the IPKF was making "good progress" and until "it had implemented the provisions of the agreement" IPKF "would not be withdrawn". Deshmukh indicated to the President that India would be ready to withdraw the IPKF "by mid- or late 1990." This was thoroughly disappointing to Premadasa who now decided to follow an aggressive approach to the de-induction question.

The death of the TULF leader Amirthalingam was a great setback to India, since he was always projected as a moderate face of Tamil aspirations and a rallying point for the bulk of the non-LTTE Tamil opinion. His funeral was attended by a large number of Indian dignitaries from India and in the process a great indiscretion was committed by many of them. Most of them except for Natwar Singh did not care to obtain a proper Sri Lankan visa and Colombo quite rightly questioned the propriety of it and described it as a violation of her sovereignty.

Following the general elections in India, the Congress Party led by Rajiv Gandhi was replaced in New Delhi by the Lok Dal government headed by Vishwanath Pratap Singh. The LTTE, which had burnt its bridges with Rajiv Gandhi government, saw this as an opportunity to mend fences with New Delhi, to avoid permanent impairment of relations. On December 4, 1989, Anton Balasingham, the second most important leader of the LTTE in reaching out to the new administration told the United News of India that the LTTE were keen to remove the "misconception" that it was hostile to New Delhi. He said that if the new administration adopted a conciliatory approach to the LTTE there was every possibility that the friendly ties between the LTTE and the Indian Government would be re-established. Balasingham sought to blame the estrangement of its past relations with New Delhi on the bureaucracy, and hoped that "the new administration would ensure that they have new people who will understand and accommodate" the LTTE's point of view. When reminded that it had been the Tigers' case till then that India should stop interfering in the island's affairs, he said:

> "This must be made clear, because there is so much misconception. The LTTE is a friendly force towards India. We have never been hostile. The LTTE objected only to the foreign policy determinations of the Rajiv Gandhi administration, particularly certain crucial provisions of the India-Sri Lanka accord and the manner in which it was implemented".

In another conciliatory move, the LTTE made a formal application for recognition as a political party amidst speculation that the Sri Lankan Government would dissolve the North-East Provincial Council. On December 10, Balasingham in an interview published in the *Sunday Observer* said the LTTE "will not go against the cordial relationship between India and Sri Lanka". He said, "we will not be an obstacle to those two countries strengthening their relationship." Addressing himself to New Delhi, he said "we did not want Indian military interference in the ethnic problem of our country. And at the same time we request the new Indian Government to adopt a fresh foreign policy orientation towards Sri Lanka taking into consideration the interests and aspirations of the Tamils and Muslim citizens of this country." He confirmed LTTE's application for being recognised as a political party to the Election Commission and said, "within a few days the new party would be announced."

As pointed out above, the preliminary round of discussions between Sri Lankan Government and the LTTE had concluded in May. To set the agenda for a substantive round of talks, the President was keen to evolve a national consensus and had asked the various political parties and interest groups to make their suggestions, which were discussed at an All-party Conference on September 13, 1989. The President informed the Conference that a national consensus had emerged with regard to the following issues:

" *Bringing to the mainstream of politics those forces that are today outside the democratic process;
* Preventing violence;
* Restructuring peace and normalcy;
* Restructuring the political, economic and administrative systems;
* Ensuring equal rights for all people, regardless of considerations of creed or community; and
* Eliminating the socio-economic disparities that still remain in the country."

These were unexceptional principles to which no one could take umbrage and yet they lacked in specifics capable of providing a solution to the ethnic problem. The President therefore, asked the parties to come forward with specific suggestions. On September 18, 1989 when the President reported on the Conference to the parliamentary party of the UNP, he expressed his readiness for new solutions and a change to secure peace for which "we must be prepared to make any sacrifice". In the next few days the President remained busy meeting with the representatives of the various political parties and discussing with them their suggestions to usher in peace.

<22>

Deinduction of the Indian Peace Keeping Force

Before the year 1988 ended, it was clear to everybody that the IPKF operations had got bogged down. The Indian policy in Sri Lanka came under fire in the Indian Parliament and provoked denunciation in Tamil Nadu. It too had become apparent in India and Sri Lanka that the ethnic conflict had no easy and early solution. Correspondingly, the disenchantment of Sri Lanka became more and more cacophonous with the presence of IPKF. The question of ending the IPKF mission engaged the attention of both the people and Government of Sri Lanka. The Government of India was peeved that the IPKF should suffer the opprobrium of having to withdraw without accomplishing its allotted task. Whenever the question of withdrawal was raised in public, India looked for cover or hedged her position on the issue with unconvincing and shifting arguments. The Indo-Sri Lanka agreement, which mandated the induction of the IPKF, did not envisage a situation where the deployment would become a prolonged necessity and demand for its withdrawal an embarrassment. India had agreed to the IPKF deployment essentially to make the surrender of arms palatable to the LTTE, since surrendering them to Sri Lanka army would have appeared a surrender of a vanquished to the victorious. It was also intended to be a guarantee to the beleaguered and doubting Jayewardene that India meant business. The turn in the fortunes of the IPKF created an irritation, which no one had bargained for. Since India and the new administration of Premadasa looked at the problem from different spectrums, clash of perceptions was perhaps inevitable and unavoidable.

It was on November 1, 1987, that probably for the first time in a BBC interview Rajiv Gandhi was asked if there was any timetable for a withdrawal. He was stumped by the question. He did not expect, so soon after the induction of the IPKF, a question on its withdrawal. Caught off-guard, he naturally had no categorical answer and said, "This is really up to President Jayewardene. It will partly depend on the law and order situation as it develops and what forces he has under his command." Discounting the danger of getting bogged down, Gandhi said that he and President Jayewardene were aware of that and therefore "this should be a short, sharp exercise and our boys should be back soon."

On December 7, 1987 in a UNI dispatch from Cairo, Sri Lankan newspapers quoted Rajiv Gandhi telling the Egyptian newspaper, *Al Gumihryia,* that the withdrawal of the Indian army from the Island depended on President Jayewardene's wishes and the return of normalcy. These responses convinced everybody that there existed no agreed timeframe for the IPKF's withdrawal and if India chose she could prolong her stay on the Island as long as she wished. There was no compatibility between the wishes of the President and the "return of normalcy". There was a storm in the Sri Lankan parliament when on December 8, 1987 Leader of the opposition in parliament, Anura Bandaranaike drew the attention of the House to the statement of General Harkirat Singh, General-Officer-Commanding the Indian forces in Sri Lanka that the IPKF would "not go from Sri Lanka until the Tamils are satisfied and their aspirations are met". The General too had added for good measure that the IPKF took orders from nobody except from the Government of India.

Obviously, there was a communication gap between New Delhi and its commanders in the field. Gen. Harkirat Singh's statement was indiscreet albeit a ground reality. For cosmetic reasons, this policy was unsustainable in public and caused acute embarrassment to Colombo. To ward off the opposition offensive, Colombo took refuge under Rajiv Gandhi's observations to *Al Gumihryia* and told the House on December 10, 1987,

> "The IPKF is in Sri Lanka at the invitation of the Government of Sri Lanka. The IPKF must necessarily operate in Sri Lanka under the over-all direction of the President, who is Commander-in-Chief. They will leave Sri Lanka when the President requests them to do so."

In January 1988, the President of Sri Lanka was Chief Guest at the Republic Day celebrations in New Delhi. His presence in Delhi provided an opportunity for a detailed discussion on the implementation of the Indo-Sri Lanka agreement. A spokesman of the Indian Ministry of External Affairs said in New Delhi that both sides had agreed that there should be an early creation of conditions for the return of the refugees to their home in Sri Lanka and necessary modalities for this were agreed upon. However, the spokesman in responding to a query declined to comment on the likely duration of the stay of the IPKF in the Island. As violence escalated and the IPKF found itself hamstrung in disarming the LTTE, the question of its withdrawal came frequently under spotlight. On March 16, 1988 replying to a question in the Lok Sabha on the apprehensions expressed in Sri Lankan Parliament on the likely stay of the IPKF in the Island, Minister of State in the Ministry of External Affairs Natwar Singh said:

> "The IPKF has gone to Sri Lanka at the request of the Government of that country to implement the Indo-Sri Lanka agreement and ensure the security and safety of all communities living in the Northern and the Eastern Provinces of Sri Lanka. The question of the duration of the IPKF's stay in Sri Lanka will have to be decided in that context. There is no question of the IPKF staying in Sri Lanka permanently."

Two days later on March 18, Natwar Singh making a statement in the Rajya Sabha said that the IPKF "do not want to stay there a day extra" than necessary to restore peace and tranquillity in the Island. On March 27, in an interview to the Colombo daily *Lankadipa*, High Commissioner Dixit asserted, "one thing we must bear in mind here is that Indian forces are here on the request of the Sri Lankan President. It is not because we want to be here. As soon as its tasks under the agreement are completed, they will go back."

These were disquieting statements since they left open the possibility of indefinite stay of the IPKF in the Island. What were the aspirations of the Tamils? When they were deemed met? What was the measure of President's satisfaction or when the tasks allotted to the IPKF were completed, or for that matter when the ethnic peace was restored, were all subject to varying interpretations to suit the convenience and agenda of each party. These were the questions, which did not lend to unanimity of views. If on the other hand had there been tangible progress in disarming the LTTE, or signs of peace visible on the horizon, the stay of the IPKF, if not welcome at least would not have been irritating. This was not to be. As the IPKF failed to disarm the LTTE and its operations got bogged down thus opening up the possibility of its prolonged stay, the demand for its withdrawal became loud. To keep the domestic critics appeased, Colombo felt it necessary to keep on broaching the issue of the IPKF withdrawal with New Delhi on all possible occasions. In May 1988, when the Minister of Lands Gamini Dissanayake visited New Delhi, he did not fail to take up the issue of withdrawal with the Indian leaders. On return home, he told the daily *Observer* on May 14,

> "...we discussed the issue and as earlier indicated by the Sri Lanka Government it was reiterated that the Sri Lanka Government will decide when they (IPKF) will leave after normalcy in the two provinces is established.
>
> "As before Mr. Gandhi mentioned to me again that the IPKF will leave whenever President Jayewardene requested them to do so, and our President feels that their presence was no longer necessary."

On May 28, two days before the arrival of the Indian Defence Minister Krishna Chandra Pant in Colombo, Sri Lankan Home Minister K.W. Devanayagam in a letter to him, came out with the worst denunciation of the IPKF and its failure to carry out the assigned task despite its sacrifices. He cast doubts on its ability to combat terrorism and in fact went on to quote public perception that it was even in collusion with some of militant organizations, which were responsible for the killing of innocent Muslims and Sinhalese in the Eastern Province while the IPKF looked the other way. In short he said:

"The IPKF and its presence are agitating the minds of many people in this country. I have reports to support the contention...in short the highlighting of the absence of information of the IPKF activities leads the public to believe that it is not likely to help combat terrorism."

Two days later, May 30, 1988, Indian Defence Minister Pant landed in Colombo. Inevitably the role of the IPKF came under the scanner. Both sides paid tribute to it for its role in the "preservation and consolidation of the territorial integrity of Sri Lanka in the face of violent separatist actions". Despite some stray voices, New Delhi apparently succeeded in convincing Sri Lanka on the need for IPKF's continued presence. Despite public appreciation of the role of the IPKF, the Government of India came under heavy pressure from Colombo for its withdrawal. The joint communiqué issued at the end of the Defence Minister's visit said:

"As the situation in the Northern and the Eastern Provinces continues to improve, the IPKF force levels will be reviewed, depending on operational requirements and the situation on the ground. In view of the encouraging situation in the North and the East, the Indian side conveyed that forces not required would return to India in the near future. The two sides agreed to consult each other from time to time in this regard."

Within days, on June 7, 1988 India announced the withdrawal of a contingent of the IPKF, which it was stated was not required "operationally". It was made out to be "part of the on-going process of constant reappraisal of operational requirements to implement the Indo-Sri Lanka accord." Sri Lanka media described the withdrawal as Phase-I of the pull-out of the IPKF. A day earlier on June 6, High Commissioner Dixit told a press conference in Colombo that the pull-out would reduce the number of the Indian forces in Sri Lanka. Since July last year there was a steady build-up of the Indian troops in the Island. It started with 6,000 and had escalated to around 52,000. "From now the strength will come down", Dixit said. He rejected any suggestion that the strength of the Indian force in Sri Lanka exceeded beyond this figure at any time and added hopefully, "the troops pull-out is the beginning of the end of the suspicion of Indian intentions".

Paying tribute to the IPKF, President Jayewardene acknowledged to the UNP Parliamentary group (June 6) the services rendered by the peace force in fighting to preserve the country's unity and independence. It was a left-handed compliment when he said that owing to the presence of the IPKF in Sri Lanka the lives of a large number of Lankan servicemen, who would otherwise have been killed in combat, had been saved, while many members of the IPKF had been killed and wounded. Loss of Indian lives was apparently of no consequence to the President! On June 8, Lalith Athulathmudali, the Minister for National Security and Deputy Minister of Defence confirming the withdrawal to Parliament, left no one in doubt that it was taking place because of the insistence of Colombo during the visit of the Indian Defence Minister. His announcement was quite embarrassing to the Government of India. He said, "there is a requirement for the Indian troops to return to India when their task of disarming the LTTE is over and conditions in the North and the East return to normalcy". He went on to add that such a review took place during the visit of the Indian Defence Minister and hence the reduction in the strength of the Indian military. It was obvious to everybody that neither of the two pre-conditions precedent to the troops withdrawal articulated earlier had been met and yet India was made to withdraw! Rubbing salt, the LTTE told the *Hindu* on July 29 that none of the expectations raised by the agreement had been fulfilled, and the accord had failed to "safeguard the interests and aspirations of the Tamils." The JVP, on the other hand, in reflecting on the accord, said that India attempted to set up an independent Eelam state in "a third of the Sri Lankan territory in the North and the East now occupied by the Indian aggressive forces."

Prime Minister Rajiv Gandhi whose prestige was at stake, to save his face, was understandably repeating ad nauseam that the withdrawal was as a result of better situation prevailing in the Island. When H.K.Dua of the *Hindustan Times* (23 July 1988) asked him about the pull back of Indian troops from Sri Lanka, Gandhi said:

> "The IPKF is in Sri Lanka at the request of President Jayewardene as an instrument of implementing the Indo-Sri Lanka agreement. Its presence is also necessary to ensure the safety and security of all the communities in

Sri Lanka. The presence of IPKF and its possible withdrawal should be seen in this perspective. However, as the situation continues to improve, the IPKF levels will be reviewed and whatever troops are not operationally required, will be brought back."

The deployment of the IPKF again came under scrutiny in the Rajya Sabha on August 29, 1988. The BJP stalwart and expert on defence affairs, Jaswant Singh expressed his party's annoyance at the situation. He was at pains to suggest that by this "not only are India's security interests not being sub-served, in fact they are being harmed". He charged that there was no "recognizable or intelligible purpose behind the involvement of the IPKF in Sri Lanka and there is no attainable military aim." He went on to say that no country had ever benefited from a long war which is what we are ending up by going in Sri Lanka". The India's bugbear, Ranasinghe Premadasa, never one to let any opportunity slip to damn India for her role in the Island's ethnic problem, told the Sri Lankan community in Hong Kong (his remarks were carried by the official *Daily News* on September 28, 1988) that while the IPKF came to Sri Lanka at the invitation of the President of Sri Lanka, India had confirmed that "the IPKF will leave any time our President wanted." He reiterated that their presence was "to fulfill the obligations on the part of India to restore normalcy in the North and the East." Setting a time-frame for the withdrawal, he said, "I am told they will be here only till such time the Provincial Council Elections for the Northern and Eastern Provinces are conducted for which nominations have been already called." This observation of the Prime Minister became an important element since soon he was expected to replace the incumbent President following the elections to the Presidency. And sure enough he succeeded Jayewardene.

In the Presidential election-manifesto, the UNP had made withdrawal of the IPKF as an important item on its agenda. The UNP's nominee for the high office, Ranasinghe Premadasa in his election campaign pledged that on being elected he would take necessary steps to see that the IPKF was withdrawn immediately from the Island. A few days before Jayewardene was to demit office, Rajiv Gandhi and Jayewardene met in Islamabad for the

South Asian Association for Regional Cooperation Summit (December 1988). By now it was apparent to everyone that with the election of Premadasa to the Presidency, pressure would mount on India for the withdrawal of the IPKF. India could hardly have been oblivious of the imperatives of the real politics. If Rajiv Gandhi was looking for a face saver from the outgoing President, it was not there. Jayewardene and Premadasa had an uneasy existence since the July 1987 agreement. Premadasa feeling suffocated under its shame had no chance of softening. Jayewardene was not unaware of it. He therefore did not feel encouraged to intercede with him to save Rajiv Gandhi's face. In Islamabad, Rajiv Gandhi drew blank. Taking discretion the better part of valour, New Delhi sought to make peace with the ground realities. A statement issued by the Government of India on January 1, 1989 in New Delhi (after the return of Gandhi to New Delhi from Islamabad) made a promise to further reduce the IPKF presence in Sri Lanka. It said:

> "As the situation in the Northeastern Province improves further; as the devolution of powers becomes effective; as the Indo-Sri Lanka agreement gets progressively implemented and as the mischief making potential of extremist elements opposed to the agreement is reduced, Government is hopeful of making further withdrawals in consultation with the Sri Lanka government."

As pointed out above, with the emergence of Premadasa on the scene, with his commitment to throw the IPKF out at the earliest, the interests of the LTTE and the new administration in Colombo converged on the question of the IPKF withdrawal. Both had seen the IPKF as an occupation force. The LTTE particularly, had perceived the IPKF role as adversarial. It was clear to the LTTE that its ambition of Eelam could only be achieved if it succeeded in throwing out the IPKF. As long as Jayewardene occupied the Presidency, he had no choice but to remain steadfast to the role of the IPKF. Premadasa had no such commitment. He was keen that he redeemed his election promise of throwing the IPKF out of the Island at the earliest. He was not unaware that one of the conditions precedent to withdrawal articulated by India at the highest level was the restoration of normalcy in the North-Eastern Province, which was far from achieved. He therefore surmised that unless the

LTTE played ball, there was no chance of claiming normalcy even remotely. India was bound to drag her feet as otherwise her credibility in the eyes of other countries in South Asia would stand miserably eroded. She would not, in future be able to play her role of a regional super-power. Foreign Minister Wijeratne could discern a tone of desperation through the LTTE's messages, April 3 and 11, chose to respond by inviting it to come to the negotiating table-suggesting to it "when a nation in wrecked by internal conflict, only outsiders will reap the benefits." New Delhi watching the poker game from the sidelines felt but isolated and helpless to influence the events in any manner. It was no longer calling the shots as during Jayewardene's Presidency. That privilege had passed on to the LTTE for a change and India felt belittled.

It was not the LTTE alone that was spoiling the party for New Delhi. The JVP too smelt an opportunity to spite India and take its revenge for its imprudence to help Colombo in 1971 in putting down its insurrection. When there was no visible sign of Indian troops reduction after the initial withdrawal, the JVP upped the ante for Premadasa and called upon the people to drive the IPKF out of the Island. Playing it cool, the Government reminded the people that it was itself quite keen on the early withdrawal of the IPKF.

In a surprise move, on June 1, 1989 the President in a public declaration and that too on the holy occasion of the pinnacle unveiling ceremony at Chittavivekashramaya Temple in Wickremasinghapura, Battaramulla called upon India to withdraw her troops from the Island by the end of the very next month, "July, 1989". He said "having a foreign force in an independent country is a slur on its self-respect; it devalues the freedom of the country". A force that had sub-served Colombo's interest for over two years suddenly became a "slur on its self-respect". He reminded India that Prime Minister Rajiv Gandhi had already said "they will be pulling out the peace keeping force from Sri Lanka" any time the President wanted. Referring to the peace talks with the LTTE, the President asserted there was now no rationale for the continued presence of the IPKF in Sri Lanka. Besides, he said Sri Lanka expected to host the postponed SAARC Summit Conference in that year. He lamented that Sri Lanka could not do so with "self-respect", if "a foreign army is operating in the country". Since the IPKF would be marking its two-year presence in Sri Lanka at the end of July, it was imperative that the "IPKF troops leave Lanka by the end of July", he demanded. The President added if it was a great help to have received the IPKF at the request of the former President, "recalling the Peace Keeping Force back to India will also help us greatly at this moment".

In order not to give any excuse to the IPKF to prolong its presence in the Island, the President appealed to the people "to act with patience and desist from violence during these two months". To inject urgency to his demand for de-induction, on the very next day, June 2, Premadasa not only reiterated it but also repeated the reasons for the same in a formal letter to the Prime Minister of India. To mount further pressure on New Delhi, he informed Gandhi that he was deputing his Foreign Secretary to the Indian capital to complete the formality of consultations and explain the rationale of his decision. He indicated that future relations between the two countries be based on a treaty for which he said, "we have submitted several proposals". Without further ado, Wijeratne landed in New Delhi.

New Delhi was incensed. An official spokesman on June 2, reminded Colombo that New Delhi had for some time on its own, initiated the process of withdrawal of the IPKF depending on certain parameters, and therefore, the government was "puzzled" at the proposal of the President at this stage. Infuriated New Delhi told Sri Lanka loud and clear how inept it was to conduct diplomatic relations on such a delicate matter in this unilateral and highly embarrassing manner! To convey its irritation the Indian High Commission in a press release issued to coincide with Wijeratne's return to the capital Colombo from New Delhi said that India could not be pushed like this. To underline the message that there was a synergy between the IPKF withdrawal and the implementation of the agreement, the Indian High Commission on June 7, said:

> "On the question of withdrawal of the IPKF, India has repeatedly reiterated its desire to withdraw the IPKF at an early date. It was agreed that consultations would continue so that conditions can be created as envisaged in the Indo-Sri Lanka agreement to facilitate IPKF withdrawal."

That President Premadasa had failed to evolve a national consensus on the withdrawal question was clear like daylight. Within the country doubts were expressed on the wisdom of his action. On June 7, the Communist Party listed several steps, like security of the Tamils, devolution of powers etc., which needed to be ensured before the IPKF departed. The next day EROS said that troops withdrawal should be dependent on security of the Tamils. The SLFP endorsing the withdrawal request in Parliament on June 9, expressed serious doubts whether in the event of the IPKF withdrawing, Sri Lankan security forces were equipped enough to handle the insurgency in the North and the East. The Government appeared least bothered about the price of withdrawal. It just wanted to see the back of the IPKF.

In the acrimonious correspondence that ensued between the two Governments at the highest level each side tried to outwit the other. On June 2, the spokesman of the Indian Ministry of External Affairs said India was puzzled by the request. Rajiv Gandhi in his response of June 20, reminded the President of the circumstances under which the IPKF was sent and said "this was the time when the situation seemed headed inexorably towards the break up of Sri Lanka". The Indian Prime Minister insisted on linking the withdrawal to the progress achieved in the implementation of the agreement. He said that India had already taken the initiative to pull back the IPKF in stages to coincide with the implementation of the agreement leading to the devolution of powers to the Provincial Councils. He unsuccessfully tried to convince the President of the need to "jointly draw up a mutually agreed schedule for the full implementation of the Indo-Sri Lanka agreement and the complete withdrawal of the IPKF". His insistence that the two had "to be joint, parallel exercises" found no echo in Colombo. In talking to N. Ram of the *Hindu* on June 5, Premadasa justified his request because of threats from the JVP and his commitment to the electorate. New Delhi remained unconvinced. It was therefore no surprise that Sri Lankan Foreign Secretary during his visit to New Delhi failed to convince India of the need for early withdrawal.

As a measure of additional pressure, the parliamentary group of the UNP adopted a resolution reinforcing the Presidential request. On June 15, the Ministry of Foreign Affairs in a statement restated the President's demand. The LTTE too chipped in with its own endorsement. To crown all these efforts, the President on June 16, issued a special message to the people of Sri Lanka dilating at length on his theme of the IPKF withdrawal, and said "the IPKF should be withdrawn from our country as quickly as possible. There is no argument about that" since he believed the IPKF had not only failed to restore peace in the North and the East but this failure had also resulted "in peace being disturbed in other parts of the country".

India anxious not to appear to be dragging her feet, refused to be pushed around. She felt peeved that there was no prior consultation and the manner of the call was humiliating both to India and the IPKF. India regretted the precipitate and unilateral demand for withdrawal, despite IPKF contributing towards implementation of the agreement and in the peaceful conduct of successive elections, "threats of terrorist violence in the Northeast" notwithstanding. If it had not been possible to achieve total peace, Rajiv Gandhi placed the blame on the doors of Colombo and said, "All the Tamil groups, barring one, had given up the demand for Eelam". Rajiv was certainly not so naive as not to understand that it was the obstinacy of that one group, which mattered the most and was holding the agreement to ransom. He did not wish to yield any ground to Premadasa so easily. He added, "If the process of devolution of powers to the Provincial Councils had been implemented in time and had the deliberate attempt by the Sri Lankan Government to alter the population balance in the Tamil areas by the continued state-sponsored colonization to Tamil areas been stopped, the extremists would have been further isolated and marginalized and the violence ended".

Not one to give up so easily, Premadasa returned the charge of the Indian Prime Minister in his letter of June 30, 1989 insisting that Sri Lanka had faithfully implemented her obligations. As a proof of Colombo's sincerity he pointed out that the proposals "for a political settlement of the ethnic problem negotiated from 4-5-1986 to 19-12-1986, as well as the residual matters to be finalised between the Government of Sri Lanka and the Government of India have all been accepted and incorporated in the relevant amendments to our Constitution and the Provincial Councils Act". Squarely blaming the IPKF for the delay "in giving effect to certain proposals within the timeframe envisaged by the agreement", he maintained this "had been occasioned by the inability of the Indian Armed Forces to ensure a cessation of hostilities and violence in the North and the East."

Both Premadasa and the LTTE sought to cut the ground from underneath the feet of India on the question of restoration of peace in the North-East. On June 28, 1989 Premadasa pointed out to Gandhi that since the LTTE had "announced complete cessation of hostilities against the Sri Lanka Government with immediate effect", therefore India must "ensure that the IPKF does not take any offensive action against the LTTE which will tend to prejudice the negotiations that are currently in progress". The message had unfortunate ring around it. Sri Lanka now wished to convey that with the LTTE's fresh commitment to talks and therefore to peace, the pre-condition for Indian withdrawal had been met, and there could be no further excuse for IPKF's continuance in Sri Lanka. On top of it, the adoption of the 13th Amendment and the Provincial Councils Act all relevant matters concerning the ethnic problem and negotiated between the two Governments in the 1987 accord stood implemented. The beleaguered Rajiv Gandhi was not prepared to relent so easily. The structure of peace, which he had so assiduously and enthusiastically built and had called it the "peace of the century", lay in ruins. Though embarrassed, he sought to belittle the claim of Premadasa stating that there was nothing new in the LTTE announcement regarding "cessation of hostilities" as the same had already been achieved two years ago. On June 30, replying to Premadasa, he put it thus:

> "The Indo-Sri Lanka agreement provides for a cessation of hostilities between the Tamil militant groups and the Sri Lankan Forces, and also for the Sri Lankan Forces to stay in barracks in the North East Province. Both these were achieved on July 30, 1987. Thus there has already been an effective cessation of hostilities between the Sri Lankan Forces and the LTTE. I am glad that the LTTE has now formally conceded this reality."

The President was incensed. He saw in India's response an attempt at procrastination, an effort to prolong Indian presence on the Island. He reminded Gandhi (July 4, 1989) that his claim that the cessation of hostilities had been reached in July 1987, was spurious since that "cessation" was a short-lived phenomenon. Injecting further animosity, he warned Rajiv Gandhi that seeking a mandatory role for the IPKF by his own interpretation of the agreement and insisting on its continued stay in Sri Lanka "would constitute a serious interference in the internal affairs of a friendly sovereign country and a gross violation of the peremptory norms of international law".

Rajiv Gandhi who had staked his personal prestige on the 1987 accord found himself at his wits end. He decided to send his Special Envoy B.G. Deshmukh, the Cabinet Secretary with his letter of July 11, 1989 proposing "joint consultations" for the withdrawal of the IPKF with a "simultaneous schedule for the implementation of the Indo-Sri Lanka agreement", failing which India would "have to decide the details of IPKF's withdrawal unilaterally consistent with our responsibilities and obligations under the Indo-Sri Lanka agreement".

Premadasa set out four premises to Deshmukh, which he formally repeated to Rajiv Gandhi in his reply of July 12, and they were briefly (1) the IPKF came to Sri Lanka at the request of the President of Sri Lanka and was under his command; (2) the accord was strictly a bilateral agreement; (3) presence of the IPKF and devolution of powers to the Provincial Councils were not inter-related, the latter being an internal matter falling under the sovereign jurisdiction of Sri Lanka and "any military force to ensure the process of devolution is complete" had no legal sanctity; and (4) India had failed to stay by the agreement since contrary to the obligation enjoined upon India not to permit the use of her territory for activities prejudicial to the interest of Sri Lanka, there were Tamil elements campaigning for Eelam being tolerated in India. Besides, he was insistent that the IPKF had failed to deliver both in respect of cessation of hostilities and surrender of arms by the LTTE within the timeframe envisaged in the agreement. It was unfortunate that a force, which came to restore peace, got entangled in armed conflict, Premadasa averred. To India's dismay, Premadasa described the IPKF stay as "prejudicial to a political settlement with the LTTE" and charged that government's failure to evict the LTTE was abetting "certain groups in other parts of the country" to indulge in violent activity. In another letter a week later (July 19), Premadasa described as "unlawful taking of civilians lives" by the IPKF since they have "publicly announced a cessation of hostilities" against the government. Premadasa had already put his demand for deinduction of the IPKF non-negotiable asserting "the only condition that should be satisfied for the withdrawal of the Indian Armed Forces is a decision by the President of Sri Lanka that they should be withdrawn".

The protracted correspondence took the two leaders nowhere. It was a dialogue of the deaf. Both stressed their respective points of view without regard to the other's sensitivities and previous commitments contained in sacred agreements arrived at between governments. But one flaw stood out conspicuously. The circumstances in which the agreement was negotiated had left much to be desired. It was discussed behind closed doors under the threat of a big power to the smaller one to fall in line at the pain of facing consequences, which did not exclude military intervention of the regional super-power. To that extent it was not an agreement between two equal powers freely arrived at. If Sri Lanka had no alternative then but to accept the diktat of the bigger power, now the smaller power in order to push through with its wishes sought to embarrass the bigger power which was caught trapped in the jungles of Sri Lanka redeeming its unredeemable pledge to disarm a formidable guerrilla force. Rajiv was not unaware that the agreement was signed behind the back of Premadasa who did not feel obliged to stand committed to it. Finally, Premadasa threatened that "I as President of an independent sovereign Republic would have no option but to treat the agreement as being inimical to Sri Lanka's sovereignty and national interest" if in the opinion of the Indian Prime Minister "the agreement should be construed as creating an obligation for the Indian Armed Forces to remain in Sri Lankan territory without the concurrence and against the express wishes of the Sri Lanka Government".

While this lengthy correspondence was being exchanged, the ground situation refused to change to India's advantage either. Then the worst happened. The intelligence sources of the IPKF stumbled against some astounding information. In raids on the hideouts of the LTTE, the IPKF discovered arms and equipment that Sri Lankan army had supplied to the militants under the specific orders of the President. Premadasa had moved to strengthen the LTTE to enable it to give the IPKF a good drubbing, make it realize that it stood no chance of defeating it, demoralize it completely and then throw it out. In humiliating the IPKF, the President wished to avenge his personal discomfort that he had to suffer when Jayewardene inducted it against his wishes.

India had to suffer another embarrassment when its staunch supporter, the TULF leader, Amirthalingam, was bumped off by the LTTE. He too had opposed the withdrawal of the IPKF since it played an important role in ensuring the safety and security of the Tamils. In an interview given to the Kochi-based weekly the *Week* of June 18, 1989, TULF leader had pleaded "if IPKF has to go, then first train a provincial force and arm it" and advocated its stay "for another year at least". This too went against the grain of the LTTE. It eliminated Amirthalingam not long thereafter on July 13, 1989.

In the face of such a truculent and trenchant attitude of Premadasa, Rajiv Gandhi saw no point in carrying on the correspondence any further. The stridency and raucousness in the President's approach emboldened the LTTE to have a swipe at the IPKF. It had the audacity to offer a cease-fire to the IPKF "provided there was a definite timeframe for their withdrawal." Queering the pitch for the IPKF, the President warned that if it failed to withdraw by July 29, it would be confined to the barracks. To mount international pressure on India, Colombo decided not to attend the SAARC Foreign Ministers' Conference in Islamabad in July 1989, and warned that it would be constrained not to host the SAARC Summit in Colombo later that year if the IPKF failed to leave the shores of the Island.

While India was officially persisting with the IPKF, on the ground nothing seemed going right for her despite "losing a large number of army personnel" and "spending huge amounts as well", as the Cabinet Secretary T.R Seshan told D.R. Kaarthikeyan, an IPS police officer (then posted as Inspector General of the Southern Sector of the Border Security Force) in June 1989. He asked him to make an on the spot assessment of the situation in Sri Lanka. After a fortnight visit to the Island where Kaarthikeyan met everyone and anyone who mattered, his assessment was in favour of talking to the LTTE and withdrawal of the IPKF. At a meeting convened by the Cabinet Secretary in New Delhi to discuss his report there was some reluctance to agree with him. He persisted with his advice and told the high level meeting:

> "I am talking about the ground reality. The fact is that they (LTTE) are popular with the people and they control the area. The EPRLF group of Chief Minister Varadaraja Perumal is loyal to India, but lacks both popularity and strength on the ground. The morale of the IPKF is low. Even some senior army officers told me that they are not able to boost the morale of the ranks, as they themselves do not know why the IPKF is there and why the Indian armed forces should fight a war against the people of Indian origin and kill them and get killed by them. Many of the junior officers and other ranks were of the view that we should leave the issues to be sorted out between the Sri Lankan Tamils and the Sinhalese. So my recommendation is we withdraw the IPKF forthwith, leaving the matter to be sorted out between the Sri Lankan Tamils and the Sri Lankan government. If for any other strategic reason India should continue to get involved in Sri Lankan affairs, then the only option available is to talk to the LTTE. If we do not want to talk to the LTTE, then we should withdraw the forces immediately." (Triumph of Truth—The Rajiv Gandhi Assassination: The Investigation: D.R. Kaarthikeyan and Radhavinod Raju; New Dawn Press: 2004, p.194)

Unfortunately, New Delhi was bitten by the distrust of the LTTE. Kaarthikeyan's recommendations went against the grain of the New Delhi's Sri Lanka policy. His advice was like a cry in the wilderness and the whole exercise proved abortive.

So far as Colombo was concerned, India found herself rushed off her feet. The President unmindful of the consequences of his action appeared bent upon taking on the elephant, which he rightly perceived had been incapacitated to hit back. To save the situation, the High Commissioner Mehrotra had a 50-minute stormy meeting with Premadasa in his effort to wean him away from the brink and respect the sensitivities of India. He assured him of Indian withdrawal but under a negotiated schedule to give it the veneer of respectability. Premadasa could detect a veiled threat in the advice of the High Commissioner, and decided to be a little more discreet. His willingness to sit down with the High Commissioner to negotiate the broad perimeters of the withdrawal defused the situation substantially. The mortified Premadasa too signalled his agreement to send his Foreign Minister to New Delhi to discuss the details of withdrawal.

On July 28, 1989, the two countries formally announced that on the request of Sri Lanka, India would recommence the withdrawal of the IPKF with immediate effect from July 29, 1989 a deadline set by Premadasa for complete withdrawal of the IPKF. The Foreign Minister of Sri Lanka was invited to New Delhi to "discuss the time schedule for the withdrawal of the remaining IPKF contingent in Sri Lanka". Though the President failed to get the complete IPKF withdrawn by the date set by him, at least he succeeded in enforcing a partial withdrawal and speeding up the withdrawal process. A triumphant and jubilant President announced, "all communities in Sri Lanka, the Sinhalese, Tamils, Muslims and Burghers as well as the world community who value the independence of our country will be quite overjoyed and relieved".

The SLFP welcomed the agreement and felt "relieved that a major confrontation with India has been averted at the last moment". Further negotiations led to another agreement on September 18, 1989 setting up a Peace Committee "to afford an opportunity to all political and ethnic groups in the North-East Province to come together to settle their differences through a process of consultation, compromise and consensus and to bring all groups into the democratic process, thereby ending violence and improving conditions for the physical safety and security of all communities". A Security Coordination Group was set up to ensure that there was no adverse impact on the law and order situation during the phased deinduction of the IPKF. The Government of India announced its intention to accelerate the process to complete the deinduction by December 31, 1989.

At the end of 1989, there was a change of government in New Delhi. Vishwanath Pratap Singh at the head of a coalition government replaced Rajiv Gandhi's Congress Government. By now the deinduction had not progressed to a level that it created confidence in Colombo. The President was more than troubled that the deinduction would not be completed by December 31, as originally committed by New Delhi. Hardly had the new Prime Minister taken office, than the Minister of Foreign Affairs, Wijeratne, appeared in New Delhi at the head of a high-powered delegation with a message from the President for the new Prime Minister. He conveyed to him the importance Colombo "attached to the early de-induction of the IPKF and also some other concerns relating to recent developments in the North-eastern Province of Sri Lanka". Unfortunately for Wijeratne there was disappointment in store, since he could not get any firm assurance from the new administration that the de-induction would by completed by the end of the year, which was hardly three weeks away. On the other hand, he was told that:

> "... a response would be conveyed to the Sri Lankan Government after a full examination of all issues involved especially the safety and security of all communities in the North-eastern Province of Sri Lanka. The whole spirit should be one of trust and cooperation and a joint endeavour for the mutual fulfillment of obligations assumed by both governments."

On December 18, 1989 the Indian High Commissioner, Lakhan Lal Mehrotra briefing journalists said:

> "IPKF will be withdrawn by the end of December from the Central Sector including Mullaitivu, Vavuniya and Killinochchi but no dates have been fixed for the withdrawal of the IPKF from the rest of the area. Prime Minister has said that he would like the schedule of withdrawal to be jointly worked out by India and Sri Lanka."

An embarrassed Wijeratne told journalists "we did not expect a firm commitment so soon from the new government", but remained optimistic that the withdrawal would be completed by the contemplated date. When asked by journalists whether it was logistically possible for the IPKF to pull out two and a half divisions within a matter of 23 days, he said, "where there is will, there is a way". In view of what the Indian High Commissioner told the journalists of the discussions in New Delhi, Wijeratne was obviously being needlessly optimistic.

Wijeratne was feeling frustrated. He betrayed it by refusing to meet the Indian High Commissioner to re-draw a schedule for the deinduction. He told journalists on December 21, he had requested the High Commissioner to "put down in writing if he had anything to say and if at all there is to be any discussion, it would be only with the Indian Prime Minister or the Foreign Minister". He blamed the Indian bureaucracy for muddling up the withdrawal programme. In a defiant mood, he charged the IPKF trying to leave behind a puppet army, the Tamil National Army (TNA), which was being trained and armed by it. To up the ante for Sri Lanka on the question of TNA, LTTE leader, Anton Balasingham, warned Colombo that unless TNA was disbanded, the LTTE would not disarm. In the LTTE style, he wished to reassure the President of the LTTE's commitment to "multi-party polity" once the IPKF left and the "proxy army called the TNA" was neutralized. Assuring LTTE's desire to "work out a security arrangement with the Sri Lanka government whereby their armed cadres can be absorbed in a legal manner" a promise was held out that "after becoming a political party" the Tigers would "give up their demand for Eelam."

India's failure to complete the withdrawal by December 31, 1989 was irritating Colombo. Colombo was indignant when India set the new date of March 31, 1990 to complete the de-induction. Foreign Minister Wijeratne once again dashed off to New Delhi in an attempt to persuade India to complete the process earlier than March 31 and if possible by January 31, 1990, a few days before the anniversary of Sri Lanka's independence, February 4. Before leaving for New Delhi, he told journalists on January 4, that the proposed date of March 31 was unacceptable to Colombo. He recalled to the Indian leaders the promise made by the previous Prime Minister and insisted that India honoured it. He was not amused when told that Gandhi had "not considered the logistical problem". On return from New Delhi, Wijeratne said nothing officially. Enough information was leaked out to assure the people in Sri Lanka that the Foreign Minister's trip was after all not completely unproductive. An AFP report from New Delhi said that Wijeratne left the Indian capital after two days' of talks, which included a 45-minute meeting with the Prime Minister on a hopeful note reassured with India's commitment to an early troops withdrawal.

While agreeing to the deinduction, India cautioned Sri Lanka against any failure on her part to provide security and safety to the Tamils from the areas vacated by the IPKF. Taking umbrage to Indian warning, Wijeratne was quick at his repartee and blamed the IPKF for having created the conditions, which could endanger the safety and security of the Tamils. Nevertheless, it did not take long for disenchantment to set in. On January 12, 1990, at a press conference Wijeratne expressed his displeasure at New Delhi's failure to honour Rajiv Gandhi's pledge to effect the total withdrawal by December 31, 1989. He however drew some satisfaction from the promise made by the new External Affairs Minister, Inder Kumar Gujral, that he would personally see if the withdrawal could be completed before the new stipulated date.

Preparing for the withdrawal, New Delhi remained worried about the safety of the Tamils since Lankan accusation that RAW was trying to destabilize Colombo by killing key men in the government was seen as offering an alibi for the possible exodus of refugees after the IPKF withdrawal. A statement of the official spokesman of the Indian Ministry of External Affairs of February 17, 1990 therefore felt it necessary to caution Sri Lanka against any failure on her part in guaranteeing the safety and security of the Tamils. Feeling let down by New Delhi on the deinduction question, Colombo was at this time in a defiant mood. On February 22, Wijeratne returned the compliments and accused New Delhi of creating conditions, which endanger the safety and security of the Tamils in the Northern and the Eastern provinces and said that New Delhi should instead caution the IPKF and not Sri Lanka. Holding the IPKF responsible for the present situation in the North and the East, Wijeratne said, "the problem ...is that the Tamils are fighting Tamils, because the IPKF has trained and armed the EPRLF, ENDLF and the TELO to fight the LTTE." To up the ante, a few days earlier Stanley Dominic leader of the LTTE's Political Wing in order to undermine the IPKF warned that "in the event of their failing to move out (of Sri Lanka) we will be compelled to attack them".

In such a depressing scenario, the tributes paid by former President Jayewardene at a banquet hosted by the Indian High Commissioner Mehrotra in honour of the General Officer Commanding the IPKF, Lt. Gen. Amarjeet Singh Kalkat, on March 17 came as a whiff of fresh air. In the presence of Wijeratne, the former President said that the IPKF had come at his specific invitation and in the process of its operations it had lost 1500 lives and that Sri Lanka "can never forget this". But soon it was discovered that New Delhi and the state government in Tamil Nadu had different perceptions of the role of the IPKF in the Island. When the IPKF returned to India, the DMK government of Karunanidhi refused to give it the honour of a befitting reception.

On March 24, 1990 when the last contingent of the IPKF left from Trincomalee, besides the Defence Minister of Sri Lanka Ranjan Wijeratne, the three service chiefs of Sri Lankan armed forces were present to bid it farewell. The High Commissioner Lakhan Lal Mehrotra in his farewell message paying tribute to the IPKF, said, "History will record your achievements in golden print and the memories of those of the IPKF who have laid down their lives to preserve the unity and territorial integrity of a friendly neighbour will last in our hearts for ever. A proud and grateful nation awaits your arrival back on Indian shores". With that closed an unfortunate chapter in Indo-Sri Lanka relations, which had begun with the signing of the Indo-Sri Lanka agreement on July 29, 1987.

The IPKF came out of Sri Lanka after paying a heavy price. Its task remained unfulfilled. The reputation was sullied and battered. In human terms the price was quite high. Total number of all ranks killed was 1,155 of which the officers were 55, an indication of the leadership qualities the Indian army provides. Number of disabled was 36. The number of wounded was 2,854. The IPKF killed 2,592 Tamil guerrillas, wounded 1,159 and captured 1,185.

LTTE had the last laugh. Velupillai Prabakaran in a statement on April 1, 1990 describing the departure of the IPKF as the "historic turning point" said:

> "We have successfully foiled the Indian military intervention. Now the Indian occupation forces have completely withdrawn from our homeland. The termination of the Indian intervention is a grand victory to our struggle...For more than two years we fought a ruthless war shedding our blood against a formidable military force, against a mighty power in Asia..."

Nevertheless, the LTTE did not wish to shut the doors completely on India. To keep a window open for future relations it sought to assure New Delhi that it was not antagonistic either towards the Government of India or the people of India, but it was hurt at the "misguided polices" of the earlier regime, which compelled it to oppose them. While saying so it spelt out the basis for future relationship,

> "The policy makers in Delhi should realize that the legitimate struggle of our oppressed people will not in any way contravene the geo-political concerns of India nor will it undermine the internal stability of the Indian State. We fervently hope that on the basis of this understanding the new Indian administration would make sincere efforts to restore friendly ties with our organization. We desire the Indian government and the people of India should support and recognize the legitimate struggle of our people."

But it was left to Rajiv Gandhi, now out of power, to give the veneer of some dignity to the IPKF. In an interview to the Kolkata-based *Sunday* (19 August, 1990), he said,

> "I would like to point out that the IPKF in Sri Lanka was not fighting for the Tamils against the Sinhalese. It was not fighting for the Sinhalese against the Tamils. It was fighting for the unity and integrity of Sri Lanka. It was fighting for a certain stability in our region, without other people interfering in our area. And the definition of that stability was a joint definition by Jayewardene and myself. It was not something that India had unilaterally laid down. That problem that is going to come up with the line that this government is taking...is that all is going to be lost."

Rajiv Gandhi was more forthcoming on the significance of the role of the IPKF in his address to the All India Congress Committee during its July 1990 session when he had warned that had the LTTE succeeded in its separatist agenda in Sri Lanka, separatist tendencies in the Indian State of Tamil Nadu could have sprung. Rajiv Gandhi wished to drive home the point that the IPKF's fight in Sri Lanka was for the unity of India.

‹23›

The North-East Provincial Council

The elections to the North-East Provincial Council, which under the 1987 agreement were scheduled before December 31, 1987, were finally held in November 1988 that too after considerable pressure from India. Rajiv Gandhi was anxious to demonstrate to the Indian public and perhaps more to the international community that the stalled agreement of 1987 was still alive and kicking, despite Indian failure to disarm the LTTE and restore even a semblance of peace in the north-east region of the Island. That even the Tamils were getting disillusioned with the IPKF was a source of worry for New Delhi.

The elections that should have been held in both the Tamil provinces, were held in the Eastern Province alone and that too without LTTE's participation. The LTTE enjoyed complete control in the Northern Province and it was considered prudent not to risk elections there. Its impact naturally was negative. An election in the east alone confirmed to every one that the IPKF's control in the north was tenuous and the LTTE was calling the shots there. It made lack of commitment of all the parties to the agreement obvious and conspicuous. It left the impression and perhaps rightly that the formation of the North-East Provincial Council was more of a crisis management than a fair and honest implementation of the agreement. Even this limited exercise could be held under the intimidating eyes of the IPKF, who lorded over the entire process. It became difficult to rebut the charge that the IPKF rigged the elections in favour of its chosen party Eelam People's Revolutionary Liberation Front (EPRLF), which swept the polls. Since north was the symbol of Tamil nationalism and aspirations, its exclusion was politically unfortunate. It not only eroded the legitimacy of the North-East Provincial Council itself, but also its representative character. It too exposed the inability of the IPKF to restore normalcy in the Tamil heartland after more than one year of operations. A council representing the north and the east would have perhaps Jaffna as its capital city, thereby giving the Tamils a sense of pride and restored the historic glory of Jaffna. Choice of Trincomalee as the capital did not evoke any emotional chords among the Tamils.

The exclusion of mainstream Sinhala parties from participation in the electoral process too put a question mark on the representative character of the Council. Therefore, the Council, which should have had the goodwill of both the communities living within the north-east, failed to present itself as that vital bridge on which both walked together to embrace each other. This failure, on the contrary, widened the gulf between the two communities. This was perceived as a good enough reason for Colombo and Trincomalee to stand apart. The Council and its Chief Minister remained the creations of India and instruments of Indian hegemony and chauvinism. Under the circumstances, the confrontation between Colombo and the Council surprised no one.

The choice of the Chief Minister of the newly constituted NEPC was neither prudent. Chief Minister Perumal was neither a Jaffna Tamil nor from the East. He was a Tamil of Indian origin, who had settled himself in Jaffna. The timing for the birth of the NEPC was critical too. It emerged at a time when Premadasa who had no commitment to the agreement, ascended the throne in Colombo. A year earlier, as envisaged in the Indo-Sri Lanka agreement and with Jayewardene in the saddle, would have made all the difference. Perumal, who was perceived as a creature of the IPKF depended too much on it for his survival. He looked to New Delhi all the time, which sent signals to all the communities that he was heading a proxy administration. Colombo found the whole set up too distasteful for its liking.

That the North-East Provincial Council set up in Trincomallee lacked popular support too became clear from the views of

D.R. Kaarthikeyan. (Kaarthikeyan later headed the Special Investigation Team that investigated the assassination of Rajiv Gandhi.)

Despite the support that Perumal extended to Premadasa in his election for the Presidency, the two drifted apart since the agenda of the two were poles apart. While Perumal was walking on the crutches of India and the IPKF, Premadasa was committed to throw the IPKF out of the Island no sooner had he entered the Presidential Office. On December 17, 1988, a couple of days before Premadasa was declared elected to the Presidency, Perumal presented his first policy statement to the Council expressing his dissatisfaction with the 13th Amendment. His announcement that he would commence negotiations for improving the devolution package not only with Colombo but with the Government of India too, was indeed unfortunate. It was imprudent and uncalled for to have started the life of the Council on an agitational note. The question of devolution was a highly emotive issue. Prudence required chewing and digesting what had been achieved before asking for more. Any reopening of the question of devolution needed to be left to a more opportune time in the future with proper spadework and through consensus.

To have involved India not only exposed him to the hard core Sinhala elements but irritated the new President who had no love lost for India. Perumal could not have been unaware of the JVP's influence on the Sinhalese articulated on the anti-IPKF and anti-Indian platform. All this betrayed Perumal's political naivety, which he often displayed as he got caught in the quicksands of murky relationship with Colombo and as the Indian Peace Keeping Force prepared to leave the Island after being kicked out by the contumacious President.

In January 1990, he went to New Delhi to consult with the Indian authorities on matters concerning the North-East Council. This was highly undesirable for the Chief Minister of a province in a sovereign country. He neither informed the Central Government of his intention to do so nor did he observe the norms of immigration and customs that any citizen of a country needed to abide by. On return to Trincomalee, he too violated the immigration and customs regulations. Wijeratne was not the one who would let an opportunity escape his malevolence easily. To expose Perumal and embarrass India he told the press on February 8, 1990: "we don't know whether the North-East Chief Minister brought gold, drugs, illegal arms or currency" from his visit to New Delhi. Taking a dig at the IPKF for promoting illegal actions of the Chief Minister, the Foreign Minister when asked whether the Sri Lankan security personnel and customs officials in Trincomalee did not have the right to check the persons leaving the country, Wijeratne said, "when Mr. Perumal gets into an IPKF plane and scoots off, our officers don't have the opportunity of checking him". IPKF could hardly shrug off the charge of promoting illegal activities of the Chief Minister. This was an added excuse for Colombo to ask for the IPKF's ouster. India too must hold herself accountable for his misconduct in acting above the law. It neither thought it necessary nor desirable to curb the activities of Perumal, which were in violation of normal laws of a sovereign state. India too committed the indiscretion of entering into negotiations with him on matters, which were within the domestic province of Sri Lanka. He was the Chief Minister of a region of a sovereign state and India had no reason to entertain him over the head of Colombo thus further straining relations with President Premadasa, who was estranged in any case. The effort should have been to reduce the area of conflict than to widen it. Indian action only ensured widening of the gulf.

Earlier on February 4, on the 42nd Independence Day of Sri Lanka, the NEPC boycotted the celebrations following a call from the ruling EPRLF controlling the administration. A bomb exploded where the NEPC Governor, Nalin Seneviratne, hoisted the national flag in Trincomalee headquarters of the provincial administration.

Shortly after Perumal had returned from his New Delhi sojourn, EPRLF issued a Charter of nineteen demands, which must be fulfilled within a year as otherwise, he threatened, the North-East Provincial Council would constitute itself into a constituent assembly to create a Tamil Eelam. Whether Perumal had consulted India on this issue remained a matter of speculation, but the fact that it was done soon after his return from New Delhi could not stop the tongues wagging. Strangely enough, this was totally against the Government of India's policy to respect the territorial integrity and national sovereignty of Sri Lanka. That India connived at what Perumal was doing perhaps was more an indication of New Delhi's frustration at the developments in Colombo than a studied reversal of any policy. In the end, EPRLF policies not only hastened the demise of the experiment in Tamil self-rule but also of the Indo-Sri Lanka agreement, which was sold as fulfilling the Tamil aspirations without doing damage to Sri Lanka's territorial integrity. It vindicated Sinhalese apprehensions that the Tamils' demand for merger of the North and the East was only a stepping-stone to secession and Eelam.

Speaking to Colombo-based *Weekend* within hours of moving the resolution in the North-East Provincial Council on March 1, 1990, Perumal said: "we have now given the last chance to the Government of Sri Lanka" and if Colombo did not yield on the demands, "we will sever all links" with the central government. He also made it known that he had sought the recognition of many countries, and was awaiting their response. Regarding the presence of Sri Lankan security forces in the north-east, he said after one year "we will declare them a foreign force".

This development was a bolt from the blue for Sri Lankan Government. On March 6, 1990, it came under relentless attack in parliament and was accused of creating a sorry deadlock. Sirimavo Bandaranaike was in a belligerent mood and blamed the present situation on the Indo-Sri Lanka Peace agreement of July 1987. Striking a self-righteous note she said that the SLFP had "opposed the accord bitterly" at the beginning itself and had "warned the government of the dangers arising therefrom". The Minister of Foreign Affairs responding to the debate attributed the EPRLF's mischief to the Government's determination not to let it create the Tamil National Army with the support of the Indian Peace Keeping Force. The silver lining he claimed was India's renewed commitment to the unity and integrity of Sri Lanka and significantly added he had told the Indian High Commissioner that, as a proof of New Delhi not backing Perumal it should withdraw his security cover. He stunned the House when he gave the High Commissioner's response: "it is best that India takes these people away from Sri

Lanka soil." Wijeratne claimed. He retorted, "Jolly good. Do it if you can." He challenged India to stand by her offer. He reiterated once again in the Parliament, "We confirm that India should take away their friends, the so-called Vardaraja Perumal and his minions from Sri Lanka." He asserted Perumal would not survive without the IPKF support. Clearly in Sri Lankan Parliament India was being officially accused of double standards—supporting Perumal while swearing by the unity and integrity of Sri Lanka. This stance of India was unfortunate. Did she intend to leave behind confusion and chaos and destabilize Sri Lanka for being unhelpful on the question of deinduction of the IPKF? In the face of an open challenge to her credibility, India chose to observe silence.

Perumal, putting up a brave face, declared that he would continue the "struggle" even after the departure of the IPKF". "We have no truck with the IPKF in declaring a free, independent state. Let them go. But we will stay and fight", said the Chief Minister in a pretence of pomposity. He repeated the warning that if the 19-point Charter were not accepted in one year, he would declare Sri Lankan army in the Province a "foreign force". These were brave words indeed. But pompous Perumal had little doubt about his ability to survive without the Indian support, which became clear in the next few days.

Apprehending trouble with Colombo after the withdrawal of the IPKF, the Chief Minister left Sri Lanka on March 10, in an executive jet from Trincomalee after being airlifted to the China Bay by an Indian Air Force helicopter. The IPKF had informed Sri Lanka Air Force that an Indian Air Force MI 8 helicopter would perform forced landing exercise in the Trincomalee area. Sri Lanka Air Force was warned against being alarmed at its maneuvers. The helicopter during one of its landings behind the North-East Provincial Council Secretariat picked up Perumal, his wife, and his father-in-law. Its next forced landing had occurred near a jet aircraft enabling Perumal and his party to get into it. Soon the jet had taken off for Mauritius. The following day, an Illushin cargo aircraft, which landed at China Bay had picked up about 250 of the Chief Minister's supporters and flown them to Orissa in India. On March 16, the official spokesman of the Ministry of External

Affairs disabused press reports of Indian connivance and manipulations. Describing them as tendentious, he said, "The IPKF is doing its duty in evacuating refugees on the orders of the Government of India and with the concurrence of the Sri Lankan Government". New Delhi only succeeded in deceiving itself by such a claim. The underlying message was that Sri Lankan Government too had connived at Perumal and his co-hearts leaving the country. Apparently Sri Lanka, reading the Government of India's mood did not wish to create another diplomatic crisis, by blocking their exit, and give IPKF an excuse to prolong its stay. Sri Lanka was happy to see the back of Perumal and company. Good riddance to bad rubbish! By helping the Chief Minister to abandon Sri Lanka and seek refuge outside, New Delhi did not cover itself with glory. Taking a holistic attitude, the Government of India on April 5 reiterated yet again its commitment to the unity and integrity of Sri Lanka and denied it supported "any call for Eelam in any form."

The crisis was precipitated because Perumal wanted that a "provincial police force" under his control though not authorized by Colombo be in place before the IPKF left. The EPRLF did not wish to return to the situation where it would be dependent on the Sinhalese army and police for its safety particularly under the shadow of new nexus created by the convergence of the interests of the LTTE and Colombo. The government had recognized the Civilian Volunteer Force (CVF), as an instrument for law and order duties but was dead set against accepting another paramilitary organization, the Tamil National Army (TNA) trained and armed clandestinely, as Colombo maintained, by the IPKF as part of the EPRLF outfit. Sri Lanka remained apprehensive on the need for another outfit adding to already existing plethora of militant and armed organizations, which it charged was forcibly conscripted by the IPKF. New Delhi failed to allay Colombo's nervousness about TNA's bona fide and IPKF's role. It refused to accept the IPKF's claim that it had only trained the personnel of the CVF. India naively denied even the existence of the TNA and pretended not to be aware of the source of its financing or training. But it was there and operated under the very nose of the IPKF. It was presumptuous on the part of the IPKF to deny its existence. The LTTE had observed at close quarters the emergence of the TNA as a formidable rival force. In an offensive against the TNA, the LTTE on October 9, 1989, accused the Government of India of creating an illegal paramilitary organization "to protect its puppet provincial regime and fight the Tamil Tigers". Meanwhile clashes between the LTTE and TNA became frequent and bloody in which the latter had mostly a bloody nose. By the time the experiment of a "merged" province of the Tamils collapsed, the LTTE succeeded in ensuring that the TNA was eliminated and posed no challenge to it.

Under the Provincial Councils Act of 1987, one of the safeguards to guarantee some autonomy to the Provincial Councils was that the Central Government could not dissolve Provincial Council by an executive fiat. Perumal's UDI now provided the alibi to get rid of the Council, where more than one half of the total membership expressly repudiated or manifestly disavowed obedience to the Constitution. This happened on March 25, 1990. With that collapsed the first experiment of "united" Tamil state in Sri Lanka.

Exit of the EPRLF leadership and withdrawal of the IPKF, which took place almost simultaneously, left the field free for the LTTE. The political arrangement including a provincial police establishment, which had been considered during the last couple of years was not yet in place. The Tamil National Army had already been decimated by the LTTE. The government was unable to deploy security forces in strength to take over the law and order duties. In asking the IPKF to withdraw, the President had acted only on impulse and with a sense of ultra-nationalistic fervour. The LTTE's offer of peace and a negotiated settlement were a subterfuge to get the IPKF out of the Island. Once the LTTE strategy succeeded, it had no use for negotiations. It hurried to fill the vacuum in the North-East.

The collapse of the truce between the government and the LTTE led to violence on a large scale. Like a wounded lion, Ranjan Wijeratne roared that the government would make no more attempts to negotiate with the LTTE or declare another cease-fire and instead would fight to the finish. Taking a swipe at the IPKF, he said that LTTE survived the IPKF because the latter did not want to annihilate and eliminate it. With the outbreak of violence on a large scale and the government air strafing to relieve the beleaguered troops, it was return to the old days. The civilian population could hardly escape the ferocity of the renewed fighting. According to some reports 5,000 civilians in Jaffna town were wounded in the strafing by the Air Force planes and helicopters. In the face of escalating violence, Colombo did not wish to give in and declared on June 17, 1990 "there will be no cease-fire until the LTTE stops its nonsense, the military machine will continue to move". While the Government could not give any figure of civilian casualties, unconfirmed reports put the number of civilian wounded at about 5,000 in Jaffna town alone.

This was an unexpected but unfortunate situation, which the Government of India found in Sri Lanka soon after the IPKF withdrawal. The Indian Cabinet and the Political Affairs Committee of the Cabinet were seized of the developing situation. Prime Minister Vishwanath Pratap Singh consulted the Tamil Nadu Chief Minister Karunanidhi. A statement issued on June 28, 1990 while expressing Government of India's "concern" and "anguish" at the "increasing intensity of the conflict in Sri Lanka and the growing escalation in the level of violence," sought to affirm to Colombo that "it will not allow its territory to be used by any group of militants as a base for their activities." Non-involvement of India in the Island's happenings was inherent in the present phase, particularly so soon after the IPKF withdrawal. India, however, emphasized the other elements of her Sri Lanka policy. These were:

(1) India could not be a mere spectator to the goings-on in the Island, notably of the heavy loss of civilian lives in the Tamil majority areas;

(2) She would exert diplomatic pressure on Sri Lanka to ensure against escalation of violence and loss of civilian lives; and

(3) India stood for the unity and territorial integrity of Sri Lanka.

A thankful Premadasa therefore, when greeting India on the occasion of 43rd anniversary of her Independence, did not forget to acknowledge Indian assurances and said:

> "We are deeply grateful for the assurance given by the Government of India to the effect that your great country stands for the unity and territorial integrity of Sri Lanka. Also India's assurance that there would be no interference in our internal affairs and that Indian territory, will not be allowed to be used by militant groups for subversion against Sri Lanka, is greatly appreciated by all our people. These sentiments strengthen us in the belief that India has a significant role to play in ensuring the stability of our region."

The scale of violence however, refused to climb down. On August 3, 1990, the LTTE entered two mosques and massacred at least 170 Muslims who were praying in Kathankuddy town of eastern Batticaloa. Colombo was understandably incensed. Wijeratne on August 9, 1990 described the LTTE as "criminals" who had to be "exterminated". Anguished and concerned at the growing violence and ever-increasing number of casualties, a troubled Indian Prime Minister V.P. Singh made a personal appeal for immediate cessation of hostilities and return to the negotiating table. The violence had spewed an increasing number of refugees into Tamil Nadu.

The new situation ignited the Indian Parliament once again. On August 29 and 30, 1990 the Rajya Sabha reverberated with the angry accusations of the members of Parliament. Sri Lanka was accused of trying "to wipe out the entire Tamil civilian population." A harassed Minister of State for External Affairs, Hari Kishore Singh was hard put to stem the tide of members' ire. An enraged House refused to be pacified with the homilies from the Minister. The presiding officer of the House had repeatedly to intervene to cool the frayed tempers. A senior member of the House, H. Hanumanthappa expressing the exasperation of the members with the government's stand said, "After all the anguish, anger, and concern which has been expressed in the last two days, the whole thing was watered down by the Minister's reply."

In the midst of all this mayhem at the end of January 1991, the Indian Minister of External Affairs Vidya Charan Shukla visited Colombo. Recovering from the earlier wounds, he vowed neither to militarily get involved in the Island's ethnic conflict, nor allow Indian territory to be used as a base for terrorist activity. Coincidently, when Shukla was still in Colombo, the DMK Government in Tamil Nadu was dismissed. This was an additional signal to Sri Lanka that the flow of arms and ammunition, fuel and other strategic items from that state in India to the north of the Island would dry up, which would greatly help in containing terrorist activities in the Island.

On January 29, 1991 the Indian Foreign Secretary S.K. Singh told a press conference in Colombo that the two countries had different perceptions of the situation in the north. India having disengaged herself from the ethnic conflict, felt prudent to enter into a more enduring relationship with Sri Lanka, which would ensure long-term prosperity of the Island nation. It was the strengthening of economic bonds by developing greater trade relations that New Delhi wished to concentrate upon. This matter was the focus of attention of the leaders of the two countries during Shukla's visit. Possibilities of cooperation, specifically in the field of joint exploration of oil, tea export etc. were discussed. There was a general consensus to further develop and enhance cooperation in the economic, financial and commercial spheres. It was agreed in principle to set up a Joint Commission at the ministerial level. It was formally set up in August 1991, during the visit of Sri Lankan Foreign Minister Harold Herat to New Delhi. Some years later, in 1998 in the same spirit, India and Sri Lanka entered into an agreement to provide for free trade between the two countries that opened the possibilities of greater commercial interaction.

24

Assassinations and the Second Peace Process

In May 1991, Rajiv Gandhi, the former Prime Minister of India, was assassinated in Tamil Nadu. It was suspected that the LTTE was behind this heinous crime. India was in the midst of her general elections to elect a new Parliament and it was expected that the Congress party led by Rajiv Gandhi was on the comeback trail, which would put Gandhi in the saddle once again in New Delhi. LTTE had perceived Gandhi to be the main hurdle in its struggle for an Eelam. It was its calculation that his return to power would bring back the old Indian hostility towards the organization. The LTTE was not known to have any compunction in eliminating anyone who it perceived would be a problem for it. The list of people who fell to the LTTE's dragnet was a long one. Its top brass could not think of any other solution to its looming problem that faced it if he succeeded in returning to power. It happened that way only. From the very beginning the needle of suspicion pointed towards the LTTE and the Indian police did not take too long to work out the case. Once it was confirmed that the LTTE had indeed committed the crime, entire Indian perspective on the LTTE changed. The Indian public opinion was particularly piqued and irritated that despite the fact that the IPKF was made to fight the LTTE with its hands tied at its back, and allowed itself to suffer ignominy, because India was careful not to let the outfit be destroyed altogether, it had chosen to act treacherously. Had the IPKF been allowed a free hand it was not impossible for it to have achieved LTTE's liquidation. But that did not appear to be the objective of India.

Having actively entered in the arena of ethnic conflict first to promote a meaningful dialogue between Colombo and the Tamils and then in constructing the 1987 Peace accord, India only wished to cordon off the region from any outside interference. Though India had initially trained and armed the LTTE and other militants, despite its professions to the contrary, the idea was to merely build a pressure point, which would make it more difficult for Colombo to ignore Tamils' legitimate grievances and make it more deferential to their woes and give them some respectable space in the Island's polity. That it did not work as planned is another matter. In course of time the LTTE developed fangs true to its name. By the time India signed the 1987 agreement, the LTTE was not only in a position to oppose its benefactor but defy it too. India perhaps was not prepared for this surprised discovery. She failed to make a realistic assessment of its strength and ability to stand alone and defy the regional power. As the LTTE defied India, New Delhi felt that its intransigent and recalcitrant ward could be disciplined with a little drubbing. New Delhi only wished to make it amenable to its agenda, come to the negotiating table and help in working out an agreement, which would meet the aspirations of Tamils while maintaining the territorial integrity of Sri Lanka. While pursuing this course, India did not wish to blunt the alternative instrument for resolution of the ethnic conflict, should Colombo remain niggardly or renege as in the past on Tamils' demands. The TULF's failure to get justice from the Sinhalese in the past had convinced Tamils in India that it was LTTE's spirit of sacrifice, which was keeping the Tamil struggle alive and kicking and making everyone hear their shrieks. To that extent, LTTE succeeded in keeping its constituency in South India alive and vibrant. That LTTE had a different perception of itself remained a mystery to those who promoted and supported it. The Indian intelligence agency, RAW, must get the rap on its knuckles for its failure to properly assess LTTE's abilities and capabilities. On the other hand, the LTTE was irked that its position had been undermined by New Delhi by posing as the guardian of the Tamils by arrogating to itself the right to decide what was best for the Tamils. While India remained wedded to the territorial integrity of Sri Lanka, the LTTE had no such compunction since the dream of Eelam was predicated upon the break-up of the

Island's political integrity. The Government of India and the LTTE were following two different and contradictory strands in their approach to the Tamil problem and the clash in their perceptions was inevitable. In the post-1987 period, there too was a polarization in the public opinion in India towards the Tamil struggle on the Island. The non-Tamil opinion was resentful of the LTTE first opposing the IPKF and then joining hands with Sri Lankan President to eject the IPKF out. Tamil Nadu and Tamil public opinion had different perception of the drama unfolding on the Island. They were critical of New Delhi's developing animosity towards the LTTE who were a self-sacrificing lot. To them New Delhi appeared to be more concerned about the territorial integrity of Sri Lanka than to the sufferings of the Tamils and their sensitivities. It was no wonder that Tamil Nadu Chief Minister refused to do the IPKF the honour of a reception in Chennai on its return home after being deinducted from Sri Lanka in March 1990.

After the assassination of Rajiv Gandhi, the resentment against the LTTE turned positively hostile even in Tamil Nadu. Indian public saw greater virtue in the Sri Lankan government using force to meet the LTTE challenge. In India, the LTTE henceforth came to be perceived a villain of the piece, drug peddler, a monster indulging in wanton violence, and a megalomaniac fascist organization. In the Indian Parliament, the sympathy for the LTTE evaporated altogether. There were no more voices of commiseration. They gave way to hostility and antipathy and there was no dearth of members of parliament who pleaded with the Government of India to provide assistance to Sri Lankan Government to deal with the LTTE menace. On September 11, 1991, Jayanthi Natarajan, a Tamil Member of Parliament, even warned the Rajya Sabha of LTTE attacking coastal villages of Tamil Nadu. Velupillai Prabakaran became the principal accused in the conspiracy to assassinate Rajiv Gandhi and hence the request to Colombo for his extradition. Finally, on May 14, 1992 the LTTE was formally banned in India and continues to be a banned organization since then. The ban could not have been imposed until the organization was involved in terrorist activities in India; the statement of S.B. Chavan, the Indian Home Minister in the Lok Sabha on May 14, 1992, accused the LTTE of indulging in "several terrorists acts in India" by organizing the Tamil young men into an organization called the Tamil National Retrieval Troops (TNRT). The decision to ban the LTTE, received all round support in the country, particularly from Tamil Nadu. The DMK, however, chose to maintain silence. The AIADMK Chief Minister, J. Jayalalithaa expressed her gratitude to the Prime Minister and the Union Home Minister for banning the LTTE and described the decision in the best interest of preserving the unity of the country. K. Ramamurthi, Member of Parliament and President of the Tamil Nadu Congress Party too endorsed the statement of the Chief Minister and said this was the right step to protect the unity and sovereignty of the country. The Secretary of the Tamil Nadu State Unit of the Communist Party of India (Marxist) welcomed the ban but cautioned the Government against using the ban to crush dissenters or harass the genuine Lankan Tamil refugees. The *Indian Express* in an editorial accused the Government for taking a long time to come to this decision and reversing the policy of support to the LTTE, which was "a major political blunder". The *Hindu* in its editorial of May 17, 1992 said "the ban has come not a day too soon." Taken by surprise at the turn of the events, the LTTE became vituperative and described the Indian decision as lacking in "foresight, diplomacy and tact". It cautioned India: "this precipitate action may adversely affect India's global interest in future." Indian discomfort was complete in that the LTTE hitting below the belt, indicted her of intervening in the "Tamil national question, i.e. in the affairs of a foreign country" by sending "an occupying force into the Tamil homeland and under the guise of a peacekeeping force". Uncompromising in its criticism, it said:

> "It is the Indian government, which attempted to destroy the Tamil tigers and the Tamil national freedom struggle. In this war of aggression, it killed tens of thousands of Tamils. Therefore it was the Indian Government and the leadership of the Indira Congress in particular, that intervened in the internal affairs of our country which had serious consequences."

The change in the fortunes of the LTTE, particularly in relation to India, created a dilemma for the Government of Sri Lanka. There was a reciprocal demand in certain quarters in the Island for a similar ban on the LTTE. It avoided a decision since "the government did not wish to prejudice the issues and take a precipitate unilateral action". The observation of the Indian High Commissioner, N.N. Jha, that the "Indian action was a symbolic gesture with international ramifications" indicated lack of seriousness on the part of India in choosing to ban the organization. Sri Lankan Prime Minister D.B. Wijetunge's repartee that for Colombo it was a serious business since its security forces were involved in a fierce fight to eradicate terrorism upset the Indian High Commission. The public opinion in Sri Lanka including that of the main opposition party the SLFP believed that to resolve the ethnic issue, LTTE could not be ignored. It was therefore Government's position not to rush into taking a decision but to wait and watch. That "wait and watch" continued in Colombo till the dawn of January 1998 when Colombo reacting to LTTE bombing of the Island's holiest Buddhist shrine, the Temple of the Tooth Relic in Kandy, proscribed it.

On May 24 to India's embarrassment the government-owned *Sunday Observer*, voiced charges made by the General Secretary of the People's Front of Liberation Tigers (PFLT), Yogaratnam Yogi over "People's Forum", a weekly program broadcast over the Voice of Tigers, the clandestine LTTE radio. Yogi charged that after failing to bring down the Premadasa government through the former Minister Gamini Dissanayake, and his clique—a reference to last year's impeachment move against the President—India was using the ban to sabotage the talks between the Government and the LTTE. Yogi too had accused India of financing a leading newspaper group and others to destabilize the government. It may be recalled that on February 15, 1990 Foreign Minister, Ranjan Wijeratne, had publicly claimed the arrest of "about hundred persons by the security forces in connection with the attempt engineered by Indian intelligence agency RAW to assassinate key figures in the government and destabilize the country". The Indian High Commissioner on the same day (May 24, 1992) dismissed the charge as "utter nonsense and fabrication", as alleged by the *Sunday Observer* in its story. It is interesting that when the Government of India sought to publish its notification to ban the LTTE in the official media in Sri Lanka to make the ban known as widely as possible, the *Sunday Observer* refused to carry the notification even when it was a paid insertion, without assigning any reason.

For quite some time Indo-Sri Lanka relations continued to be cool. The Government of India licking its wounds watched from the sidelines the aggravation in the situation in the Island. The structure of relations built during the 1983-87 period crumbled. The visit of President Premadasa to New Delhi in October 1992 as Chairman of the SAARC was utilized by India to discuss bilateral relations as well. The joint communiqué issued at the end of his visit looked trite. President Premadasa vetoed any mention of the 1987 agreement in the joint communiqué. He was loathe to the agreement from the beginning and it was therefore not much of a surprise. India swearing allegiance to the Accord included it in the banquet speech of her President on October 1, 1992 as a "sincere attempt to resolve the ethnic problem that had sadly gone on for well over a decade". India continued to believe that merger of the Northern and the Eastern provinces with proper devolution of powers was vital for an effective and lasting solution to the ethnic problem. This point was underscored in the talks that Prime Minister Narasimha Rao had with the visiting President, much to the latter's irritation. Meanwhile, the Parliamentary Select Committee of the Sri Lankan Parliament appointed to work out a formula or solution, which would resolve the ethnic issue peacefully, drew a blank. The Committee, dominated by the Sinhalese members, was averse as in the past to accommodating the minimum Tamil aspirations. This was despite the fact that the Tamils had climbed down sufficiently from the hey days of 1985 when they would have nothing less than the right to self-determination as a price for their continued association with the majority community. The 4-point formula, put up by the Tamils before the Committee on June 17, 1992 was:

1. An unified politico-administrative entity for the permanently merged North-East Province.
2. Substantial devolution of power ensuring meaningful autonomy to that unified unit.
3. Institutional arrangement within the larger framework of the un-bifurcated North-East Province for the Muslim people ensuring their cultural identity and security.

4. The Sinhalese people to enjoy all the rights in the merged province that other minorities have in the rest of the country.

There was no breakthrough nor was there any silver lining on the black and cloudy horizon. In January 1993, President Premadasa made a pilgrimage visit to India. His talks in New Delhi during a stopover failed to break the ice. The relations between the two countries remained cold. India regretted her inability to attend the SAARC summit scheduled in Colombo. The LTTE continued to believe that the political situation on the Island was "gloomy" as in the past. In an interview broadcast on the BBC on March 4, 1993 Prabakaran pledged his commitment to peace "from the bottom" of his heart. He said that to find a final solution to this intractable problem there "should be a fundamental change in the attitude and approach of the Sinhala government".

On May 1, 1993, in a sudden turn of events, a LTTE suicide squad assassinated the enigmatic President Premadasa. Rajiv Gandhi had paid with his life for distrusting the LTTE; Premadasa now paid with his life for trusting it too much. After a short interregnum, the UNP was ousted from power and the reins of administration in Colombo passed into the hands of youthful Chandrika Bandaranaike Kumaratunga, the daughter of the two previous heads of the government—S.W.R.D. and Sirimavo Bandaranaike. She headed a coalition of political parties—People's Alliance. The principal party in this alliance was the Sri Lanka Freedom Party. She stormed into office pledging a new deal to the Tamils to end the ethnic conflict once and for all. On August 19, 1994 she extended her "hand of friendship" to the LTTE; and in a rapturous message to the nation, she declared that she would "build a society without any discrimination where all the minority communities would enjoy equal rights as equal citizens".

There was euphoria all-round and the LTTE too responded positively. It offered to accept a "substantial package" as an alternative to its demand for an independent Eelam state. LTTE's chief spokesman, Anton Balasingham surprised everyone when clarifying he said that this meant that regional autonomy or self-government "guaranteed by the Constitution, and recognized by the international community". This was a first helpful signal from the LTTE, which had in the past always insisted on Tamil Eelam. More surprise was in store when Balasingham blamed the TULF for raising the demand for a separate state. He sought to distance the LTTE from the TULF and the slogan of Eelam saying that the original demand for Eelam came from the TULF and the LTTE came later and carried forward the issue of self-determination. The same argument was repeated by the LTTE when it entered into another peace process under the Norwegian facilitation in 2002.

On August 30 to send a positive signal to the LTTE, Kumaratunga in an interview to the *Hindu* of Chennai said that as a first step towards peace her government had unilaterally lifted the embargo on "most essential items to Jaffna...and except for a few (items) which go into the making of arms, we are allowing the rest to go".

Ensured of a positive response from the LTTE, the new Government showed understanding of the compulsions of the situation and India's stake in any peace process. It sought the Indian endorsement to her peace efforts with the LTTE. On October 6, an unidentified source in Colombo told the *Sunday Observer* that Colombo had been assured of India's support for the peace process. The official clarified that while India had declined to publicly endorse the peace process, the Indian Government had indicated that it would not stand in the way of the negotiating process. India was quietly consulted as Colombo made initial overtures to the LTTE. The official clarifying the Indian response said, "I will not say that India has blessed the proposed talks with the LTTE. But I can certainly say that she will not interfere". India's reservations had to be understood in the context of LTTE's involvement with the assassination of her former Prime Minister Rajiv Gandhi and consequent ban on it. There was an unannounced visit by the Information Secretary, Lionel Fernando to New Delhi that produced the desired results. Once India gave a green signal, replies were sent to the LTTE's message for talks, delegates were named and dates fixed for the first round of talks. The LTTE too was keen that the proposed talks should be blessed by India and the Bishop of Jaffna Rt. Rev. Thomas Savundaranayagam sounded India on its behalf and appealed not to block the peace moves. The September 10, 1994 press release of the LTTE welcoming the "victory of the People's Alliance at the recent Sri Lankan elections, also announced the "readiness of the LTTE to hold unconditional talks with the new Government". As a gesture of goodwill, the LTTE released ten Sinhalese prisoners held by it. It offered a meeting between Prabakaran and President Kumartunga if she visited Jaffna. The LTTE too acknowledged and welcomed the Government's decision to restore electricity, repair highways, and renovate irrigation schemes and offered its full cooperation in this task.

Notwithstanding some of the above positive developments, Prabakaran's public stance remained ambivalent. On September 13, 1994 he told the BBC that the LTTE were not placing any pre-conditions for talks, but he insisted on complete lifting of economic embargo and cease-fire before the talks could take place to create a peace ambience. Holding an olive branch to the Muslims who were displaced from their homes in Jaffna due to killings by the LTTE, Prabakaran offered his regrets and said since they "belonged to the Jaffna soil", LTTE would "permit them to come back" when conditions return to normal.

For next eight months, the government and the LTTE were engaged in lengthy correspondence with Kumaratunga and her personal representative and meetings with the officials for talks to prepare for a discussion on the substantive issues of peace and resolution of the ethnic problem. The Government, on its part, removed the embargo on a number of items excluding some strategic ones, which had a dual use for civil and military purpose.

The LTTE continued to underline the need for an agreement on cessation of hostilities. It was reemphasized during the preliminary talks on October 13 and 14. On November 12, the LTTE unilaterally declared one-week cease-fire to coincide with the swearing in of Chandrika Kumaratunga as the new President of Sri Lanka, in the hope that the Government would reciprocate the gesture. On November 16, the LTTE in a press release once again underlined the need for such an agreement to prevent various violent incidents. After prolonged arguments, an agreement for an indefinite cessation of hostilities was finally signed on January 7/8, 1995. Separate committees for each area—Jaffna, Mannar, Vavuniya, Mullaitivu, Batticaloa-Amparai and any other areas as deemed necessary—were agreed to be set up to inquire into any instances of violation of agreement.

Other pre-conditions stipulated at different points of time and piecemeal included removal of embargo on some of the remaining items, removal of ban on fishing in the northern waters, removal of military check-post at Pooneryn, which the LTTE said hindered free movement of people from the mainland to the peninsula, free movement of LTTE armed cadres in the North and the East etc. The Government went extra mile to meet some of the demands. Additional items were identified for free movement into the LTTE areas. Restrictions on fishing in the northern waters were relaxed. A formal agreement for cessation of hostilities was signed as indicated above. On the crucial issue of LTTE's demand for free movement of its armed cadres, the Government was unyielding. On the question of military check-post at Pooneryn the government was willing to make some adjustment in the location of the post, so that the movement of civilian traffic was considerably eased, which it did but that did not satisfy the LTTE. The government however, remained adamant and unyielding on the demand for its removal altogether.

The LTTE was not impressed by the concessions made by the government, and dragged the President into the luxury of a lengthy correspondence. It indulged in hair-splitting, without coming to grips with the core issue of political settlement. On February 22, 1995 after the correspondence had dragged on for too long, the President proposed to Prabakaran the "use of the good offices of a neutral and uncommitted person who would serve as an intermediary" between the two "to carry directly any ideas, proposals and explanations we might wish to convey to each other concerning the elements of a political solution to the ethnic problem". After consulting with the French President, she proposed the name of a retired French diplomat, suggested by him, for this purpose, who, she claimed, was not known to her. LTTE reacted negatively to the suggestion. Prabakaran insisted that the talks be held in a transparent manner between the representatives of the two sides and not through a private individual in "secret". Balasingham likened the President's suggestion to foreign mediation but rejected it since it was mediation by a foreign individual while it preferred mediation formally by a foreign government. Private mediation, the LTTE charged, amounted to lack of trust by the government in the organization.

Idea of private mediation was reflective of the Government's frustration, as the Foreign Minister Lakshman Kadirgamar said: "We were obliged to try this step only to break the impasse and the logjam in the talks." He said though three rounds of talks had taken place, the LTTE was not ready "to begin the discussions on a political package and the Government was keen to get started on this". Stung by the charge of foot-dragging, the LTTE returned the compliment in a statement of 26 February 1995 and accused the Government of creating difficulties in the path of peace. The statement said despite the fact that an agreement on cessation of hostilities had been signed more than a month ago, cease-fire had not come into force and the monitoring committees were facing difficulties in their functioning for lack of logistical support from the Government. A day earlier on February 25 in a letter to Chandrika, Prabakaran himself had made a similar accusation and said that the Government was not giving priority to the needs of the people but to military subterfuges. A LTTE press release of February 26 once again charged Colombo of insincerity in implementing measures to mitigate hardships of the people and engaging in "cosmetic exercise". In returning the charge a Colombo statement of March 6, 1995 underlined Government's sincerity and ascribed the tardy progress in the peace talks to the LTTE, imposing new conditions periodically.

The exchange of polemics did not augur well for the peace process. The President who was personally committed to ending the ethnic conflict was left gnashing her teeth when on March 16, 1995 she received a letter from Prabakaran threatening to break the peace talks if "a favourable response" was not received before March 28, 1995 to his various litany of grievances mentioned above. Despite being personally hurt she was keen on preventing a breakdown since she had invested heavily in the peace process. To salvage it, she suggested direct talks, which she said, "would help arrive at positive decisions". She even suggested the names of government representatives and dates (March 23, 24 and 25) for talks at Jaffna and requested Prabakaran to nominate his representatives for this purpose. Prabakaran's response was brusque and worrying for the President. He once again threatened to close the chapter of peace talks saying, "I do not think a further dialogue is necessary" to clarify any issue.

Breakdown of the second peace effort

Kumaratunga was apprehensive and worried. Her dream of resolving the ethnic issue by peaceful means and expeditiously was in tatters. She decided to use the Indian card to save the peace process. She was scheduled to go to New Delhi on a state visit before the March 28, deadline set by the LTTE. On the eve of the visit there were enough media reports prompted perhaps by the government to put pressure on Prabakaran of a possible request from New Delhi for his extradition during her Delhi visit. While assuring Prabakaran that he had nothing to fear on this account, Colombo made sure that the sword of extradition stayed hanging on Prabakaran's head to keep him on line. On March 22, 1995 the government discounted reports that the President would discuss this issue in New Delhi. The reports of his extradition were described as tendentious with a view "to sabotaging the peace initiative pursued by the government and to create a mistrust between the Government and the LTTE". Foreign Minister Lakshman Kadirgamar, making his contribution, sought to discount any such possibility stating that the Government had not received such a request so far from New Delhi. Reassuring Prabakaran, Kadirgamar said that even during his own recent visit to Delhi there was no discussion on his extradition. He stressed that in fact Prime Minister Narasimha Rao encouraged the peace initiative and said "If you solve your problem, it will be one problem less for us".

On March 28, 1995 at the end of her visit, Kumaratunga told a news conference in the Indian capital that "the question of extradition did not come up, because the legal processes are still not finalised". This was contrary to the facts. The extradition was indeed discussed. The public stance was a clever ploy to reassure Prabakaran so that he remained on board the peace process. She left the possibility of extradition on a later date (when the processes were complete) open to keep Prabakaran guessing. This had the desired effect, at least for the time being. On March 30, Prabakaran appearing conciliatory showed his willingness to resume the dialogue as from April 1, 1995. He extended his deadline for breaking the talks to April 19, 1995. He however remained adamant on the question of removal of the military check-post at Pooneryn because of its "critical importance" for free and unhindered movement of the people.

In yet another effort to placate the LTTE, the Government appeared to soften its stand on two crucial issues of removal of the Pooneryn check-post and free movement of armed LTTE cadres by offering to discuss them further. The LTTE unfortunately was not mollified. The LTTE construed this statement as government's failure to create conditions for peace talks and reiterated its decision to call off the talks forthwith charging the Government of procrastinating on the vital issues of concern to it.

A press release of the LTTE' Political Committee, issued the next day reiterated what Prabakaran had conveyed to the President in his letter the previous day. It blamed the failure of the talks on the inability of the government "to solve any of the contentious issues satisfactorily within the timeframe given by the LTTE". A week later (April 27) in an interview broadcast on the BBC, Prabakaran justified his action by suggesting that "we made this painful decision at a time when our people had lost all hopes that peace would return to the Tamil homeland and the Tamil problem would be resolved". Showing lack of inherent faith in Colombo, he said,

> "I wish to make a point here. That is, giving pledges and implementing those pledges are two different things. It is true that President Chandrika gave us pledges. But she has not taken constructive measures to implement them. In the past Tamil people have been betrayed several times by previous Sinhalese regimes. Agreements were made but not implemented. Pacts were signed and abrogated. This is our history."

The President was distraught at this sudden turn of events. In a pensive mood she told the New Delhi fortnightly *India*

Today, "she did not expect anything else from the Tigers. It is the most ruthless and most effective guerrilla organization in the 20th century". Her predicament was best reflected in her statement to the fortnightly when she said whether one liked it or not, one had to be realistic and deal with him. "The man today controls one-third of our country, two-thirds of its coastline", she said in resignation and went on, for the first time, to hold Prabakaran responsible for the killing of the former Indian Prime Minister Rajiv Gandhi.

Thus, another sordid chapter in the disgusting story to negotiate peace to the ethnic conflict ended abruptly leaving bitterness and bad taste all round. The skeptics described the abortive talks as a strategic move on the part of the LTTE to gain a breathing space to re-group and re-equip themselves, in which they admirably succeeded leaving everybody wondering and askance. Once the peace talks collapsed, President Kumaratunga had no compunction in putting the blame for the assassination of Rajiv Gandhi on the shoulders of Prabakaran to bring out the devil in him, something no one in responsible position in Sri Lanka had done before. Soon India felt free to put in the request for LTTE chief's extradition. On June 3, 1995 the Sri Lanka Foreign Secretary confirmed that a formal request had indeed been received for this purpose. Besides, Prabakaran, India sought the extradition of two other LTTE leaders —Tigers' intelligence Chief Pottu Amman and LTTE Women Wing's leader Akila.

❮25❯

Extradition of Prabakaran

The request for extradition of the LTTE leader had its own history. Not sure of Colombo's cooperation, New Delhi dithered before putting in the request. The Designated Court at Chennai where the Rajiv Gandhi assassination case was being heard, issued proclamations and warrants of arrest against Prabakaran under Section 8(3)(a) of TADA (Terrorists and Disruptive Activities Act) on January 31, 1992. These proclamations were published in Sri Lankan newspapers in 1992. The Court directed the accused to appear before it on or before February 28, 1992. As expected, Prabakaran and the other accused failed to appear before the court. On May 20, 1992 the Special Investigating Team (SIT) filed the chargesheet against V. Prabakaran, in the designated court in Chennai. In July 1992, Sri Lanka Foreign Minister Harold Herat visited New Delhi. India raised with him the question of Prabakaran's extradition and asked Colombo's reaction if such a request were made by New Delhi. He informed New Delhi that Sri Lanka would follow the law in the case of his extradition but before activating any legal process, India should make a formal request. In April 1994, a Red Corner notice requesting the arrest of Prabakaran was circulated through Interpol.

Senior officials of the Indian Ministry of External Affairs informally consulted their Sri Lankan counterparts on the question of extradition. In the absence of any extradition treaty between the two countries, there were two options. The request could be made either under the existing bilateral legal arrangement or under the SAARC Convention on Suppression of Terrorism. The Sri Lanka Extradition Law No. 8 of 1977 as extended to include the Commonwealth countries, provided one alternative. Reciprocally, the Indian Extradition Act of 1962 was extended to Sri Lanka by Gazette Notification of August 17, 1978. Under this bilateral arrangement, extradition could be sought in accordance with Section 8(1) of the Sri Lanka Extradition Law which required India to furnish the full case documents acceptable to Lankan courts for the consideration of the authorities. Once Colombo accepted such documents on the recommendations of the Attorney General, the Court of Committal of the Island was authorized to issue a warrant of arrest of the accused. The major pitfall in this process was obvious. The trial could not proceed in the Court of Committal in absence of the accused. This was made abundantly clear by Sri Lankan legal authorities to their Indian counterparts in February 1992.

The other option of SAARC Convention on Suppression of Terrorism went beyond the Sri Lankan law on extradition in that it enlarged the scope and number of exclusions from the political exception clause and had wider amplitude of offences for which this clause could not be invoked. There was additionally an expediency clause under the SAARC Convention, which allowed a government to deny extradition if it was inexpedient to accede to such a request. New Delhi decided to rule out the SAARC option and bat on the first. Government of India directed the Central Bureau of Investigation (CBI) to prepare the necessary documentation for making an extradition request to Colombo. The CBI suggested to the Ministry of External Affairs "utmost consideration of various issues at the highest level before a considered decision is taken by the Government". The essence of the CBI advice was that the trial in the Rajiv Gandhi assassination case in India was being held "in camera" and as such passing even minimum evidence to Colombo would prejudice the outcome of the trial in India. The CBI felt that there was no guarantee that the material filed by the Government of India was likely to be found sufficient by Colombo. It also warned the Government to keep in mind the fact that even if Colombo wished to help India, Sri Lanka was in no position to apprehend and hand over the accused to New Delhi.

It was obvious to New Delhi that Colombo was apathetic in its cooperation. Sri Lanka did extend some cooperation to the Special Investigation Team (SIT) during its several visits to Colombo in connection with the investigations in the case. However Colombo balked when CBI Legal Advisor wanted to visit Colombo in June 1992 to hold discussions with the Sri Lankan Attorney General. Colombo made it known that there could be no informal consultations between the two sides on the extradition question until a formal request for extradition was received.

Given these constraints, the Government of India was not sure of the advisability of making a request for extradition. It apprehended that should Colombo decide not to cooperate, it could turn down the request on the specious plea of the documentation not being tangible enough to grant the request. Above everything else, it was the question of political will on the part of Colombo to cooperate with New Delhi in this sensitive matter. Having made the request it would be most embarrassing for the Government of India if Sri Lanka failed to cooperate due to her own political compulsions such as keeping the option of a dialogue with the LTTE wide open. The Government of India was not unconscious of the fact that India had in 1982 procrastinated on Colombo's request for Prabakaran's extradition for his involvement in the shoot-out incident in Pondi Bazar. Similarly, Colombo had in the past made unsuccessful requests to the Government of India to extradite the Tamil militants using the Indian soil for their violent activities against Colombo. It may be recalled that if the Treaty of Peace and Co-operation between the two countries to replace the letters exchanged with the Indo-Sri Lanka Peace Agreement of July 1987, could not be successfully negotiated, it was precisely on account of different perceptions of the two Governments about their obligations on the extradition issue. The Core Group of the Indian Ministry of Home Affairs considered the pros and cons of the case for extradition. It decided that notwithstanding the arguments against making such a request, extradition procedure should follow as a logical step in the due process of law. The prevailing political situation too demanded that political imperative needed to be met. Despite this, the Committee of Secretaries after considering the matter in all its ramifications at its meeting on July 27, 1992 decided not to go ahead with the extradition request at that juncture and deferred it. It was not until 1995 when New Delhi noted that both Colombo and the Tigers had burnt their bridges and the peace process initiated by President Chandrika had collapsed, that New Delhi decided to resurrect the issue of extradition.

On June 3, 1995 a letter from the Government of India to the Foreign Minister of Sri Lanka, containing the request for arrest and extradition of LTTE leader Velupillai Prabakaran for the assassination of Rajiv Gandhi was delivered in Colombo. Same day Sri Lankan Foreign Secretary, Rodney Vandergert, told the *Sunday Observer* that he had accepted the extradition request on behalf of the Foreign Ministry. A full supportive dossier was submitted along with the letter of request. Apart from Prabakaran the Indian letter sought the extradition of LTTE Intelligence Chief Pottu Amman and leader of the Women's Wing of the LTTE Akila. Sri Lankan Foreign Secretary told the *Observer* that according to the procedure, the documents now received would be submitted to the Ministry of Defence who would take up the case with the Attorney General's Department. He further said that after study of the supportive material received, if additional information was required, that would be called for from India for presenting the case in the Court. Vandergert did not hide the fact that Colombo was taken by surprise by the Indian request since he was given a notice of in-coming message only a few hours in advance of the actual arrival of the documents. The Indian High Commission remained tight-lipped about the sudden move on the extradition front. When the journalist asked the Deputy High Commissioner of India, Cheri George, for reasons for the sudden move, he did not say anything except for confirming the extradition request. A *Reuter* report from New Delhi said that the Indian Commerce Minister, P. Chidambaram had informed the Parliament that the Government of India had sent the extradition request through a special messenger. *Reuter* quoted the Minister saying that an Indian Special Court hearing the Gandhi assassination case had "granted fresh non-bailable warrants of arrest on the said three accused for their apprehension and extradition to India". An AFP report quoted Indian political circles to suggest that the move was an attempt by Narasimha Rao's Government to ward off political pressure from within the Congress Party, which was unhappy, since Rao was seen reluctant to pursue the case with vigour. Sonia Gandhi, the widow of Rajiv Gandhi and her close circle of Congressmen who included quite a few disgruntled elements had made this an issue to embarrass Rao. It was sought to be a message to those Indians who had begun to criticize the Sri Lankan military offensive against the LTTE.

On July 31, 1995 the Minister for External Affairs Pranab Mukherjee confirmed to the Lok Sabha that Sri Lanka Government in processing the Indian request had forwarded the extradition papers to the Ministry of Defence, the nodal Ministry for handling the extradition affairs, which "in turn have sent the request to the Attorney General of Sri Lanka for his legal opinion in the matter." He however, added that New Delhi had received no formal response from Colombo in the case.

It has, however, to be understood that India in making the request was not unaware of the legal, political and physical hurdles in getting Prabakaran extradited. Efforts to tame Prabakaran during the IPKF operations had come a cropper. The IPKF had to withdraw from the Island under unfortunate circumstances and without completing its most important task i.e. disarming the LTTE. It was the LTTE and its supremo who had the last laugh in the race for gaining an upper hand. When the LTTE was banned in India, Colombo did not consider it necessary to outlaw the organization. Sri Lanka was quite conscious that banning it would amount to closing all options of a political process in the future, since the LTTE by its policy of annihilation had eliminated any alternate Tamil voice with whom the government could deal with. It was this compulsion that dictated Colombo's attitude to the LTTE and its leader Prabakaran. Now of course, with the collapse of the peace process Colombo felt free to deal with the matter in its discretion without being encumbered by other considerations.

Sri Lanka's political opinion both in the Government and in the opposition in the past, had felt that India was being cussed on the question of LTTE and Prabakaran's extradition. It was perhaps only to embarrass and undermine the Premadasa Government, which was responsible for the discomfiture of the

IPKF. Since the Indian High Commissioner in Colombo, N.N. Jha, had described the Indian ban on the LTTE as a "symbolic gesture with international ramifications", Prime Minister D.B. Wijetunga had accused India of not being serious about the matter. On May 21, intervening in the debate in Sri Lankan Parliament on the extension of Emergency, the Prime Minister referring to the security operations in the north-east had said, "This is a serious fight. Our soldiers in the security forces and our policemen too are fighting and sacrificing their lives to protect the innocent people... Therefore at this juncture, the government does not wish to prejudge the issues and take percipitate unilateral action." It is interesting that when India sought to get the notification banning the LTTE in India published in newspapers in Colombo to give the ban a wider publicity, the Lake House newspapers, controlled by the Government, though initially agreed to carry it, later reneged without assigning any reason for the same.

Sri Lanka remained ambivalent on the question of extradition even when Chandrika Kumaratunga came to power in Colombo, particularly when she had stormed into office with an agenda to establish peace through dialogue and accommodation with the Tamils. She had no hesitation in recognizing the LTTE as the only body of Tamils with whom she could open a dialogue. On a visit to India in March 1995, when talks with the LTTE were still on track, she told journalists in New Delhi who asked her whether Prabakaran would be arrested if sighted, "the problem is sighting him", and even if sighted, it would "depend on the circumstances". On August 13, 1995, after the talks with the LTTE had broken down, she still felt arresting Prabakaran "whose extradition had been sought by India was difficult". She asked, "If a hundred thousand Indian troops could not arrest him, how can we?" Sympathizing with India she said the idea of extraditing him was "laughable" and "it won't work."

On October 3, 1995 the Indian Minister for External Affairs Pranab Mukherjee told journalists that Indian request for extradition was "still on track", and "we have asked Sri Lankan Government to expedite it." Taking a charitable view of the delay Mukherjee said the delay was understandable considering the fact that India had provided Sri Lanka with 27 kilograms of documents relating to the case. In October 1995, both the Indian Prime Minister Narasimha Rao and Sri Lankan President Kumaratunga were in New York for the UN General Assembly meeting. The question of the extradition of Prabakaran figured in their talks in New York. According to one source who was present during the talks and quoted by the media, when Narasimha Rao reminded Kumaratunga of the extradition case, the latter reportedly told Rao, "You know what an elusive character he is. In fact, why don't you come and get him." Rao apparently shook his head and said, "No, thanks. We have already burnt our fingers once by getting involved in Sri Lanka and lost more than 1, 200 of our finest soldiers. We have no intention of repeating this mistake".

On October 17, 1995 Sri Lankan Minister of Justice and Constitutional Affairs, G.L. Peris told Parliament that the Attorney General was examining the Indian request. On November 21, Sri Lankan Inspector General of Police announced a reward of Rs. 5 million to any person supplying information leading to the arrest of Prabakaran. The police assured that the identity of the informer would be protected. In order to make the incentive attractive, it was announced that the reward would be available in any currency desired by the informer.

The Tamil groups were greatly disappointed at India's demand for Prabakaran's extradition. They lamented that hope of resuming a tattered peace process howsoever remote had been dashed by this single act of the Government of India. They said that if the doors to peace were shut by the LTTE, they had been locked by the Indian request. The groups bitterly opposed to the LTTE, like Eelam People's Democratic Party, however, welcomed the move. The Sinhala opinion broadly welcomed the move for extradition. In the past, however, if the public statements were any guides, former President Ranasinghe Premadasa would have summarily dismissed any Indian request for extradition. The late President had told a public meeting in April 1992, "Just because the younger brothers (Tamils/ Prabakaran) did wrong at time, the elder brothers (Sinhalas/ Premadasa) will not hand them over to next door (India) for the purpose of making them obedient". As pointed out above in June1992, Colombo had refused permission to a legal advisor to the Indian Central Bureau of Investigation to visit the country to discuss issues concerning extradition. Three years down the line, the wheel had moved full circle. The hard-line Sinhala opinion now wanted the government to help in the arrest and extradition of Prabakaran and his colleagues, as it was important to have India as an ally in the war against the LTTE. Though both India and Sri Lanka had ruled out Indian military intervention, external help to end the militancy refused to go away. To ensure Indian help in some unforeseen eventuality, Colombo felt the extradition would bolster Sri Lanka's position in New Delhi. Chandrika was not unmindful that a request of this kind from New Delhi would be another pressure point on LTTE, which stood isolated from the international community.

The Indian request for extradition of Prabakaran, despite lapse of time, still stands on the agenda of India-Sri Lanka relations. There is hardly any doubt that there is little chance of its being realized. When Sri Lanka's Prime Minister, Ranil Wickremasinghe, visited New Delhi on June 10-11, 2002 the spokesman of the Ministry of External Affairs maintained that New Delhi's demand for extradition of Prabakaran remained "operational" and that there was "no change" in Indian policy on the subject. Earlier, Tamil Nadu had too shut all options for the Government of India. On April 16, 2002 Tamil Nadu Legislative Assembly adopted a special government sponsored Resolution that Prabakaran should be extradited to India to stand trial in the Rajiv Gandhi assassination case. In keeping with Chief Minister Jayalalithaa, flamboyant style of functioning, the resolution demanded if the Sri Lankan Government was unable to capture Prabakaran and extradite him, the Central Government with Colombo's permission should send the Indian army to provide help to the Sri Lankan army and take all steps to capture Prabakaran. The Indian External Affairs Minister Yashwant Sinha during his visit to Colombo in October 2003 when asked by journalists reiterated that New Delhi was "pursuing" the extradition question with Colombo. While that might be New Delhi's official position for the record, there is no doubt that the demand has moved on the backburner, at least till the peace process under the Norwegian auspices reached end of the road one way or the other. As is well known, India has blessed the Norwegian initiative and assured Colombo of

India's goodwill in finding a solution to the ethnic conflict. By queering the pitch on the extradition question New Delhi could not be seen spoiling the party.

Sri Lankan Government meanwhile lifted her ban on the LTTE to kick-start the peace talks under the Norwegian aegis to meet the LTTE pre-condition to join any peace process. But the ban by India and other countries, however, stood in place. Consequently, there was no legal softening of any sort towards Prabakaran personally, at least for the time being. Prabakaran's lack of remorse at Rajiv Gandhi's assassination at his well-publicized press conference in April 2002 did not help matters. Not wanting to be explicit, he only confirmed what was believed to be his complicity in the crime by refusing to comment on "a tragic incident that happened ten years ago".

The confirmation of LTTE's involvement in the assassination case of Rajiv Gandhi was also provided by the Eastern Commander of the LTTE, Vinayagamoorthy Muralitharan *alias* Karuna, during his short lived revolt against the organization's leadership. In an interview to the *Hindu* (March 14, 2004) he ripped off the pal of evasion that the LTTE had placed on the assassination by evading responsibility. He nailed the LTTE for the Indian Prime Minister's assassination, describing it as the biggest mistake of the organization and added,

> "We should have stopped with fighting against the Indian Army. Going back and assassinating Rajiv Gandhi—killing him in Tamil Nadu—is not acceptable. I consider it the gravest mistake of our intelligence wing."

This by itself did not add much to the case of murder per se, which in any case stands concluded in India coming to the same appalling conclusion. Nevertheless, it provided conclusive evidence from the horse's mouth of the complicity of the Tigers in the heinous act. To that extent, it added to the already existing mountain of evidence that the Indian investigative agency collected following the assassination thus making things more difficult for the Government of India to show any clemency or leniency to either Prabakaran himself or his organization, now or later.

A lot of water has flowed down the Yumna since the assassination. After thorough investigation of the case by the Special Investigation Team (SIT) constituted by the Government of India, 41 LTTE men including Prabakaran and Pottu Amman were identified with the criminal conspiracy to assassinate Rajiv Gandhi. It may be mentioned that some of the accused who were either dead or absconding were not put on trial (Prabakaran and Pottu Amman were declared absconders and hence not tried). Both the Designated Court (constituted under the Terrorist and Disruptive Activities (Prevention) Act (TADA) for the trial of the case) and the Supreme Court, which heard the appeal, had no hesitation in concluding that the LTTE alone was responsible for the assassination of Rajiv Gandhi. Twenty-six accused that were charged by the prosecution before the Designated Court were convicted on January 28, 1998 of all the charges for which they were arraigned and sentenced to death. However, the case received some setback in the Supreme Court when it determined that the assassination could not be covered under the TADA. (The Court too did not admit government's Review Petition in this regard.) The Supreme Court sentenced only one accused to death. (It was subsequently commuted to life imprisonment.) Three accused were sentenced to life imprisonment. Others who were found guilty of lesser offences, the period of detention already undergone by them was set off and their release ordered forthwith by the Supreme Court. However, Supreme Court's observation that "there is not even a speck of doubt in our minds that the criminal conspiracy to murder Mr. Rajiv Gandhi was hatched by atleast four persons comprising of Vellupillai Prabakaran, Pottu Amman, Sivarasan and Akila" has far-reaching importance, both judicially and politically. Judicially, whenever and if ever any one of them is put on trial, there will be little space available for any trial court to come to any other conclusion. Politically, this verdict leaves little option for any government in India to show any political accommodation to Prabakaran or the LTTE.

There was a new twist in the Prabakaran drama. On October 31, 2002 a Colombo court handed down a 200-year sentence to Prabakaran in a 1996 Central Bank bombing case. This shuts any possibility of his extradition to India in the future should he be arrested if the current or any future peace process failed to find a settlement of the ethnic question. If on the other hand, a settlement to the ethnic entanglement were ever found, the position of Prabakaran in Sri Lanka would undergo a dramatic change. He is bound to control the new administration in the North-East. He would be an important element in any settlement and possibly turn into a Tamil and perhaps a Sri Lankan hero. No doubt Sri Lankan legal process would have a fresh look at the sentence awarded to him. Can an important leader of a neighbouring country, particularly of a community, which has ties of ethnicity with the people of India across the narrow waters of Palk Strait, be a criminal in the eyes of the Indian law? Well, that would be a dilemma for India to sort out!

‹26›

Devolution Package

As the peace process collapsed, and the hostilities resumed, the question of Indian help to pull Sri Lanka's chestnut out of the fire surfaced once again. However, the President remained ambivalent about India's position. In an interview to the New Delhi fortnightly *India Today* (May 15, 1995), while Kumaratunga appreciated India's stand that it was an internal problem of the Island, yet insisted that India as a friendly neighbour was concerned and understandably took the position that she would not interfere "unless the Sri Lanka Government wants them to. And even then I think they would think ten times before that, which should be the correct attitude". As far as India was concerned there had been conflicting signals emerging on this vital question in the light of the past experience. On May 19, 1995 the Indian Minister of State for External Affairs Raghunandan Lal Bhatia told the Press Trust of India in Amritsar that "Sri Lanka has approached a number of countries for help and India is considering what it can offer". But he ruled out dispatch of Indian troops to Sri Lanka and suggested that the possible help could be in the form of "military consultations, information, and training" of Sri Lankan armed forces. Earlier in May, India had set up a naval blockade across the Palk Strait in a bid to prevent LTTE boats from smuggling arms and fuel from India to Sri Lanka. On June 7, 1995 the Indian External Affairs Minister Pranab Mukherjee in an interview to the *Times of India* ruled out Indian intervention in Sri Lanka and confirmed that there had been no such request either from Colombo. Underlining Indian anxiety Mukherjee said, "we are concerned at the resumption of hostilities and the use of advance weaponry by the LTTE...we are watching the situation with close interest...and believe that a political solution has to be found within the framework of unity and integrity of Sri Lanka". Asked whether he was ruling out another Indian intervention, Mukherjee replied "yes, but I would not put it positively. The question does not arise since there is no request from Sri Lanka".

This was the second time almost within a month that the Indian External Affairs Minister had to rule out Indian intervention in the face of persistent reports that President Kumaratunga had indeed asked Indian assistance during her stay in New Delhi to attend the SAARC Summit. Five years later, after the fall of the Elephant Pass, when a military debacle stared Sri Lanka in the face and Colombo sent emergency and desperate messages to New Delhi for help to save the situation, New Delhi while appearing to prevaricate, consciously opted against any active involvement and decided to look the other way, when countries such as Israel and Pakistan extended military help, something that was anathema to India in the past.

Following a two-track policy of coalescing military action with a move on the political front to keep the political process going, President Kumaratunga on August 3, 1995, in an address to the nation, announced a package of devolution proposals envisaging the establishment of Regional Councils. Commending the proposals to the nation, she offered them as an "effective constitutional framework for the devolution of power to regions based on credibility, clarity, and an internally consistent and coherent value system, which is capable of effective implementation and include structures for the just resolution of centre-region disputes". Her address was full of hopes and gave promise of a new deal. She reiterated her commitment made in her address to the Nation on January 6, 1995 and repeating it said,

> "We have a vision of Sri Lanka where all communities can live in safety and security, where human dignity is valued and equality of treatment is an accepted norm of public life. We believe that all communities must be given the space to express their identity and participate fully in the life of the nation, whether it be at the national, provincial or local level..."

She spelt out the five principles on which her exercise for devolution was based:

(a) An effective constitutional framework for the devolution of powers to regions based on credibility, clarity and an internally consistent and coherent value system, which is capable of effective implementation and include structures for the just resolution of center-region disputes.

(b) To encourage the regions and communities which inhabit them to become constructive partners of a stable and pluralistic democracy.

(c) To ensure that all persons may fully and effectively exercise all their human rights and fundamental freedoms without any discrimination and in full equality before the laws.

(d) To give recognition to Sinhala and Tamil as official languages and to thereby accord equality of status to the official languages and to recognize English as a link language.

(e) To protect the identity of distinct communities and create conditions for the promotion of that identity including right to enjoy their own culture, profess and practice their own religion and nurture and promote their own language, and to transact business with the state in the national language of their choice.

Even before the President announced the proposals she had encountered opposition from the hard-line Sinhalese elements. On July 28, 1995 influential Buddhist Clergy had urged the President to delay the plan to devolve powers to the minority Tamils until the LTTE were defeated. On the other hand, the UNP for a change, showed understanding but refused to let Chandrika walk away with all the credit. A UNP delegation that had a 90-minute meeting with the President appeared positive and insisted that a solution to the north-east problem should be political and not military but insisted the President share the credit for the new move with the UNP. The UNP General Secretary, Gamini Athukorale claimed that it was "the UNP which started the devolution process". On the day the Cabinet accepted the proposals, a delegation of the National

Salvage Front, which included the JVP met the President and said they had "no quarrel" with the devolution process but before that was done, democracy should be restored in the country. The Lanka Sama Samaja Party, the Communist Party of Sri Lanka, and Sri Lanka Mahajana Party, which met President Kumaratunga on July 2, extended support to the devolution proposals. The TULF, however, wanted some improvements in the package and desired that the unit of the devolution be discussed separately and later. Expectedly, the LTTE officially rejected the package as a plan of betrayal and an attempt to isolate the LTTE from the Tamils. On August 12, Anton Balasingham was quoted on the radio "Voice of the Tigers" to say that "we are not at all worried in analysing the political package which was not submitted to us and to our people. The government announced the proposed political package and declared war at the same time and as such it is not giving way to stable solution and peace but will lead to long-term battle. The proposal is a plane betrayal and this solution would have been achieved during the period of negotiations with the LTTE."

On August 3, 1995 a Ceylon Worker's Congress delegation led by S. Thondoman, Minister for Livestock Development met the President. Thondoman repeated his surprise suggestion made a few days earlier that she entrusted the administration of the north-east to the LTTE leader Prabakaran for five years. The Memorandum "Devolution Package—Response of the Ceylon Workers' Congress" containing this proposal suggested that "the warring parties—the Government and the LTTE" should become "negotiating partners" if the "devolution package is to be accepted and implemented." The Memorandum underlined the capability of the LTTE, which relentlessly spearheaded the struggle for Tamil rights for over twelve years "to wield power, exercise authority and maintain law and order". Putting the onus "to build up the legal framework and to develop democratic institutions for the sharing of power and exercise of authority" on the LTTE, the Memorandum put the responsibility of providing support to the LTTE "for the steady evolution of the democratic process" on the Government of Sri Lanka. Thondoman also suggested that the whole of the Island should be divided into four regions to facilitate administration and to make the devolution process viable. The regions should be

(1) North-East, (2) North-Central, (3) North-Western and (4) Central Uva and Sabaragamuwa and Western and Southern.

On August 11, India expressed her strong support to President Kumaratunga's proposals to end the dragging ethnic conflict and described the package as a "bold attempt" to end a bloody separatist drive by Tamil guerrillas. A spokesman for New Delhi said, "the devolution package deserves the most serious consideration of all concerned", and added, "The Indian government has taken note of the proposals for devolution of power for a political solution to the ethnic issue...India has consistently stood for a peaceful political solution of this crisis".

There was international support for the package too. The European Union extending its support to the President's initiative said, "the EU hopes that the far-reaching proposals the Government has set out, will be considered carefully and constructively by all parties. This could open the way for an early return to peace, normality and development throughout the entire country." The International Relations Committee of the United States House of Representatives unanimously adopted a resolution supporting the government's peace process.

In order to create a broad consensus for the package, the President expressed her desire to go the extra mile and announced that if the LTTE would accept the democratic process and the devolution proposals, the government was prepared to offer a cease-fire to the LTTE. She rejected any proposal to ban the LTTE for the present. Despite the fact that India lost much of the initiative in the Sri Lanka imbroglio, Colombo had never been unmindful of the Indian sensitivities. It always made sure that in every initiative India's blessings were ensured and that New Delhi was kept on board and on the right side. Whenever there was a change of Government in New Delhi, and since 1996 there had been too many, Sri Lanka found herself first in the Indian capital trying to preempt the possibility of the new government being influenced otherwise. It happened when Deve Gowda became Prime Minister, again when I.K. Gujral formed the government and yet again when the Bharatiya Janata Party led National Democratic Alliance saw itself installed in New Delhi. On each occasion she received assurances of her unity and territorial integrity.

The year 1996 saw yet again the installation of Dravida Munnetra Kazhagam (DMK) under the leadership of M. Karunanidhi in Tamil Nadu. The party was an alliance partner in the United Front Government under Prime Minister Deve Gowda. Karunanidhi personally and the DMK were known sympathizers of the LTTE. However, after the assassination of Rajiv Gandhi, the Party had slightly distanced itself from the LTTE. Karunanidhi's remarks to the EPDP leader Douglas Devananda on May 2, 1996 that although he was supportive of the interests of the Tamil community in Sri Lanka, he would not extend any support to the LTTE since "we have had enough of the LTTE and we are now fed up with him" were music to the ears of the Sinhalese regime in Colombo.

Paradoxically, while India's assurance to respect the Island's territorial integrity and unity were welcome in Colombo, her assurance of non-interference in the internal affairs of the Island did not create a very comfortable feeling. Colombo was painfully aware that unless LTTE were defeated or weakened militarily, there was little chance of any meaningful political dialogue and settlement. Colombo also knew well that this formidable task the Sri Lankan security forces were unable to perform by themselves. Colombo held India responsible for creating the LTTE monster. The President and other leaders declared more than once publicly that India was guilty of this unpardonable sin and they would not allow India to wash her hands of the mess. Sri Lanka expected India to play a positive role in combating the LTTE menace. President Kumaratunga agreeing with the suggestion of the editor of the *Frontline*, N. Ram (January 1, 1999) that India was morally obliged to help Sri Lanka to find a solution had said, "I would tend to agree with you. I think India does have a moral obligation, given the fact that they were also partly responsible for the commencement of the war. Not India, but the Indian government of that time".

In January 1997, External Affairs Minister Inder Kumar Gujral visited Colombo and extended assurances of India's non-interference. The Government owned *Daily News* refused to give an unqualified welcome to this pronouncement and said on January 20, 1997:

> "Mr. Gujral is on record as having said that India does not want to interfere in Sri Lanka's internal affairs. This, of course, is an international principle, which has to be respected for the better conduct of international relations. But such formal principles should not prevent a friendly neighbour from discharging responsibilities. Sri Lanka's sovereignty and territorial integrity cannot be secured without India's assistance".

Another government owned paper *Sunday Times* holding India responsible for the present situation argued that merely saying that "India will not interfere in Sri Lanka's internal affairs is not enough" and opined "having interfered, India must undo the damage it inflicted on its southern neighbour". It was an amusing situation. The media and the Sri Lankan leaders who earlier accused New Delhi of interfering in the internal affairs of the Island, were now arguing in favour of India getting involved to discharge her responsibility to her neighbour. Colombo was not willing to let India take shelter under the Gujral doctrine to escape its "responsibility".

Caught in this new situation, New Delhi remained keen to stay out of the ethnic riddle. Gujral insisted that the conflict was an internal matter and the Tamil Nadu Chief Minister personally and the DMK party as a whole had endorsed this position. He was quite assertive that India would not allow her territory to be used by the LTTE for hostile activities against Colombo. Colombo was no longer shy of looking at India's commitment to the territorial integrity of the Island from the prism of its own angle. They regarded Indian support as compulsive and not altruistic. The Colombo media recalled that the first cry for separatism in India echoed from Tamils in South India. They pointed out that the implications for India for a separate Tamil state in Sri Lanka comprising less than two million Tamils were ominous. There were other separatist movements in India as in Kashmir, the Punjab, and Assam, which did not augur well for her, if they received support from abroad.

In March 1998, after the mid-term poll, the Bharatiya Janata Party led National Democratic Alliance (NDA) government assumed office in New Delhi. As in the past, Sri Lankans were again the first to land in the capital ostensibly to greet the new government but in fact to receive the renewed assurances of India's position towards the ethnic issue. They never returned dissatisfied on this account in the past and this time too they were not disappointed. The new leadership had no difficulty in repeating all the assurances of the past and make Colombo feel happy. The fresh issue of Gazette notification on May 14, 1998, continuing the earlier ban on the LTTE for another two years in India was an assurance, which the Lankans welcomed gleefully. A grateful Sri Lanka remained uncritical when Buddha smiled on May 14, 1998 at Pokhran and India conducted nuclear tests to the amazement of the whole world.

❮27❯

Epilogue

As the stalemate continued in the ethnic conflict, the LTTE showed its periodic signs of fatigue. In his Martyrs' day message of November 27, 1998 Prabakaran lamented that the Tamil problem remained unresolved despite so much of sacrifices and bloodshed. He felt compelled to call for peace and said, "we are open to the civilized method of resolving conflict through rational dialogue." Given the lack of trust between the Tamils and the Sinhalese and the failure of the earlier efforts to achieve peace in direct talks with the government, he showed preference for "third party mediation for political negotiations," but "without preconditions". Again on September 30, 1999, the LTTE in a press release accepted that "international third party mediation is crucial and necessary for a negotiated political settlement of the Tamil national question".

Since the withdrawal of the IPKF and the failure of the two peace initiatives, President Kumaratunga had been in a quandary on how to break the impasse and bring the recalcitrant and contumacious LTTE within the mainstream of the political life of the country to end the ethnic conflict that had consumed over 60,000 lives, a much larger number wounded, hundreds of thousands displaced within and outside the Island and destruction of unlimited material resources. The President was quite conscious, given the past history of the ethnic conflict, the credibility gap between the government and the LTTE had widened. The real problem before the government was how to restore that credibility and create the confidence without which no talks could possibly succeed. It was for this very reason that during the 1995 peace process, when the talks with the LTTE drifted aimlessly, Kumaratunga had proposed the intervention of a retired French diplomat. The offer was then rejected by the LTTE on the plea of transparency saying, that it could not negotiate on the back of the people. It, too, had apprehensions about the impartiality of the Frenchman. It is pertinent to point out that while the LTTE was averse to private mediation, which the suggestion implied, Colombo showed aversion to any foreign official intervention in a dispute between itself and its citizens, particularly after the experience of the aborted Indian mediation.

With history of failed offensives and the long history of the conflict, the President was not unmindful that the LTTE could neither be militarily defeated nor weakened, nor was it possible to impose a settlement on it against its wishes. After each reverse it had bounced back with greater vigour, vitality and exuberance thus gaining the reputation of the most formidable guerrilla organization in the world. The LTTE might have lost an odd battle in its long struggle but had not been defeated decisively nor would it capitulate to negotiate on terms unacceptable to it. It had not only shown its teeth but also sunk them deep into anyone who dared challenge its supremacy. One has to take into account the fact that since the LTTE's success in sabotaging the 1987 India-Sri Lanka Peace Agreement and the humiliation it succeeded in heaping on the IPKF, the LTTE's claim as the only organization capable of representing the Tamil interests had become unchallenged. The LTTE during its long struggle eliminated all other rival Tamil groups, militant or moderate, struggling for the rights of the Tamils. The TULF was the oldest and most representative of the Tamil organizations and during its long existence had chosen to adopt the parliamentary route to get justice for the Tamils. The LTTE, one by one, wiped out its top leadership over the years. Whatever was left of it, meekly surrendered to it by accepting it as the sole representative of the Tamils. If the government had to negotiate with any Tamil organization, it did not have much of a choice. A solution acceptable to TULF or any other Tamil organization had no meaning unless acceptable to the LTTE. On the other hand, what was acceptable to it, others had no choice but to accept that without question. Having said that it too remained a fact of life that most of the people accepted its leadership more out of fear than respect for it. Faced with this situation, Colombo's options were limited. They had little choice. It is instructive that during the parliamentary elections-2001, the TULF along with some other Tamil parties entered into an alliance, on a common platform recognizing the supremacy of the LTTE. The LTTE consequently achieved its long-dreamt objective of being the sole representative of all the Tamils in the Island. It was a different matter that later the TULF fearing being completely sidelined, tried once again to regain the lost ground but it was too late and faced a split. In the April 2004-elections, the TULF once again accepted the LTTE as the sole representative of the Tamils by joining in the Tamil National Alliance and surrendered the initiative to the LTTE. In the process it wrote its own death warrant.

The LTTE 'earned' for itself this unenviable position through both blood and terror. The Sinhalese— the State and the people—besides the international community too likewise had no choice but to recognize it as the authentic voice of the Tamils. It successfully created a state within a state, controlling territory; running a parallel administration that levied and collected taxes, enforced its own laws and system of justice. Some of the countries, which declared it a terrorist organization and banned its activities on their soil, did so to put pressure on it to join the mainstream of the political life of the country and help in the restoration of peace and tranquillity. They had been careful no to treat it as a pariah. Each one of the countries with interest in the area, whether the United States or the countries of the European Union or the EU itself, did not ignore the LTTE despite imposing ban on its activities in their countries. The ban was an instrument to curb the streak of violence in it, while pressurizing Sri Lanka the urgent need to meet Tamil aspirations. A number of diplomats based in Colombo and other dignitaries visit the LTTE-held area in the North and keep contacts with it with the tacit approval of Colombo, thus giving it some legitimacy. However, the stigma of a terrorist organization haunts it. On its own the LTTE did precious little to convince the world that it has given up its stripes and was willing to settle to a political career. Consistent refusal of the LTTE to dismantle the military camps set up in the post cease-fire period near Trincomalee in violation of the cease-fire agreement, renewed efforts to rearm and strengthen itself militarily, refusal to give legitimate space to the Muslims by continuing hostility towards them, assassination of Tamil political rivals and perceived agents of the government, did not create enough confidence in the civil society that the LTTE was willing to settle for a political solution in a democratic milieu. The continued recruitment of children among its cadres has neither beholden it to the human rights groups and international organizations. The civil society, too, did not wish to leave the Tigers in any doubt that unless it renounced violence, both the legitimacy and respectability it hankered would elude it.

Anxious to eliminate all vestiges of terrorism from the face of the earth after September 11, 2001, the United States declared the LTTE a terrorist outfit. Washington however, used the ban principally to push it to the negotiating table and has been doing everything to sustain the peace process despite roadblocks. The statement of the deputy spokesman of the State Department, Philip Reeker on August 6, 2003 that by its boycott of the current peace process, the LTTE was "undermining hopes for peace" and that "Washington was concerned with some aspects of Tiger behaviour" was intended to nudge the LTTE to return to the negotiating table and warning it against resuming its violent activities. The US State Department's fresh designation on October 23, 2003 of the LTTE as a terrorist organization along with 25 other international terrorist outfits, to fulfill a statutory requirement to continue the ban, sought to convey the same message. Clarifying the ban on the same day Richard Boucher, the spokesman of the State Department reiterated, that "although the LTTE are engaged in a peace process with the Sri Lankan Government, one which is supported by the US, Washington has determined that the group continues to engage in terrorist activities" and hence the redesignation. This came as a great disappointment to the LTTE in its search for legitimacy. Ever since the current peace process started, the LTTE used every opportunity and ploy to get itself out of the isolation imposed on it by the international community. That Colombo was forced to withdraw its ban to kick-start the negotiations was a different story. Interestingly and ironically on September 29, 2003 Sri Lankan Minister of Constitutional Affairs had thrown broad hints to the US Deputy Secretary of State Richard Armitage for withdrawal of the American ban on the LTTE but was rebuffed and told that USA would revoke the ban only after the LTTE renounced terrorism and ceased to perpetrate terrorist acts. No wonder while the President's party, SLFP welcomed the American announcement of October 2, 2003, the reaction of the UNP or its government was muted. This once again demonstrated lack of domestic consensus on a vital issue. The claim made by the former Deputy US Permanent Representative to the UN and a former American Ambassador in Colombo Peter Burleigh that the United States took the lead internationally in attempting to isolate and weaken the LTTE and his country's efforts crystallized when the LTTE was added to the list of the terrorist groups was a truism. Speaking on the role of the US in South Asian conflicts at a seminar in Colombo's Bandaranaike Centre for International Studies on March 21, 2004 he said:

> "That step by the US made illegal the supply of financial and other support from US citizens to the LTTE. It also has some impact on similar actions taken by other governments, where like the US, there are substantial number of Tamil expatriates. While this US action probably had some real financial impact on the LTTE, perhaps, more importantly it had a psychological and practical impact which probably made the LTTE leadership more inclined to seek a negotiated settlement."

It is not for nothing that unlike in the past, the LTTE while avoiding the talks, and expressing dissatisfaction with the slow progress had avoided the temptation to return to the path of violence. By dragging its feet on one issue or another, it tested not only Colombo's but also the patience of the international community, while attempting to gain time for the international situation to turn in its favour. Interestingly and unlike in the past and for the first time, the LTTE in rejecting Colombo's proposals for an interim administration, went to great lengths to hammer out counter proposals for a political structure that would meet their objective and undertake the reconstruction and rehabilitation work in the Tamil areas with the money that was committed at the Tokyo Conference in June 2003. This change in its attitude and approach was significant and raised hopes that LTTE after all may have realized the limits of dividend that violence could pay in the post-9/11 world arraigned against terrorism in all its manifestations and across the globe. The civil society across the globe is not willing to accept resort to violence to gain an objective, howsoever justified and laudable in the eyes of so-called liberation movement(s).

Colombo's position had been vulnerable on various counts. Chinks in its armour stood exposed more than once—on the fall of the Elephant Pass in 2000 and again during LTTE's crippling attack on the Colombo air force base and the civilian aircraft in October 2001. It once again realized that its ill-trained, ill-motivated and demoralized security forces were no match for the highly trained and motivated Tigers and therefore the inevitability of negotiating with the LTTE.

Colombo taking note of the LTTE's position on "international third party mediation" and keen to bring the Tigers to the negotiating table was cognizant that some sort of intervention from a third party had become inevitable. However there was some initial hesitation on the form of this intervention. As pointed out above private intervention was ruled out by the LTTE in the past. Colombo did not wish to leave anybody in doubt that while it favoured facilitation, it was against any form of mediation, which bordered on arbitration. On October 17, 1999 Foreign Minister Kadirgamar articulated Lanka's position on this question in the Colombo based *Sunday Observer*. He rejected mediation since it amounted to judgmental decisions and conclusions concerning the merits of the dispute and could lead to recommendations that might be totally unacceptable to the state. He emphasized that it would be very difficult for a sovereign State to accept a mediator, thus understood, in a dispute with a group of its own citizens. President Kumaratunga too ruled out mediation in an interview to the editor of the *Hindu* (October 18, 1999) and showed her preference for facilitation.

The fiasco of the fall of the Elephant Pass in 2000 and the crippling LTTE attack on air-force base in Colombo the next year and Indian inability to respond to Colombo's entreaties for meaningful help thereby acquiescing in Colombo turning to Israel and Pakistan, an abomination for New Delhi in the past, left Colombo with little option. India at this time was caught in the web of domestic coalition politics. It was a different matter that the estrangement of the DMK, a partner in the ruling

National Democratic Alliance, from the LTTE due to its killing of moderate Tamil leaders expanded New Delhi's options but it remained loath to commit itself to any military response. The re-notification of the ban on the LTTE on May 14, 2000 for another two years, as per the statutory requirement was an assurance to Sri Lanka that India, while unable to militarily respond to its needs, remained distanced from the Tigers. It too, was a message to the Tigers that its sins had not been forgotten in New Delhi. This delivered a negative message that New Delhi unable to break fresh ground remained prisoner of the past and therefore unable to make any meaningful contribution in resolving the ethnic conflict.

India's failure to sharpen a response to the developing situation in the Island too belied her claim as the regional power. That she was averse to leave the field free for any outside country to tread on her turf to promote a solution by mediation or facilitation was no longer relevant. As pointed out above, Sri Lanka unable to tame the Tigers militarily or otherwise was desperate for an outside agency, which would bring the LTTE to the negotiating table and keep it there. The latter having been at the receiving end of the Indian stick since 1987 and now smarting under the Indian ban had lost confidence in Indian fairness. It perceived that New Delhi was more concerned with promoting its own strategic interests than finding a solution to the Tamil problem. Prabakaran specifically articulated this later at his press conference on April 10, 2002, when he said: "We too decided that Norway would be an appropriate facilitator because of its neutrality and that it has no strategic interest in the region". The implication was clear and left no one guessing that the LTTE continued to believe that India only subordinated the Tamil interests to her own regional strategic concerns. LTTE ideologue Anton Balasingham keen to soften the impact of Prabakaran's message of no-confidence in India, amplifying Prabakaran's remarks assured India that LTTE was not permanently estranged from New Delhi. Administering a sugarcoated pill to humour India he said,

> "Without India this problem will not find a permanent settlement. India is the regional super-power and we need India's backing and support. We do not want to

have any unfriendly relationship with India because we have suffered a lot as a consequence of contradictions between India and the LTTE. So, we want to renew our friendship and engage in a positive relationship with India."

Both Prabakaran and Balasingham however remained conscious that the assassination of Rajiv Gandhi had alienated India from the LTTE cause as distinct from that of the Tamils. Keeping an eye on the future and not wanting to burn bridges completely with India, Balasingham took pains to emphasize the common ties of race that bind Sri Lankan Tamils with the Indian Tamils. He said at the same press conference: "As a race of people, we are Tamils and we have our roots in India. India is our fatherland. We have respect and love for India and its people". He pleaded for a new relationship with India overcoming the past.

Balasingham repeated the same theme of "forgive and forget" on December 6, 2003 at a meeting organized in London to commemorate the annual "Heroes' Day". Expressing LTTE's desire to establish "friendly relations with India" he pleaded that in the past both sides had made mistakes and therefore "let us put the past behind and look forward". Beseeching for a "radical change in India's attitude", Balasingham assured New Delhi that it would "not act in any way prejudicial to India's geo-political and economic interests". He also sought to assure India that if she were to give up her unfriendly posture towards the LTTE, the latter would welcome New Delhi playing a "significant role in the current peace process". He therefore asked India "to adopt a new creative approach and initiate friendly relations with our organization".

Balasingham's statement has to be read in the backdrop of the "arrest" of Indian fishermen by the LTTE off the coast in Northern Sri Lanka under its control on November 29, 2003. Their release through the intervention of Norway brought home to India that she had the LTTE as the presiding deity in its neighbourhood and she learn to live with this fact, even if it was an uncomfortable one. The LTTE in trying to coerce India to end its hostility towards it was glossing over the intricacies of Indian domestic politics. It failed to understand that the ruling goddess in Chennai was alienated from the LTTE and would not countenance any friendly demeanor by New Delhi. Besides, the Indian public had yet not forgiven the LTTE of its peccadillo of committing the assassination of Rajiv Gandhi. The Congress Party presided over by the widow of the late Prime Minister was a strong force to reckon with in the domestic politics of the country and any softening towards the LTTE would create avoidable complications. Already, the Tamil Nadu Chief Minister Jayalalithaa taking a serious note of the LTTE's indiscretion in "arresting" Tamil Nadu fishermen had provoked her to urge New Delhi to conduct joint naval exercises with the Lankan navy to eliminate "unauthorized" naval operations in the international waters by naval arm of the LTTE, the Sea Tigers. She also warned New Delhi about the "explosive impact" of LTTE's terrorism on the Indian internal security, which was becoming more vulnerable and fragile by the day due to the inter-play of various terrorist organizations.

Nevertheless, on the fall of the Elephant Pass in April 2000, India realized that Colombo unable to find a military solution appeared desperate for help in promoting talks with the LTTE and smelt an opportunity to seize the initiative from the Norwegians who were waiting on the sidelines for quite some time. While not wishing to get militarily involved, New Delhi offered to facilitate the talks should both the LTTE and Colombo approached her. Norway not wishing to involve herself in unseemly competition with India was more than willing to let India try once more the peacemaker's role. Oslo told Sri Lanka that if "anyone particularly India, wants to play a role in this process, it is perfectly all right from their side". Foreign Minister Kadirgamar told *Daily News* on May 23, 2000 that Norwegians had "recognized India's valuable position in this region, they have recognized the inevitability of Indian involvement in this issue. You cannot have a political solution to this problem without atleast the consent of India". But Kadirgamar was not happy the way India had offered to facilitate talks. Instead of making any formal offer through an official communication or in conversation with any senior Minister or functionary of the government, the Indian External Affairs Minister Jaswant Singh merely made the offer in an off- the-cuff remark to a T.V. news channel and left it at that. Sri Lankan Foreign Minister bemoaned the lack of diplomatic subtlety. India did not follow up her offer officially. As expected the offer was neither picked up by Colombo nor by the LTTE. The Indian initiative, made half-heartedly, was a non-starter.

Having failed to gain ground in Colombo, New Delhi had no alternative but to feel satisfied that both Sri Lanka and Norway had conceded the Indian *locus standi* and were keen to take New Delhi on board as the train chugged along. The LTTE was neither averse to this. The USA too, conceded India's interest, a point well articulated by both the Deputy and the Assistant Secretaries of State of the US State Department, during their visits to the sub-continent in May and November 2000 respectively. The military situation, after the fall of Elephant Pass stabilized in favour of Colombo. President Kumaratunga regained her poise and confidence to tackle the LTTE menace. In the new scenario India returned to the scene yet again to see if there was a role for her. She no doubt realized her limitations but did not wish to be left out completely while others came and fished in her waters.

It was to assert this interest that the External Affairs Minister Jaswant Singh, appeared in Colombo in June 2000, to once again assure the "continued commitment of the Government of India to the unity, sovereignty and territorial integrity of Sri Lanka". Sounding helpful, Jaswant Singh offered to President Kumaratunga "assistance in the humanitarian and economic spheres to ease any constraints that may be currently faced by Sri Lanka" and announced a credit facility of US $ 100 million. Elaborating on return to New Delhi on June 12, the Minister said that India would provide "advice" to the government and political parties in Sri Lanka without encroaching on the country's sovereignty or aiding it militarily. He offered to consider the appointment of a Special Envoy for Sri Lanka to facilitate the process of advice. But Colombo had no interest in mere advice and the offer of a Special Envoy did not take off.

India again found herself ticked off by Colombo, when the Indian High Commissioner Gopal Gandhi indiscreetly expressed "disappointment" at air raids made by Sri Lanka Air Force "in self- defence" on LTTE targets at the end of June and beginning of July 2001 to "pre-empt" LTTE attack in Jaffna peninsula.

India's advice that "there was no alternative to peace" did not go down well with Colombo. Colombo taking umbrage to Indian response described it "unrealistic and unacceptable". Colombo was miffed that New Delhi unable to bail it out, should express disappointment while failing to take note that the bombings were "pre-emptive and in self-defence". Therefore Sri Lanka described American response as "principled and realistic" and Indian stand "unacceptable and unrealistic". Bemoaning Indian attitude, the Government statement castigated India and declared that it was the "unquestioned right" of any sovereign state to defend its territorial integrity and made a point of mentioning that it was a right India had "often" exercised. Sri Lanka did not fail to note that the United States too had expressed "concern", but respected "the right of any nation to defend its territorial integrity", which implicitly accepted Colombo's explanation. Colombo held the High Commissioner personally responsible for this imprudence since it was felt that he failed in his duty to correctly brief and advise New Delhi. Presidential Secretariat sent discreet hints to New Delhi that Colombo would find it difficult to do business with its representative who lacked understanding of Sri Lankan position. Not long thereafter in a routine reshuffle of some postings, Colombo found itself doing business with a new High Commissioner.

As the year 2001 was racing to a close, there were fast paced developments within the Island. In the elections to the Parliament, the opposition succeeded in edging out the incumbent government of the President's party. A new United National Front government under Ranil Wickremasinghe of the UNP took office to the chagrin of Chandrika Kumaratunga.

Wickremasinghe's assumption of office of the Prime Minister of Sri Lanka introduced domestic antagonism in the country's politics, and the manner in which he handled the peace process impacted it negatively. It was for the first time since the introduction of the present Constitution by Jayewardene in 1978 that the parliamentary and the executive heads of the polity were from two different and historically antagonistic parties. Therefore, instead of complementing each other, which was the need of the hour, the two were seen acting as rivals in running the administration. The Prime Minister signed the Cease-fire

Agreement with the LTTE on February 22, 2003, without consulting the President who was the executive head of the government. He held discussions with the LTTE by holding back the details from the President. The President's suggestion to appoint her representative at the talks received scant attention from Wickremasinghe. The President who was ultimately and constitutionally responsible for the final settlement was understandably upset. In short, the actions of the Prime Minister failed to promote a harmonious relationship between the two pillars of the executive who needed to stand together to hold the structure of the peace that Wickremasinghe thought he was building.

Assuming the reins of government in Colombo, Ranil Wickremasinghe with the past experience as a guide, felt convinced that even if India had opted to stand out, her interest in any solution of the conflict as a regional power could not be denied. He remained anxious to keep Indian goodwill intact. On taking office in Colombo he lost no time to visit India (December 2001). He not only obtained New Delhi's blessings to any peace initiative launched through the good offices of Norway, but also asked Norway to make sure that New Delhi was kept in the picture. The LTTE anxious to proceed with the fresh peace initiative too wished to use the opportunity to see if it could maneuver to get out of the Indian proscription without showing any remorse for its past. It proposed that its chief negotiator, Anton Balasingham, was allowed to take up residence in Chennai for medical considerations and India hosted the talks for reasons of logistics. Left to itself the Government of India did not appear averse to the idea, despite being aware of LTTE's unsavory past. But as pointed out above, given the antagonistic predilections of the ruling party in Tamil Nadu, the AIADMK upped the ante and scuttled any such possibility. The memories of the LTTE misusing the hospitality of Tamil Nadu in the eighties were still fresh in the minds of the ruling establishment in Chennai and the public in general. The assassination of Rajiv Gandhi too had antagonized the Tamil public opinion against the LTTE. It is noteworthy that even the rival opposition party the DMK, one time LTTE's benefactor, too had lost sympathy for it. New Delhi, therefore, found hamstrung in taking an independent line and show any accommodation to the LTTE. The baggage of domestic politics had become a millstone round New Delhi's neck.

Be, as it may, the Norwegian facilitations picked up. The government and the LTTE signed a Memorandum for cease-fire on February 22, 2002. Unfortunately, in signing the Memorandum for cease-fire the Prime Minister went against the proclaimed policy of the President, and thereby he took the risk of running into problems with her. Cleverly maneuvering through the fragmented Sinhala politics, the LTTE succeeded in gaining some sort of political space, despite international ban remaining in place. As an unvanquished force LTTE clinched for itself the status of an equal partner with the government in the negotiations that followed. The holding of talks in different world capitals, each meeting being hosted and tacitly supported by governments and international agencies, catapulted the LTTE into prominence and gave it a position on par with the Government of Sri Lanka. It was no wonder that the LTTE felt humiliated when it was excluded from the Washington Conference in April 2003 and since then boycotted the peace talks altogether.

Nevertheless, each round of talks emitted positive signals and brought cheers around the Island to its war-weary people. Prabakaran's Heroes' Day message of November 2002, was equally encouraging when he said: "we are prepared to consider favourably a political framework that offers substantial regional autonomy and self-government in our homeland on the basis of our right to self-determination". Prime Minister touted it a "paradigm shift" in the LTTE's position. In the euphoria of the day it was forgotten that in the past too the LTTE had pledged itself to a federal solution to renege from it later to the chagrin of everybody. On March 2, 1993 in a BBC interview and on February 5, 1995 in an interview to the *Sunday Island*, Prabakaran and Balasingham expressed similar sentiments respectively. Similarly, on March 26, 1995 Lawrence Thilakar, the international spokesman of the LTTE had said, "if there is a federal solution, we will consider it." One has to remember that in the initial stages of conflict resolution federalism was a dirty word with the Sinhalese and they were loath to talk of it. But pushed to the wall, the term had gained some respectability in Colombo. The Constitutional proposals of August 2000, which conceded the concept of federalism without saying so did not pass muster with the UNP and fell through in the inter-play of Sinhala politics. Times changed and it was now the UNP that shouldered the responsibility of hammering out a peace settlement. Interestingly and for the first time, the LTTE while boycotting the peace talks in April 2003 agreed to spell out their terms for a settlement. It was the hope of all that in making its proposals, it would keep the broad perimeters of federalism in mind and not deviate from the basic principles.

As the peace talks made some progress, New Delhi had the mortification to see the foreign intervention widening to include high profile countries like Japan, the United States, the United Kingdom, France besides the European Community itself. Colombo's request for British inputs to restructure the Island's security forces and legal consultations for an interim administration were scarcely a palliative for New Delhi. The consultations among the LTTE and its sympathizers within the Diaspora and international experts on constitutional matters in Paris in late August 2003 and by all accounts hosted by the French Government, to sharpen its (LTTE's) response to the Colombo's proposal for an interim administration in the North-east, left India wondering whether she was now condemned to be a mere spectator and only hear out what others wished to do in her backyard.

India drew satisfaction from the fact that despite standing on the sidelines, her interest in the peace process has been acknowledged and accepted in more than one way. It was best articulated by President herself in an interview with the *Hindu* (April 12, 2003) of Chennai. While making light of the interest of other countries, she said:

> "India is the one country that would be justifiably interested in Sri Lanka. Sri Lanka's future in this matter, for reasons that are known, I don't have to spell them out. The historical reasons, the geographic proximity, the linkages, the economic and everything else. Therefore, India should play a very proactive role politically, I don't mean militarily."

This explains why Colombo remained solicitous of Indian interests in Sri Lanka. This held good both for Prime Minister

Wickremasinghe and President Chandrika Kumaratunga, who periodically found enough excuses to visit New Delhi to keep India abreast of the developments in talks with the LTTE from their individual perspectives. Needless to say the perspective of the two Sri Lankan leaders differed substantially. The Norwegians were too not found wanting in this respect.

Wickremasinghe's anxiety to increase the area of accord and harmony with New Delhi found expression in his decision of February 16, 2003 to bring in the legislation to provide citizenship to the Tamils of Indian origin holding Indian passports but had been staying on in Sri Lanka for long and their natural increase numbering around 1,68,000. They were held up in Sri Lanka since their repatriation process was linked to the return of the Sri Lankan refugees from India and also because the ferry-service between the two countries had been disrupted. It may be recalled that Balasingham had in the famous press conference of April 10, 2002 included the citizenship question of these Tamils as part of the LTTE agenda for ethnic settlement. By the present move (the necessary legislation for this purpose has since been adopted by the Island's Parliament), the government intended to ensure that atleast one irritant in the peace process was out of the way. It too had the effect of denying the LTTE the leadership role of the Tamils of Indian origin while helping Wickremasinghe to strengthen his credentials with New Delhi since their repatriation would have opened the old wounds. In any case, New Delhi had long ago declared that it deemed the problem of Tamils of Indian origin still stranded in the Island as closed. With the present action the problem officially too now stood closed.

The Norwegians accepting the importance of Indian interest made sure that New Delhi was kept informed and it supported the process all along. Eric Solheim stated the obvious on November 18, 2003 in New Delhi on his way to Norway from Colombo after stating that the peace process was on hold until the two Sinhala parties sorted out their differences. He had no difficulty in acknowledging that New Delhi was kept informed at every stage of the negotiations. He was candid enough to admit that though India was not involved in the peace negotiations directly, she would have to come in at some stage and he did not see any prospect of lasting peace till issues concerning India were also addressed.

The plan for an interim administration presented by Colombo having been rejected by the LTTE, the latter for the first time presented its own proposals to Colombo on October 31, 2003. It envisaged the setting up of an Interim Self Governing Authority (ISGA) with sweeping powers. This precipitated a crisis in the Island's politics and brought the President and the Prime Minister, who were living in an uneasy co-habitation arrangement hammers and tong at each other. The proposals did not merely ask for control of the administration but defying all canons of federalism, were a prescription for splitting the country. The President who always feared that the Prime Minister had been too soft on the LTTE to win peace at any cost and anxious to put a halt to any more government munificence fired her first salvo. She stripped the three ministers of the Cabinet of their important portfolios of defence, interior and communication when the Prime Minister was on an official visit to the USA and assumed their direct charge.

The LTTE's proposals not only sought the monopoly of powers in all walks of life and administration for itself but also failed to assign any role to Colombo in the ISGA. If the norms of settlement set in the Oslo accord of December 2002 and India-Sri Lanka Joint Communiqué of October 2003 issued at the end of Prime Minister Wickremasinghe's visit were applied, they come nowhere near them even remotely, but instead seek to put in place an unparalleled new constitutional set-up for the north-east completely independent of the central government. They too do not come any way near the LTTE's own declared intention of seeking substantial autonomy based on federal principles. The central government's role was limited to giving annual funds for the north-east and nominating some representatives on the LTTE dominated, (not Tamil dominated) ISGA. The Government of Sri Lanka was denied any role with regard to important matters like international agreements relating to trade and natural resources, police and justice administration, auditing of accounts, land administration, taxation and finance and local administration with regard to the north-east. Sri Lankan government was prohibited from entering into any fresh agreement with regard to the north-east and its resources on which the ISGA would exercise complete control so much so that it would even exercise complete control of and access to the coastline of the north-east. In short what the LTTE suggested was a completely new administrative set-up with "plenary powers" outside of the jurisdiction of the Sri Lankan Constitution, in which the LTTE would be supreme and the Sinhalese and the Muslims and the State of Sri Lanka on its sufferance. What the LTTE asked was a licence for unilateralism with no scope for national interface between various communities. The ISGA instead of creating an interactive society would unbind whatever links there were between the Tamils and the other communities in the region. It sought to bring into reality the cherished concept of homeland of the Tamils in the North-East to the exclusion of everybody else.

Colombo, in its own proposals made to the LTTE earlier for the interim administration, had excluded matters pertaining to police, land, taxation, and security. While it was true that Colombo too had given a majority role to the LTTE in interim administration, there were safeguards for other communities like minority veto on matters that affected the interests of Muslims and the Sinhalese living in the North-East, because the two communities between them constituted 60 per cent of the population of the Eastern Province. It may be pertinent to recall that the Muslims draw their entire strength in the East and if they were not to have any voice there, they would be reduced to nullity, particularly given the antagonistic past in which the Muslims suffered at the hands of the LTTE.

The LTTE's proposals came after a long wait by the civil society both within Sri Lanka and abroad. The expectations that since the LTTE had for the first time in the history of the ethnic conflict taken upon itself to come out with its own prescription for the solution of the perennial problem, it would atleast while demanding maximum for itself, be solicitous and accommodative of the sentiments of other communities, and would respect the territorial integrity of the Island, (hopes raised as a result of the agreement arrived at in December 2002 in Oslo), were belied. The apologists of the LTTE took the line that the proposals were at best a negotiating position and not the final position of the LTTE and therefore could be a starting point to carry the stalled peace process forward. But a closer reading left little scope for optimism. The final paragraph of the proposals (No. 23) warns that if no settlement is reached at the end of fourth year, they "shall engage in negotiations in good faith for the purpose of adding, clarifying and strengthening the terms of the Agreement." This implied that this document could not be watered down now or later. Since all disputes on interpretation of this document if not settled between the two parties were subject to international arbitration, would give the LTTE the status of a sovereign entity on par with the State of Sri Lanka. In short the LTTE sought to create a de facto a state of Tamil Eelam for the interim period, de jure declaration coming in due course.

The LTTE's proposals had resulted from the crisis of confidence between the mainstream Sinhala parties led by the President and the Prime Minister, already living in an uneasy relationship. The UNP Prime Minister Ranil Wickremasinghe with an eye on the next presidential election, and keen to monopolize the credit for himself and his party for a peace settlement forgot the basic truth of the ethnic politics of the Island. Since the two Sinhala parties drew their sustenance from the same constituency, it was the vote-bank politics and urge for competitive populism that led both of them to pursue policies and programmes, which while sharpening the Sinhalese radicalism, impinged on the basic rights of the Tamils as equal citizens of the State. It was this grievance of the Tamils that had led to their alienation initially and finally a call for Eelam in the Vaddukoddai Resolution of 1976. In the long history of the ethnic conflict there has been no dearth of opportunities when the Tamils could have been won over with little accommodation, but each time the Sinhala party in the opposition sabotaged any chance of settlement to deny the ruling party the kudos.

Despite being unpalatable, there was little choice. Outright rejection of the proposals would result in complete breakdown of the peace process. It became necessary to pretend to give them some consideration in the expectation that the LTTE would be willing to come down from the high pedestal and cooperate in a settlement that would while preserving the unity and sovereignty of Sri Lanka, fulfill their aspirations too. The SLFP while accusing the UNP of whetting the LTTE appetite, fully aware of the constraints of the Sri Lankan security forces to find a military solution, did not decry the proposals. It was hinted that these proposals could provide the starting point for resumption of the stalled talks. The President, who as a first step took control of the crucial Defence portfolio, articulating the government's point of view on the talks said in an interview to the *Frontline* news magazine (December 5, 2003) that "my principle—some people in my party don't agree with me—very frankly is that even the most unacceptable position of your adversary can be a basis to begin discussions. That does not mean that we can accept or pretend to accept the proposals. The LTTE's proposals as they are, unless they are willing to amend them during negotiations, cannot come within the Constitution of any country in the world because it is asking for another state. It can only come within the constitution of a separate state."

No country including India came forward to take the LTTE to task for its audacity to propose a secessionist solution. Interestingly, the censure came from the European Union and in no unmistaken language. The EU Commissioner for External Relations, Chris Patten on a visit to Sri Lanka said in Colombo on November 25, 2003 that the international community expected the LTTE not only to give up violence, stop child recruitment, and political killings but also to remain committed to a federal solution as agreed to at Oslo in December 2002, within the framework of the territorial integrity and sovereignty of Sri Lanka. Mincing no words, he told Prabakaran the next day, when he met him in Kilinochchi, that "it was quite difficult to associate them (LTTE proposals) with any form of federal solution I am aware of" and that it was highly impertinent of his organization to have made a "final negotiation position" instead of putting forth "a set of suggestions" for resolution of the ethnic conflict. He asked the LTTE supremo to "renounce violence, stop cease-fire violations, accept federal solution and address the issue of a Muslim delegation to the peace talks". Patten also told Prabakaran that if it were established that the LTTE were guilty of cease-fire violations, it would call into "question the good faith of the LTTE in the peace process". Interestingly, the LTTE briefing on the talks, as in the past, was brazen and Prabakaran while not giving any commitment on resumption of violence insisted that whether "Sri Lanka returns to war is completely in the hands of the Government. It is not at all in the hands of the LTTE to ensure there is no return to violence." Evidently the LTTE refused to be browbeaten by Mr. Patten's reprimand. This was also evident from the annual Heroes' Day speech of Prabakaran on November 27, 2003.

The LTTE leader in his speech said nothing that would allay the doubts and fears about the proposals particularly in the context of the EU Commissioner Patten's charge that the proposals did not inspire confidence about the intentions of the LTTE. His speech repeatedly described the Sri Lankan security forces stationed in the North-East "the Tamil homeland" as "occupation army" where "oppressive conditions of alien military occupation prevail(ed)". In his long discourse, Prabakaran justified his asking for sweeping powers because "large areas of the north-east are already under our effective jurisdiction and efficiently administered" by it. Simply put he suggested as an interim solution, the extension of the LTTE administration in the government-controlled areas to bring the entire north-east under its de facto control. His Heroes' Day message except denying that the proposals were a secessionist prescription remained vague about the north-east's relations with the rest of the country under the LTTE's new dispensation. He did not spell out the nature of the north-east's administrative synergy with that of the central government or its legal position under the Island's Constitution.

Given the international scenario against violence, Prabakaran left an escape route open by making a cosmetic suggestion that the LTTE's proposals were only "a basis for negotiations". But he made no reference to the LTTE's commitment to the concept of federalism or to uphold the territorial integrity or sovereignty of Sri Lanka. Refusing to sheathe the sword of Damocles, he warned "if the Sinhala chauvinistic ruling elites continue to deny the rights of our people and oppose reconciliation and if the conditions of oppression continue", the Tamils would "have no alternative other than to secede and form an independent state invoking the right of self-determination of our people". He ended his message on a note of caution for the Sinhala political leadership "not to create the objective conditions that would drive our people to seek this ultimate option". But one thing stood out in his address. He rightly accused the present stalemate on the lack of consensus between the two main Sinhala parties. His warning that this alone was capable of derailing the negotiating process had a ring of truth. This truth was established several times in the past and there was a real apprehension of history repeating itself.

Prabakaran, alienated from President Chandrika in the past, was naturally putting the blame for the present impasse on her shoulders. Wickremasinghe was quite obliging and it was the President who, in his opinion was acting a villain of the piece. Kuamratunga was apprehensive of the fissures in the Sinhala constituency. Prima facie, the President's action appeared to threaten the peace process. However, her suggestions for a national government, and subsequently for a Joint Peace Council (JPC) co-chaired by both the leaders as a policy body supported by Advisory Council on Peace (ACP) composed of representatives of all political parties, clergy, professionals and the latter body further supported by technical committees was an ideal one. This procedure would have involved all the political elements in the country in the decision-making with no chance for anyone to renege later. It could not be fortuitous that the suggestion for the JPC came from the President a day after the interview given by G.L. Peiris to the *Hindu* and the *Frontline* (November 27) making a similar suggestion that "direct and vigorous input by the President and the People's Alliance" through "an overall committee jointly chaired by the President and the Prime Minister to consider the parameters within which the negotiations should be held." He underlined the importance of such a joint approach by saying "it is evident that when one is negotiating a substantive solution there must be a cross-party consensus otherwise there will be no implementability".

Had such a consensus solution emerged it would have borne the signatures of the main elements of the majority and minority communities. To that extent it would have wider acceptance. Such a scenario was expected to take care of the Muslim opinion as well. The President's suggestion that while the Prime Minister supervised day-to-day discussions with the LTTE, the policy inputs were provided by the JPC was quite constructive. Her readiness to share the Defence responsibilities with the Prime Minister through the appointment of a Minister in that Ministry under her "over-riding powers" went a long way to propitiate the Prime Minister but, alas, it failed to elicit a positive response from the UNP. This would have enabled the two parties to sit together to create the much-needed southern consensus, lack of which in the past had been the bane of all efforts at peace. This would have addressed the Tamil grouse that the lack of Sinhala consensus invariably spelt doom of many a peace initiative in the past. This too had the potential to eliminate any chance of the LTTE trying to play one party against the other to disrupt the emergence of consensus at the political level and justifying its call for secession.

But the obduracy of the Prime Minister to show even an iota of deference to any suggestion emanating from the President was frustrating to the latter. Left with no alternative she made up her mind to appeal to the voters over the head of the Parliament by dissolving it. It was her assessment that it would offer her an opportunity to place a prime minister of her party as head of the parliamentary wing of the government, who was amenable to her discipline. To strengthen her hands before jumping into the electoral fray she successfully stitched an alliance with the radical Sinhala party, the JVP to form a United People's Freedom Alliance (UPFA). It was a desperate move of the President and betrayed her frustration with the unaccommodating and uncompromising Prime Minister who suffered no qualms of conscience in undermining the elected and executive head of the government. One has to remember that in the past JVP was guilty of fomenting an insurrection in the South and was also responsible for the assassination of her husband. This move betrayed her desperation since she had felt marginalized as she helplessly watched Wickremasinghe pandering to the shenanigans of Prabakaran in order to win an illusive peace at all costs.

The crisis of Sri Lankan political scene was best summed up graphically by a former editor of The *Daily News* H.L.D Mahindapala, in an article in the same paper on December 20, 2003:

> "Ranil Wickremasinghe is prepared to share power with Prabakaran, an un-elected and convicted criminal wanted by India and Interpol, and not with the elected President of the nation operating within the democratic norms.

> Wickremasinghe is even prepared to hand over, without a contest, the illegal demands of Prabakaran that violate the constitution and the foundations of the nation but he is not prepared to hand over three portfolios to the President who is legally and constitutionally entitled to administer them under her authority. He is willing to cohabit with the terrorists banned by his own safety net but not with his childhood playmate and a national leader who had won the approval of the people twice."

In such a vitiated political scenario of distrust not only between the Tamils and the Sinhalese but also among the various factions of the Sinhalese, the LTTE needed to respond more positively. Merely insisting that its proposals were not secessionist did not wash at the bar of non-Tamil national and international public opinion. It was hardly a secret in the Island that the LTTE, taking advantage of the interregnum, had successfully altered the balance of military preparedness in its favour by making fresh recruitment even among children, acquisition of military hardware and creation of fresh military camps in the east. The LTTE could not be unaware that if in the past a settlement of the ethnic problem could not be arrived at, the Sinhalas alone were not to be blamed. Its pig-headedness too contributed a lot in that unfortunate situation. It refused to appreciate the ground realities of the political set- up in Colombo that created political spasm in the Sinhala politics and brought the SLFP and the JVP together.

As pointed out above, the LTTE should remember that 9/11 has changed the perception of the world opinion against any semblance of violence whatever the justification. The ban imposed on it by some important countries in the West and India did make it feel suffocated. The global war against terrorism whatever its character, the UN Security Council Resolution No. 1373 against terrorism, freezing of funds of the terrorist organizations, the close coordination established between the LTTE and other terrorist organizations came under the scanner and it was well advised to give up the path of violence for the redressal of its grievances and achieve its objective with the support of the international civil society. In deciding to go in for the talks, the LTTE was anxious to extract a price indicating lifting of ban. It found the going difficult. If Sri Lanka lifted her ban to kick-start the peace talks, a precondition imposed by the Tigers, other countries were under no such obligation. They certainly would soften their stand and rethink the ban if it pursued the peace agenda with the seriousness that was expected and required of it. By acting obdurately and stubbornly, LTTE only reconfirmed its image of a spoiled brat wedded to fascist ideology and violence to achieve its agenda. The climate around the world was against any form of terrorism and violence to achieve howsoever justifiable ends. The world watched with ever-growing concern the LTTE's acquisition of fresh consignments of arms and recruitment of children among its cadres to strengthen its depleted manpower. It would be well advised not to test the patience of the civil society in Sri Lanka and other countries who were otherwise quite sympathetic to the Tamil cause in general. The problem with the LTTE was that it considered sympathy for the Tamils synonymous with itself. If it persisted in its intransigence, and refused to tone down its draft proposals, it ran the risk of losing its most important capital, the goodwill even among the Tamil sympathizers across the world.

Has this something to do with the nature of the LTTE's organizational structure and its leadership? As a militant organization wedded to terrorist methods to achieve its objectives, it is a closed organization. It never hesitated to use ruthless methods to demoralize and intimidate its adversaries including the civilians living in areas under its control. It motivated its cadres on strictly ethnic platform and without using religion as a motivating force. Organizationally it created the most effective intelligence and counter-intelligence network, which baffled its adversaries and demonstrated its success in one operation after another. Its innovative abilities and efforts to keep abreast with latest developments in science and technology in modern warfare and successfully combine it with the guerrilla warfare did pay rich dividends.

In terms of leadership too, it is not democratically placed. Its decision-making has lot to do with its functioning. The entire process of decision-making is concentrated in the hands of one single person, the charismatic Prabakaran. Charisma breeds dictatorship and dictators by their very nature have the tendency

to monopolize power. For them sharing power is not just a political concession, but blasphemous. It represents total defeat—the loss of lifetime's accumulation of power as well as the complete deflation of what is often a megalomaniac sense of pride and self-importance. Giving into anything less than complete military defeat becomes unthinkable. Shut-off from reality and surrounded by cronies and sycophants, such leaders frequently engage in self-delusional fantasies—that their agenda was sacrosanct, which everybody should accept ungrudgingly. That there would be no intervention to their detriment and some third force will halt the standoff if it comes about or that their own military force will somehow deter the enemy, fuels the spirit of the uncompromising mindset.

External military threats often strengthen dictators' hold and inflate their sense of purpose and determination. Dictators presume themselves immortals. They become immune to pressure. Efforts by external forces to foster democratic mindsets in dictatorial settings are fruitless. It is crucial to realize that dictators usually fall when their own people push them out. When dictators allow no political space, the ability of outside forces to encourage change becomes limited. The LTTE has been in that unfortunate state since its inception, where the word of Prabakaran had been the consecrated gospel. Those who dared to differ were not thrown out but simply wiped out. There is a long list of Sinhalese and Tamil leaders who met their violent end either for daring to disagree or challenge Prabakaran or refusing to accept the LTTE's agenda. There is little chance of any change coming about in the decision-making process in the LTTE as long as Prabakaran heads the organization. And there is no chance of his being replaced in his lifetime. The organization draws its strength from his character and personality. There is lack of democratic thinking in the organization and in the foreseeable future, neither is there any chance of it emerging. This is the bane of the LTTE!

The State of Sri Lanka has paid dearly for its follies. The dominant Sinhala community must be held responsible for promoting a conflict, which was completely avoidable. The Tamils were only 12 percent of the population against 74 percent Sinhalese and were no danger to the latter's dominant position. If only the recommendations of the Official Language

Commission in 1953 had been implemented and Tamil given it due place as recommended by it, the early apprehensions of the Tamils expressed at the time of independence regarding their future would never have found place in the politics of the country. If only the colonization policy in the Eastern Province was devoid of ethnic overtones to affect the demography, it would have helped to create national wealth and boom for the economy instead of a curse, as it turned out to be, thanks to the motivated agenda built into it. If only the "Only Sinhala" policy of S.W.R.D. Bandaranaike was motivated not by electoral gains, the polarization in the Island's politics would have been avoided. The Tamils after failing to get the safeguards from the British at the time of independence had reconciled themselves to co-existence with the majority community and participated in the national life of the country alongside of the Sinhalese. The majority community instead of following a broad agenda of accommodation towards the minorities repeatedly spurned their cooperation. The Tamil demand that their symbol "Nandi" was accommodated along with the Sinhala "Lion" on the new national flag was scuttled leaving the Tamils sulking. Not honouring various pacts and agreements signed to address the Tamils, grievances did not help to bring the two communities closer to each other. The dominant role that the Buddhist clergy assumed with the blessings of the State closed the small space that was available to the Tamils and they found themselves suffocated in the new state structure that gradually replaced the old order to their disadvantage. The "standardization policy" followed in admissions to the technical courses to squeeze out meritorious Tamil students, alienated the Tamil youth altogether. This was perhaps the last straw that broke the camel's back and the youth took to militancy and violence and there was no looking back.

The ethnic conflict extracted a heavy price. The democratic system on which the Island prided came under heavy strain and stood completely subverted. The undermining of the democratic institutions turned the Island into an authoritarian state. The draconian 'Prevention of Terrorism Act' and similar other legislations and long years of the country being under a State of Emergency led to the exercise of arbitrary powers by the government. This led to subversion of civil liberties, the essence of democracy. Frisking of individuals and searches of houses

and stoppage of traffic and roadblocks became routine in the daily life of the harassed citizens. Thousands of people, both civilian and uniformed, Tamils and Sinhalese, were killed and the number of wounded and crippled was too large to be counted. Lakhs were displaced and became homeless refugees within and outside the country. Over a lakh fled to neighbouring India for refuge. A permanent cleavage permeated into the society in general which stood divided into two distinct communities with no hope of their getting together to forge links of national unity and integration. The two communities which during their two-millennium existence on the Island had only developed antagonistic relationship, failed to overcome the past to forge new links to create an interactive society, a precondition for a vibrant democratic system.

In pursuing the "Only Sinhala" policy since 1956, first by the SLFP and later by the UNP too, led to the emergence of competitive politics in the majority community. The majoritarian politics of the two Sinhala parties completely politicized the ethnic question, thus making it impossible to evolve a bipartisan approach to conflict resolution. This led the process of national reconciliation to affect adversely the emergence of a Sri Lankan society based on shared socio-economic interests to produce a national political culture. It jeopardized any chance of Island's politics being articulated on the platform of national reconciliation. On the contrary it led to confrontational politics at all levels, thus preventing the emergence of a national political culture. The alienation of the Tamils too polarized the minority politics. The old guards of the Tamil politics, the TULF, who reposed faith in parliamentary process to redress the wrongs done to the community, unable to secure or protect the rights of the Tamil youth were gradually marginalized, giving rise to militancy among the youth who took to arms thus injecting unending violence in the body politics of the country. And the country had to pay a very high price economically. At the end of the day, the old moderate Tamil opinion represented by the TULF having allowed the initiative to pass on to the LTTE, is fast fading away and its remnants are fighting a losing battle to keep their heads above water.

On the economic front, the damage had been irreparable. The reform of the economy, which commenced from 1977,

transformed the economic system and the incentives structure in an attempt to create an enabling environment for the private sector. While tariffs, trade restrictions and taxes were reduced, prices deregulated, business freed of unnecessary controls and regulations, foreign capital encouraged with generous incentives, the increased macro-economic instability coupled with ethnic violence and consequent political instability during the eighties prevented the reaping of full benefits from the reforms. Sri Lanka therefore failed to produce economic performance in terms of human development in the same measure as other countries of Southeast Asia achieved. Sri Lanka's investment in health sector in the early years compared favourably with the countries of the Southeast Asian region, but has since declined sharply: 2 percent of the GDP in 1960 to 1.4 percent in the late nineties. The security related expenditure squeezed the expenditure on social sector. Defence expenditure, which was only 214 million US$ jumped to US $730 million in 1998, representing an annual increase of 9.9 percent. In terms of GNP, the expenditure on defence rose from 2.6 percent to 4.8 percent. Per capita increase was dramatic—US $14 in 1985 to $ 39.2 in 1998. The number of armed personnel during that period increased from 22,000 to 113,000.

Where does India stand after so much of bloodshed and sacrifices, of men and material? Sri Lanka emerged as a challenge to India's dominant position as a regional power. After the British withdrawal from South Asia in the forties, India was the only country in the region, capable of fulfilling the vacuum so created. She asserted the doctrine of regional security with herself as its guardian. Her opposition to military alliances like CENTO and SEATO was a protest against the involvement of outside forces in her area of influence. India was the largest country in every manner. Her population, area, armed forces, material resources including her industrial base etc., were bigger and larger than those of all the other countries in South Asia put together. Her borders touch all the countries of the region. She provides a bridge among them to interface and interact with each other. Indian failure as a facilitator/mediator in the ethnic conflict brought home to her neighbours limitations of her ability to provide the necessary leadership that would dispense with the need for smaller countries in her periphery to look up for

help outside of the region. If it was the aim of Indian intervention to stop outside elements a toehold in the region, it ended up in achieving just the opposite of it. Politically India stood marginalized from any role in Sri Lanka while elements outside of the region ruled the roost.

In terms of purely ethnic conflict, Indian intervention in the eighties only raised expectations among the Tamils she could not meet. On the other hand, it only added to their intransigence, in the hope that the weight of the powerful would weaken the will of the smaller and make the latter baulk. This made a difficult solution impossible. By 1976 the Tamil movement had not only developed secessionist tendencies but in fact had adopted the secessionist agenda. India, no doubt pledged herself to the territorial integrity and sovereignty of Sri Lanka, yet did not at any time ask the TULF or any other Tamil organization to officially give up that agenda by rescinding or distancing itself from the Vaddukoddai Resolution before interceding on their behalf. By acting as the intermediary on behalf of elements who had officially adopted a separatist agenda, India did not cover herself with glory. India took upon herself the task of negotiating with Colombo without ensuring a corresponding clout or leverage with the Tamils to accept a settlement negotiated on their behalf. She therefore had the mortification often to see the settlements promoted by her being spurned by the Tamils, embarrassing New Delhi.

There was complete division among the Tamils. They were divided not only between the moderates and the militants, but were split into several groups who were at daggers drawn for supremacy. The internecine war among the militants led to the killings of Tamils at the hands of the fellow Tamils. It too demonstrated lack of Indian influence or hold on them. They could neither set aside their quarrels in the common Tamil cause nor could India promote reconciliation among them. In the end the LTTE succeeded in wiping out not only the moderate Tamil leadership but also the other militant rival groups. In the process it humiliated India too. By allowing these armed elements the use of Indian territory, the politics of Tamil Nadu got polarized and criminalized.

The failure of the experiment of the peace-keeping through use of force, demonstrated the limitations of a large military force against the determined and highly motivated forces of "national liberation". India learnt at a great cost to her national honour that by projecting domestic politics in the realm of foreign relations it only propelled those forces, which she found unable to control later. In so doing India did not learn from the failures of others, the limitations of the interventionist policies in today's world.

Despite setbacks at the political and military level, India's size and resources and her geopolitical location did not allow her to be elbowed out completely. An interesting and significant development, which remained unnoticed for most part during the last decade, was a quiet change of track by India to stay engaged. Since 1990, when the unyielding and obdurate Premadasa, edged the Indian Peace Keeping Force out of Sri Lanka, and she found the political space in the Island closed to her, she decided to bide her time. Meantime it prudently decided to canalize her relations with the Island in areas where she had an inherent advantage—economic and culture. As a result of this reorientation, India's ties with Sri Lanka moved into more tangible areas in a big way. In July 1991 an agreement to set up a Joint Commission, a common platform at the government level to develop cooperation in fields of trade, industry, finance, investment, education, science and technology, tourism, and culture was set up. It has since been meeting regularly. The Joint Business Council set up under the common umbrella of the Federation of the Indian Chambers of Commerce and Industry and the Sri Lanka Federation of Commerce and Industry held regular meetings to forge closer economic relations between the business communities of the two countries at an unofficial level. In March 1995 President Kumaratunga during her New Delhi visit took time off, out of her busy political schedule to address the Confederation of Indian Industry where she enumerated the various reforms introduced by her government to facilitate foreign investments for accelerated development of the country and invited the Indian business and industry to take advantage of them. In 1997 the two countries signed an important agreement—Agreement for Promotion and Protection of Investments—to give new impetus to the promotion of Indian investments in Sri Lanka.

To cap it all, a Free Trade Agreement was signed in December 1998. It is to be noted that periodically India had been providing credit facilities to Sri Lanka to facilitate her purchases in the Indian market. But in June 2000 the External Affairs Minister Jaswant Singh during his visit to Colombo announced a major credit of hundred million US dollars. An Indo-Sri Lanka Study Team commissioned by the two governments in April 2003 to suggest a framework of measures for enhanced economic cooperation submitted its report to the Prime Ministers of India and Sri Lanka on October 20, 2003 when Wickremasinghe was on a visit to New Delhi. The two leaders then mandated that negotiations for a Comprehensive Economic Partnership Agreement (CEPA) be commenced immediately and an agreement concluded by March 2004. (Because of unexpected announcement of elections and other political developments this has been delayed.) The India-Sri Lanka Joint Commission, when it met in Colombo a week before Wickremasinghe's New Delhi visit, described the CEPA as one that "would take the two countries to a qualitatively new level of engagement by intensifying and deepening bilateral economic cooperation". It has to be seen against the backdrop of the bilateral trade crossing one billion US dollars mark under the Free Trade Agreement. Not only that Colombo has approached New Delhi for assistance for the management, rehabilitation and refurbishment of its railways including possible financial and material assistance. Colombo too has asked help in the setting up of a thermal power station based either on coal or gas. The Indian Oil Corporation has not only secured the lease of the Trincomalee Oil Tank Farm, which in the eighties was denied to it and created a lot of bad blood between the two countries, is also involved there in the marketing of oil. For some years now the Indian economic presence in the Island has become quite conspicuous. Major Indian public and private companies are playing significant role in Sri Lanka's oil, healthcare, finance, insurance and transportation sectors. To promote tourism in the Island, the mainstay of Island's economy, during Wickremasinghe's visit in October 2003 India practically opened her sky to the Sri Lankan and Indian private airlines to freely operate flights between the two countries. Sri Lanka was keen and India had not been averse, that a bridge to span the Palk strait was constructed to strengthen and facilitate trade and travel between the two countries. (It is a different matter that the Chief Minister of Tamil Nadu spoke against this proposal.) Prime Minister Wickremasinghe's suggestion of integrating the Island's economy with that of South India was a development of far-reaching significance.

The cultural field has too been exploited fully. India has set up a Cultural Centre in Colombo. An India-Sri Lanka Foundation was now funding major areas of study and research in subjects of bilateral interest. Cultural and pilgrim tourism is an area which has unlimited scope for expansion and promotion.

Politically too, the visit of the Sri Lankan Prime Minister Wickremasinghe to New Delhi in October 2003 was not an insignificant event. He welcomed New Delhi to Colombo in a big way after the absence of over a dozen years. During these years, there were quite a few occasions when Colombo missed New Delhi but could not muster courage to invite its intervention. New Delhi, bitten by the past experience, unable to make a response in an area of her prime strategic interest, had to suffer the mortification to see outside powers poaching in her backyard. Having built the economic bridge of sufficient strength, New Delhi felt confident to cross the divide that held it back all this time. Colombo never denying Indian paramount interest felt the time had come when the regional power must throw its weight behind Sri Lanka to moderate the LTTE's growing stridency. Ranil Wickremasinghe was feeling uneasy that President Chandrika Kumaratunga would react negatively to LTTE's proposal for an interim administration. She had been breathing fire down Wickremasinghe's neck that she would not allow the Government to be too generous with the LTTE in buying peace at any cost. She sent out unambiguous signals that she would not hesitate to use her executive powers should the vital and strategic national interests appeared compromised. Not that the Prime Minister would have taken any chance with the integrity of the country, but the perceptions of the two differed on the level of accommodation that was possible. Therefore from Colombo's point of view, revival of Indian interest as a moderating force in the context of the domestic power equation became equally important. What was more interesting was that in the competitive game of power politics in Colombo, India emerged as the restraining force between the two leaders sharing executive power.

India has deftly used the opportunity so provided to stage a come-back in Colombo. To the LTTE she has warned that India expected it not to cross the threshold whereby the territorial integrity of Sri Lanka was compromised. Even before the LTTE had come out with its proposals for an interim administration, New Delhi had taken care to set the threshold, which it was expected not to cross. New Delhi was clear in its mind that the "interim arrangement" should be "an integral part of the final settlement and should be in the framework of the unity and territorial integrity of Sri Lanka". These limits were set in the joint communiqué issued during the visit of Wickremasinghe to New Delhi in October, 2003. This stand of New Delhi sufficiently warmed the cockles of the SLFP, which welcomed the Indian stand since it upheld Kumaratunga's position. Not only that India told the LTTE in no unmistakable terms that she expected its "response to the proposals made by the Sri Lankan government in July 2003 will be reasonable and comprehensive". To further narrow LTTE's options, India made it clear she supported "a negotiated settlement acceptable to all sections of Sri Lankan society within the framework of a united Sri Lanka and consistent with democracy, pluralism and respect for individual rights." By making this declaration on the eve of LTTE's announcement of its response, India wanted to make her position clear to all parties. One flaw stood out clearly. India had been a little late in setting the parameters. The LTTE had already met with its sympathizers and advisers internationally and had almost sharpened its response. It was therefore no surprise that LTTE's proposal for an interim administration unveiled on October 31, 2003 was a great disappointment to India even though New Delhi desisted from taking any substantive public position on it officially.

It is noteworthy that in making the above pronouncements India was not indulging in mere verbosity. She backed up her assertions with punch. Since the deinduction of the IPKF India had adopted a hands-off policy as far as military cooperation with Colombo was concerned. This had left the turf free for others like the Pakistanis and the Israelis to fill the vacuum. New

Delhi, therefore, welcomed the proposal for defence cooperation from Wickremasinghe made in October 2003. A formal agreement though not yet signed, is still very much on the table. One would take with a pinch of salt the statement of Sri Lankan Foreign Minister Tyron Fernando made in October 2003 in New Delhi, when the proposal was first made that the proposal did not amount to "a mutual defence pact". This should in no way detract from the significance of the proposal though active military intervention from India should be ruled out.

This announcement read with the Indian statement that New Delhi had an "abiding interest" in the security of Sri Lanka and remained committed to her sovereignty and territorial integrity cast India's lengthy shadow on the peace process. New Delhi was anxious to bring home to the LTTE that though not present at the negotiating table, India would not be oblivious of what was happening around her. New Delhi even issued an oblique warning to the LTTE that its fascist agenda would be unacceptable to it and that any solution emerging from the current talks must be acceptable to all sections of the country. To that extent, the October 2003 visit of Sri Lankan Prime Minister was an important signpost, in that it marked the return of India to the centrestage of Colombo's ethnic politics as a regional power. It was also intended to be a reminder to other powers that India's silence must not be taken as an abdication of her interest in the region of her natural concern.

The story of the ethnic conflict in Sri Lanka is one of false hopes, raised emotions, disappointments turning into bitterness and bitterness into frustration and finally frustration into conflict. With each Indian intervention new illusions were created and entertained, new hopes raised and new bitterness, frustration and conflict followed. The cycle went on and would have perhaps gone on, until the shadow of 9/11 unleashed new pressures leaving the LTTE with little option but to negotiate for peace. Old habits die hard. The LTTE used to the culture of gun was finding it difficult to adjust to peace and itching to take up the gun again, which it has kept sufficiently greased. But for the international community, the longest peace process in Sri Lanka would have collapsed long ago. But do the LTTE proposals of October 31 offer any positive signs, remains a to be seen!

❮28❯

Postscript—2004

Election–2004

Unable to find reconciliation with her Prime Minister Wickremasinghe, President Kumaratunga had on February 7, 2004 dissolved the parliament and called fresh elections almost four years ahead of schedule in the fond hope of putting a candidate of her party as head of the parliamentary executive. Taking no chances, on January 20 she even forged an alliance (United Peoples' Freedom Alliance) with the radical Janatha Vimukthi Peramuna (JVP). Though the election results could not have inspired Kumaratunga, she at least got rid of her recalcitrant Prime Minister. That Sri Lanka is a fractured polity, the results of the election—2004 held on April 2 fully reflected it. The hung parliament that emerged hardly gave her the strength that she was looking for either to push through a settlement of the ethnic problem or change the Constitution, which was also high on her agenda. Her Freedom Alliance emerged as the largest group with 105 seats in a House of 225 falling short of majority by eight. The United National Front led by Wickremasinghe ended second with 82 seats. Interestingly, the Tamil National Alliance (TNA), acting as LTTE proxy, secured 22 seats from the North and the East thus strengthening LTTE's claim as the sole representative of the Tamils. That this victory was more due to the intimidation of Tamil voters by the LTTE is hardly disputed by anyone. On the Tamil front, the most significant development was the complete elimination of the moderate Tamil opinion. The TULF stood split vertically. As one would recall, the TULF in the past had enjoyed monopoly of negotiating position. The Ceylon Workers Congress representing the

Plantation Tamils bagged eight seats. The Up-country People's Front (considered close to the LTTE) and the Eelam People's Democratic Party (EPDP), (loathed by the LTTE) both got one each. The Sri Lanka Muslim Congress ended up with five seats.

The fractured parliament inevitably led to frictional politics, the blight of the Sri Lanka's history since independence. The manner in which the government failed to get its nominee elected as the Speaker of the parliament could hardly have been comforting to the President. Any possibility of change in the Constitution, therefore, should stand ruled out for the present.

The most significant development of the 2004 general elections was the emergence of the Buddhist clergy as a separate political force in the parliament for the first time. That the clergy enjoyed enormous political clout in the Island's politics was never in doubt. They influenced the course of state politics since independence of the country both in relation to the Plantation and ethnic Tamils. If the early attempts at reconciliation with the Tamils through the Bandaranaike-Chelvanayakam Pact in 1957 or the Senanayake–Chelvanayakam Pact in 1965 did not succeed, the Buddhist clergy must take much of the (dis) credit. They did not hesitate to point the gun at S.W.R.D. Bandaranaike, the founder of the SLFP and father of President Kumaratunga in pursuit of their radical nationalist agenda. While staying in the centrestage of the ethnic politics, the clergy too chose to stay out of the din of electoral politics as a separate group. Fearing that the mainstream Sinhala political parties desperate in their search for a solution to the ethnic conflict, might give away more than what they thought was reasonable, they decided to plunge themselves into active electoral fray as a separate party of their own. Thus emerged the political grouping of the Buddhist clergy—the Jathika Hela Urumaya (JHU) (Sinhala Heritage) to play their "historical role" of providing guidance to the ruling establishment more decisively. The clergy were angry that the Sinhala political parties in the past while using them for their electoral gains did not heed them when it came to the crunch. Their nine-seat tally in parliament put them in the centerstage of a hung parliament. Their refusal to join either of the two Sinhala blocs in a formal alliance but use their strength selectively and strategically to influence the decisions of the government in national interest, as they perceived them, would give them much more importance than their number in ordinary course would justify. They significantly announced on April 23 that their goal was to "prevent a division of the country" and wanted the two Sinhala parties to work together for the "betterment" of the nation. One would recall that not too long ago in 2000 the clergy had taken to the streets to protest Chandrika Kumaratunga's constitutional proposals for devolution of powers in a bid to come to terms with the Tamil aspirations. Bearing in mind the immediate context of the elections and what prompted the monks to jump into the fray, the course of negotiations with the LTTE appears treacherous. Given their declared policy of not joining any grouping but provide conditional support to the government, their clout in the decision-making in hung parliament should not be underestimated. Having said that, it also remains a fact that the 35,000 strong clergy fraternity is a house divided. Many important priests distanced themselves from the decision of the JHU to enter the electoral fray. Only time would tell how the various factions of the clergy in and out of Parliament balanced themselves in the ethnic marathon.

The United National Front suffered to a great extent on account of its lacklustre handling of the economic situation. The spiralling cost of living had come to pinch one and all and dissatisfaction was quite discernible. But more than that it was perceived that while peace was a welcome commodity and people enjoyed it too, the larger national interests were being ignored in an effort to buy peace at all costs. The LTTE too did not help the UNF by presenting its impossible proposals for a peace settlement in the shape of Interim Self Governing Authority, which people perceived as out and out secessionist.

Split in the LTTE

The Sri Lanka and the international community had a big shock in the first week of March 2004, when cracks appeared in the LTTE citadel, which hitherto was considered impregnable. For the first time in the history of the LTTE the unthinkable happened. The Tamils in the East burnt effigies of Prabakaran and his intelligence chief Pottu Amman. The short-lived revolt of the eastern leadership of the LTTE represented by its eastern commander Vinayagamurthy Muralitharan, better known as

'Col.' Karuna, took everybody by surprise. Karuna was the righthand man of the LTTE chief Prabakaran and controlled the two eastern districts of Batticaloa and Amparai. He was considered a master strategist, credited with the success of many significant campaigns of the Tigers including the fall of the Elephant Pass in 2000. He was a member of the LTTE team negotiating peace with Sri Lankan government through the aegis of the Norwegians. He was present along with Balasingham on the side of Prabakaran when the latter addressed the international media on April 10, 2002 to announce to the world that the Tamils would seek a negotiated peace. On that occasion Prabakaran had singled him out for special mention and credited him with some of the major successes of the LTTE between 1998 and 2001. Now as a rebel he split the movement vertically and gave his eastern wing the name of the Liberation Tigers of Batticaloa and Amparai.

The LTTE was known to the outside world a monolith where dissent was blasphemous and punishable with death. It was not since the revolt of Uma Maheswaren in 1979 that anyone dared to challenge Prabakaran so blatantly. More important than the fact of revolt were the reasons adduced for the unprecedented step. Karuna charged Prabakaran with ignoring the sentiments of the eastern wing cadres, discriminating against them in senior appointments, making them cannon fodder by using them in front-line operations while posting the northern cadres behind the lines in cushy and less risky and less hazardous jobs. The immediate provocation was said to be the appointment of 30 northern cadres in supervisory appointments in the organization to the exclusion of the easterners altogether. At precisely the same time Karuna was feeling unhappy because of the demand made on him by Prabakaran for additional cadres for strengthening the defences in the North for any possible showdown with Colombo since the peace talks appeared to be stalled. Karuna too was said to be miffed at the political assassinations in the East during the elections, apparently ordered by Pottu Amman without taking him into confidence. His grouse was that he was left to face the criticism for the assassinations when he was not even aware of them. In a manner of speaking Karuna was complaining encroachment on his turf by the hated Pottu Amman who considered himself next only to Prabakaran.

Of late Karuna had sniffed some foul play. He suspected Pottu Amman cooking his goose. Pottu thought that Karuna had been in his job for too long and had become too big for his shoes and therefore not amenable to his discipline. His list of charges was sufficiently long and large. He reportedly used his proximity to Prabakaran to convince him of the seriousness of Karuna's indiscretions, which included financial irregularities. Karuna when summoned to Wanni, the headquarters of the LTTE in the North, smelt a rat. Fearing elimination *a la* the Tiger style, he decided to raise the standard of revolt. He was not unaware of the fate Mahthaiya had met before him. He feared arrest. He had the nightmarish idea of being tried, tormented before physically eliminated. To ward off the worst, he probably was left with no option but to fight back.

Karuna in his revolt raised the wider issue of historical domination of the North over the East. In history Tamil nationalism was synonymous with the Jaffna Tamils playing the leading role to keep the Tamil flag aloft. It was the Jaffna kingdom that was the bulwark of Tamil nationalism in history. Jaffna was the capital of the Tamil civilization. It was the people from Jaffna who provided the intellectual edge to Tamil movements on the Island whatever the cause. They were the professionals, intellectuals, university teachers and opinion makers among the Tamils as against the Easterners who were mostly agriculturalists occupying the hinterland. They had only followed the lead provided by the highly articulate Jaffna Tamils. This historical cleavage, though resented by the East, was nevertheless accepted by it conceding the intellectual superiority of the North. Since independence from Chelvanayakam to Amirthalingam the leadership of the Tamils came from Jaffna. Karuna chose to challenge the North on an emotive issue of discrimination that his people being used as cannon fodder without being adequately compensated on par with their counterparts from the North.

More blasphemous than the charge of discrimination against the Eastern cadres was his calling in question the very rationale of the entire movement describing Eelam as a pipe dream, which had no chance of being achieved. He described Prabakaran entering into negotiations with Colombo for a federal set-up and "internal self-determination" a proof of his getting wary of the goal of Eelam. He poured cold water on the sacrifices of the LTTE for almost two decades describing the struggle as "unwinnable." He felt that its prolongation was bringing "destruction to both the sides". He even accused the organization of needlessly and mindlessly undertaking the assassination of Rajiv Gandhi thus alienating Indian public opinion against the LTTE. For him this assassination was the "gravest mistake of the intelligence wing" of the LTTE. His admission of LTTE's involvement ripped off the pall of evasion the LTTE had placed over the appalling crime. All this was profane to Prabakaran. For him Eelam was his life's sacred mission and the present phase was only a tactical move.

The revolt collapsed as suddenly as it appeared, in little over a month with not much blood spilled. Going by the LTTE's standards and history, it was expected that there would be a fratricidal war resulting in a major bloodbath. But Karuna at the last moment developed cold feet and backtracked. The well-meaning Tamils particularly the Tamil diaspora and the parents of the cadres reportedly intervened and brokered a "peace agreement", which saved the day for Prabakaran and the LTTE. The LTTE would like to forget the sordid development as a bad dream. It was noteworthy that despite Prabakaran reasserting his control in the East, there were enough straws in the wind suggesting all was not well in the State of Denmark. Not infrequent assassinations of the Tamils by Tamils from opposing camps are indicative of the fact that the challenge from the East is still alive. The warning issued by Karuna's elements still operating in the East is ominous for the Wanni leadership. Leaflets distributed by the dissidents and posted on Karuna's Website on June 4 warned that they might be down for the present but certainly not out:

> "We intend to take back control of our land in six months. We warn those who help the Wanni LTTE to destroy our lands and resources and murder our boys and girls, that they should be ready for the consequences".

The *Daily Mirror*'s front-page report of June 19 that Karuna was "reportedly busy forming a new political party" could not be comforting to Prabakaran's ears. Though Karuna vanished from the scene in early April, the ground situation is far from reassuring.

The reports of his re-emergence in a political *avatar* and espousing the cause of the Eastern Tamils are ominous. The Sri Lankan Army using former eastern cadres to up the ante for Prabakaran was a horrendous possibility for the Tigers, which could impact the peace process and its outcome. His cadres, who are now leaderless, might get a rallying point once again even if he does not don his uniform again.

Be that as it may, the footprints left by the revolt, whatever its future cannot be easily swept away. It has raised the fundamental question of the Tamil nationalism and posed a challenge to the key concept of ethno-politics among the Tamils in Sri Lanka. It gave a jolt to the theory that the Tamils of both the regions are a homogeneous people who needed a common homeland. In the past too such accusations were thrown up but not made a major issue in the larger interest of Tamil struggle against the Sinhalas. In the fifties when Chelvanayakam, the father of Tamil nationalism had made efforts to unite all the Tamils in the Island under one umbrella (His efforts in this direction sought to include the Tamil-speaking Muslims too, since he strongly and rightly believed that they are only different from the rest of the Tamils by virtue of their having embraced Islam.) The eastern Tamils felt the pangs of suffocation under the Jaffna domination articulated on the platform of the superiority of the Vellala, the dominant caste of the Jaffna Tamils. Though Prab akaran himself is not a Vellala, he belongs to the fisherman caste of Karaiyar yet his thinking has been conditioned by the Jaffna psyche of superiority. One difference, however, stands out. Chelvanayakam's style of leadership was accommodative and consensual, while Prabakaran on the contrary is authoritarian and dictatorial, leaving little space for dissent.

The north-east divide represented by the revolt would haunt the Tamils' struggle as nothing else had in the past. Prabakaran no doubt would like to forget it as a bad dream. The LTTE's claim as the sole representative of the Tamils stands dented. The Sinhalas are sure to remind Prabakaran of the ugly divide among the Tamils. The civil society that had espoused Prabakaran's case in the past found the new phenomena confounding. It was sympathetic to the Tamil cries of discrimination. It now faced the dilemma of articulating the Easterners, cry against their brethren from Jaffna. The Tamils' fight for dignity and honour has received a hard knock. When Karuna accused that his cadres from the East were made the cannon fodder, were not allowed to visit their homes in peacetime, were not promoted to supervisory posts, were used only as sentries and guards, he was raising a wider question of Prabakaran's failure to treat all Tamils alike and equal. Could the people of the East expect their future guaranteed in a merged province of north-east? In short Karuna pressed all those charges and expressed all those fears against the Wani leadership, which the LTTE had been speaking about against the Sinhalese – and had considered all that enough of justification for the violence it perpetrated on the Sinhalas. This naturally raised a question about the fate of the Easterners when left at the mercy of the Jaffna Tamils in a merged province in any future settlement!

In the short run the revolt looked ephemeral and did not impact the cease-fire. The government embroiled in elections claimed that it did nothing to upstage Prabakaran or openly extended support to Karuna. It was inconceivable that Karuna before deciding to revolt did not check out the extent of support that would be available to him from Colombo and other diverse sources, both domestic and foreign. The confession of the official spokesman of the government Mangala Samaraweera on June 24 that some individuals in the military supported Karuna while denying any "official involvement, directly or indirectly with the breakaway group" is significant in as far as it goes. "Obviously there have been military personnel involved. We are not denying it," but "the government is not officially involved", Samaraweera said. Can military personnel involve themselves in extra-military activities? This is a question that has not been addressed, though the spokesman said that the government was investigating the issue. The Deputy Defence Minister Ratnasiri Wickremanayake acting quickly too chipped in on the same day to deny army's links with the "disappearance" of Karuna. He accused that "some outside powers are trying to sabotage the government's peace efforts by such accusations against the military". The reported involvement of a UNP member of parliament in the disappearance of Karuna only underlines the murky nature of the domestic Sinhala politics.

When the revolt first surfaced in March there were reports that Sri Lankan military was backing him, that the Indian intelligence agency RAW and even the USA would extend support if he could keep himself afloat. But apparently everything was contingent on his ability to put up initially a brave front and hold his own. This explains lack of open response from Colombo to his request for a separate cease-fire agreement in the East. For whatever reasons he caved in at the very first military challenge from the North thus giving a lie to his reputation as a strategist of the LTTE for which he had received a handsome praise from Prabakaran. Others watching from the sidelines did not even feel it necessary to unsheathe their cards. This helped to localize the conflict within the Tigers. Others by holding themselves succeeded in avoiding the embarrassment of having to backtrack from supporting a flimsy character. However, one of the elected monks and leader of the Jathika Hela Urumaya, Omalpe Sobitha lamented the failure of the Sri Lankan government to exploit the rebellion and described it a "great betrayal". In a statement on April 20, 2004 he said it was a "historic opportunity to use the break-up in the LTTE to eliminate terrorism". There were similar voices in other sections of the Sinhalese too, but the Government prudently decided to watch the struggle within the LTTE from the sidelines to find out how far Karuna was gifted with the mettle the leaders are made of before jumping into the fray on his side. In so doing, it saved the peace process and saved itself the embarrassment of being accused of scuttling it.

The Norwegians at the request of President Kumaratunga, endorsed by the LTTE, landed in full force in Colombo and resumed their shuttle diplomacy to get the process on rails once again. The LTTE was no less anxious to get the talks started. It was nervous lest its status as the sole representative of the Tamils should be impacted by the dynamics of the Eastern revolt. At his meeting with the elected Tamil representatives on April 20, 2004 Prabakaran emphasized to them the imperative need to ensure that. Another point of emphasis was to work towards getting the ISGA in place in the resumed talks as a priority. As the air got thick with the talks for resumption of the peace process, the Media Coordinator of the LTTE Daya Master echoing Prabakaran's command said any future peace talks would be based on the "recognition of the concept of self-determination and traditional homeland as predicated in the ISGA proposals". He said "Sri Lankan President should accept this as a basis for the talks" and if this was accepted then the "chances of LTTE participating in the talks and peace process being taken forward without disruption are good".

President Kumaratunga anxious to build the momentum for the peace process and recognizing that the LTTE had successfully neutralized all Tamil opposition, was quick to concede the reality of its being the sole representative. But on the vexed question of the ISGA, while agreeing to let it stay on the table as a starting point, the government harboured strong reservations. In this context the statement of Lakshman Kadirgamar, who returned to the Foreign Ministry in the new government, (in an interview to the fortnightly *Frontline* of Chennai of May 21, 2004) was indicative of the President's mood:

> "They (LTTE) have put certain proposals on the table in the form of the ISGA which at the moment, we think, are far too far-reaching in many respects.... I think there would be possible alternative models to the existing ISGA proposals."

Kadirgamar indicated that while there would be total unanimity against a separate state but "I do not detect that there would be very strong organized opposition to a form of devolved government." He was hinting that the JVP could be prevailed upon to go along with the devolution proposal of the President but certainly not with the secessionist ISGA. To clarify its position independent of the Government, the JVP in its statement of June 4 repeated its opposition to the ISGA when its parliamentary group leader Wimal Weerawansa reminded the LTTE that the people had already rejected previous government's "peace process of fulfilling the avariciousness of the Tigers". He requested the donors to prevail upon the Tigers "to withdraw the precondition on interim administration". The JVP's appeal came on the heels of the Brussels Conference of the donor countries' asking early resumption of the peace talks "so that Sri Lanka could benefit from the support of the international community". There were oblique hints that if peace process did not throw up an acceptable solution quickly, the money could go elsewhere.

The LTTE was unlikely to give up its insistence on its proposals. The Norwegians who met Prabakaran on May 11 were clearly told that the ISGA must be on the top of the agenda and taken up for discussion "immediately". Balasingham who was present when the Norwegians met Prabakaran, later said that the LTTE continued to hold a different position from that of Colombo that there should be "parallel discussions" both for interim and core issues. The LTTE insisted that to start with, it would like to discuss the interim arrangement. He threw hints that a minority government was incapable of taking hard decisions required to push the peace settlement through the parliament, which would entail "fundamental changes in the Constitution", and hence the futility of taking up core issues at this stage. The LTTE therefore insisted that the interim administrative structure as proposed by it was set up so that the aid pledged by the donor countries starts flowing to address the socio-economic problems. The LTTE conveniently forgets that even the ISGA has little chance of mandatory parliamentary approval. Aware that it was already in *de facto* control of most of the areas in the north-east, if it could get an administrative structure of its asking for the whole of the region, it would practically be ruling the entire north-east without any let or hindrance from Colombo. In the ensuing peace, it would have a strong case for the withdrawal of the Sri Lankan army from its controlled areas. Once in effective control san the Sri Lanka army was established, *de jure* Eelam was not far away.

Irked by the President's offer of June 12 that the Government was "willing to explore" in collaboration with the LTTE, "interim political measures" relating to development issues in the north-east and also constitute an apex body, a National Advisory Council chaired by her for the peace process, the LTTE reiterated its opposition to such an arrangement and accused her of "political duplicity". The LTTE warned of "bloodbath" and called upon the international community to bring about the necessary pressure on the government to accept the ISGA proposals. Underlining the need of "institutionalizing" the ISGA before it could discuss the core issue, the LTTE said it was necessary to "demonstrate to the people that their urgent humanitarian needs would be effectively met with the ISGA and will help to build confidence among the people who are the real shareholders in the peace process".

It is evident that the ISGA proposals would prove a major stumbling block between the Government and the LTTE. The alliance between the SLFP and the JVP was structured on the premise, that Wickremasinghe through appeasement of the LTTE was playing havoc with the territorial integrity of the country. Anton Balasingham had then described the alliance as "a racist Sinhala outfit". Despite extreme positions taken by the two Sinhala parties (SLFP and UNP) in the past, there was no alternative for the two to sit together and hammer out a settlement that could be sold to the Tamils and that is what appears not only unlikely but impossible, given the fractional politics of Sri Lanka.

Meanwhile the ground situation in the East is causing concern both to the government and to the LTTE. If it takes the turn for the worse, it would considerably weaken the LTTE and its bargaining position. The alliance government would feel equally bold to refuse to hand over the east to the LTTE under any arrangement. The LTTE would face rough weather in a prolonged situation of stalemated peace in its controlled areas. The people undergo privations in time of stress and strife, but when the things are stable they want development, which cannot come without funds. The funds are with the donors who would not give unless there is not only peace but also structured peace capable of delivering. With every passing day, LTTE would come under pressure from the people crying for not only rehabilitation and reconstruction of what had been damaged and destroyed in the two decades of war but also to provide new socio-economic assets to take the generation next to new vistas of development. The statement of the Assistant Secretary of State for South Asian Affairs Christina Rocca in a Congressional hearing on June 24 could not be comforting to the LTTE. She categorically stated that the United States would not "remove the LTTE from its list of terrorist organizations until it firmly and decidedly gives up terrorism and policies such as the recruitment of child soldiers". She charged: "They continue to recruit child soldiers. They continue to conduct extra judicial assassinations of politicians who disagree with them. They are continuing to stockpile weapons."

India and Sri Lanka

India is caught in a difficult situation. Having decided to brand the LTTE a terrorist organization (the ban has been re-notified on May 14, 2004 as statutorily required for another two years) India would not concede any space to it. Apart from committing the sin of assassinating Rajiv Gandhi, the past conduct of the LTTE in undermining the India-Sri Lanka Accord of 1987 and even earlier sabotaging all efforts of New Delhi to help promote an acceptable solution to the ethnic problem, has been such that it comes out as unreliable and dubious organization not worthy of Indian trust and confidence. In Indian perception much of the sufferings of the Tamils could be attributed to its mulishness. New Delhi's lack of response to the entreaties of the LTTE to bury the past and start afresh has much to do with its unsavoury past. As far as the LTTE is concerned it is quite mindful of the fact that "without India this (ethnic) problem will not find a permanent settlement" and in its estrangement with India it has "suffered a lot". One has only to recall Prabakaran and Balasingham's press conference of April 10, 2002 when the latter pleading for a fresh relationship overcoming the past swore by India and reminded India of the "ties of race that bind Sri Lanka Tamils with the Indian Tamils". India once again ignored the December 2003 appeal of Balasingham to "put the past behind and look forward" even though he assured India that the LTTE would not "act in any way prejudicial to India's geo-political and economic interests".

Indian interest in Sri Lankan developments remains paramount. India cannot look benignly to the emergence of an ISGA-type administration in close proximity to Tamil Nadu and controlled by an organization wedded to terrorism. Its control over the waters where the Indian fishermen operate on daily basis would be most unpalatable. The recent arrest of some Indian fishermen by the LTTE Sea Tigers brought home to India the possibility of such a situation emerging routinely. A state within the state that ISGA would be and given its lack of accountability to international law and community is the last thing that India would wish in her neighbourhood.

Colombo too is quite conscious that emergence of ISGA-type administration would be an anathema to India and to that extent it would be advantageous to take India on board since the interest of both converged. Kadirgamar took the first opportunity after assuming charge of the Foreign Ministry in Colombo to brief New Delhi of Colombo's thinking. He broke his journey in New Delhi at the end of April, on way back from Shanghai to brief South Block. New Delhi caught in the midst of its parliamentary elections, could contribute nothing new except reiterate its earlier hope that a solution "consistent with democracy, pluralism and respect for individual rights" would emerge through internal dynamics. On the bilateral plane India and Sri Lanka reiterated their desire to negotiate expeditiously agreements in the field of economic, defence and fisheries cooperation. Earlier in January a Sri Lankan defence delegation had visited New Delhi to pursue the proposal mooted during Wickremasinghe's visit in October 2003 for a defence cooperation agreement. In March in a positive move New Delhi removed Sri Lanka from the negative list of countries to enable supplies of defence and defence-related equipment to be resumed to Colombo.

Kadirgamar found himself in Washington when the change of guard took place in New Delhi following the Indian parliamentary elections held in April-May, 2004. He did betray some nervousness initially. He was worried lest the Congress back in power should press for the extradition of Prabakaran, who stood condemned in the Rajiv Gandhi assassination case. In that case the peace process nurtured so assiduously would be in jeopardy. Putting up a brave face he said on May 13 in Washington that the relations between the two governments were "institutionalized" and the "colour of the party in power did not matter" but he chose to keep his fingers crossed on the question of extradition. The routine re-notification of the ban on the LTTE on May 14 came when there was a political vacuum in New Delhi. Colombo was left guessing about the attitude of the Congress Party, which was returning to power in New Delhi after a gap of almost eight years. Would the Congress Party headed by the widow of Rajiv Gandhi, which initiated the extradition proceedings still be keen to pursue the old case with the same vigour? Kadirgamar remembered the Congress Party's role in pulling down a government in New Delhi in November1997 on the alleged association of one of the partners in the government with the assassination conspiracy. A lot of water has flowed down the rivers of both India and Sri Lanka since then.

Foreign Minister Kadirgamar did not wish to lose any time. As in the past he was keen to ensure that Sri Lanka was first to land in New Delhi. India did not wish to disappoint him either. The release on May 27 of the Common Minimum Programme (CMP) by the newly formed United Progressive Alliance even before he landed in New Delhi was a shot in his arm. It assured support for peace talks to "fulfill the legitimate aspirations of Tamils and religious minorities within the territorial integrity and solidarity of Sri Lanka". When Kadirgamar found himself in the Indian capital a couple of days later, he was relieved that he did not have much to canvass. External Affairs Minister Natwar Singh's remarks at the May 31 press conference after meeting with Kadirgamar cheered him a lot. Natwar Singh said:

> "As you know, India is committed to the sovereignty, territorial integrity and the unity of Sri Lanka in a federal system and the Prime Minister (Manmohan Singh) has said that we very much hope that a peaceful, negotiated solution will be found, which will maintain the unity, territorial integrity and sovereignty of Sri Lanka and satisfy all sections of the people of Sri Lanka".

Kadirgamar applauded, what he himself revealed, that "not one word" was spoken on the assassination of Rajiv Gandhi in his meeting with Singh. He felt assured that New Delhi would not up the ante on the extradition question. The next day June 1, addressing his first press conference in New Delhi, the Indian External Affairs Minister said what had been left unsaid before that while New Delhi's request for extradition of Parabakaran "remained on the table", it would not be allowed to "become an impediment in the current peace process in Sri Lanka". He also gave a firm commitment that New Delhi would not agree to "Tamil Eelam" under any circumstances. In a manner of speaking, India decided in favour of peace in the neighbourhood, condoning the horrendous conduct of the LTTE in the past.

Since October 2003 the proposal for a defence cooperation agreement between the two countries is on the table. Talks were held in January when a Sri Lankan defence delegation visited India. Since March Colombo is no longer on the negative list for supply of military and military-related equipment. This was more of a symbolic gesture. Ever since the fall of the Elephant Pass in April 2000, Colombo had been allowed to make military purchases in India on a case-by-case basis. It would be recalled that during the June 2000 visit of External Affairs Minister Jaswant Singh to Colombo, a credit of US $ hundred million was extended leaving vague the areas for which it could be utilized. Sri Lankan defence personnel are admitted in Indian defence training establishments on a regular basis. Kadirgamar now picked up the threads for a defence agreement with the new government. Natwar Singh assured him (May 31) that India "will take forward defence cooperation with Sri Lanka" and the Alliance partners from Tamil Nadu would be kept informed of "all these matters including defence". Later during his meeting with the new Defence Minister Pranab Mukherjee, he articulated the suggestion further. On June 6 Mukherjee speaking in Chennai confirmed that the proposal put forth to him would be examined. Though he remained ambivalent on signing the "defence cooperation pact", Mukherjee gave enough indication that it was receiving positive consideration of the government, which was "consulting Tamil Nadu allies as well". The fact that Prime Minister Manmohan Singh too assured Kadirgamar that the proposal would be looked into, and Mukherjee's assertion that "after considering all aspects, we will take the decision," Colombo should be optimistic. Nevertheless, since Sri Lanka is no longer on the negative list, she could source much of her requirements in New Delhi confidently. A defence cooperation agreement would only institutionalize the arrangement and give Sri Lanka a greater confidence to meet the LTTE challenge. Both Natwar Singh and Pranab Mukherjee laid great stress on consulting the "southern allies" in the United Progressive Alliance in coming to a decision on the subject. In the past, these very allies had backed the policies of the previous government as partners and it is unlikely that they would have any reservations under the new dispensation now.

India would gain nothing by not signing the defence agreement. Sri Lanka too may not lose much of its sleep if it does not come through. Colombo needs it only as a palliative to deal with the LTTE with greater confidence. Since India cannot be present at the negotiating table, the agreement if signed would be a significant message to the LTTE to behave. India needs to do every bit to make sure that Colombo gains all the confidence it needs to deal with the Tigers, whose morale and self-esteem is somewhat shaken by the developments in the East. This would help close any space that antagonistic elements may be looking for on the Island. Appointment of a former Chief of the Pakistan intelligence Col. Bashir Wali as High Commissioner in Colombo has already raised the hackles of the Indian security establishment. Pakistan's every move in Indian neighbourhood is well calculated and meaningful. Wali's appointment could not be dismissed lightly as innocuous.

New Delhi is no longer burdened with the baggage of Tamil ethno-nationalism. The Tamil public opinion in India except for some stray voices would be indulgent to denying any space to the LTTE in Sri Lanka. It is in India's long-term economic and strategic interests to do every thing to bolster the morale and material strength of Sri Lanka to help her maintain her territorial integrity to which India has in the past more than once committed, even in the worst of times. This has become all the more necessary now when an important element of the LTTE - the Eastern Tamils – has shown lack of trust in the leadership of the Tigers perched in the north. Whatever the Sinhala sins in the last decades, today there is a strong southern opinion that Tamils were wronged in the past and there is a need to make amends. A defence cooperation agreement would send a strong positive signal both to the Sinhalese and Tamil public opinion, and no less to the LTTE, about India's position in the current phase.

India though not present at the peace talks, has prescribed the perimeters within which a solution arrived at would be acceptable to her. These norms are welcome to Colombo. If India goes ahead and signs a defence cooperation agreement, LTTE would be duly warned. Presently LTTE appears to be under the illusion that it has neutralized India in Sri Lanka and therefore had a free run of the place to deal with Colombo, as it liked. There is a need to disabuse it of any such notion.

The present is a difficult phase in Sri Lanka's history. New Delhi could contribute a lot without getting involved and give a positive direction to the negotiations. Sri Lanka is under no illusion about Indian direct involvement. Colombo while accepting this limitation of New Delhi, nevertheless is convinced that as a regional power India has enough stakes in the region and could not close its eyes to what happens in her vicinity. As a leading country of South Asia other countries are watching her moves carefully. If India without being interventionist succeeds in stabilizing the Sri Lankan situation, she would establish her credibility in the region.

Index